London Midland
Steam Days Remembered II

Strathwood

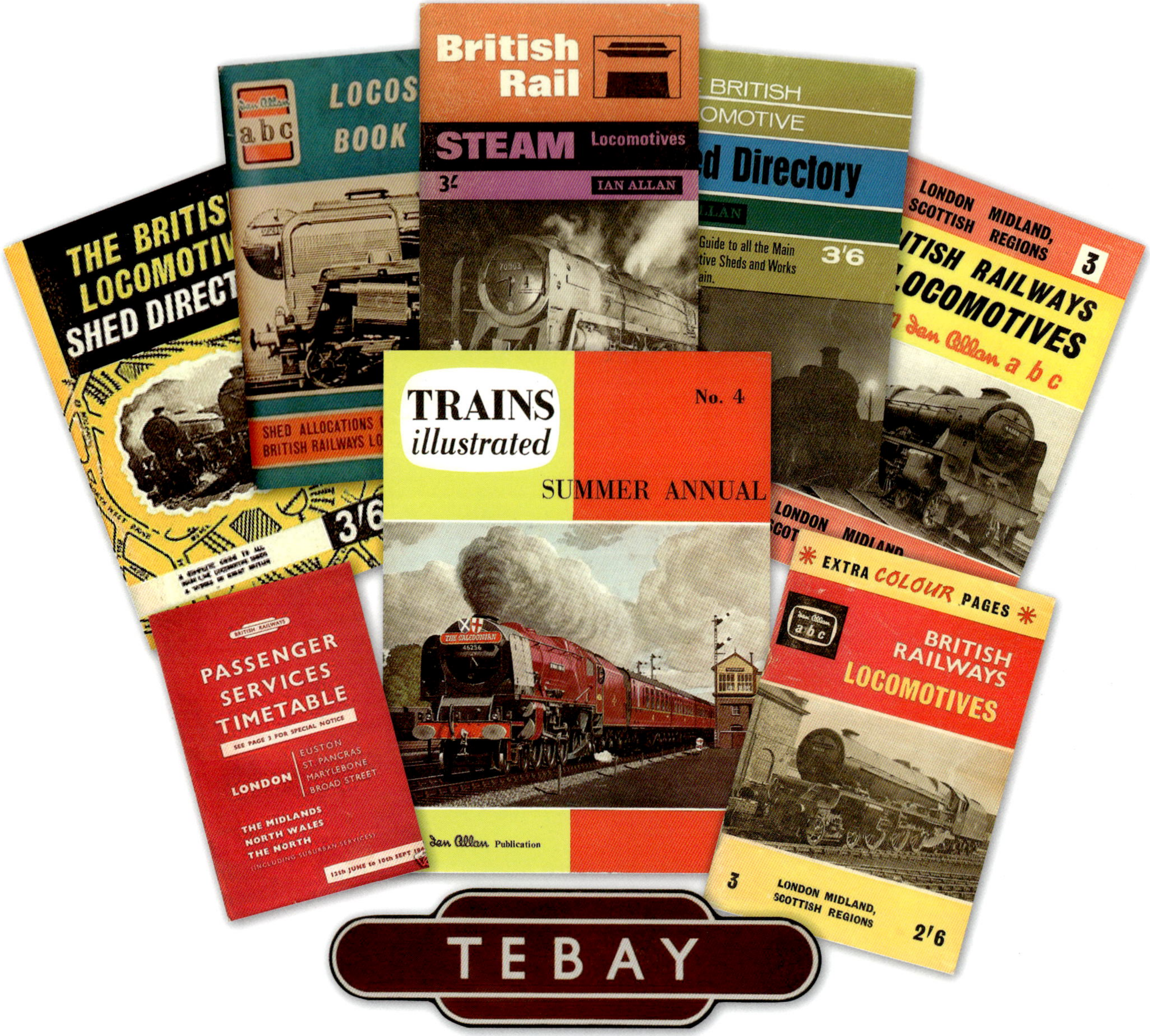
British Rail
STEAM Locomotives
IAN ALLAN
TRAINS illustrated
No. 4
SUMMER ANNUAL
Ian Allan Publication
PASSENGER SERVICES TIMETABLE
SEE PAGE 3 FOR SPECIAL NOTICE
LONDON
EUSTON
ST. PANCRAS
MARYLEBONE
BROAD STREET
THE MIDLANDS
NORTH WALES
THE NORTH
EXTRA COLOUR PAGES
BRITISH RAILWAYS LOCOMOTIVES
LONDON MIDLAND, SCOTTISH REGIONS
2/6
3
TEBAY

London Midland Steam Days Remembered II

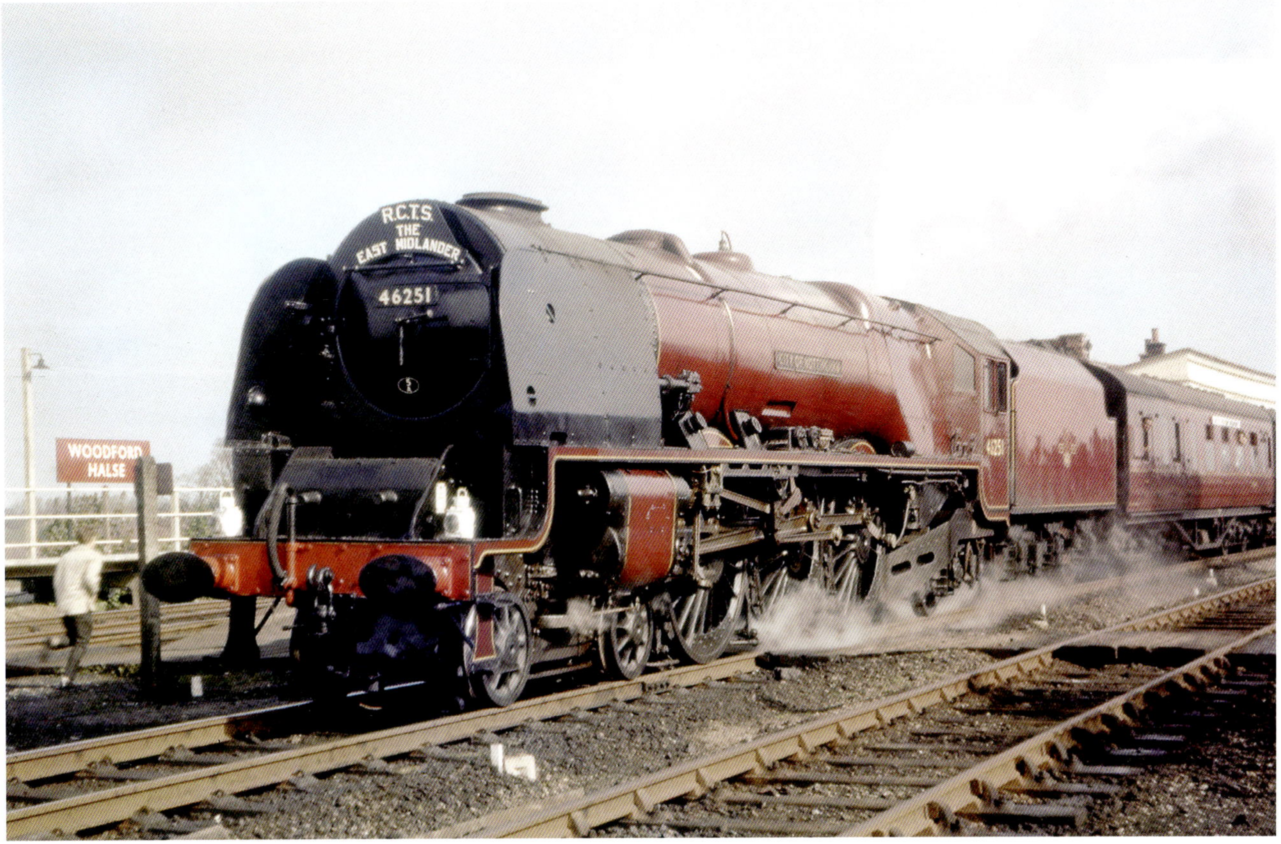

Front Cover: On its way to Didcot from Nottingham Victoria on 9 May 1964, taking a route along the former Great Central with the RCTS arranged East Midlander No.7 Railtour, was 46251 City of Nottingham, seen here briefly halted at Woodford Halse. ***Strathwood Library Collection***

Strathwood

London Midland
Steam Days Remembered II

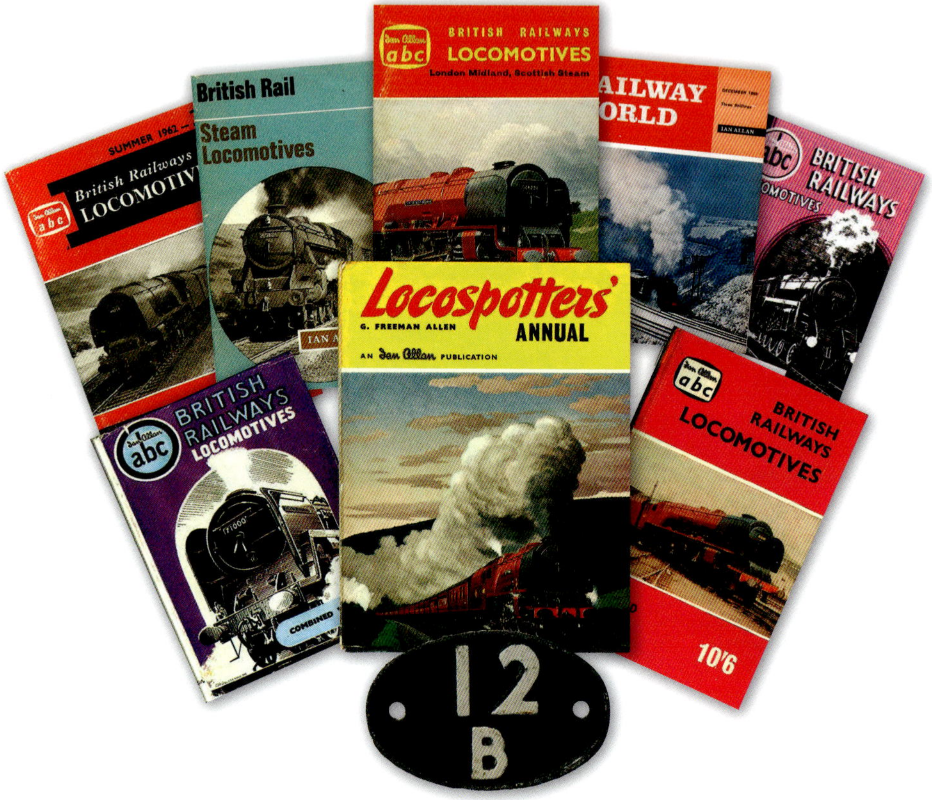

First published 2014

ISBN 1-905276-69-9
ISBN 978-1-905276-69-1

Published by Strathwood, 9 Boswell Crescent, Inverness, IV2 3ET. Tel 01463 234004
www.strathwood.co.uk

Contents

Page

Preface

In this the fourth volume in the Steam Days Remembered series we pick up from where we left off in the first volume of London Midland Steam Days Remembered this time, as we once again raid the archives to make another selection from some of my favourite shots from the fifties and sixties in colour. Once more I have called upon my old friend Roger Stanton, to share with us his experiences as a younger man growing up with steam. Indeed you will glimpse a few similarities perhaps to your own memories of the time as we venture through this collection together, back into a bygone era.

Many readers will have enjoyed Roger's first essay of growing up as a young steam enthusiast in the Midlands during the 1950s. Sadly far too many of the older guard of enthusiasts who were active at the time have now passed on, their photographic collections sometimes preserved in a loft somewhere but more often forgotten about. Or more tragically thrown out after a suitable period of mourning by the family. If you are concerned by this prospect do get in touch, and you could see your favourite shots whether black and white or in colour published in the coming months. Likewise it would be good to see more spotters from the steam era, putting down into writing their experiences for others to enjoy.

So we should give thanks to Roger and all of those who took photographs at the time and have been kind enough to allow us to see their work published today.

Kevin Derrick
Inverness 2014

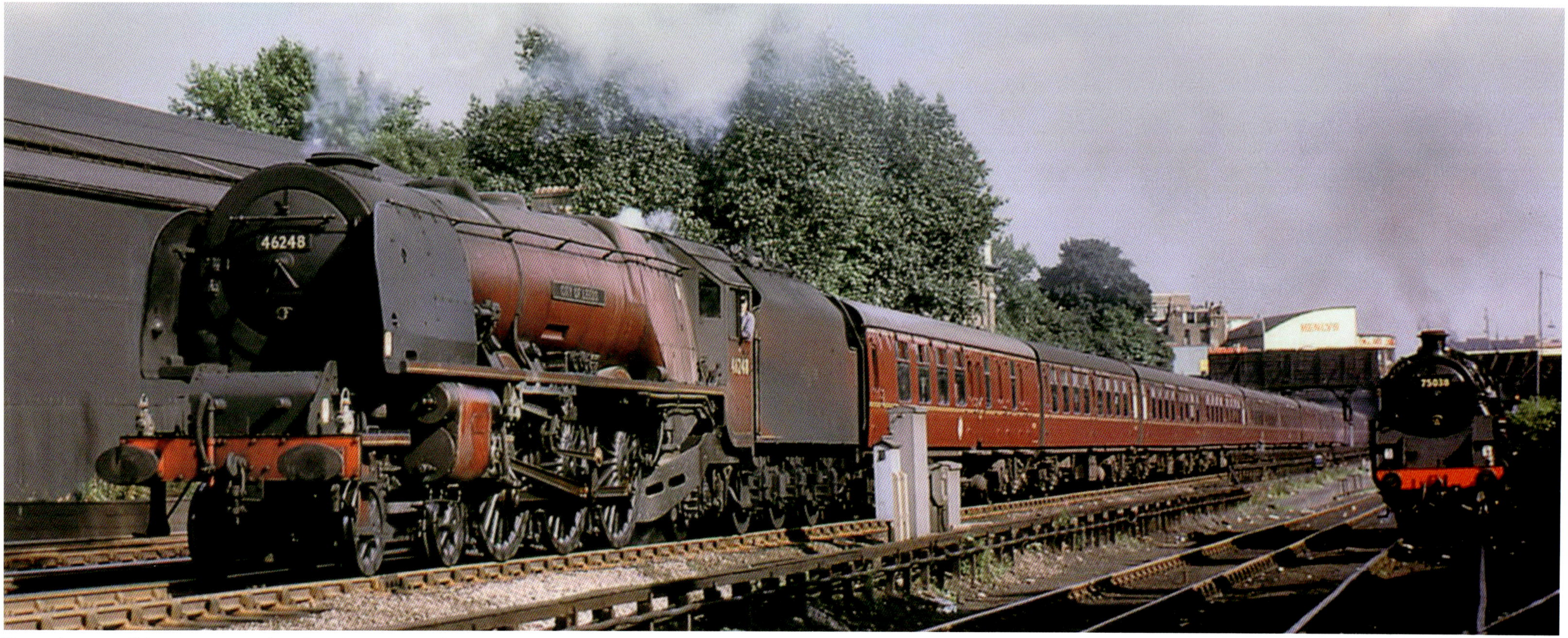

There is something mesomeric about maroon Coronations at the head of maroon coaches, as we enjoy 46248 City of Leeds, barking its way up Camden Bank with a northbound passenger service on 22 July 1962. ***Gerald T. Robinson***

Introduction - Off the Block II

As a second part to my personal railway odyssey from the first volume of London Midland Steam Days Remembered, I thought first of all to describe the various services radiating from Rugby and some of the motive power I encountered.

Apart from the mainline services there were several branch lines, and the first I'd like to deal with is the service to Leamington. Starting from the bay platforms at the north end of the station the service ran five or six times daily, and in later years was the sole preserve of Rugby's collection of Ivatt tanks. Nos 41214, 41217, 41224, 41227, 41278, 41321and 41323 all appeared from time to time. The same locos were also used on the service from Seaton Junction to Stamford, and were out-stationed at Rugby's sub-shed at Seaton. Oddly the other branch service from Seaton was worked by engines provided by Peterborough's Spital Bridge shed, and when that closed to traffic New England. There was a daily pick-up freight but the main freight traffic was to the cement works at Rugby and Long Itchington, which consisted of chalk from quarries at Leighton Buzzard bringing 7F 0-8-0s and Stanier 8Fs from Bletchley shed. Some of this traffic also used the route from Weedon on the WCML and Marton Junction, which also had a sparse passenger service until 1958, using Ivatt tanks from Warwick and Northampton sheds usually. These workings travelled past Braunston Reservoirs which I fished many times in the late 1950s and 1960s. The most unusual loco's seen were Crosti 9F, 92024 and several Midland 4Fs all from Wellingborough shed. These were probably "pinched" by Northampton shed off Corby to South Wales iron ore workings which used the old SMJ line from Blisworth. Passenger traffic on the Rugby to Leamington line ceased in 1959, but freight to Long Itchington lasted until the early 1970s, and there is a much opposed scheme being proposed by RMC Group to re-open the line as the pipeline installed in 1964 for chalk slurry has been at capacity for some years.

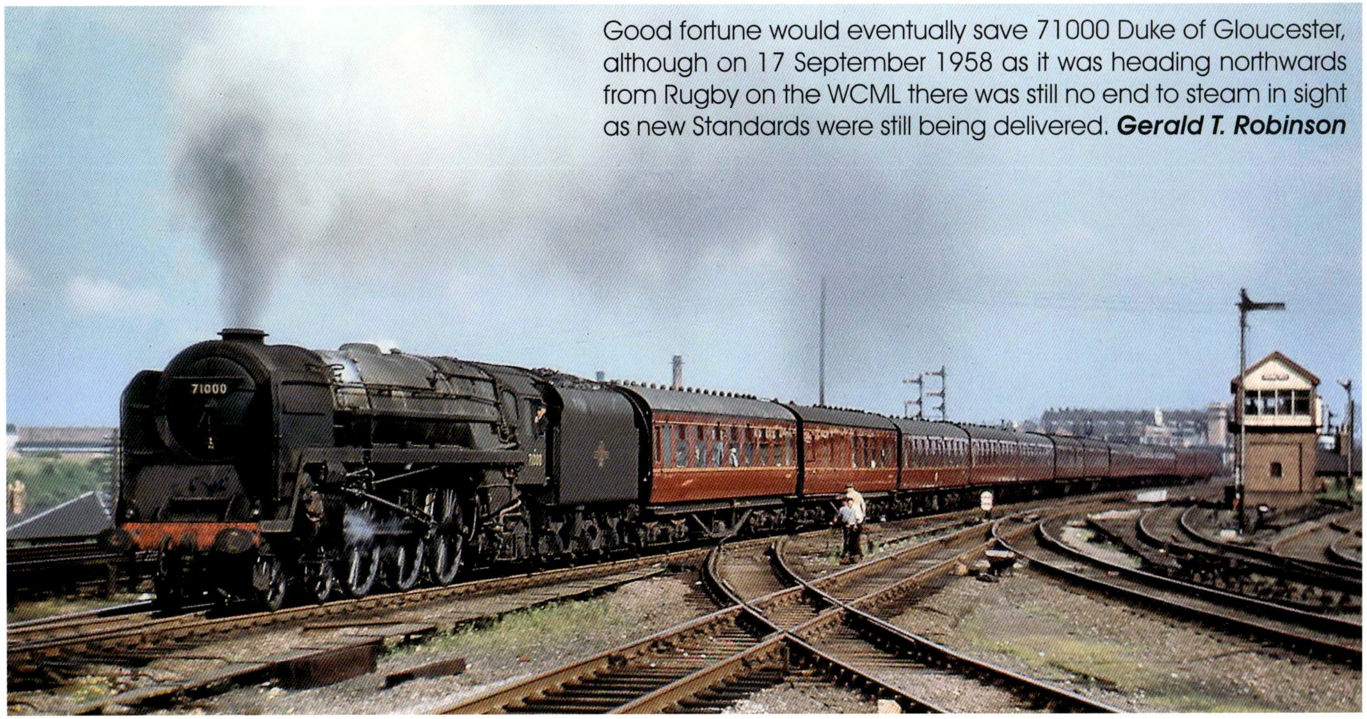

Good fortune would eventually save 71000 Duke of Gloucester, although on 17 September 1958 as it was heading northwards from Rugby on the WCML there was still no end to steam in sight as new Standards were still being delivered. ***Gerald T. Robinson***

Although the passenger traffic ceased without a big fanfare the line had it's last big day during the electrification of the WCML. It was used extensively for some months and I well remember fishing on the River Leam at Birdingbury Mill, watching an almost non-stop procession of Royal Scots, Patriots, Jubilees, Coronation and Princess Royal Pacifics along with some of the early English Electric Type 4s. R.J (Dick) Blenkinsop in one of his brilliant books recalls missing the photo of a lifetime by not having his camera with him when he could have photographed a Princess Royal and a King side by side in Leamington's two stations.

Moving round in a clock-wise manner we come to the branch from Leicester to Rugby. This was originally part of the main route north from London, and until quite recently two platforms at Euston were known as the York Road platforms. Around 1850 or so when alternative routes south were opened the line became a rural back-water and so it remained. The original London and Birmingham Railway forced the issue by refusing to accept North Midland traffic until their own traffic had been dealt with, resulting in long delays, mainly in their coal traffic from the Leicester and Nottingham coalfields. Passenger traffic in my day consisted of again five or six return workings daily, all worked by Class 4MT tank locos from Rugby and Leicester sheds. Examples of Stanier, Fairburn and Fowler versions all being used. I never saw an example of a tender locomotive used but from time to time Rugby's pilot, sometimes 46446 got a trip following a failure. Freight traffic consisted of the usual daily pickup freight with Rugby's 0-8-0s 7Fs and Midland 4F types from Leicester shed.

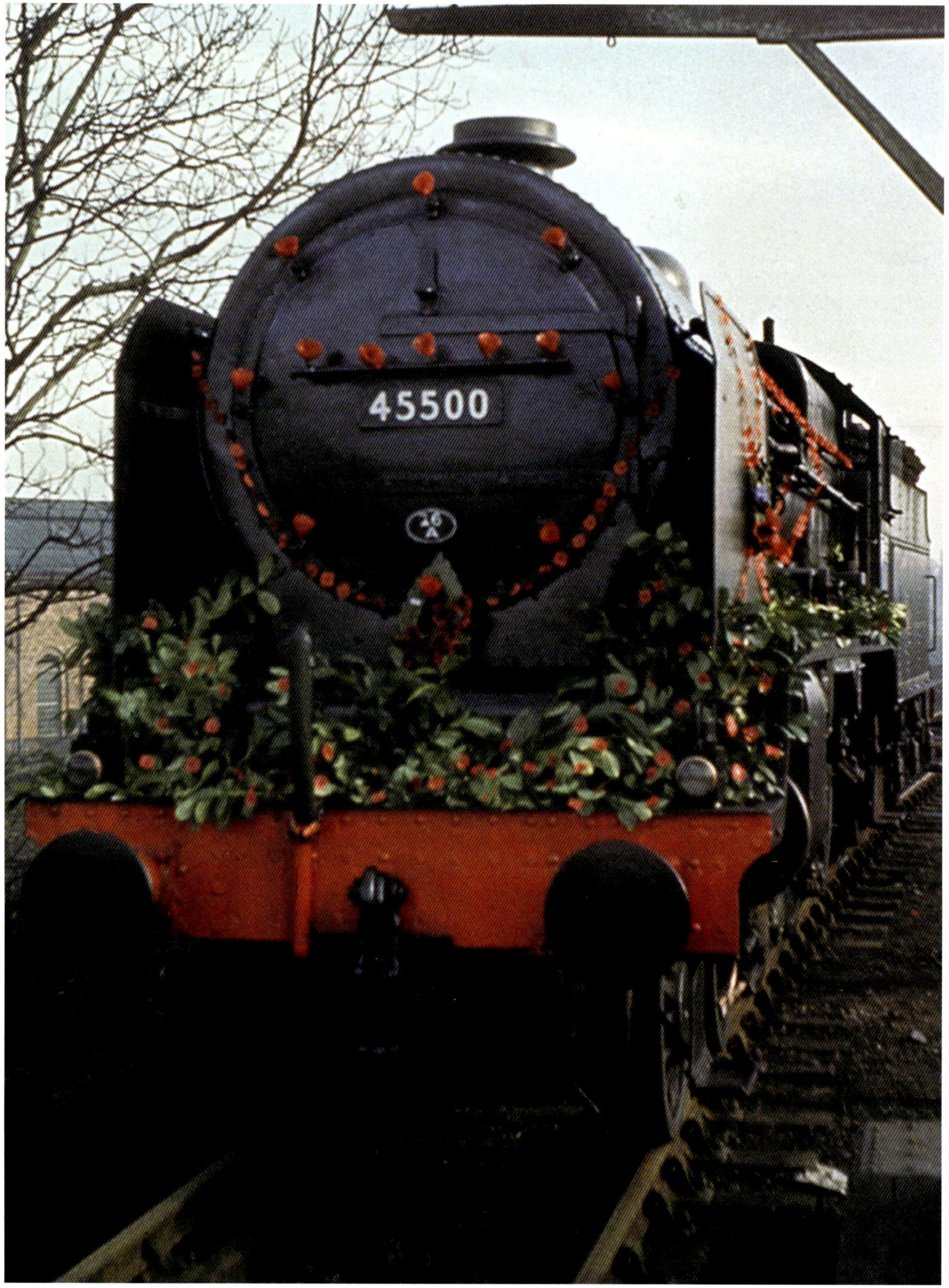

Several times a day we'd also see 8Fs usually from Kirkby-in-Ashfield and an occasional 9F from Toton, on south-bound coal workings. These workings never returned this way due to pathing complications on to the Leicester line north of Rugby, and used the line from Northampton to Market Harborough, thence up the Midland line back to Nottingham. The Northampton to Market Harborough line is of course now in partial use by the Northampton and Lamport preserved railway and is well worth a visit if in the area.

The Rugby to Leicester line closed to all traffic in 1961 and one of the reasons given was the existence of an alternative service by the GC! The eleven arch viaduct survived in Rugby but north of there all trace for many miles has disappeared, unless you know where to look.

To the south of Rugby the LNW line to Market Harborough and Peterborough swings left immediately after passing the Testing Plant and under the GC girder bridge. Again mainly a local affair it did have some seasonal traffic to the east coast consisting of Birmingham New Street to Great Yarmouth workings. After the closure of the former Midland and Great Northern line additional services used this route including freight and parcels traffic. Rugby's extensive fleet of Class 5s were usually seen along with the 4MT tanks, mainly Stanier and Fairburn as Rugby never had Fowler's allocated in my time, but the changing ownership of the line especially at the Peterborough end brought Eastern Region locomotives in increasing numbers. Classes seen were J39, B1s and on one occasion a B17, 61660 Hull City. Rugby's compounds would also have been used extensively until replaced by the Class 5s. I used the line quite a bit to go to Peterborough for spotting, and out to North Kilworth fishing on the Leicester branch of the Grand Union Canal and the canal supply reservoirs at Welford. The service staggered on until June 1966 when it was closed completely. Some traces still exist including Seaton Junction which although once in use as a scrap yard for old Cavaliers and Allegros It was is in almost an unchanged state, last time I was there it looked as though the staff just locked the doors and walked away on the last day. Visitors were NOT welcome as the owner employed several very large dogs to ensure security!

The station at North Kilworth was completely removed and restored at the site of the Warwickshire Railway Centre in Coventry, and finally the station at Yelvertoft and Stanford Park,which was substantially intact, was in use as a social club and bar at a private fishing lake! Some excellent views of this line and the others in this tome are to be found in the British Railways Past and Present series of books.

Such was the patriotism among the railwaymen at Rugby, that every Rememberance Sunday, staff would adorn a suitable locomotive such as 45500 Patriot, as here in November 1955 for a memorial service to remember their fallen colleagues. ***Bruce Chapman Collection/Colour Rail***

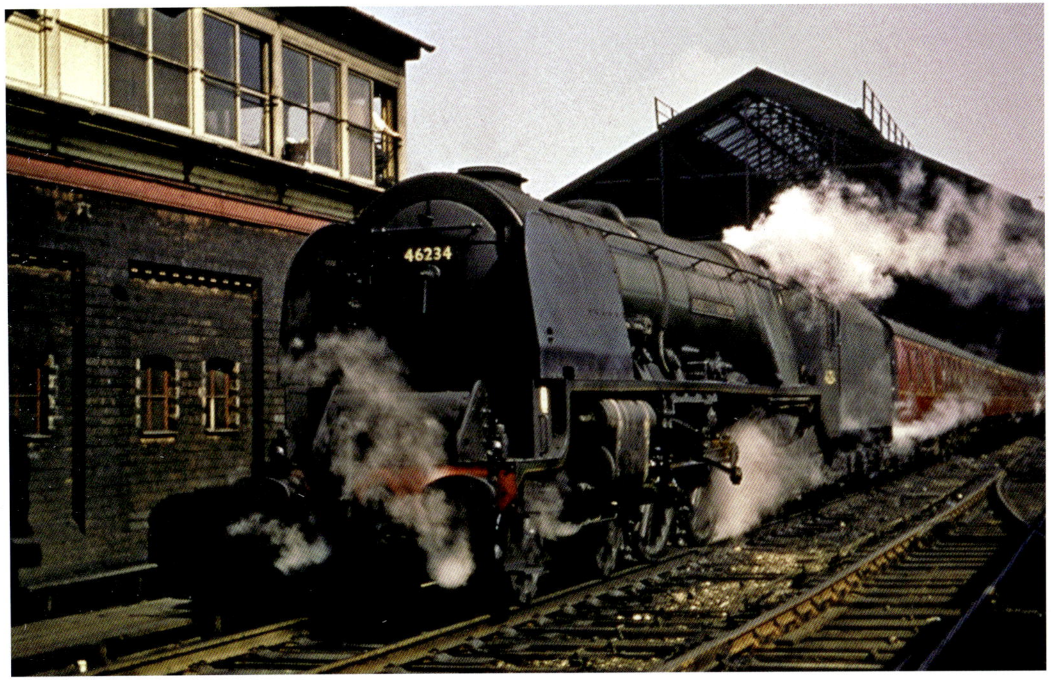

Basically four main lines radiated on the old LNW main line from Rugby. At the north end, the line to Birmingham swung away just north of bridge 283. I dealt with traffic and locomotives in the first part of my story, but I suppose the most notable feature of this line was the problems up trains faced as they had to wait for a path across the Trent Valley main line. This was eradicated when a fly-over was built as part of the electrification in the 1960s. Which sadly ruined what was a most photographic location. My lasting memory is of being on a DMU one Friday on my way to college, and glancing out of the window I saw 46208 Princess Helena Victoria on the up Welshman coming off the Trent Valley line.

This Trent Valley route headed away from Rugby and was a continuation of a four track mainline and as such was continually busy. I won't dwell too much on it as I've already covered much here, but there were many good locations for watching the trains go by. It followed the Oxford Canal for many miles and again it was possible to follow both of my main hobbies at the same time! Fond memories include seeing 45704 Leviathan speeding south in absolute showroom condition near Brinklow. As an aside I caught about 15lb of roach and skimmer bream that day! I also saw the same locomotive being attended to by the fitters the following day on Willesden shed, so I expect it had recently emerged from Crewe Works.

All the mainline London Midland passenger types used this route including the Britannias, as both Holyhead and Longsight had an allocation of these Pacifics, and if you were very lucky the occasional Clan. I know of three confirmed workings as far as Rugby of a Clan, none of which I saw, and my spotting career lurched to a halt sometime in 1964, without ever managing to see one in the flesh!

South of Rugby the mainline split into two with the Northampton line taking the easier route through the Northampton uplands. The traffic taking this route was mainly of a secondary nature including freight and parcels, but the exception to this was the fast Wolverhampton, Birmingham to Euston service. It was also used extensively for diversions when the direct Weedon route was closed for engineering. There were few stations on the route, Kilsby and Crick was closed in the 1930s. Long Buckby is still open and the only other station was Althorp Park, closed in the 1950s which would now be very handy for visiting Althorp Park and Princess Diana's resting place if that's your thing.

Left: Another Coronation this time in green as 46234 Duchess of Abercorn gets away from Rugby in 1961. ***Paul Riley/Colour Rail***

Below: A party of young lads make their way around Rugby's shed on 18 February 1961 and carefully note down Class B1, 61048's presence. ***Colour Rail***

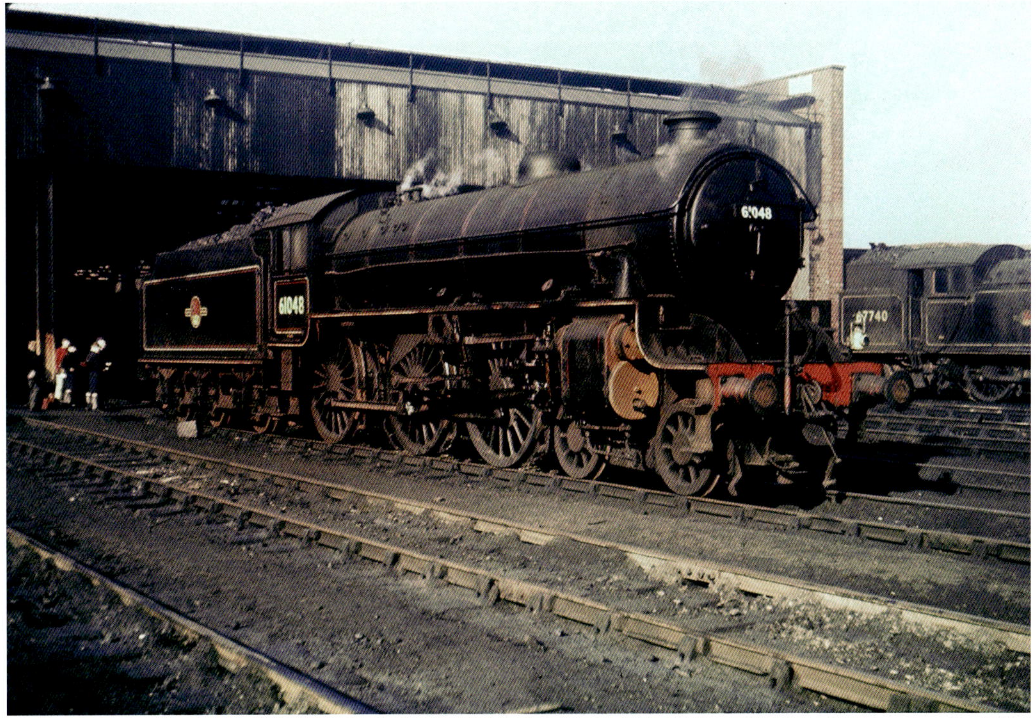

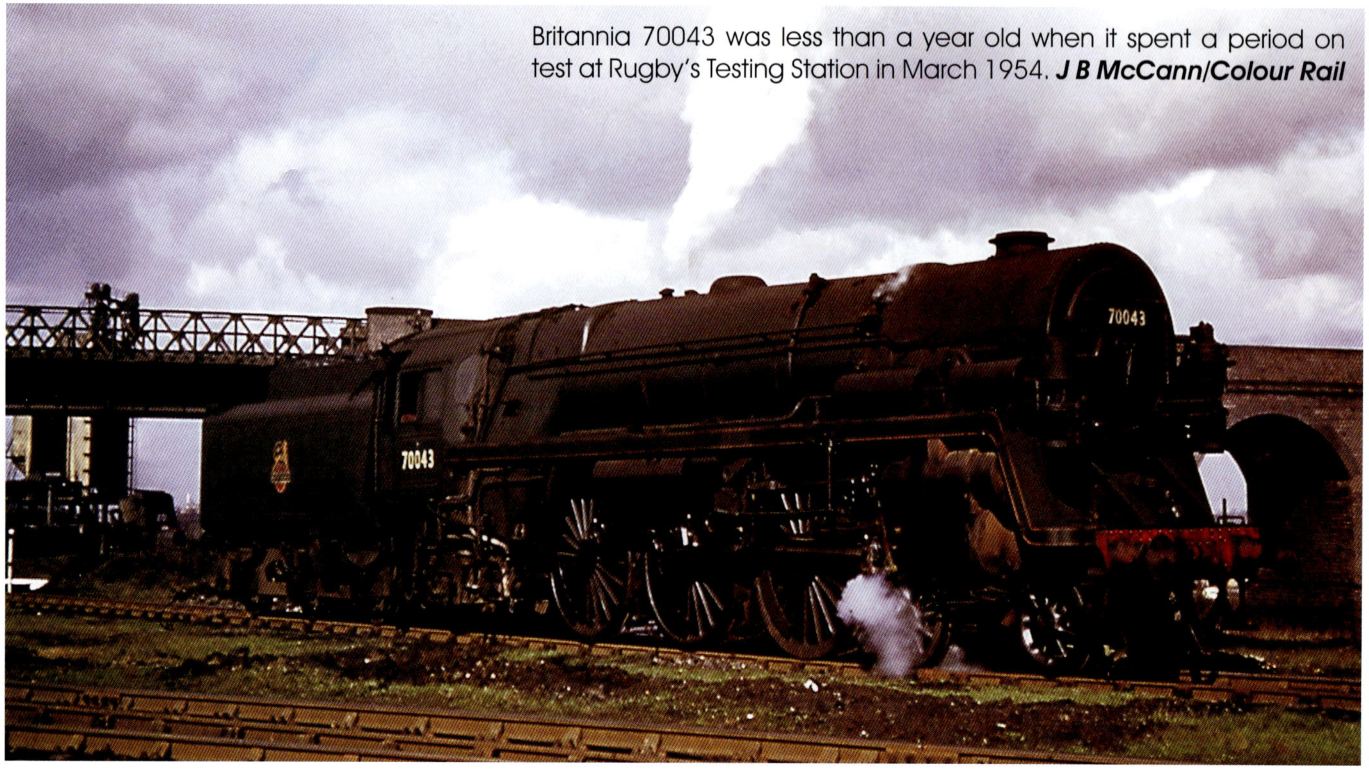

Britannia 70043 was less than a year old when it spent a period on test at Rugby's Testing Station in March 1954. ***J B McCann/Colour Rail***

The direct and older route leaves Rugby through a very interesting flyover structure built in the 1930s and heads towards Watford Gap through Kilsby Tunnel. The only station on this route in recent years was Weedon which was the junction of the line over to Leamington. I can't imagine how the planners managed to squeeze in un-fitted strings of sixteen tonners, with an almost continous procession of expresses. Factor in the southern stretch of WCML's only level crossing just down the road at Banbury Lane and think disaster, which thankfully never happened. The lines only serious accident in recent years was a high-speed derailment at Weedon in the 1950s. This route rejoins the Northampton line at Roade in the impressive cutting just north of the station, this structure is well worth a visit if in the area.

We now deal with the GC Mainline. A late comer to Rugby, crossing the LNW line on a very impressive viaduct. The only bit that survived the closures for a while was the steel structure known locally as the Girder Bridge or erroneously in the railway press as the "Birdcage" bridge. For a while it was still possible to stand on the north abutment of the viaduct looking south and imagine just how big this was, and to wonder at the expertise of the engineers as they took this line over the Oxford Canal, the valley of the River Avon and finally the extensive track layout of the LNW mainline. Imagine, if you can, back in 1957 seeing Class O1, 63576 hurtle south over the bridge on a southbound runner carrying coal or steel billets at 10 to 15 mph more than officially allowed. Nothing ever hung around on this railway. Following shortly after Class A5, 69800 on the morning Nottingham to Rugby "Ord" with K3, 61856 from Annesley on a fitted. Shortly after 61472, a B16 from York belted past on the first of the days York Dringhouses Yard to various destinations vans. Usually we would see three of these headed by two of York's V2s and a B16. However as I was to find out this railway ran all night as well, so there was much we never saw. Shortly the morning's highlight sped past A3, 60049 Galtee More heading the up South Yorkshireman, and so it went on. J11, 64388 from Woodford was possibly the slowest service we'd see that day as it pottered south on the morning pick-up. Much changed in years to follow as ex-LNER types became more scarce. I can still remember my first 9F and literally overnight the O1s disappeared!

A school holiday fishing trip to the famous "straight" behind Leicester City's Filbert Street football ground demonstrated just how much things had changed. Station pilot at Leicester Central was Stanier 4MT tank, 42556 which according to my "ref" lived in Huddersfield! The next service was hauled by 73045 from Leeds Holbeck, and by now it was clear "summats changed!". Over the years the Class 5s moved in along with 8Fs, Royal Scots, Britannias, Jubilees and I suppose the most bizarre sight I saw was 46123 running tender first on the morning "Ord" from Nottingham just before it's blessed withdrawal. As with other lines such as the S & D the final end was a blessing, and came in September 1966 with a few specials and all of the final workings hauled by clapped out Class 5s. There will be more GC observations in Eastern Steam Days Remembered.

Locomotive Observations

40001 Fowler 3MT Tanks. Very rarely seen in Rugby until 40056 and four or five others turned up to go into store on Rugby shed. They came from Hull's Botanic Gardens shed which was about to be infested with shiny new DMUs. Naturally hysteria broke out amongst local enthusiasts and soon they were underlined in the "ref". Sadly they soon disappeared from 2A to be scrapped, just as quickly they disappeared from my latest Ian Allan ABCs!

Stanier 2-6-2 3MT Tanks. Never seen despite Nuneaton 2B having some for their local services.

Class 2P 4-4-0s. Occasionally seen when some faint-hearted driver at Crewe didn't fancy his chances of getting to Euston with "sixteen on". So Crewe would pop one of their's on the front for him to push all the way to London.

Ivatt 4MT 2-6-0. Sometimes specimens seen from Nuneaton on various duties. As technically they appear to be the equivalent of one of Fowler's Crabs one would think they would be used indiscriminately, but Nuneaton drivers obviously preferred Crabs for their longer distance duties as they never wandered far.

Midland 0-6-0s (various). Not seen a lot, although one of Leicester's, ie 43846 would turn up occasionally.

Class 5. Rugby had heaps of 'em and not much for them to do really. However come the summer, half of them disappeared to all corners of UK on holiday extras. I suppose half of them would have worked through Rugby but "hard ones" were rare. However for some reason both of the named ex-Scottish ones that went to Newton Heath turned up, and were duly noted. I don't remember ever seeing another Newton Heath locomotive in Rugby. Our home shed 2A Rugby, always had one or even two specimens in good health as relief pilots, with one even reaching Carlisle dropping very little time on the Royal Scot following a failure.

Patriots. All seen at one time or another and at the end we had three or four shedded at 2A. 45537/8 and 41 ring a bell.

Jubilees. For a large steam shed Rugby had a large staff to match it's many express duties, but no allocation of large engines. Too close to London to need locomotive exchanges. However we did get a few towards the end, 45672 Anson, and 45722 Defence (which I saw on the rollers in the Testing Plant).

Jinties. Rugby always had a couple 47269 and 47677 being there for years but they disappeared when the Ivatts turned up. Several London based examples were also seen heading north for withdrawal or repair including 47300 from 33A Plaistow shed.

Stanier 8Fs. Many seen from all sorts of depots including Toton and Kirkby-in-Ashfield.

Midland 2Fs. Quite a few shedded here over the years with 58308 the first I remember seeing, but as they wore out we got more from other places no longer needing them.

Standards. Britannias seen as previously noted along with Standard 5s from Willesden and Chester. What we didn't know was that a Huddersfield based example worked south everyday on parcels to Willesden. The 76xxx's based at Neasden also worked back in the early afternoon and I saw them all eventually. 80xxx tanks were based at Watford and Bletchley and one turned up every night on an outer-suburban service before they were all sent to the Southern in exchange for their Fairburns.

WDs. It was a red-letter day if one of them turned up. The only ones I can remember were from March shed including the named 90732 Vulcan.

Diesels. In the early days 10001/1 were seen mainly on the Scottish services, usually doubleheaded but Rugby had the Bo-Bo, 10800 for a while which it ran on Peterborough services. 10201/2 and 3 turned up from the Southern to accompany the twins 10000 and 10001. The arrival of the early DMUs created a bit of excitement soon forgotten! Of course Rugby also had an allocation of D3000 diesel shunters along with D2908-13, the origins of which were North British who I've long forgotten.

Coronation Pacifics. All the English ones were "crates" but Polmadie locomotives until the very final years almost never made it this far. The same applied to Polmadie's Scots and my only local sighting, was 46104 one Sunday afternoon when fishing on the Oxford Canal at Hillmorton.

Coronation Stories

I drank in the pub called the Avon Mill and just over the road was Old Station Square where lots of railwaymen lived so I got to know a few. One night George Twynham was firing to Eric (Pinky) Perkins on the Royal Highlander out of Euston. As was their way the GPO was fifteen minutes late loading and as Eric liked a couple of tasters on the way home "he weren't happy!". A cockney fellow signing the road asked if he could get aboard and was probably greeted with "Yes, now sit over there and keep out the way". They set off with a mission, and the way George told it they used a lot of steam and coal but got back nearly all the lost time. However the cockney got off the footplate and reported them both and they got three days!

On another occasion Wagger Townsend (another drinking pal) was firing the Rugby Down Pilot, when he was told he was off to Crewe replacing an unwell fireman off an express. When asked by the driver if he'd fired one before Wagger replied that he'd never even been on one before! Furthermore he reckoned the firebox was as big as his front-room!

My last trip behind one was a Rugby to Euston local with four or five coaches. The crew obviously fancied a bit of fun as the departure from Long Buckby was as good as an AL6 electric locomotive.

Signing off for now, more can be found in London Midland Steam Days Remembered and in Eastern Steam Days Remembered.

Roger Stanton
West Australia 2014

Below: Wearing one of the many trialled new liveries for Britsih Railways in October 1948 was Class A4, 60007 Sir Nigel Gresley bringing some glamour to Rugby Testing Station. ***J M Jarvis/Colour Rail***

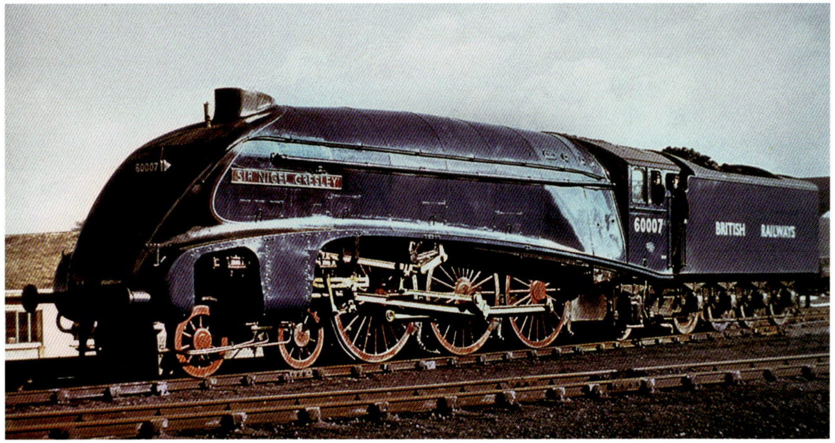

GC Death Throes

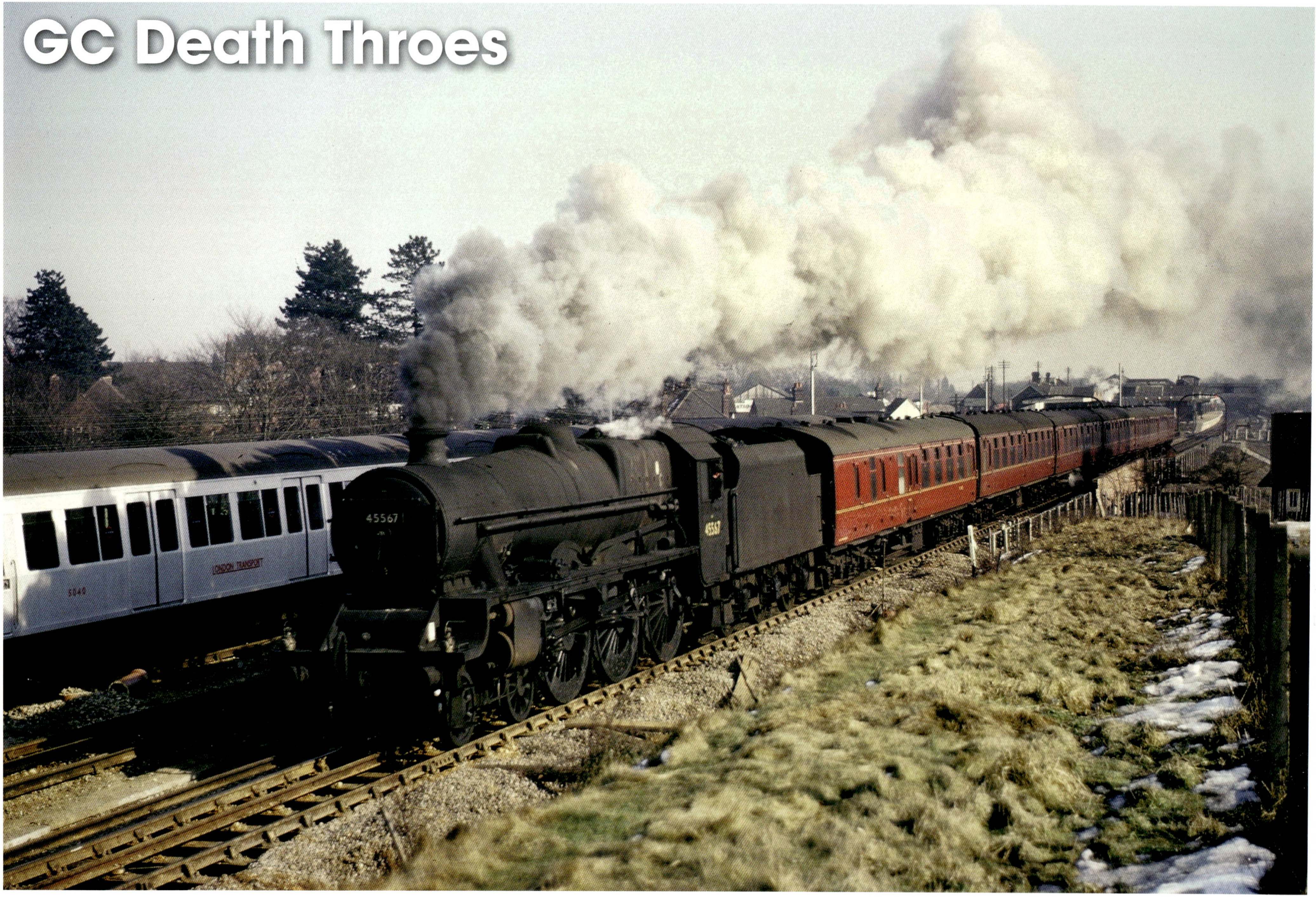

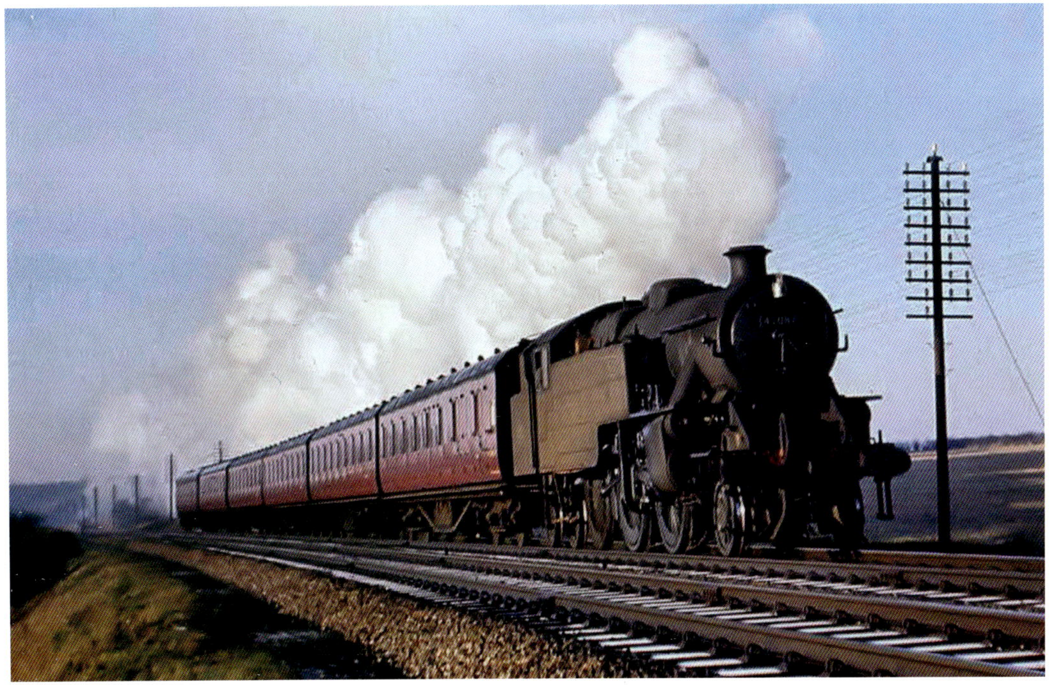

Last gasps for Fairburn tanks on locals out of Marylebone before the DMUs take over, as we catch 42087 near Beaconsfield on a frosty morning, with the 9:45am High Wycombe to Marylebone suburban passenger service 27 December 1960, then 42281 with the 10:20 Marylebone to Princes Risborough working the same morning. ***Both: Gerald T. Robinson***

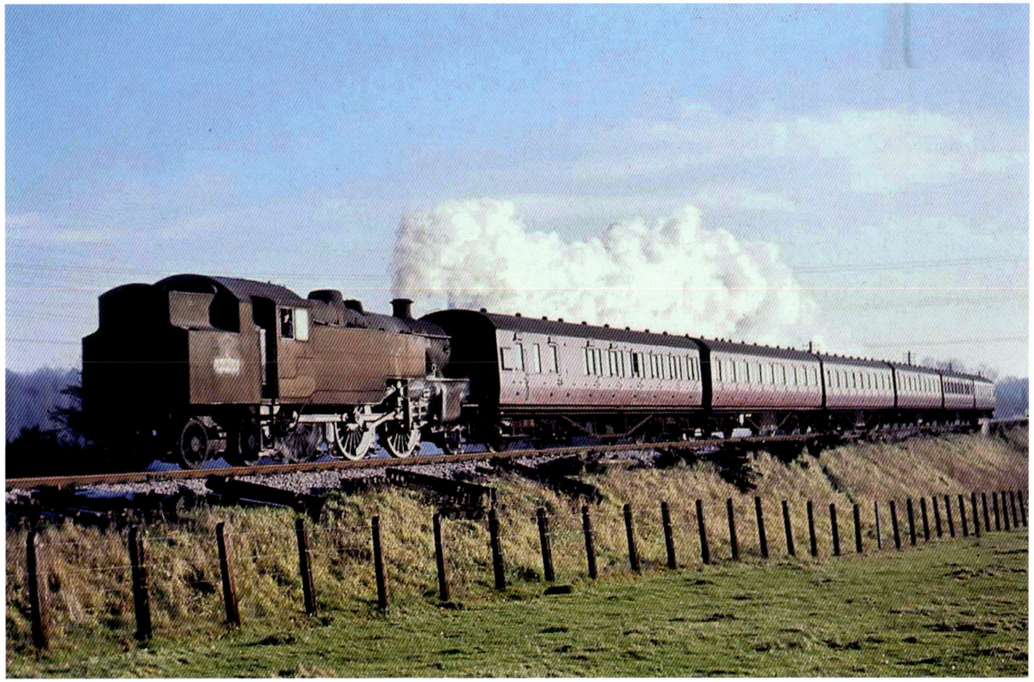

Page left: London Transport's Metropolitan Line A60 stock provides a backdrop on this chilly March morning in 1963 at Amersham, whilst Jubilee 45567 South Australia sprints along the mainline. ***Colour Rail***

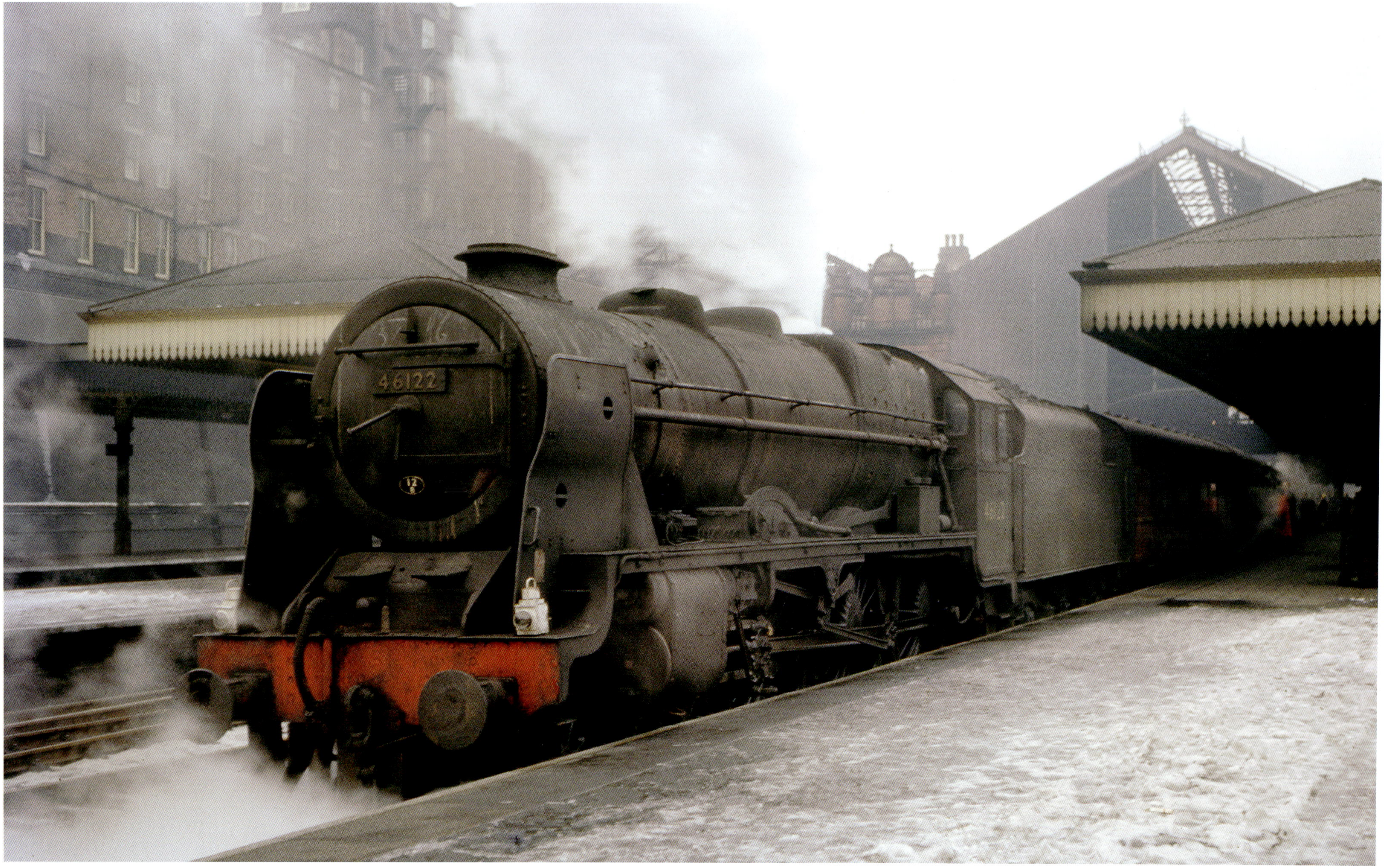

A cold day during that harsh winter in 1963 sees Royal Scot, 46122 Royal Ulster Rifleman ready for the 17:15 departure from Nottingham Victoria for Marylebone on this January evening. ***Win Wall/Strathwood Library Collection***

Opposite: Other railwaymen go about their duties around the shed in March 1964 at 2G Woodford Halse, whilst this cheery pair exchange a few words of banter as they book off duty. ***Win Wall/Strathwood Library Collection***

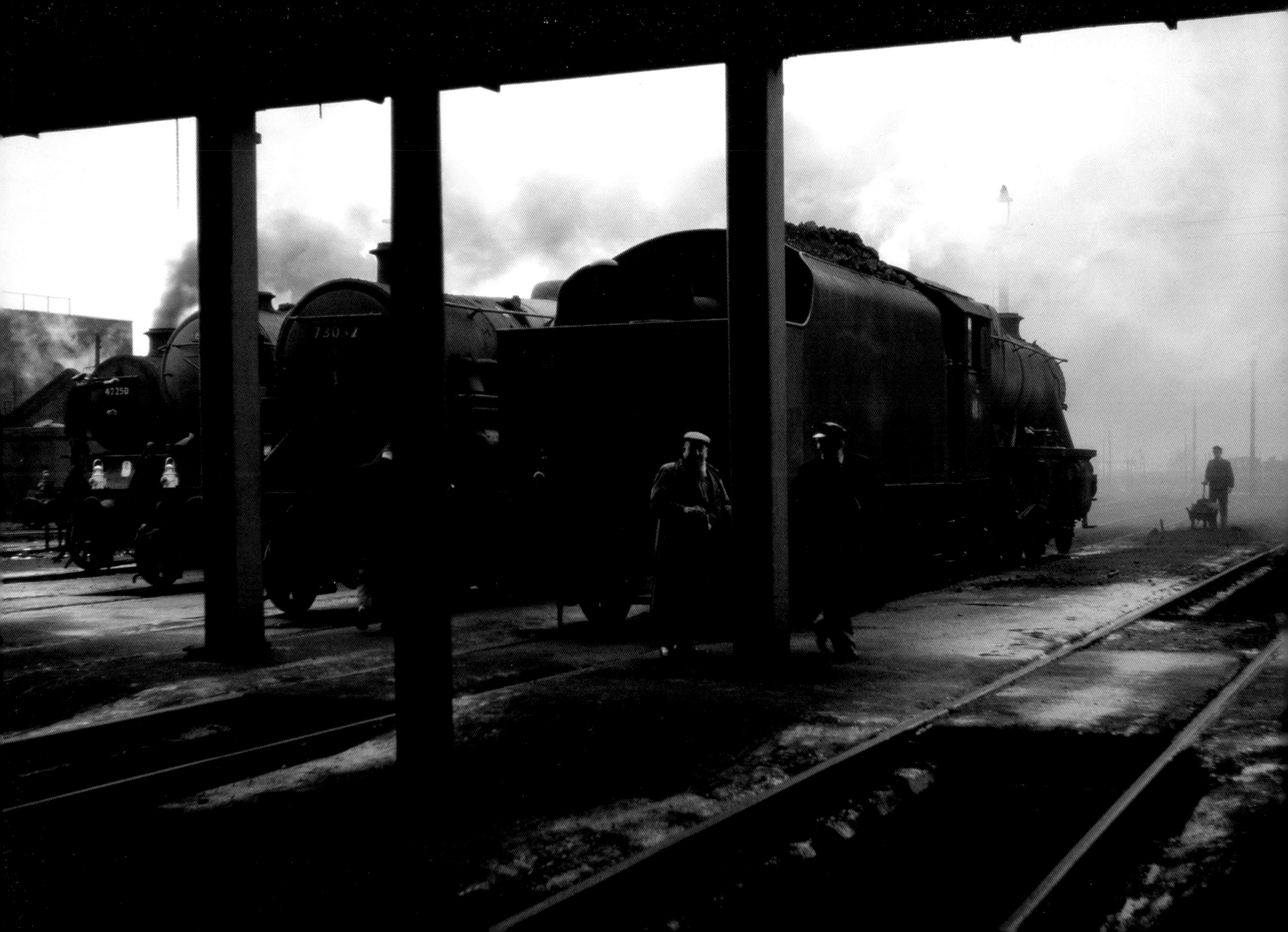
42250

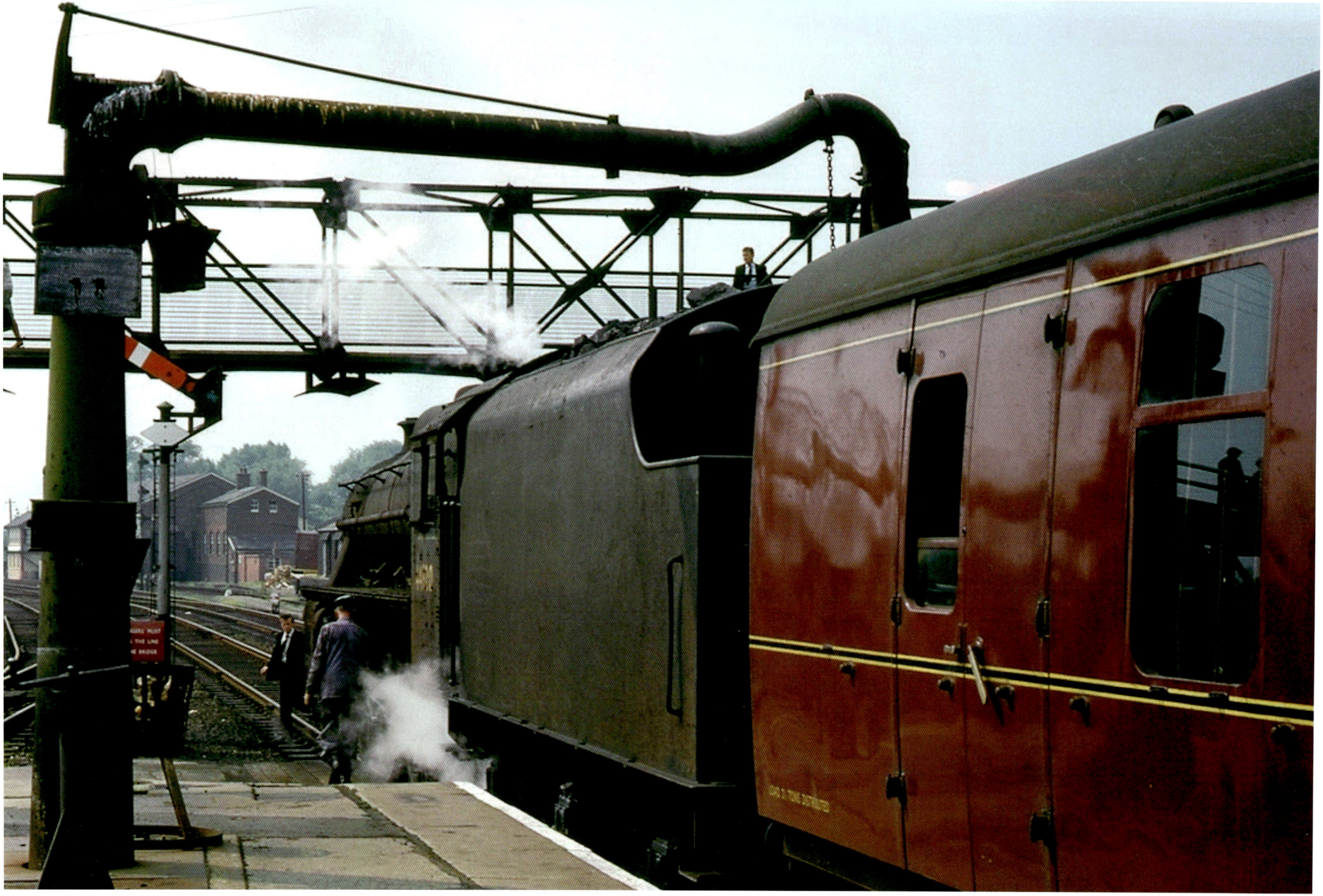

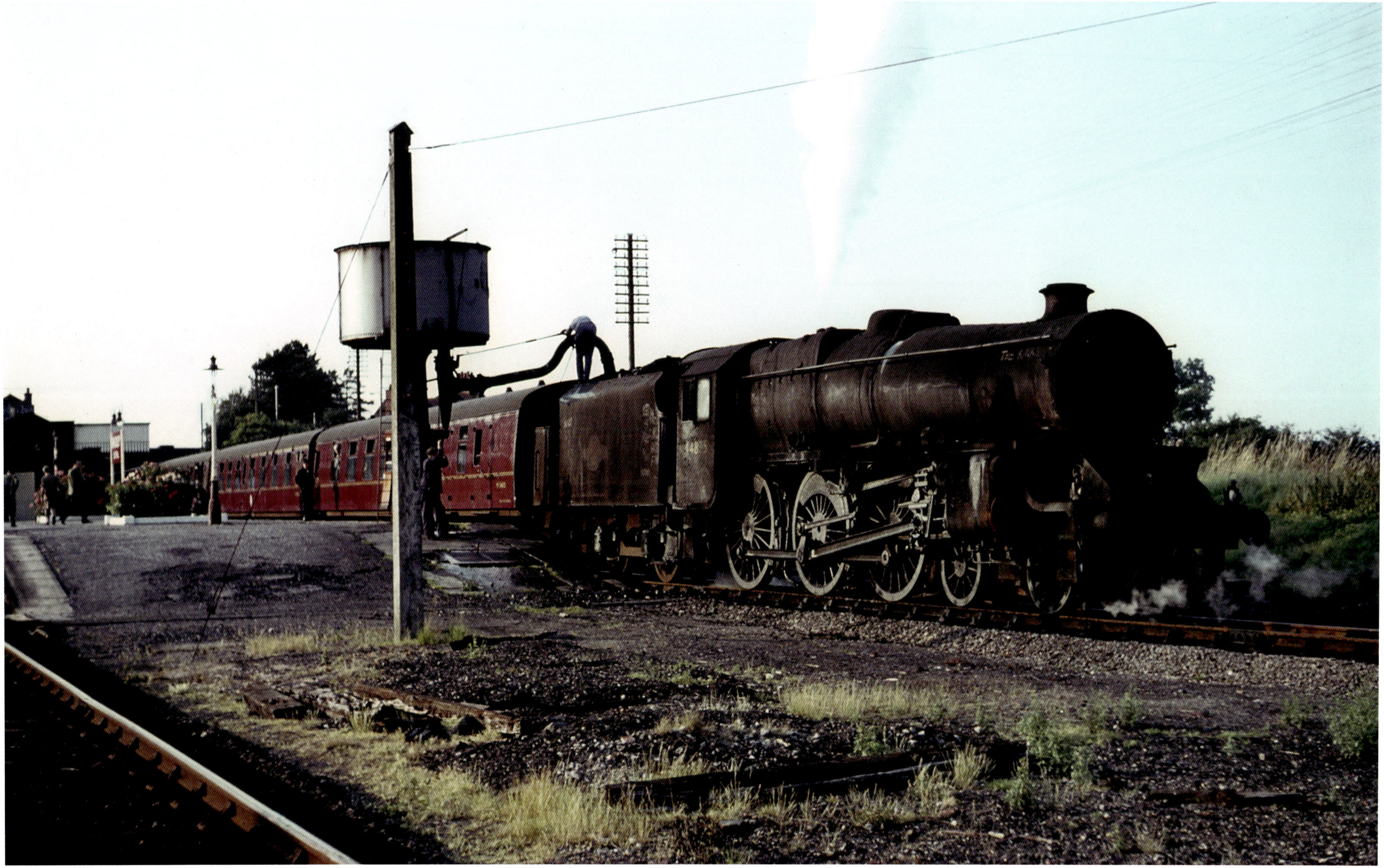

Page left: Quenching the thirst of two Black Fives, firstly with 44920 taking water whilst working the 14:38 Marylebone stopper to Nottingham Victoria at Aylesbury on 10 June 1966. ***Bill Wright***

Only a few more weeks to go for steam on the Great Central on 27 July 1966, as 44835 is attended to at Brackley with the 17:15 Nottingham Victoria to Marylebone. ***Strathwood Library Collection***

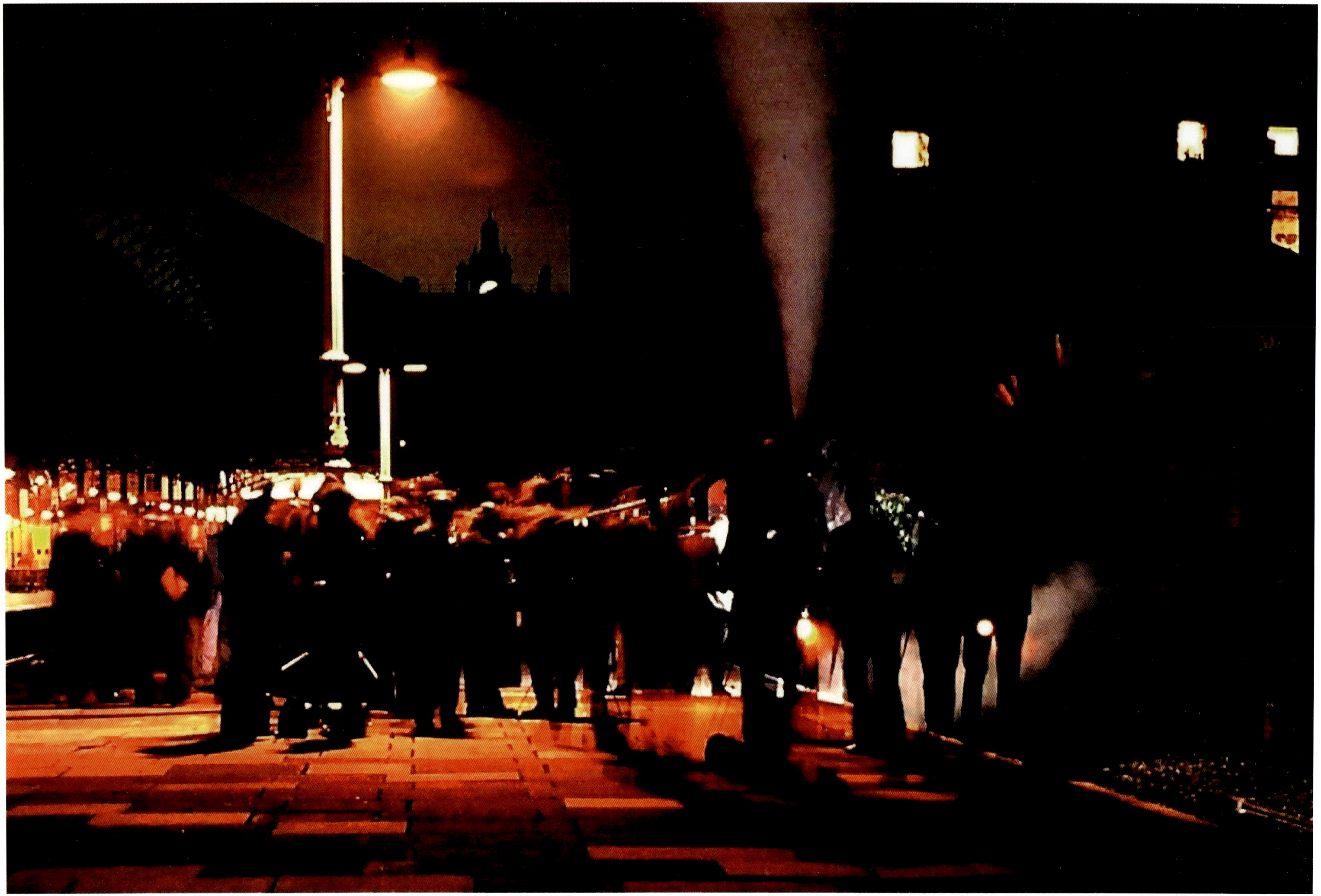

Midland's Routes

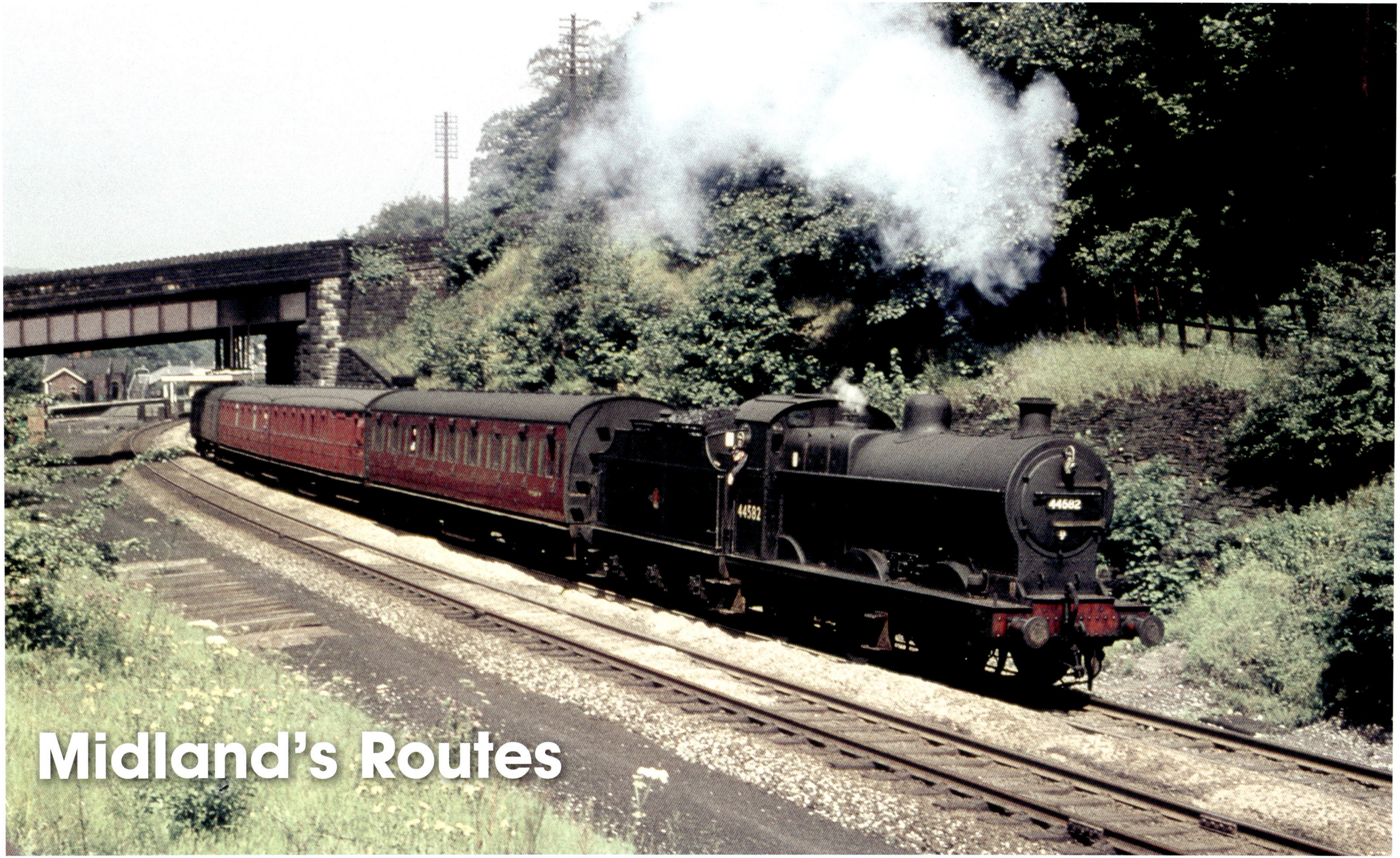

Page left: Those few weeks have passed quickly by, and cameramen and enthusiasts have turned out on 3 September 1966 at Marylebone for the last down departure for Nottingham Victoria, with Black Five 44984 adorned with a wreath for this sombre occaision. ***George Woods***

Sheffield's links with the Great Central would fade into history during the following decade, but in 1959 Fowler's Class 4F, 44582 heads south at Dore & Totley with a local along the former Midland Railway's route to the Steel City. ***Strathwood Library Collection***

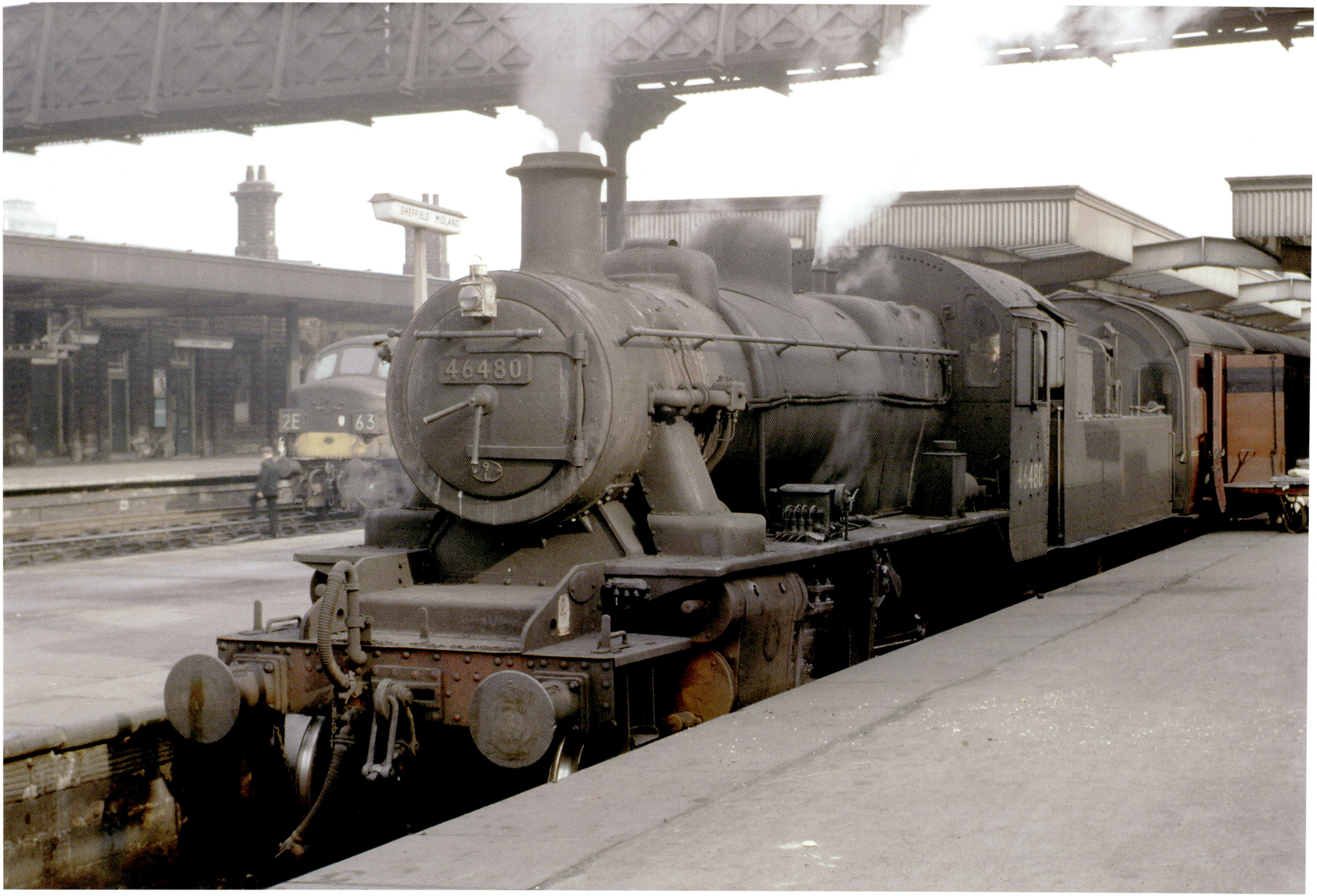
SHEFFIELD MIDLAND
46480
2E 63
46480

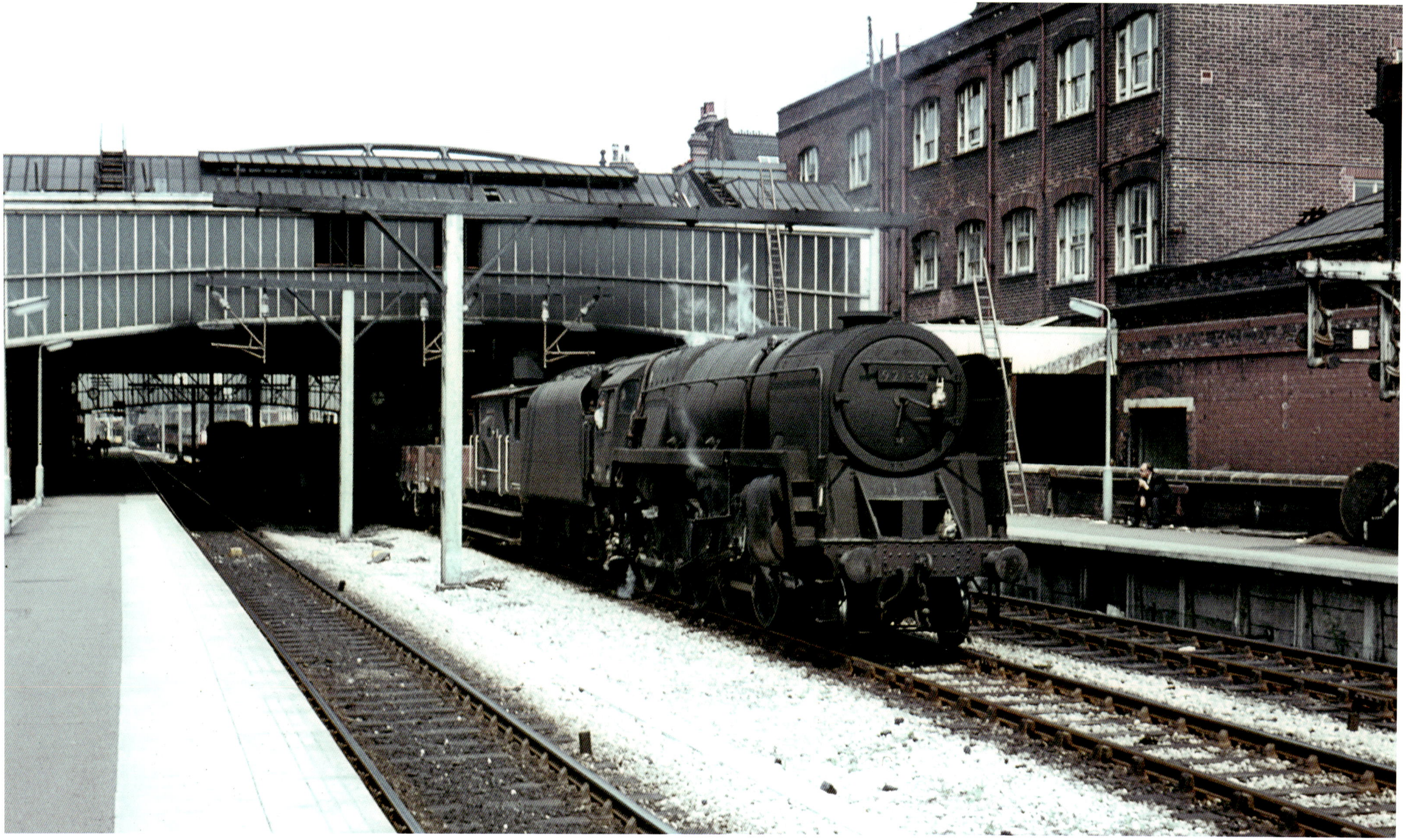

Page left: Parcels traffic is being unloaded from the guard's van behind Ivatt Class 2MT, 46480 at Sheffield Midland. Whilst a Peak rumbles away menancingly in the background as the next generation is ready to take over in May 1964. The station here was opened in 1870 by the Midland Railway and was the fifth and last station to be built in Sheffield's city centre. ***John Rowe***

Whereas the next generation at Stoke-on-Trent will be electrics to oust the likes of Class 9F, 92139 passing through around 1965. A war memorial, with brass nameplates naming the employees of the North Staffordshire Railway who fell during World War I, discreetly flanks the entrance to platform 1. ***Strathwood Library Collection***

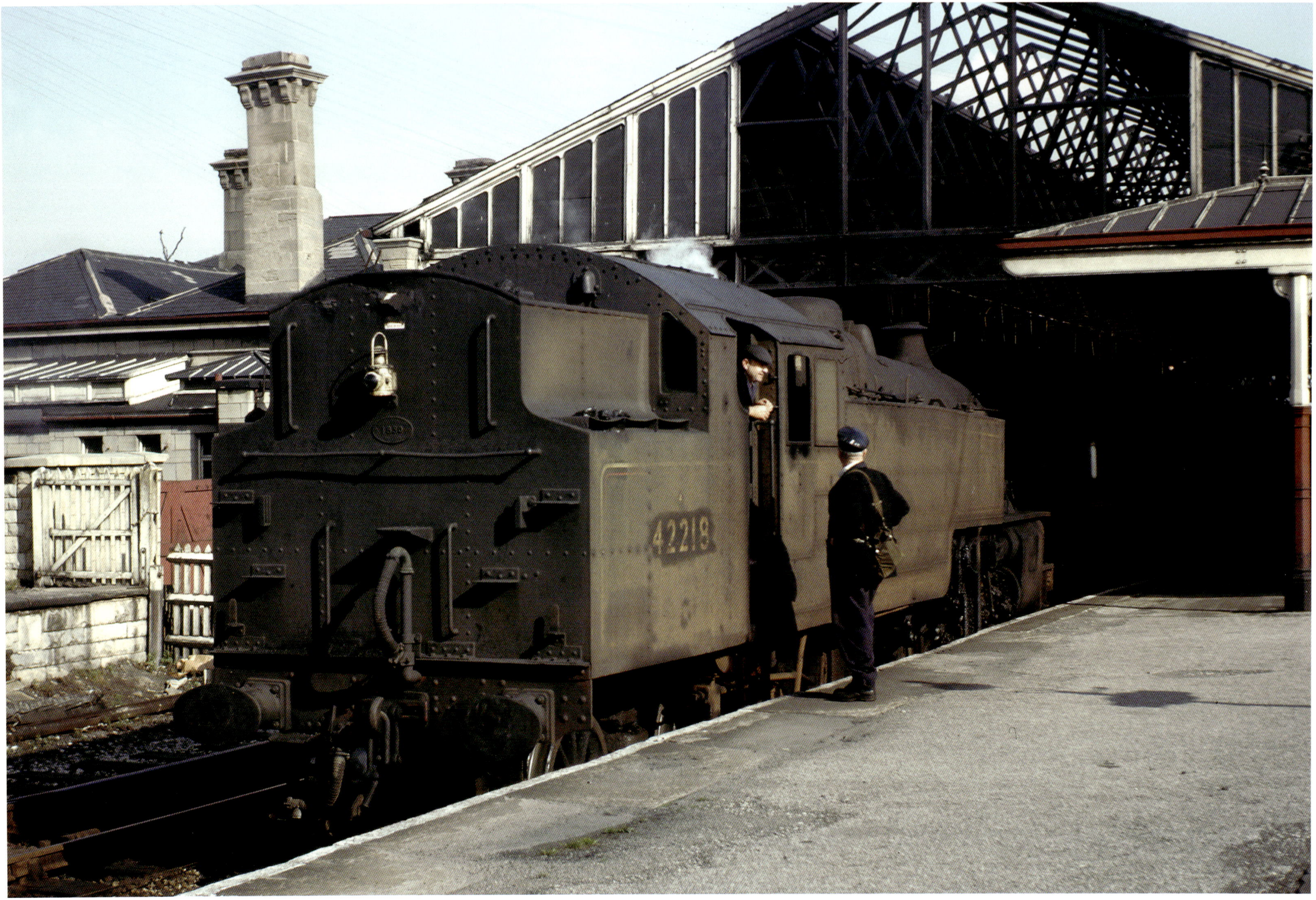
42219

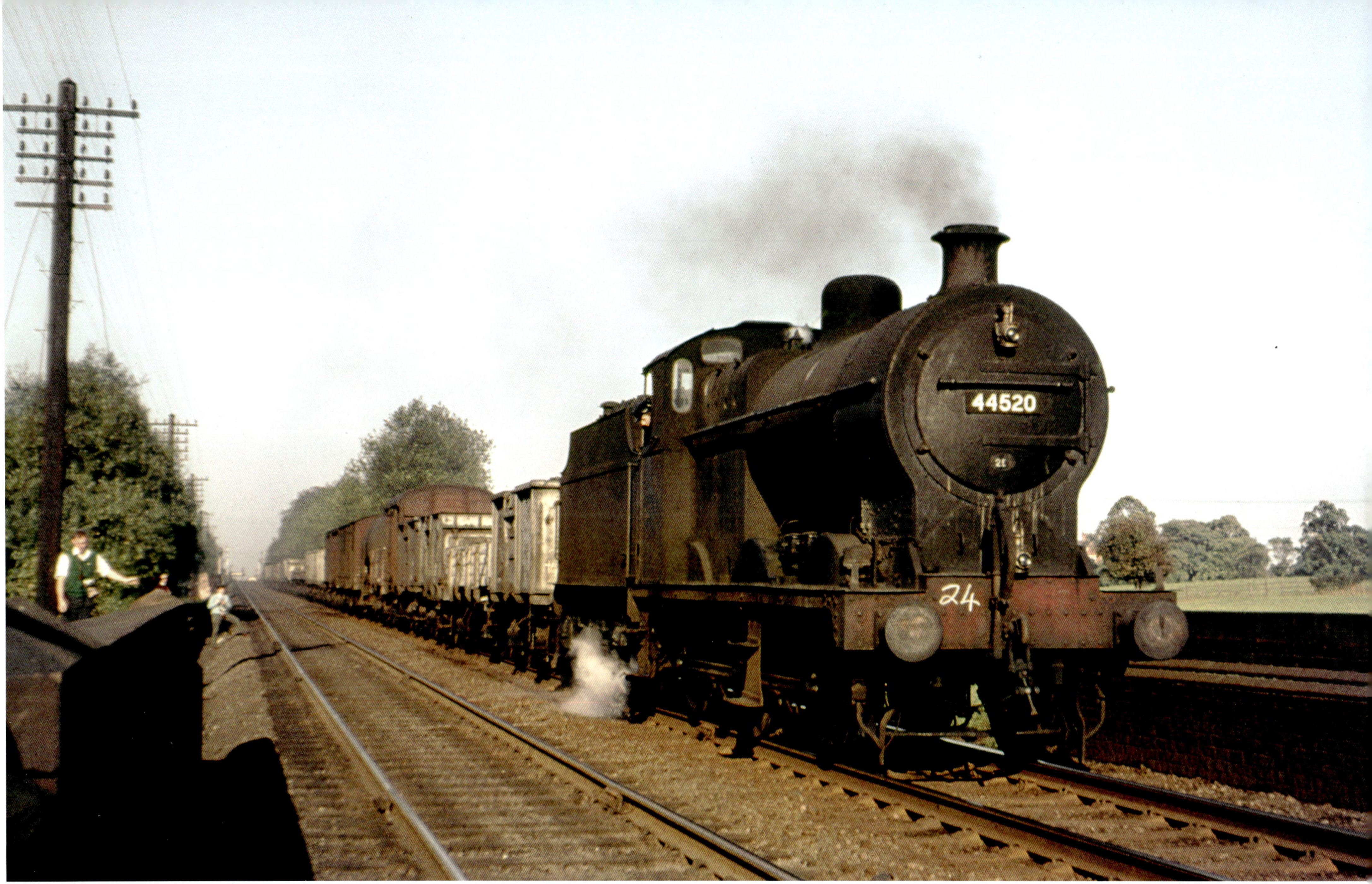

Page left: A more modest overall roof shelters Mansfield Town station in October 1964 as Fairburn Class 4MT 42218 will take onwards a Worksop to Nottingham stopper. ***John Rowe***

Fellow enthusiasts await the next northbound train to slog up the Lickey near Vigo on 12 October 1963, whilst Class 4F, 44520 drops down the bank southbound. ***Peter Simmonds***

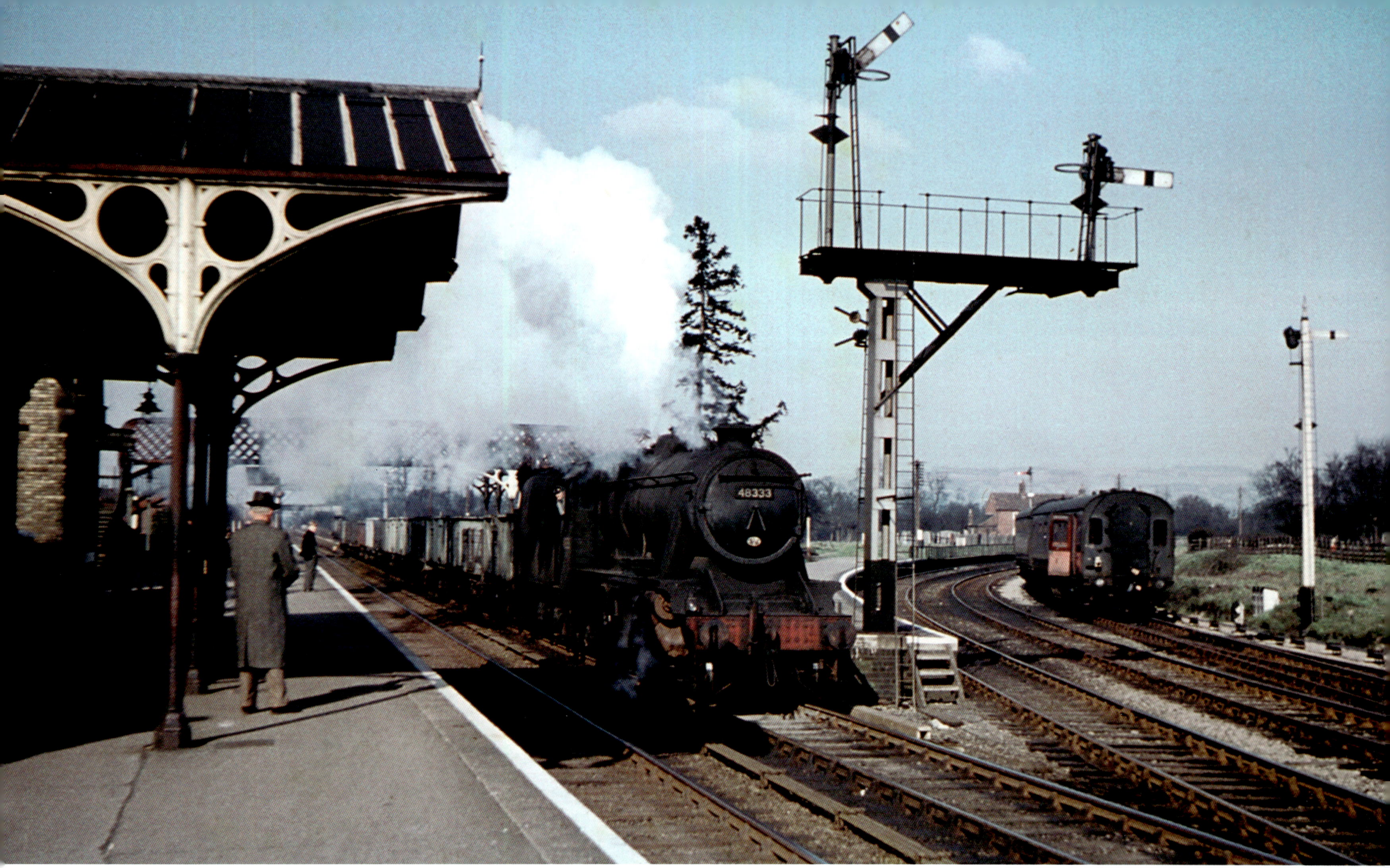

The Midland Railway's influence was still to be felt at Ashchurch on 5 March 1960, as Stanier Class 8F 48333 has a clear road with a down goods. Sadly two fatal accidents occurred near the station prior to its original closure in November 1971, the first on 8 January 1929 and the second forty years later on 8 March 1969. The station reopened on 1 June 1997 on the site of this earlier station which had lain derelict for twenty six years. ***Douglas Twibble***

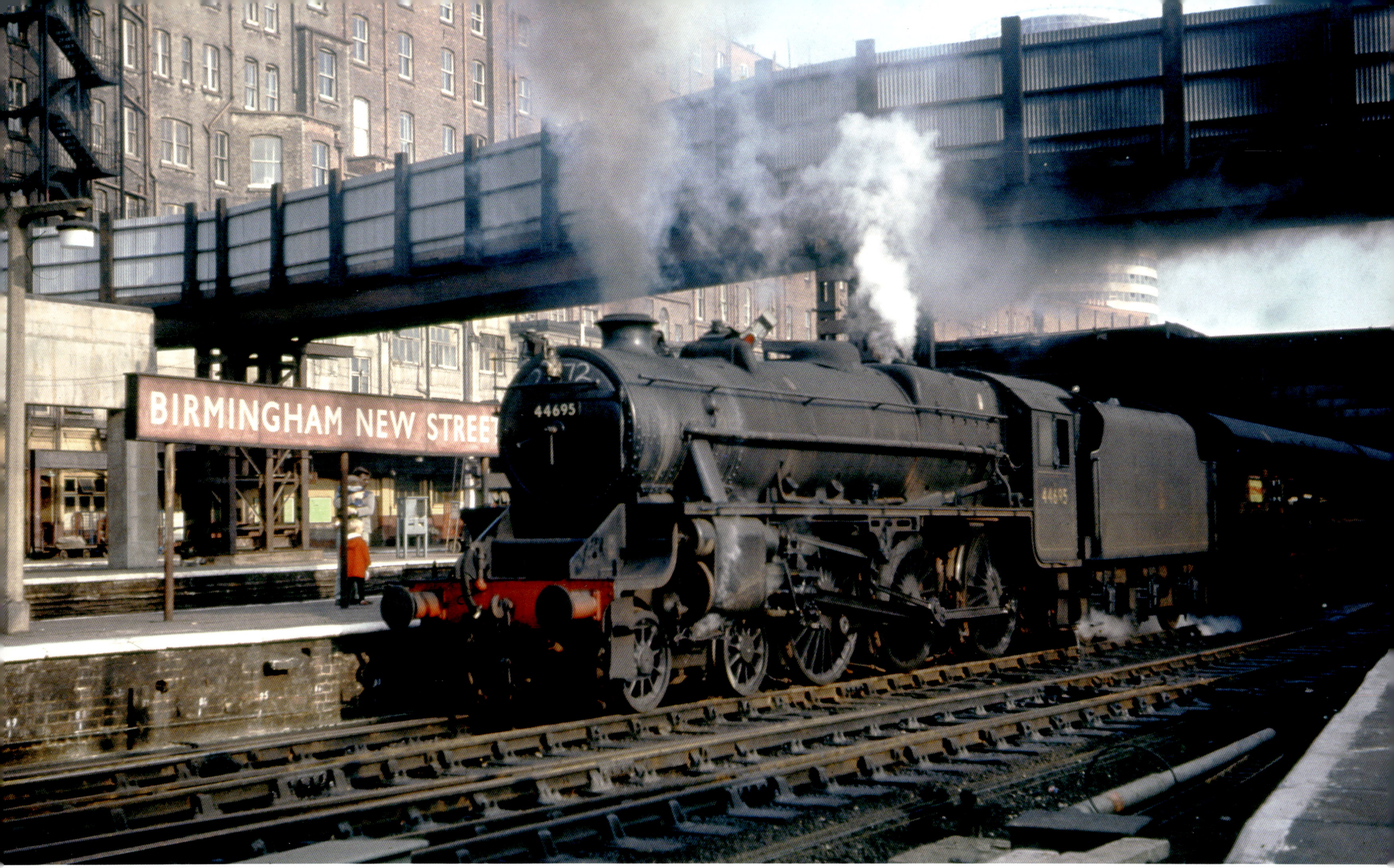

Black Five 44695 gets away past one of the old style nameboards as the rebuilding work has already started during the sixties. The original New Street station was built in the Victorian era and had the largest single-span arched roof in the world. After the 1960s exercise of rebuilding in concrete, the enclosed station, now with buildings over most of its span and passenger numbers more than twice those it was designed for, it became very un-popular with its users. ***Dave Hill***

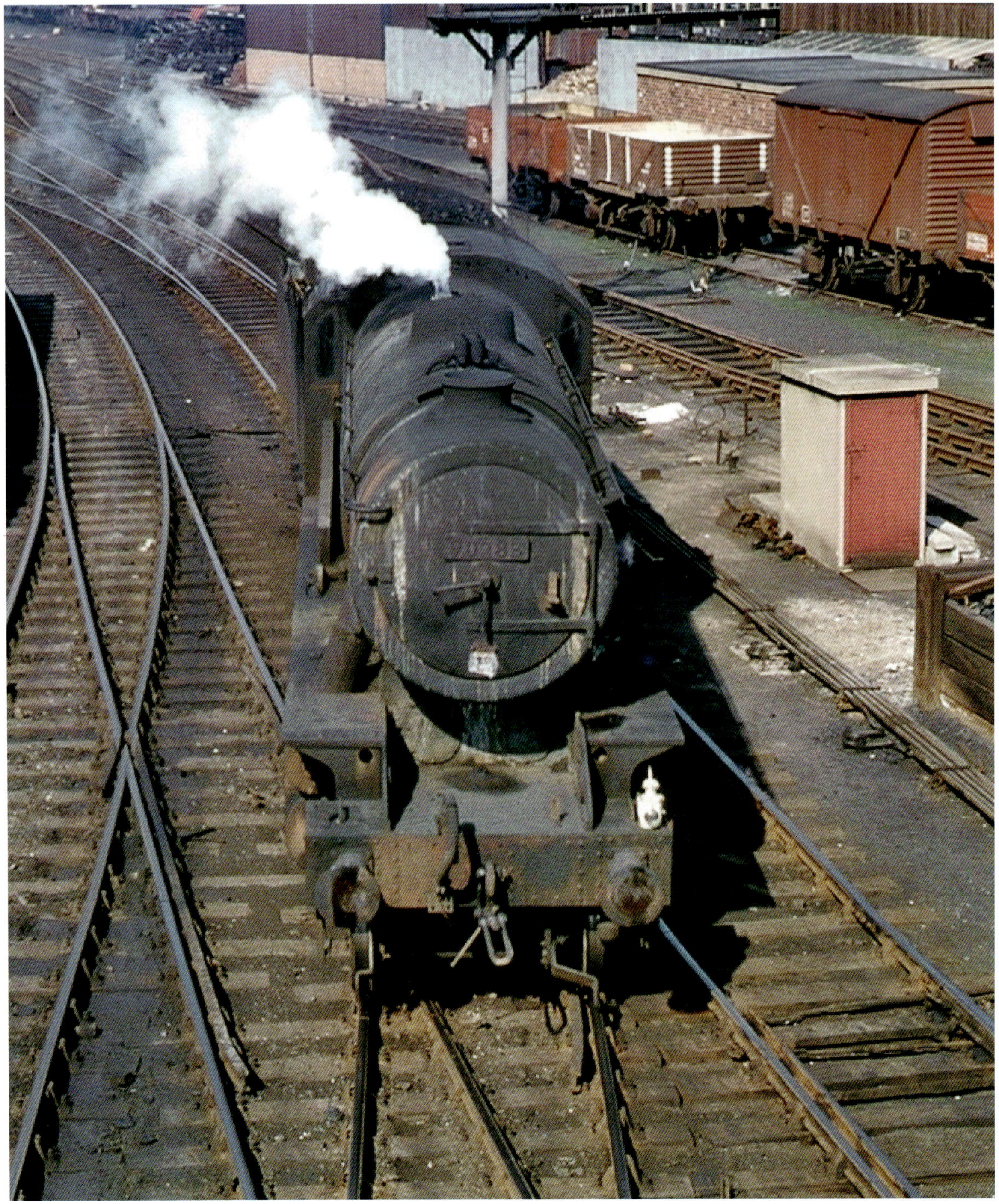

The spritual home of the Midland Railway was here at Derby where a typically shabby Austerity 2-8-0, 90283 wanders light engine past the station and under the long footbridge that linked it to the railway works on All Fool's Day in 1965. ***Bill Wright***

Opposite: Back to the last days of the old New Street station in Birmingham with the Midland Railway's extension which was another remarkable overall roof, as the lined green livery of Standard 5MT 73068 catches the sunshine in 1963. The original semicircular LNWR roof was 1,110 feet long, 205 feet wide and 80 feet high, composed of iron and glass, as built without the slightest support except that afforded by the pillars on either side. This original LNWR station roof was strengthened with additional steel tie bars during 1906-7, this was done as a precaution following the collapse of a similar roof at Charing Cross station in 1905. The LNWR roof was demolished shortly after World War II after sustaining heavy bomb damage during the Birmingham Blitz. It was replaced with temporary canopies over the platforms, which remained in use until the station was rebuilt in the 1960s. ***Tim Matthews***

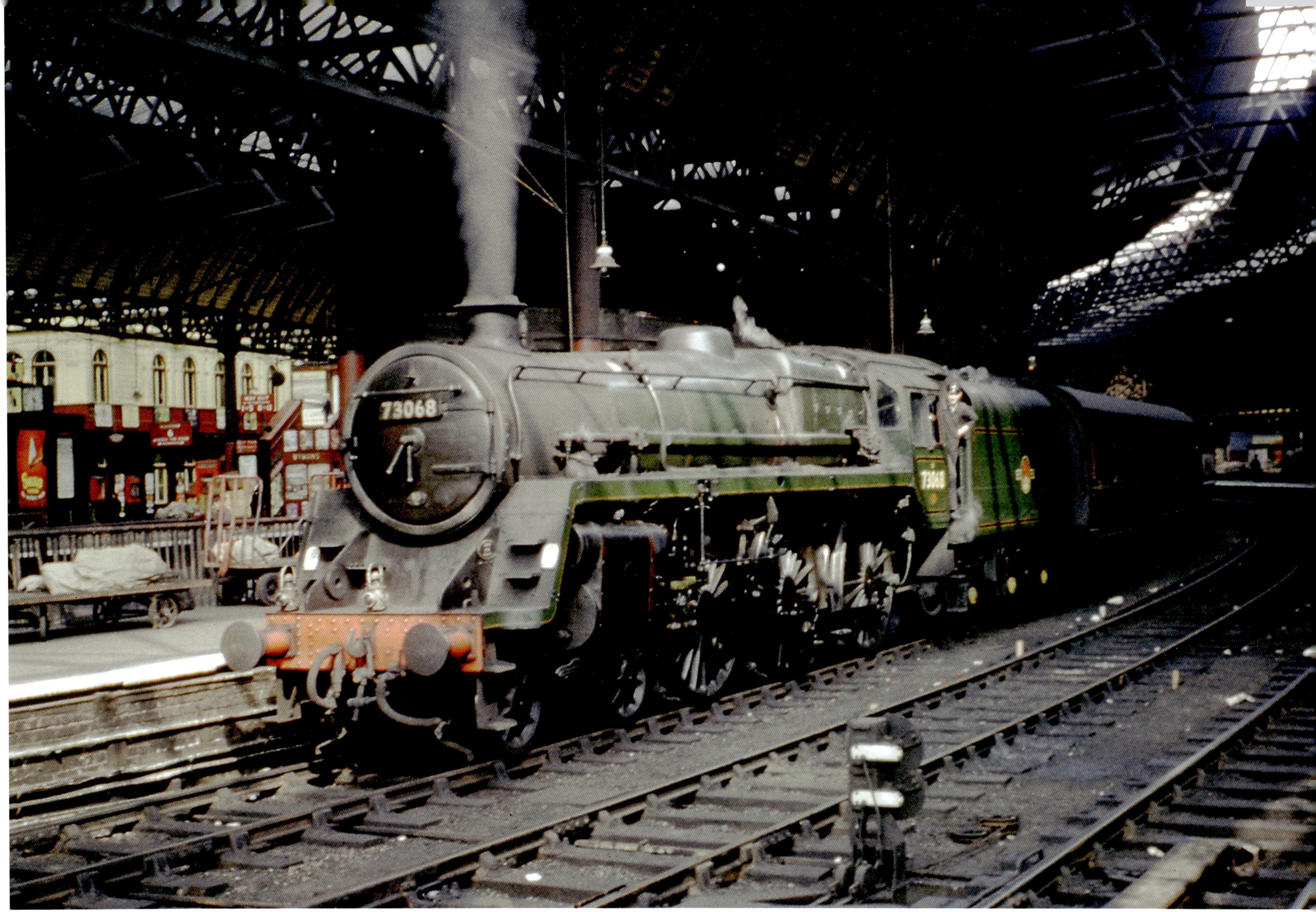
73068

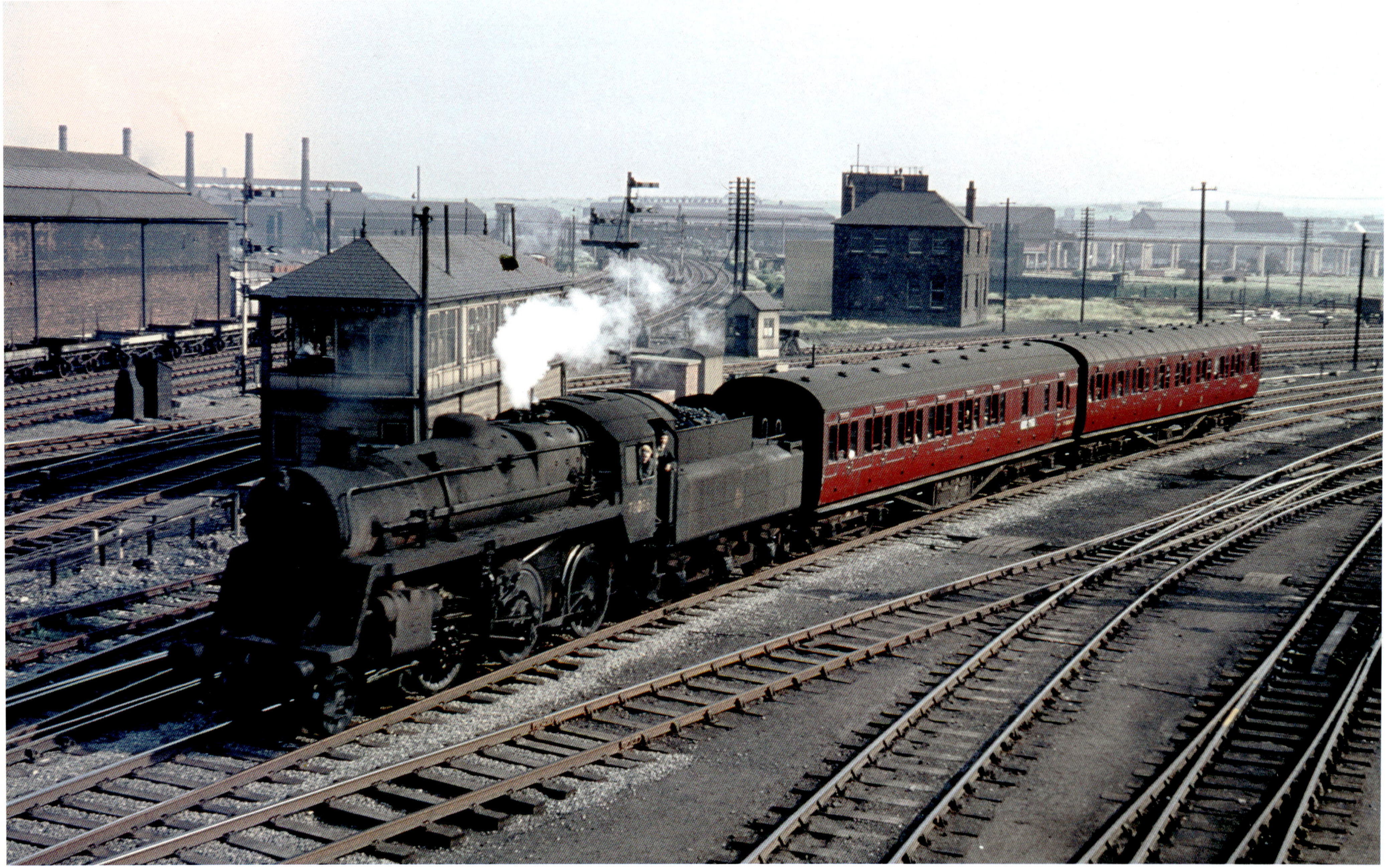

The engine crew look out upon the overbridge and our cameraman as they approach Rotherham's Masborough station, with Standard Class 4MT 76056 more than ample power for this short local service. ***Strathwood Library Collection***

Opposite: We catch up with Fairburn Class 4MT, 42218 once again on a cold and bright morning at Worksop whilst it was engaged on a Nottingham stopping service in October 1964, just days before the engine was withdrawn. ***John Rowe***

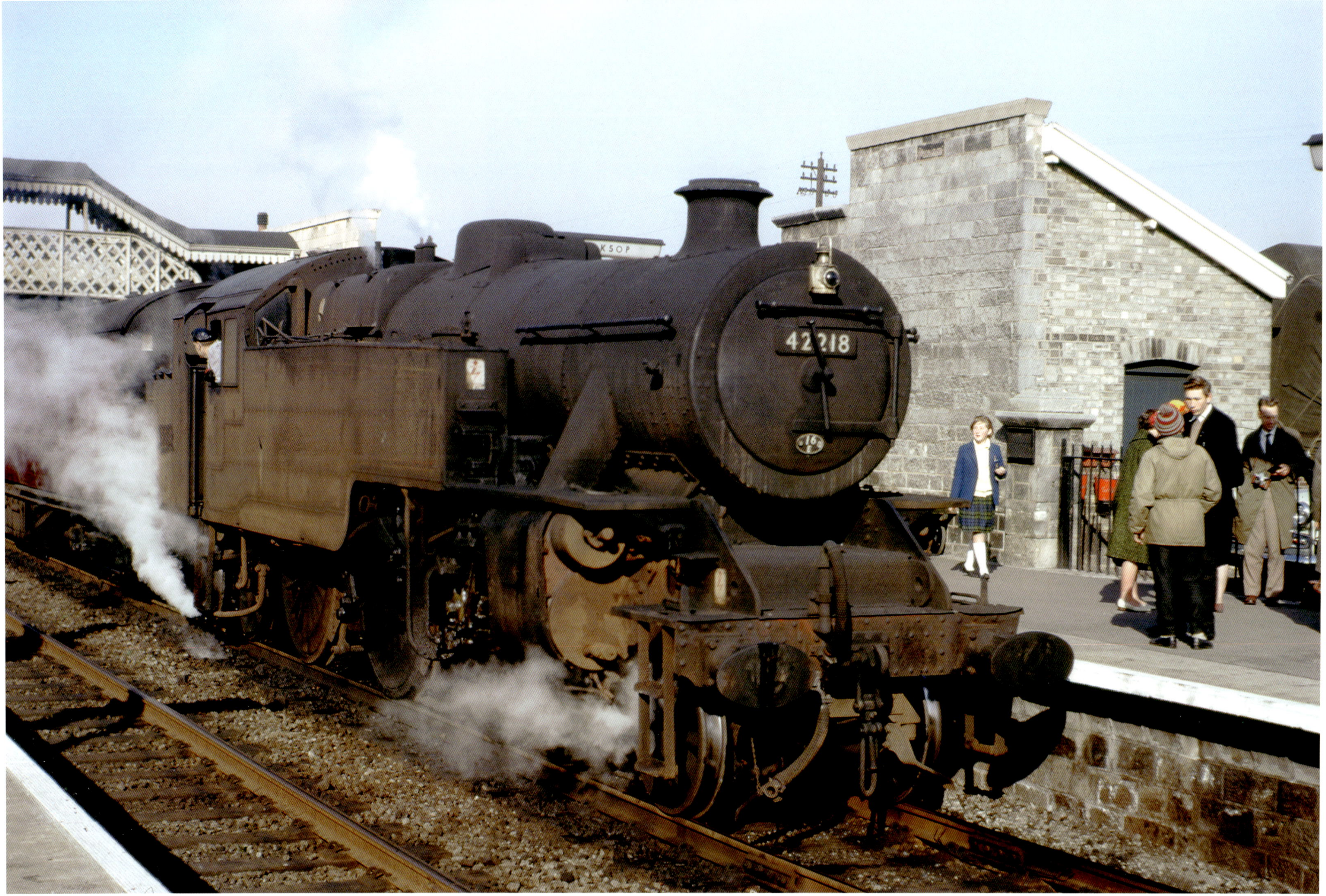
42218

Specials

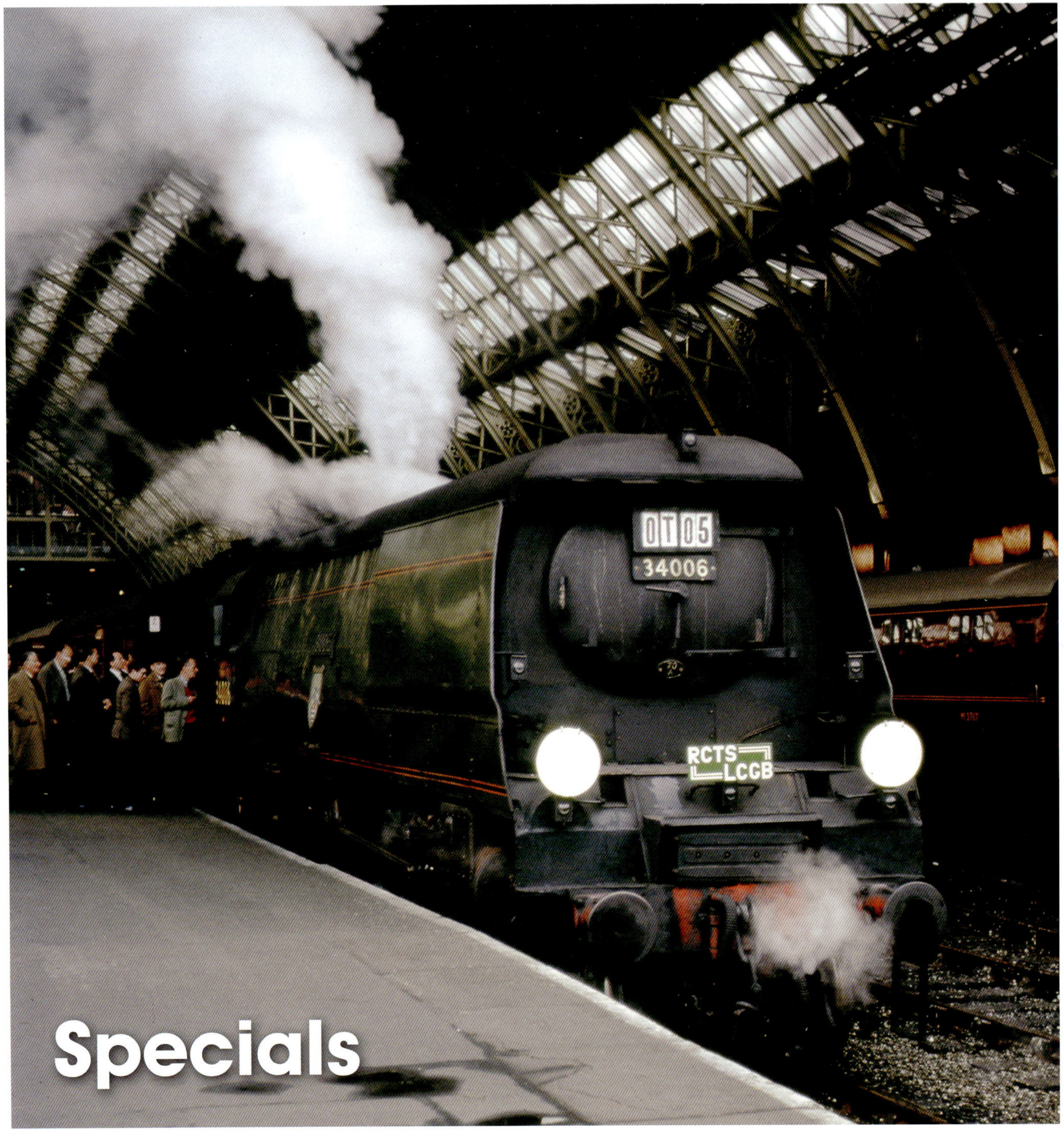

On 11 May 1963 the RCTS/LCGB ran their North Midlands Railtour starting from St. Pancras, with Bulleid's West Country, 34006 Bude at its head. The train was booked to visit Derby for the works and to Buxton, with Class B1, 61004 Oryx booked to take over at Derby to head further northwards. In the event the run behind the Bulleid did not go well, as the crew were not familiar with the locomotive and the planned visit to Derby Works was cancelled as they arrived eighty minutes down. ***Win Wall/Strathwood Library Collection***

Opposite: The previous year the RCTS had better success with their East Midlander No.5 tour on 13 May 1962, running this time from here at Nottingham Victoria to Darlington for another booked works visit, once again behind a Southern locomotive. This time it was Schools, 30925 Cheltenham with Class 2P 40626 tucked in behind. Even though 40626 did not have a valid boiler certificate which was politely overlooked, the pair of 4-4-0s made a spirited run on the return from Darlington to York, with a top speed of 83mph at Thirsk. This was inspite of the Class 2P being described as a very rough runner! ***Strathwood Library Collection***

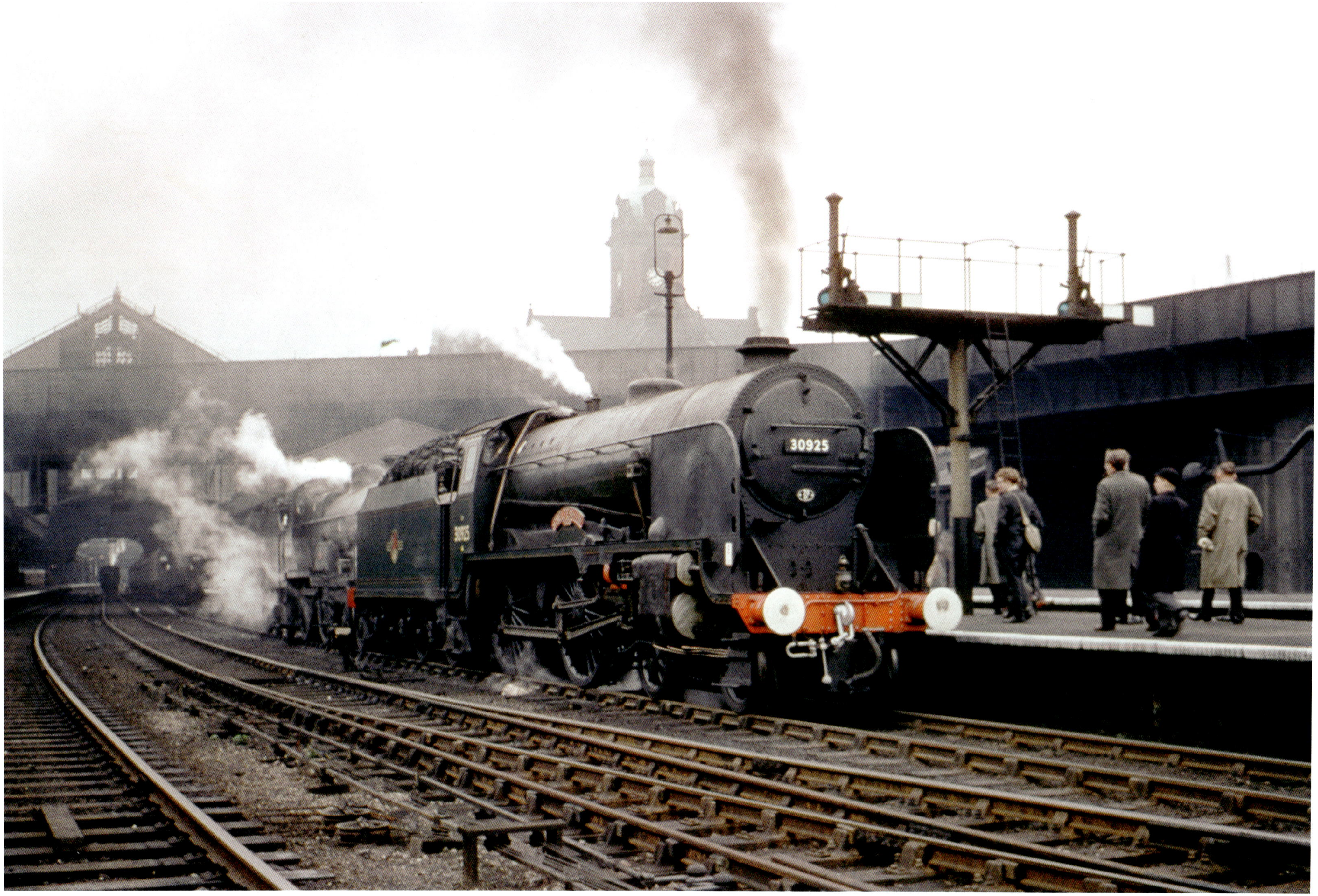
30925

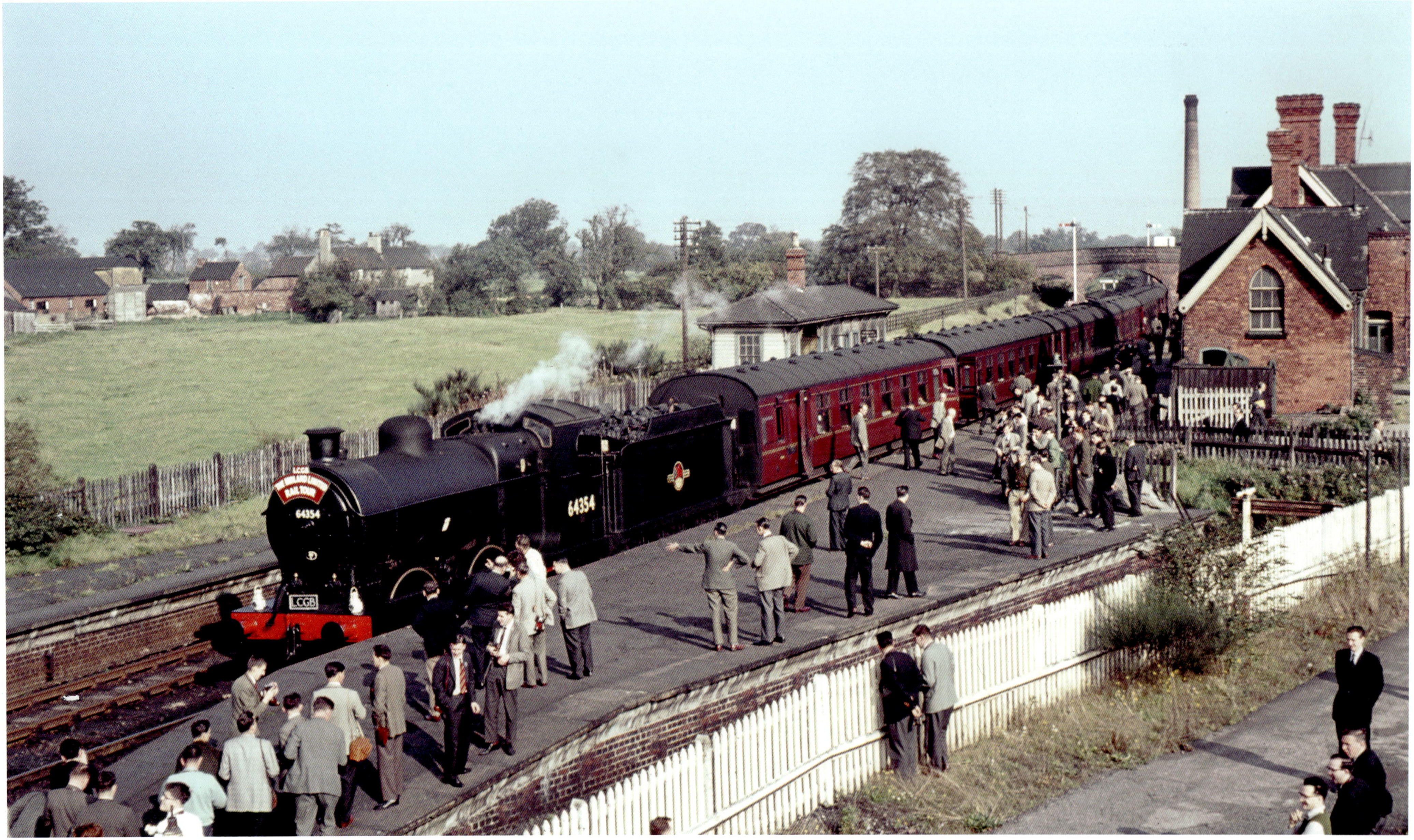

Another locomotive in its last month of service, was Class J11, 64354 when used on 16 October 1962 on one of the legs of the LCGB's Midland Limited tour. This special ran outwards from Marylebone to Nottingham Victoria along the Great Central, thence a tour of lines in the Midlands as here at Egginton Junction, before a return to London via Northampton and Bedford to reach St. Pancras. ***Strathwood Library Collection***

Opposite: A brand new Peak shares the carriage sidings at Kings Norton with our old friend Class 2P, 40646 prior to the start of the Stephenson Locomotive Society's tour named the Seven Branch Lines. Among those seven branches, was the line from Northampton to Bedford via Olney on this the last day it was open, 14 April 1962. ***Strathwood Library Collection***

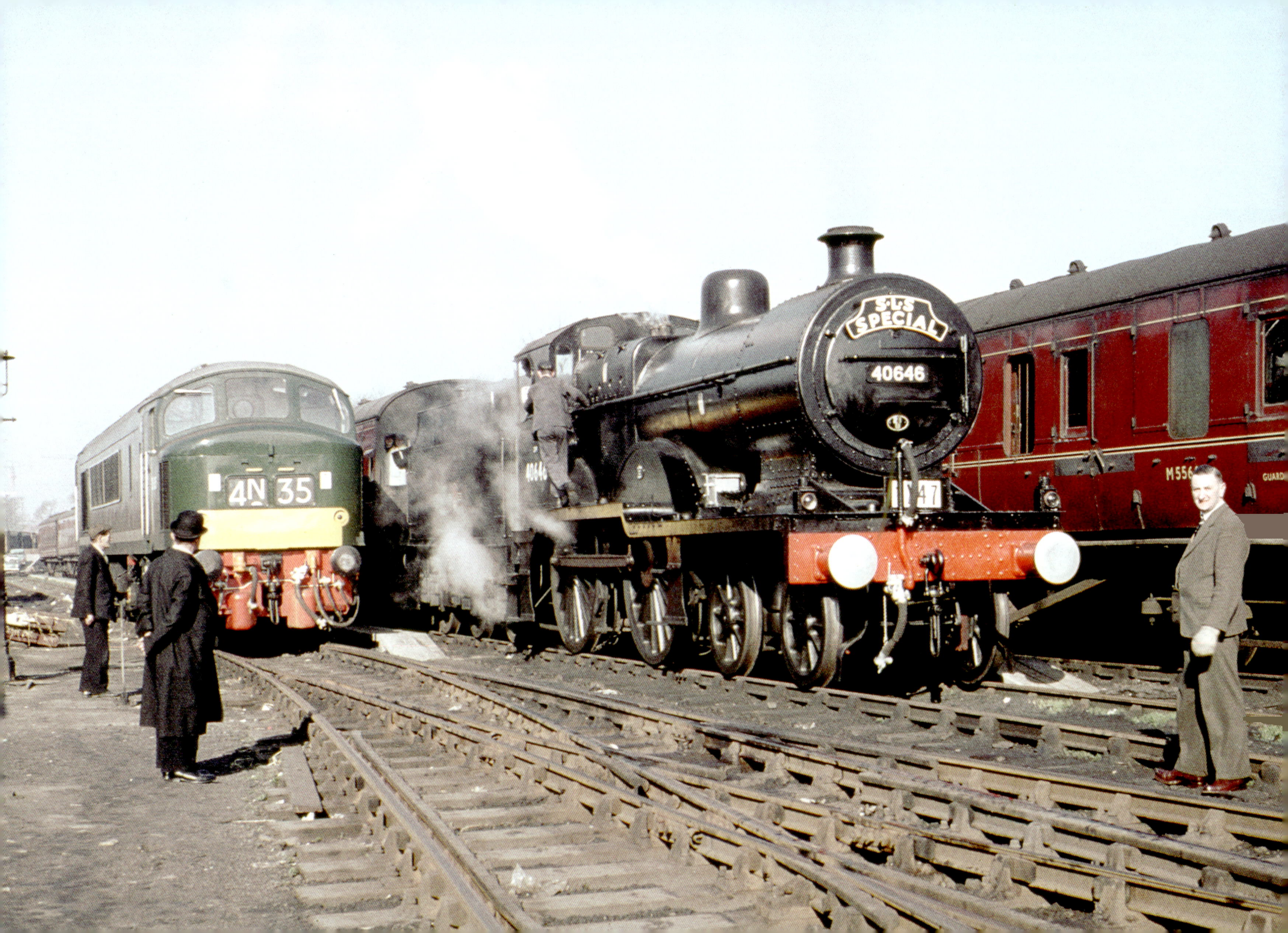
4N 35
S·L·S SPECIAL
40646

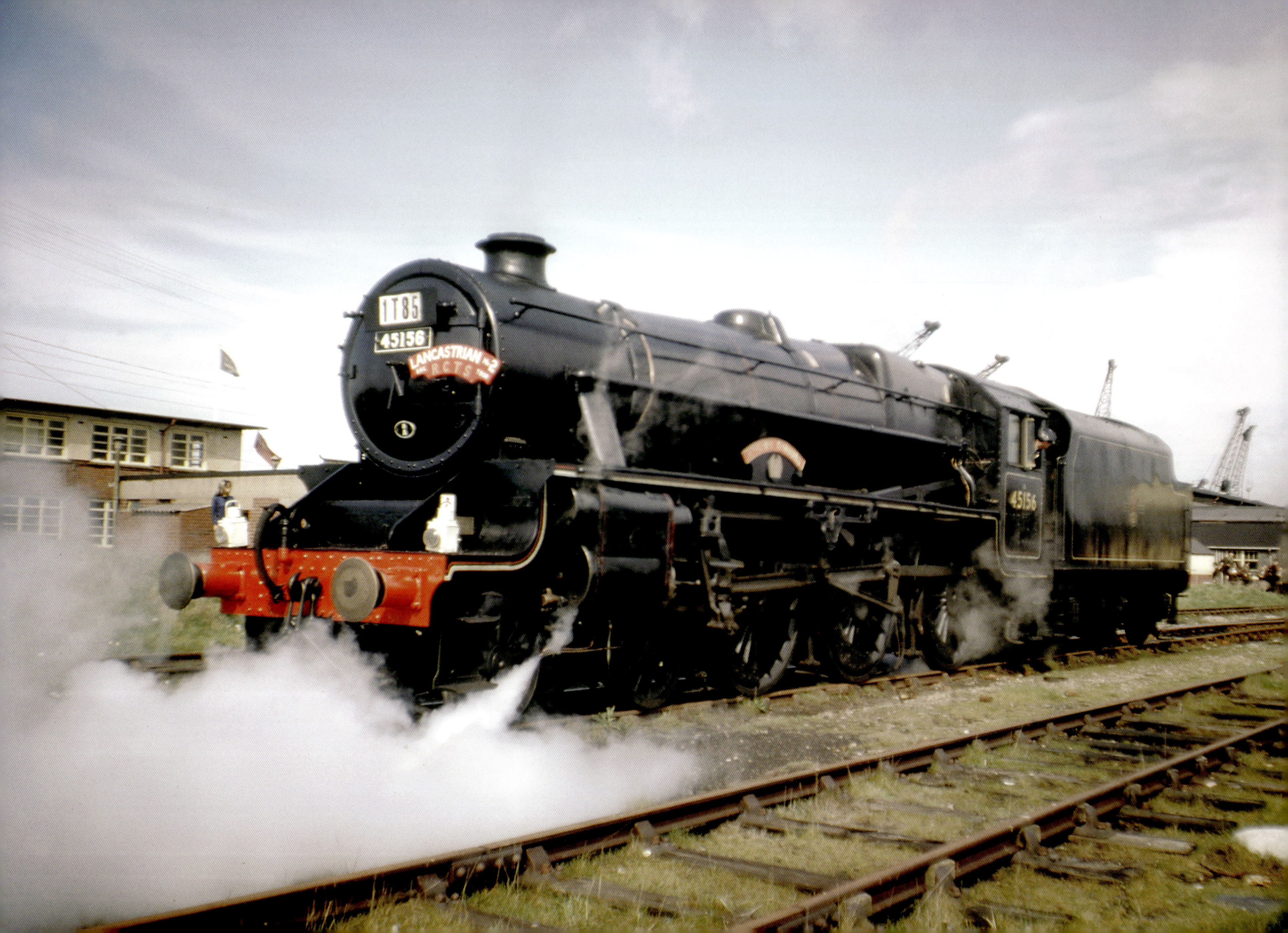
1T85
45156
LANCASTRIAN No 2
RCTS
45156

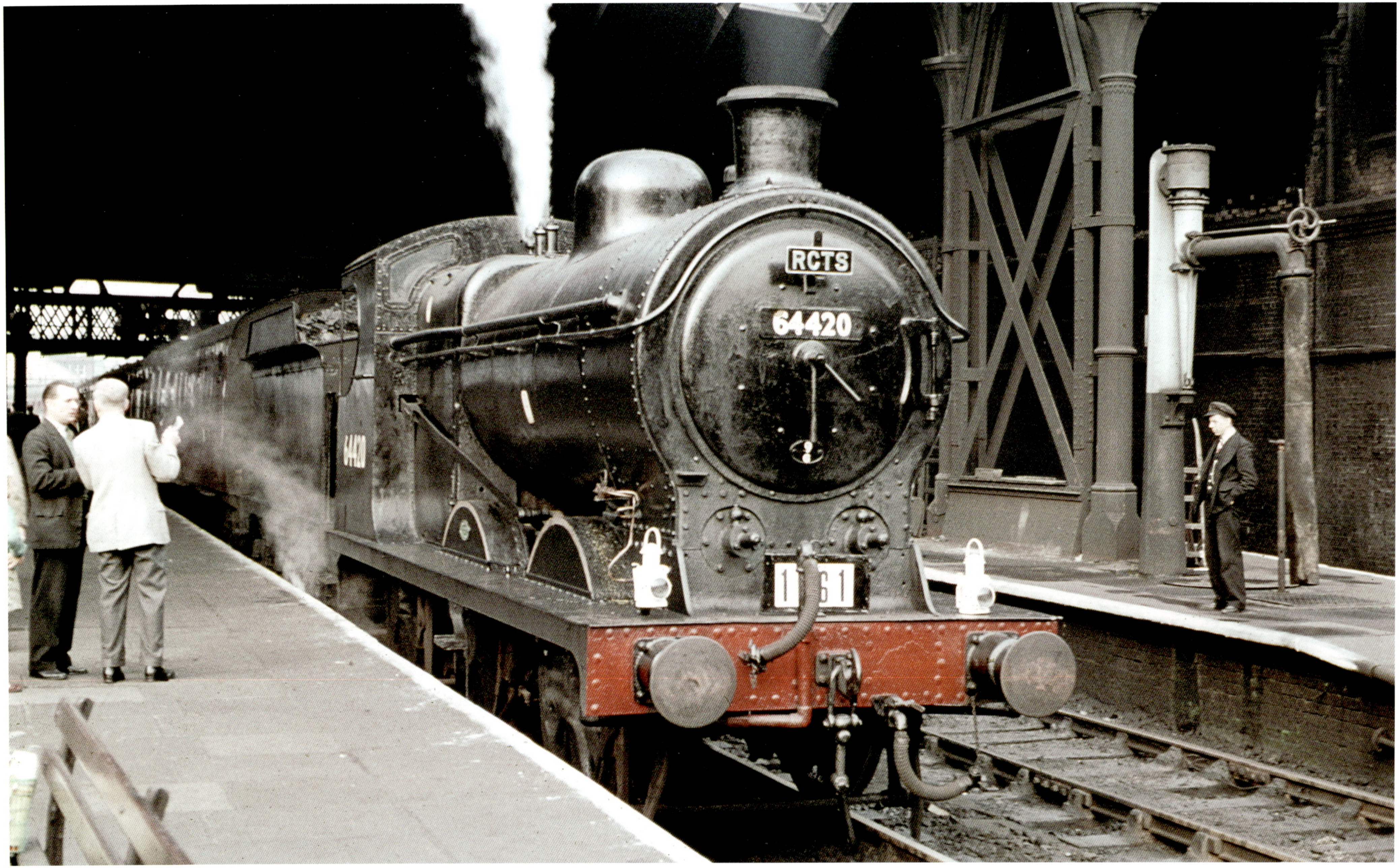

Page left: The sun was shining brightly mid afternoon on 20 April 1968, as Black Five 45156 Ayrshire Yeomanry was running round at Heysham Harbour with the RCTS Lancastrian No.2 Rail Tour. ***Chris Forrest***

On 23 September 1961 it was the turn of Class J11, 64420 to head another RCTS special, this time it was the Four Counties Rail Tour from here at Manchester Victoria. ***Strathwood Library Collection***

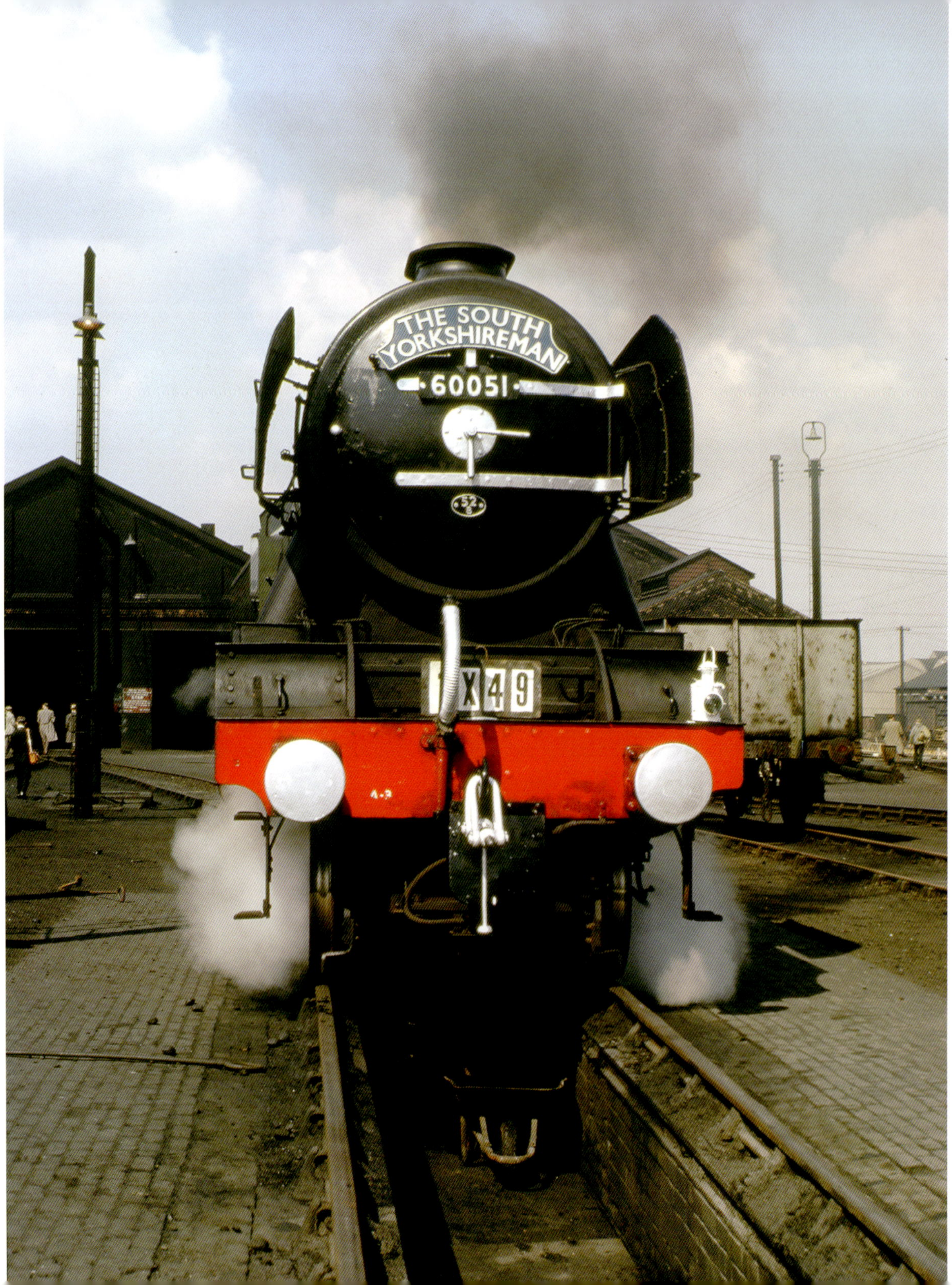

The Halifax Railfans and the Pennine Railway Society combined resources to run the South Yorkshireman No.2 tour on 18 April 1964. Star of the day was Class A3, 60051 Blink Bonny seen here taking a breather whilst the tour's particpants visited both Derby Works and here at 16C Derby's former Midland Railway engine shed. ***John Rowe***

Opposite: The RCTS commemorated the virtual end of the once numerous fleet of Midland 0-6-0 tender locomotives on 16 October 1965. Their tour visited numerous lines in the heart of the Midland system, where these engines were once so common. Such was the rarity now of the 4Fs that 43953 had to be brought in from Workington shed to power the train. This locomotive would in fact prove to be the last Midland 4F in service, retirement coming about three weeks later on 6 November. Whilst prepared to the highest standard for the railtour it became obvious towards the end that all was not well with 43953, with time being lost and the speed rarely exceeding 30mph. Maybe it was the 50mph streak on the Ambergate to Derby section after this stop at Ambergate, that perhaps overstretched the forty-four year veteran. ***Strathwood Library Collection***

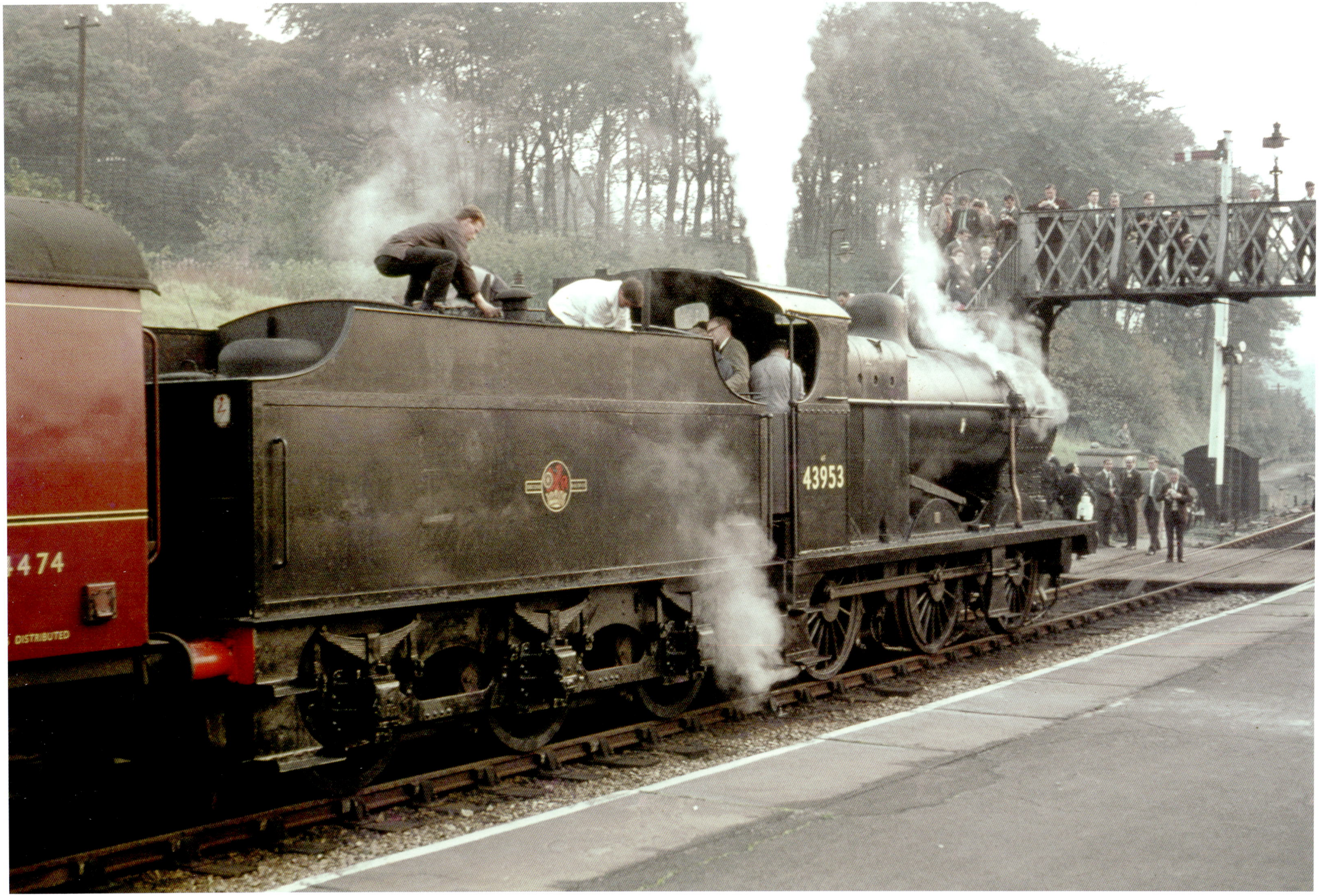
43953
4474
DISTRIBUTED

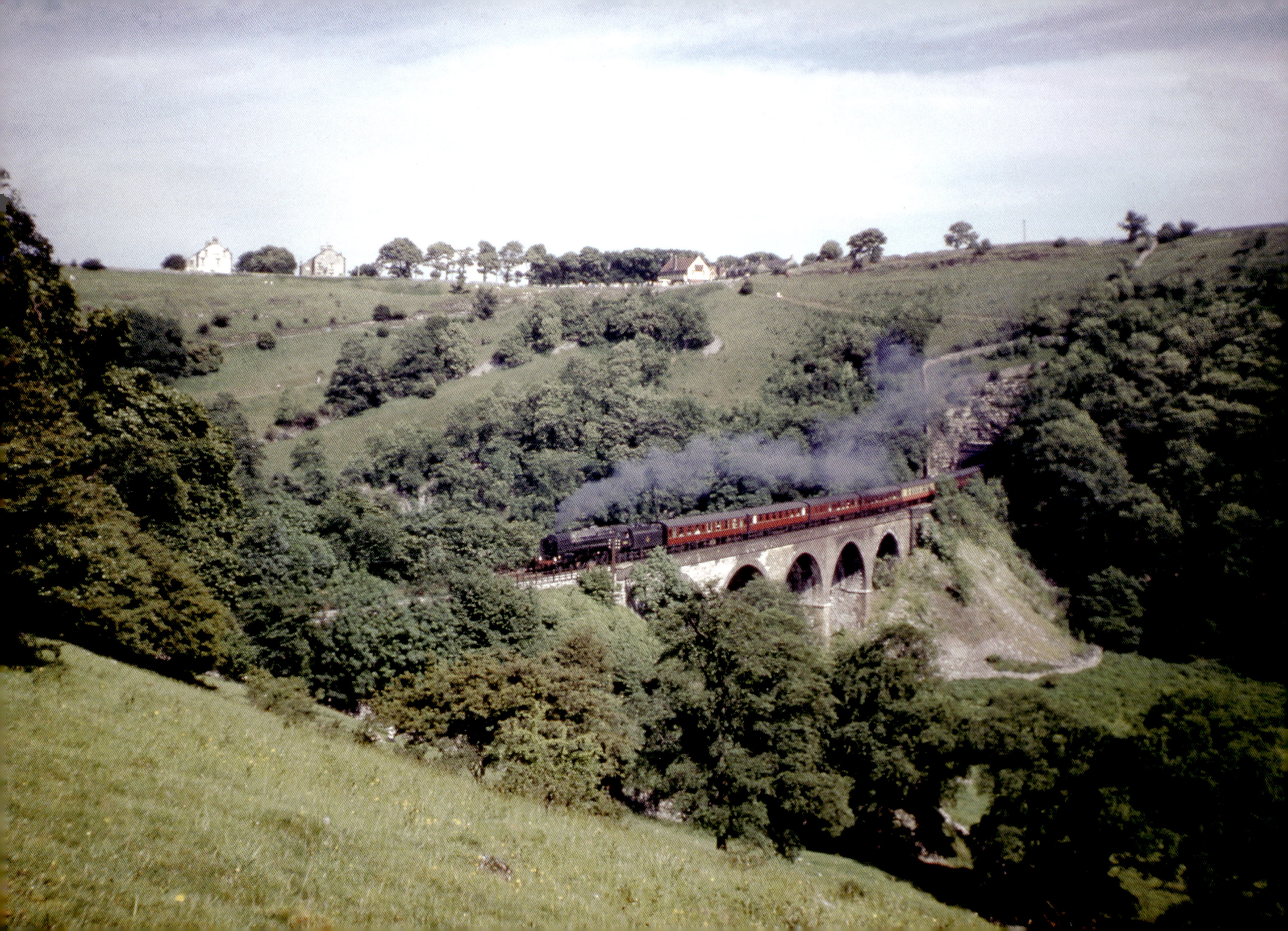

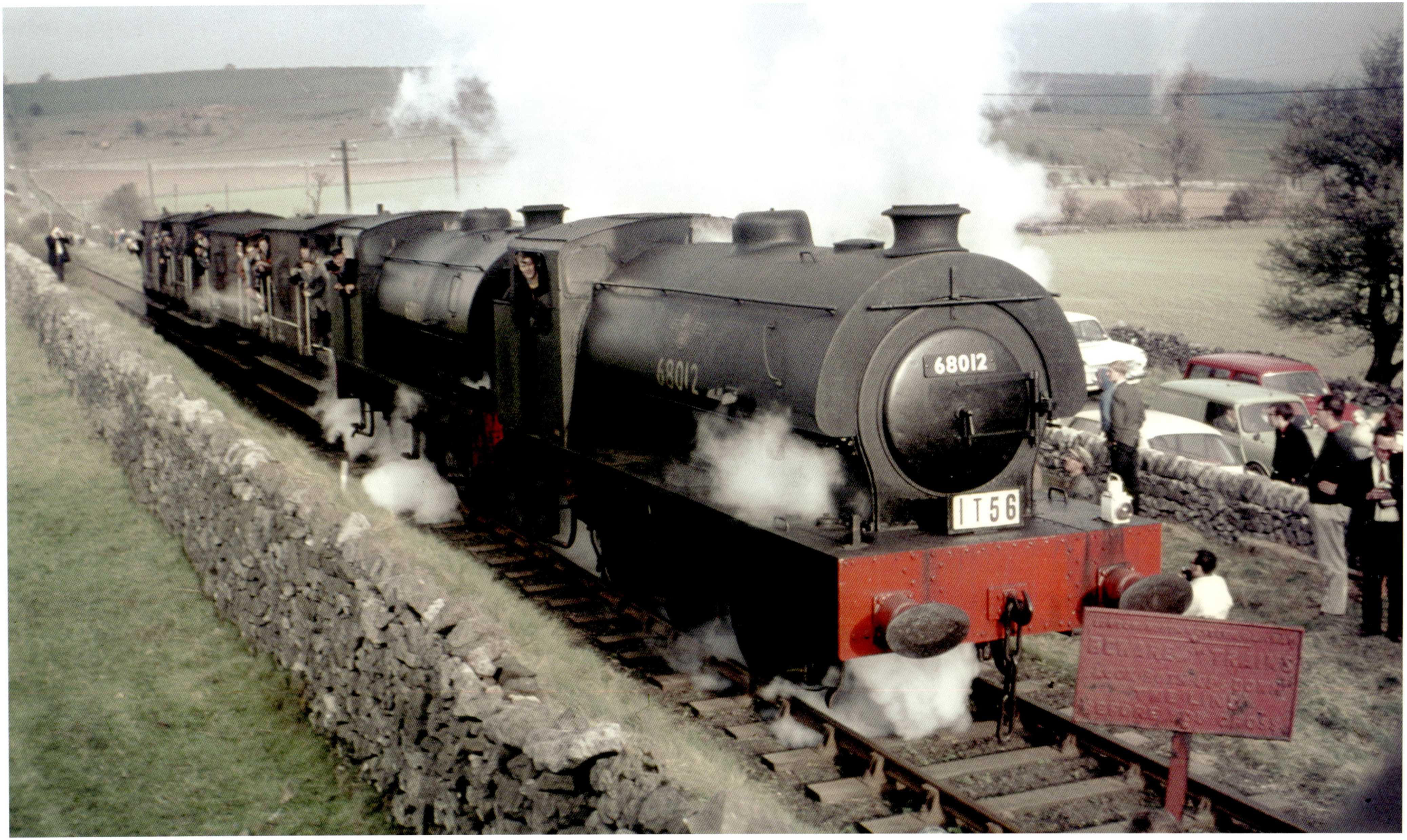

Page left: Staying in Derbyshire we see Britannia, 70013 Oliver Cromwell at Monsal Dale, which we believe was the last steam locomotive to haul a passenger train over the Derby to Manchester route on 9 June 1968. As from 1 July 1968 the route beyond Matlock to Chinley North Junction closed to passenger services with the section as far as Topley Pike closing completely. ***Chris Forrest***

Crowds of enthusiasts gather at the top of the famous Hopton Incline as Class J94s, 68006 and 68012 breast the summit with a brake van special, the line closed shortly afterwards in the spring of 1967, after one hundred and thirty six years of operation. ***Strathwood Library Collection***

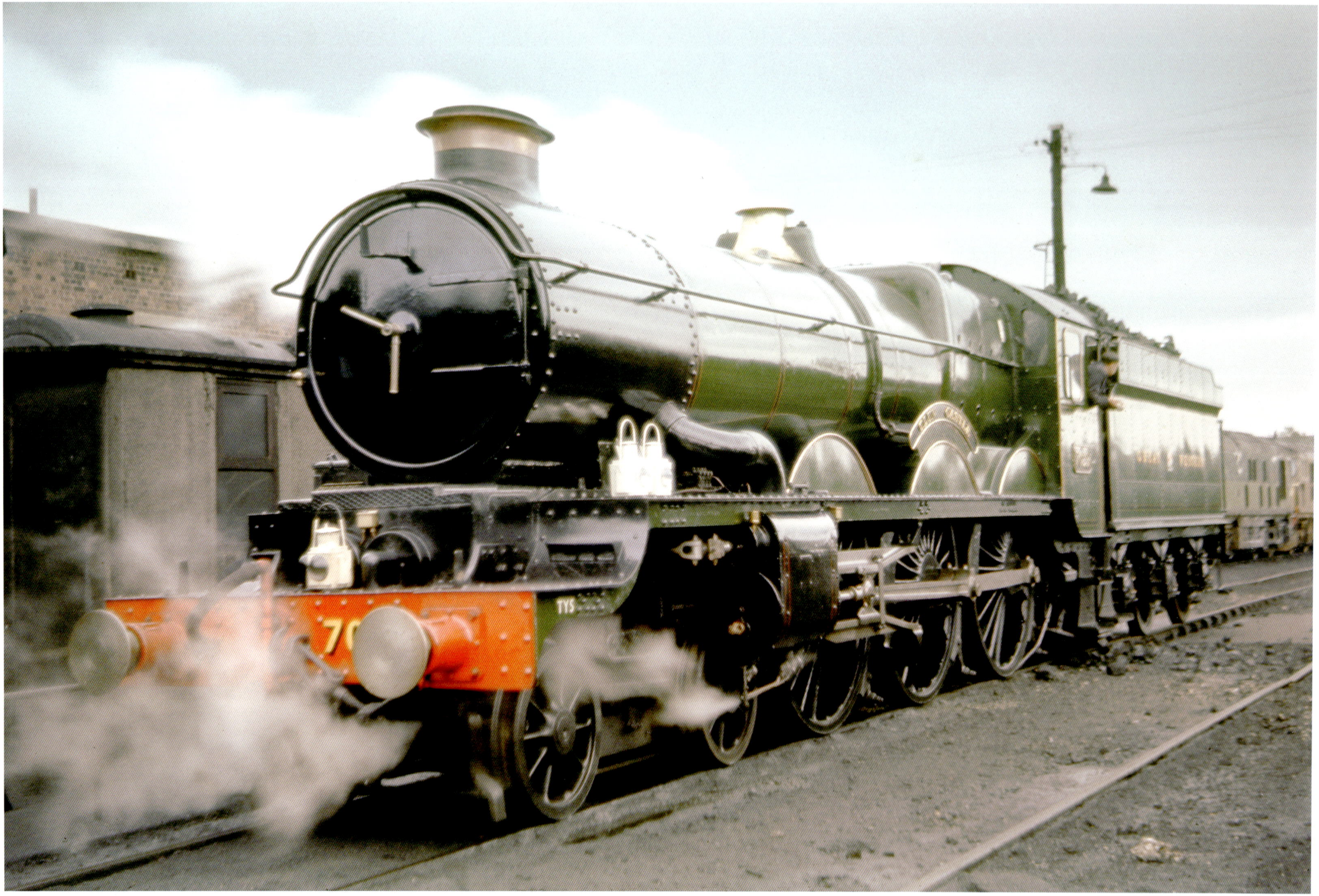

Page left: A real stranger in the camp at Carlisle Kingmoor on 30 September 1967, as 7029 Clun Castle now in the hands of Pat Whitehouse, had arranged for his locomotive to be involved in seven railtours in as many weeks at this time. This tour was in connection with the A4 Preservation Society, the Castle being in charge for the leg from Peterborough to here in Carlisle, with 4498 Sir Nigel Gresley for the run back in the opposite direction, thus allowing us this spectacle on shed at Kingmoor that afternoon. ***Strathwood Library Collection***

Another railtour to visit The Border City the previous September, was when the South and West Railway Society ran their marathon Granite City special over the weekend of the 3rd and 4th. One of the eight locomotives to be rostered on this tour was Class V2, 60936 seen here at Carlisle Citadel on the Saturday ready for its leg onwards to Edinburgh via the Waverley route. ***Late Alan Marriott/Strathwood Library Collection***

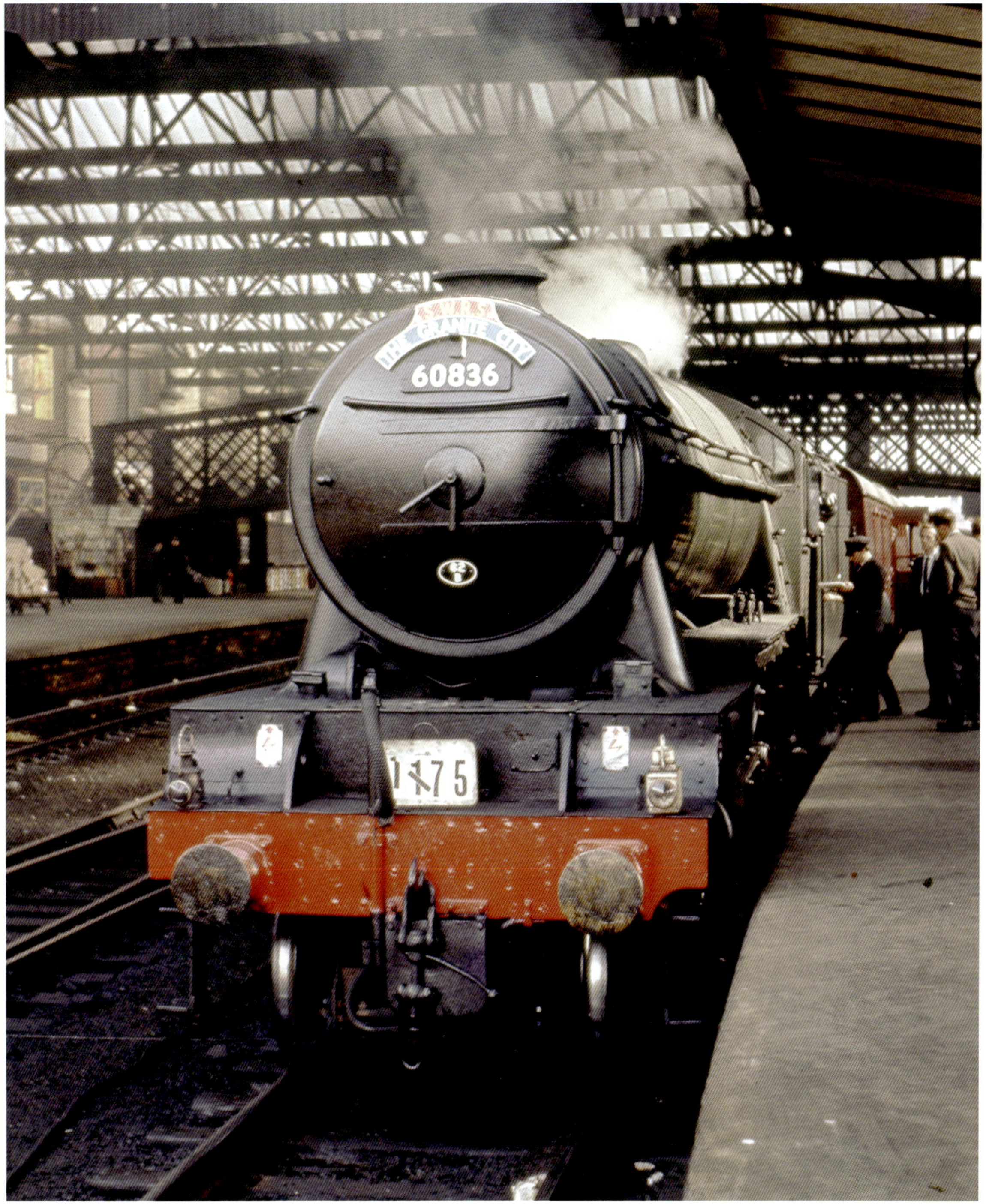

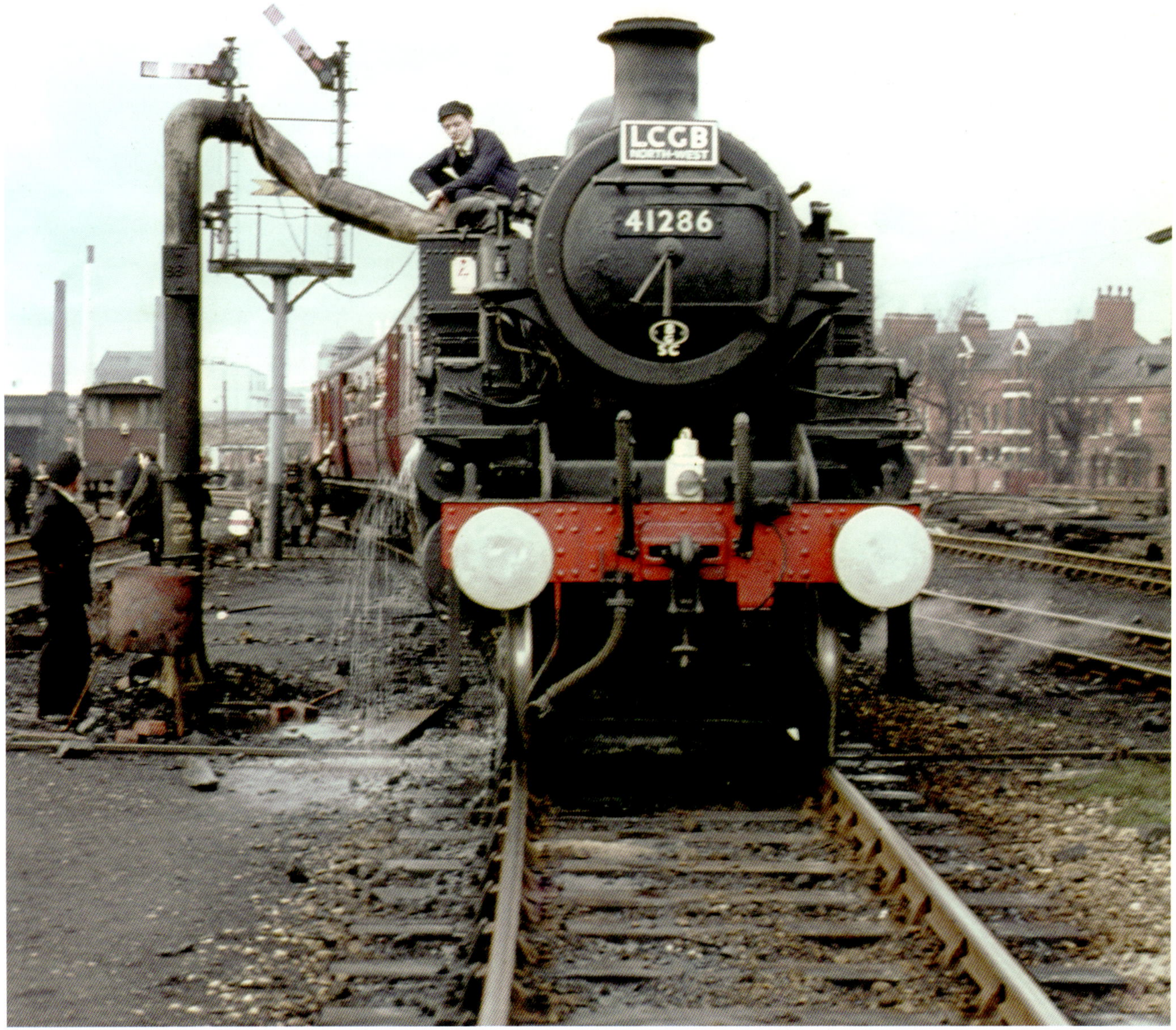

To commemorate the last push and pull workings with steam, the LCGB ran two tours due to high ticket demand both were behind Ivatt Class 2MT 41286 in September 1966. A stop was made on one of the runs here at Warrington to refresh the tanks, and as usual back then a chance for many to jump down trackside for a photograph, happy days! ***Strathwood Library Collection***

Opposite: Another farewell was marked on 5 March 1967, as the Stephenson Locomotive Society ran two trains to mark the end of the GWR Birmingham to Birkenhead service. One of these trains arrives here at Chester General from Birkenhead behind a partially cleaned Class 9F, 92203. ***Dave Livesey***

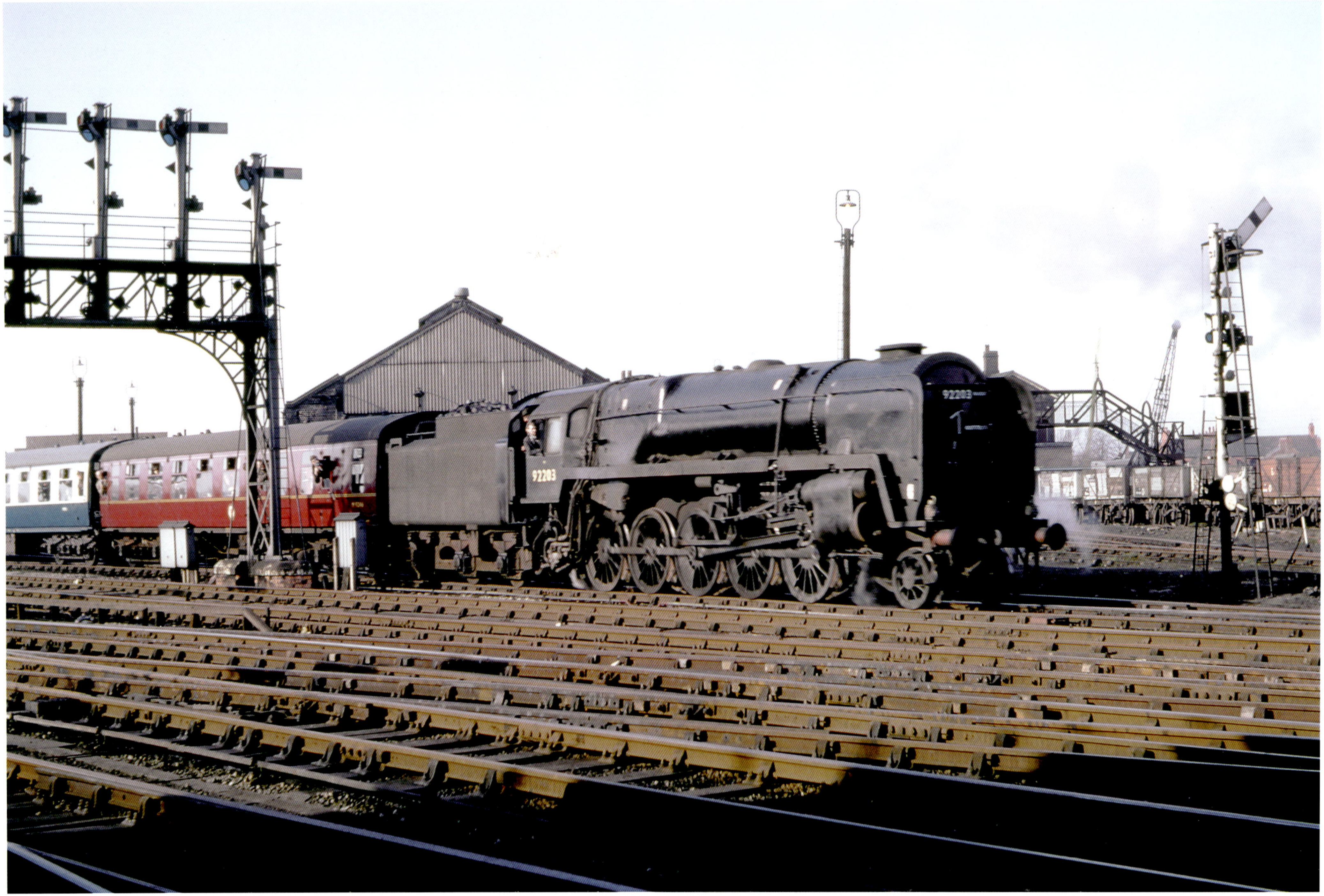
92203

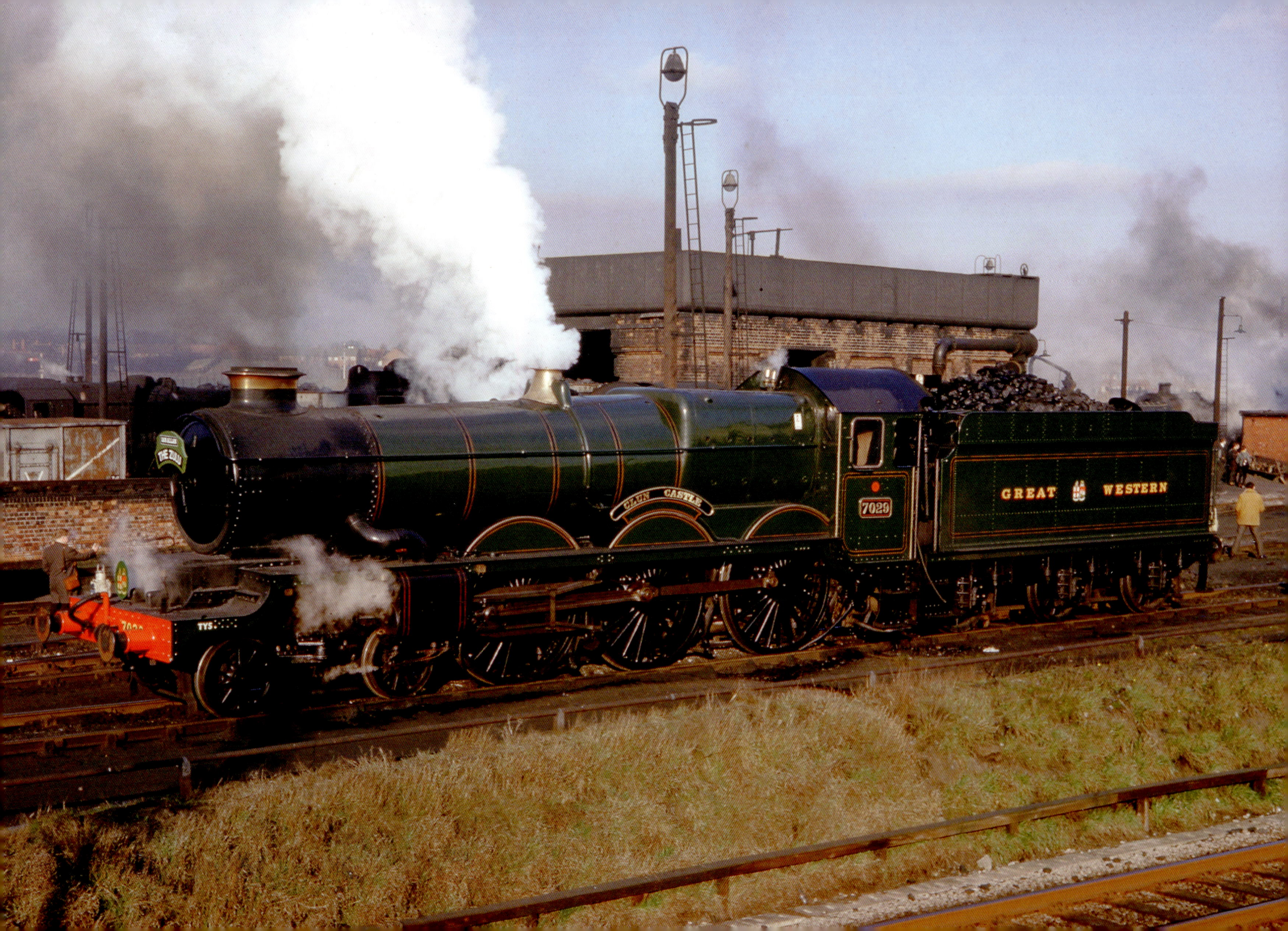
CLUN CASTLE
7029
GREAT WESTERN

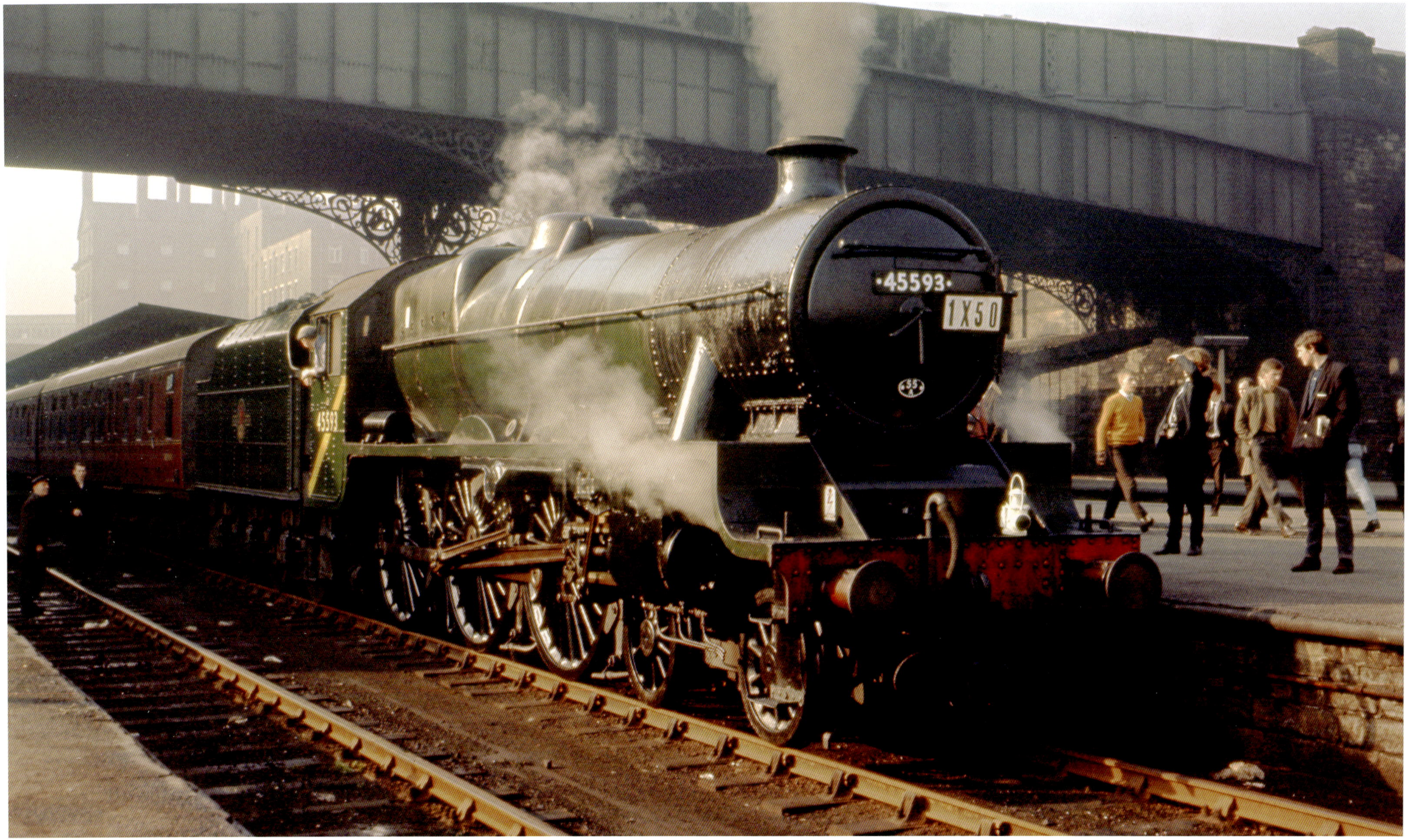

Page left: Making it a very busy weekend on this line, Ian Allan also ran two commemorative trains of their own over the route from Birmingham to Birkenhead, but starting from London first. Both 4079 Pendennis Castle, and 7029 Clun Castle seen here on shed at Chester were well turned out for their duties, which were shared.
Tony Butcher

Just about every weekend at this time enthusiasts had a choice of railtours all over the country to choose from. For example; just one of four specials on the weekend of 30 April 1966, Jubilee 45593 Kolhapur sizzles away in the sunshine at Bradford Forster Square, with the South Yorkshireman No.5 heading for Carnforth and Carlisle.
Win Wall/Strathwood Library Collection

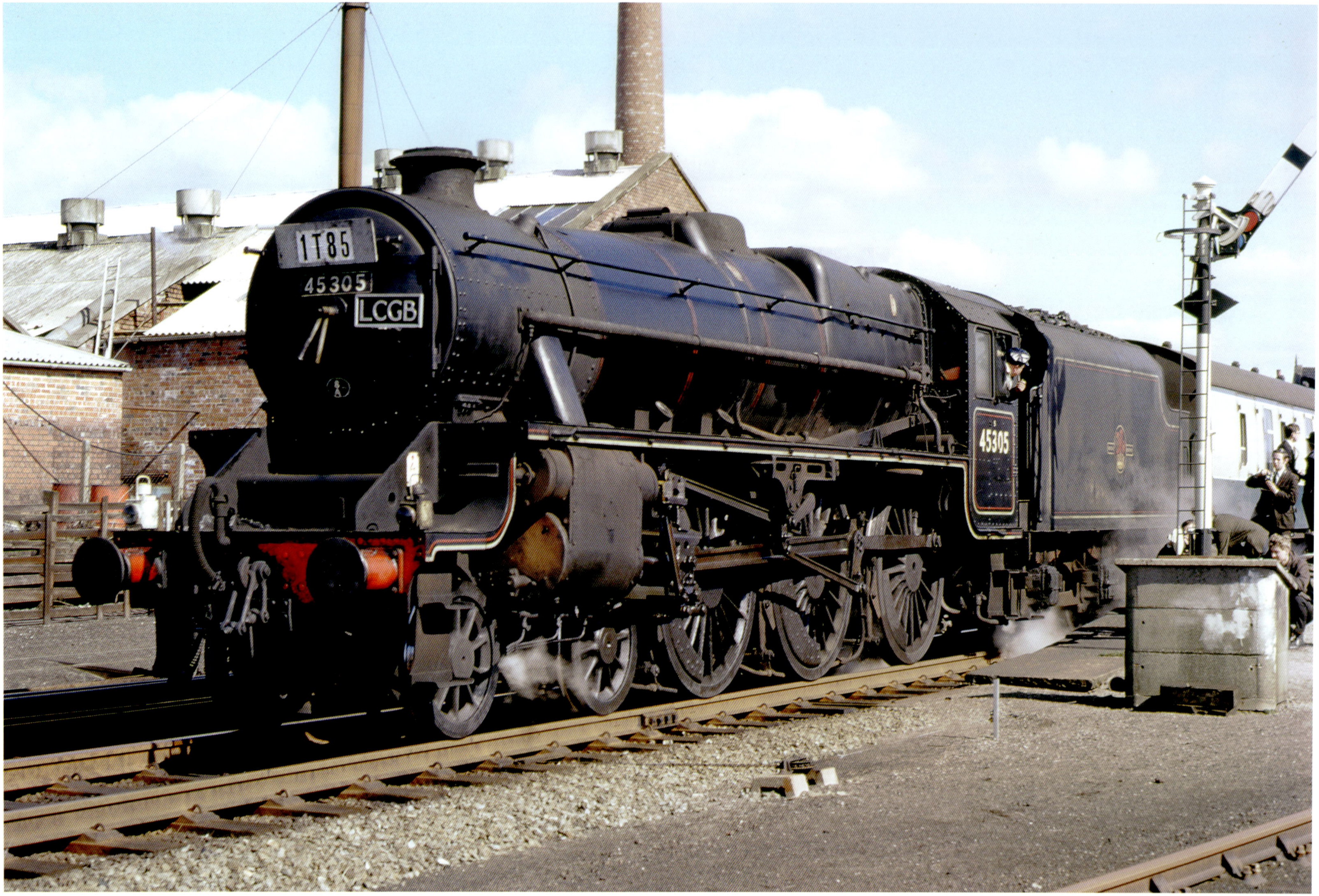
1T85
45305
LCGB
45305

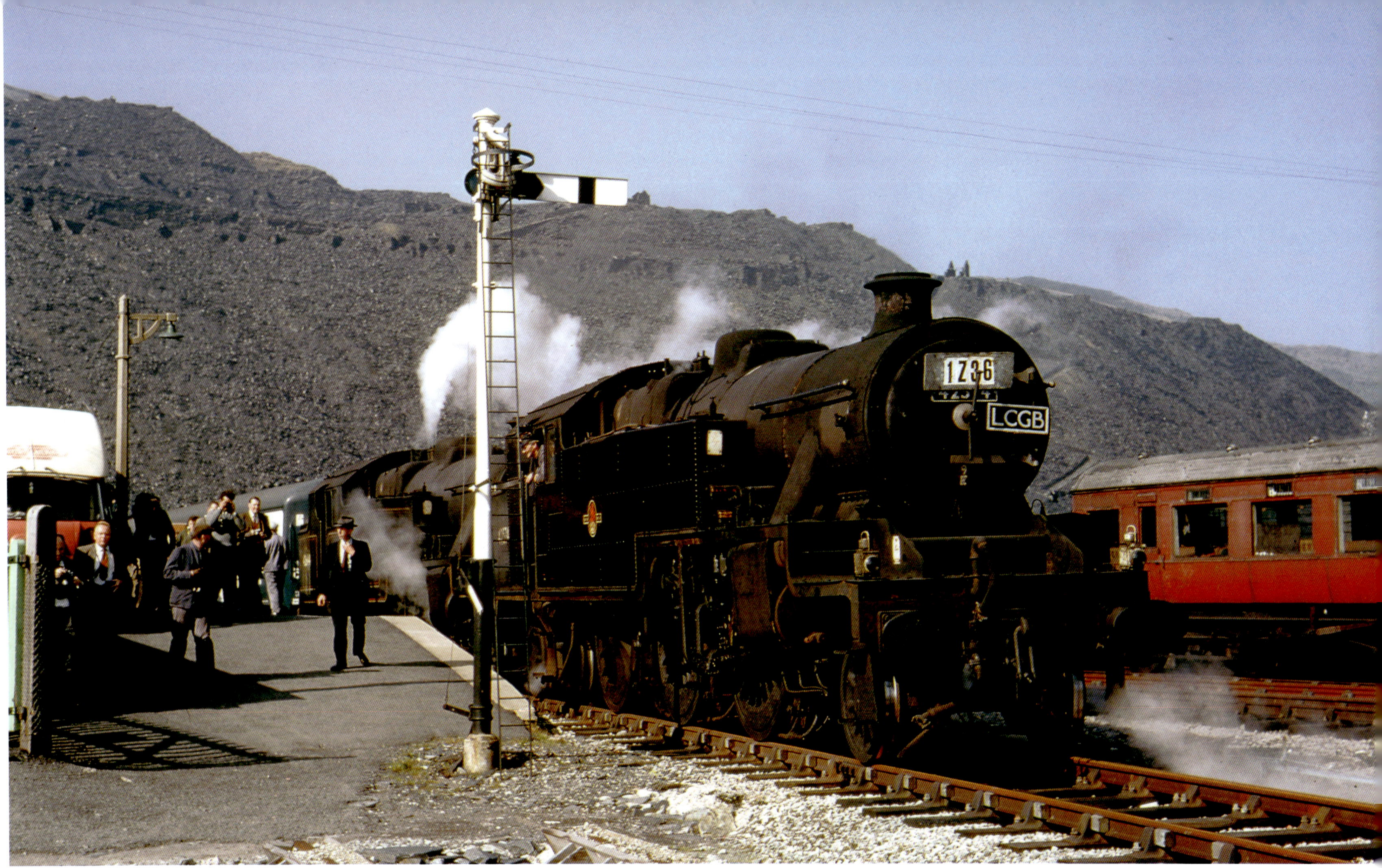

We are ready for the off at Burscough Bridge mid afternoon on 6 April 1968, with the LCGB's Lancastrian run throughout behind Black Five 45305. The route was out and back from Liverpool's Lime Street station for a circuitous journey around the county. ***Strathwood Library Collection***

The LCGB's distinctive headboard is in action once again on 24 September 1966 for their Conway Valley Railtour, Stanier Class 4MTs 42574 and 42644 were in charge of the leg from Llandudno Junction to here at the foot of the slate mines at Blaneau Ffestiniog and back. ***Tony Butcher***

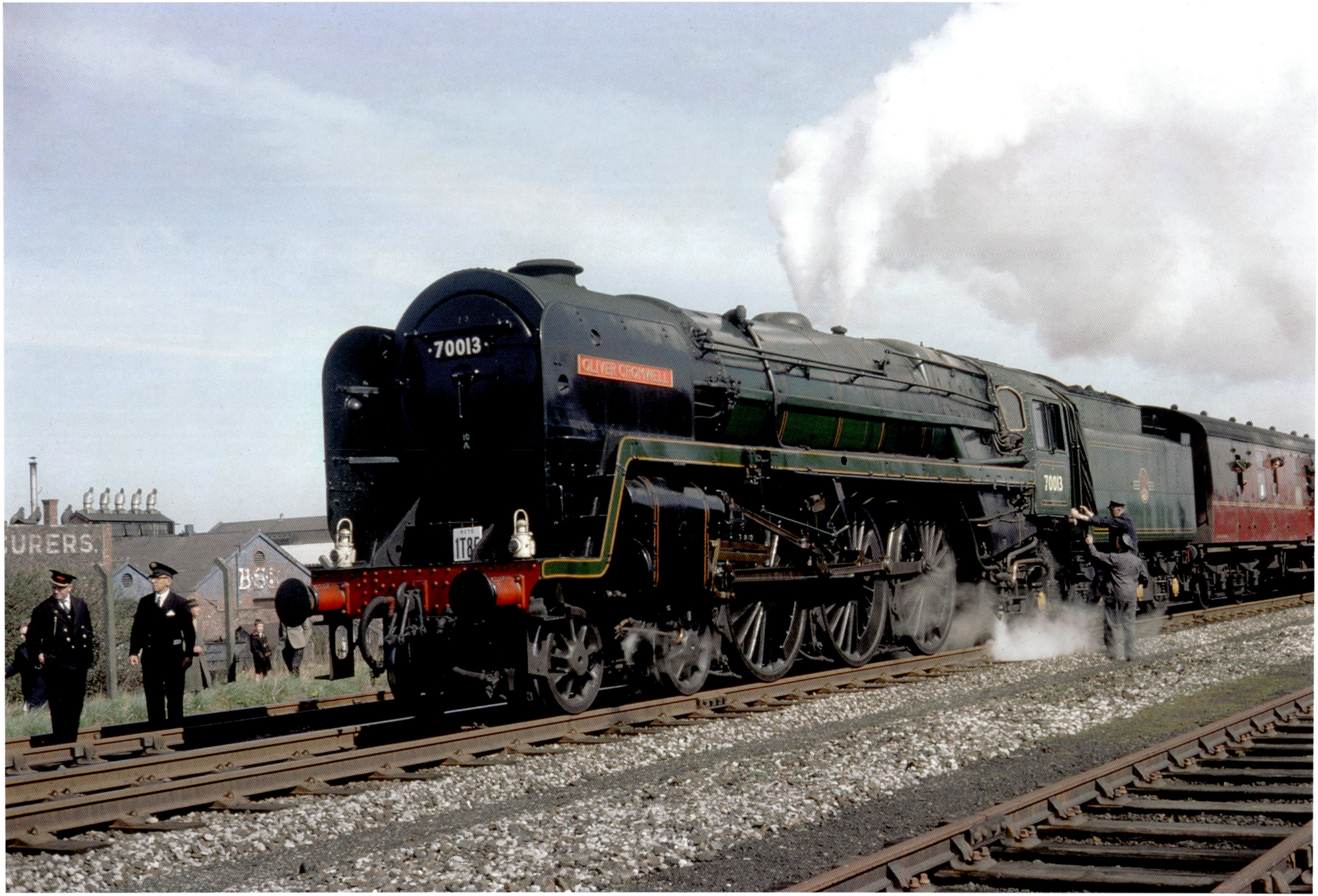
70013
OLIVER CROMWELL

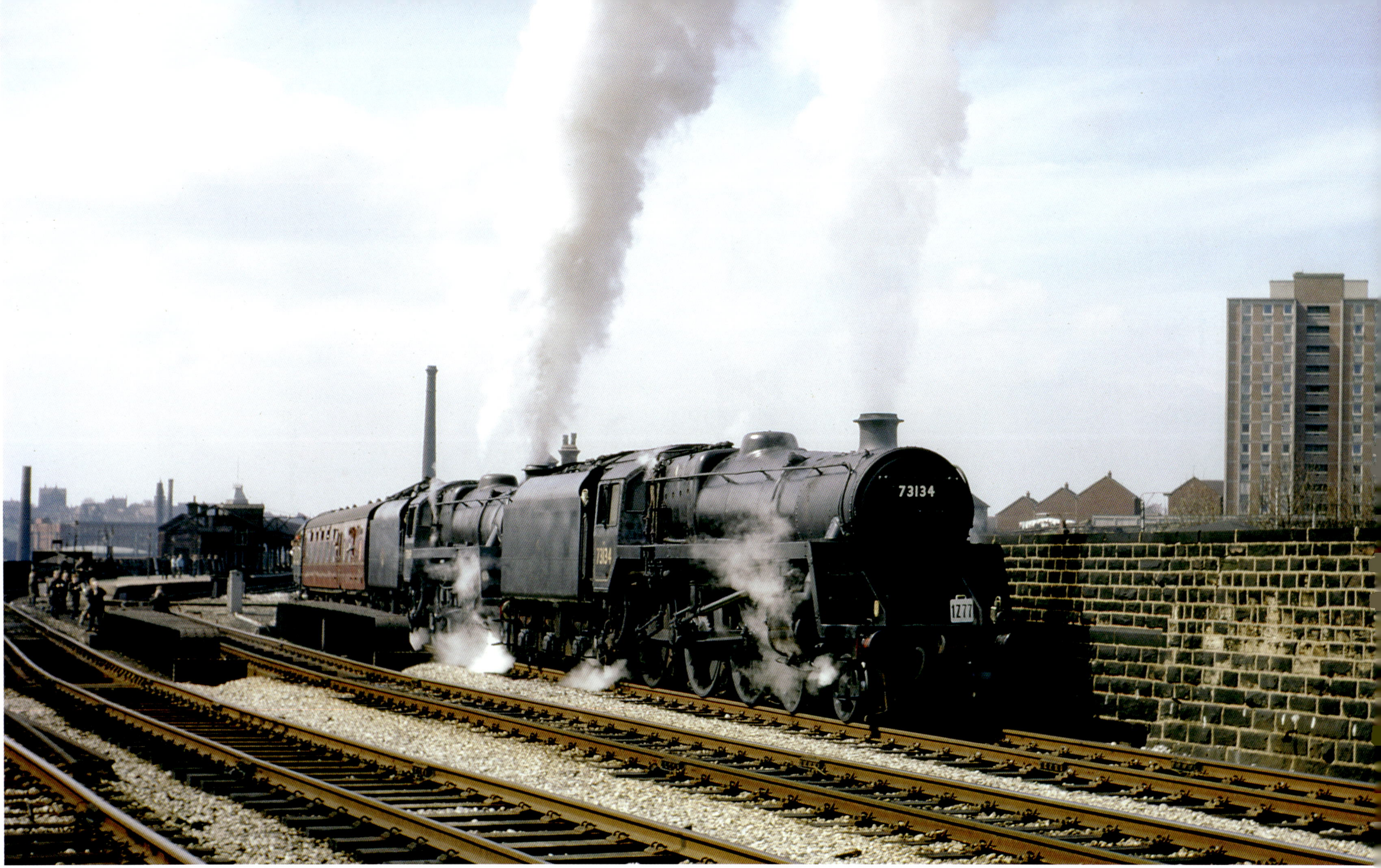

Page left: Two specials were run on 20 April 1968, as we rejoin the RCTS Lancastrian No.2 for the handover from Black Five 45156 Ayrshire Yeomanry to Britannia 70013 Oliver Cromwell at Fleetwood, as part of this two hundred and eighty mile railtour. ***Tony Butcher***

Elsewhere the same day the Manchester Rail Travel Society in conjunction with the Severn Valley Railway Society were running their North West Tour. With Standard Class 5MTs 73134 and 73069 departing from Stalybridge. ***Jerry Beddows***

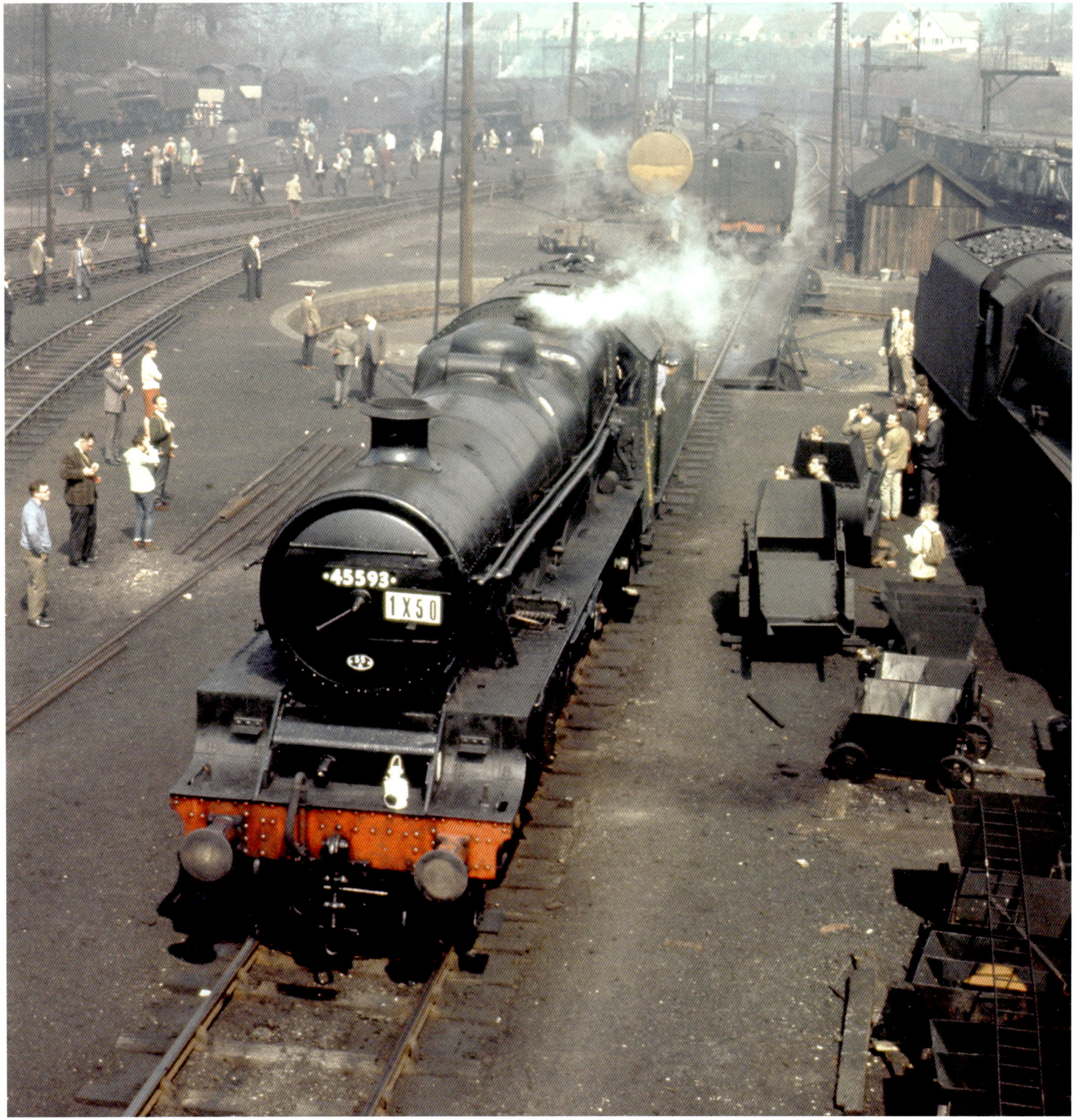

Having brought a packed train of enthusiasts from Bradford that morning as seen already on page 45, Jubilee 45593 Kolhapur has just taken on coal at Carnforth for the next leg onwards to Carlisle, meanwhile everyone is free range around the depot here in the spring sunshine. ***Win Wall/Strathwood Library Collection***

Opposite: The following year and fellow spotters are well rugged up in the winter sunshine for an unoffical visit to Crewe South on 19 February 1967, as two filthy engines are recorded in light steam. Steam activty would linger on here at 5B Crewe South for most of the year until 6 November when the shed closed. ***Colin Rodgers/Strathwood Library Collection***

Shed & Works Visits

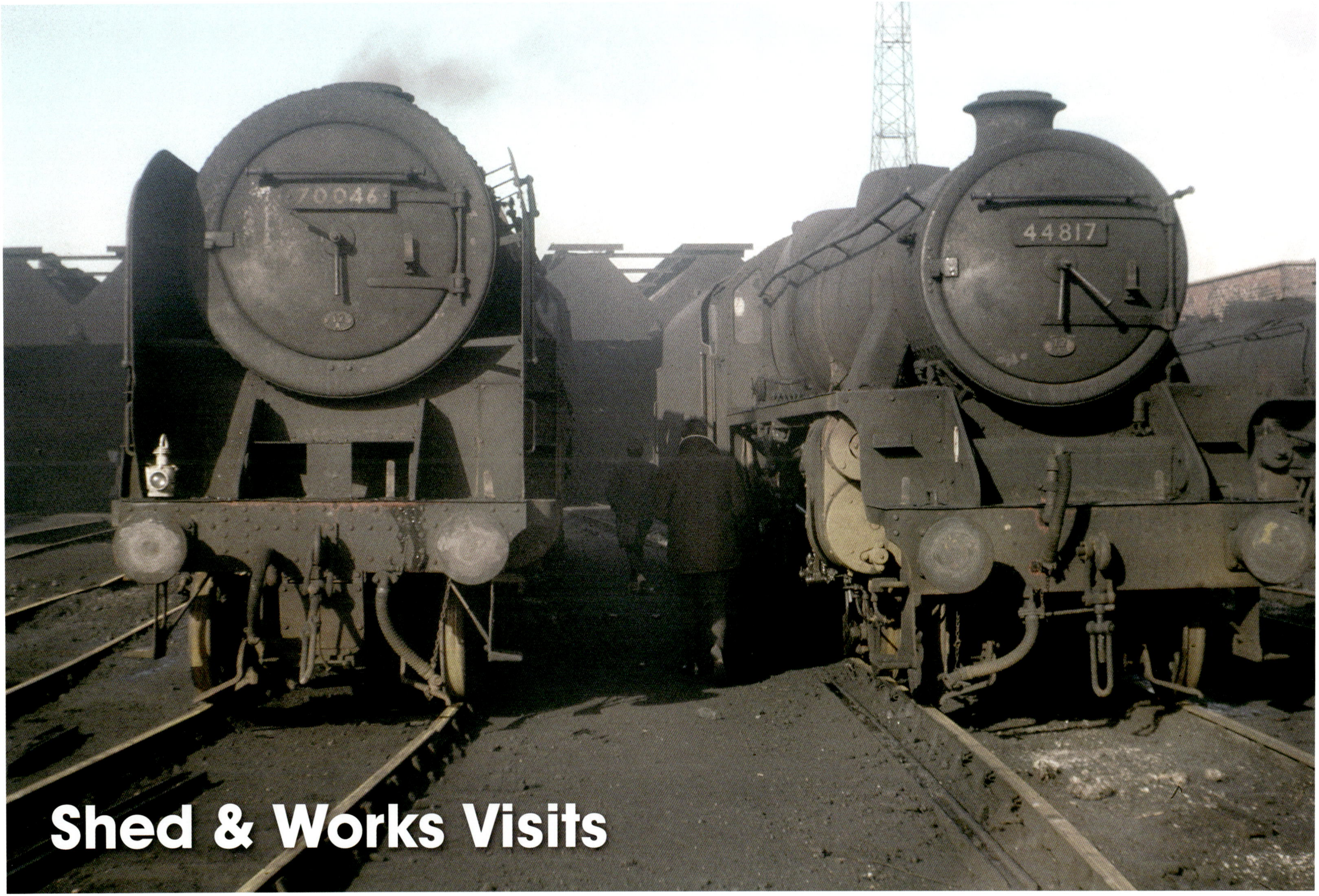

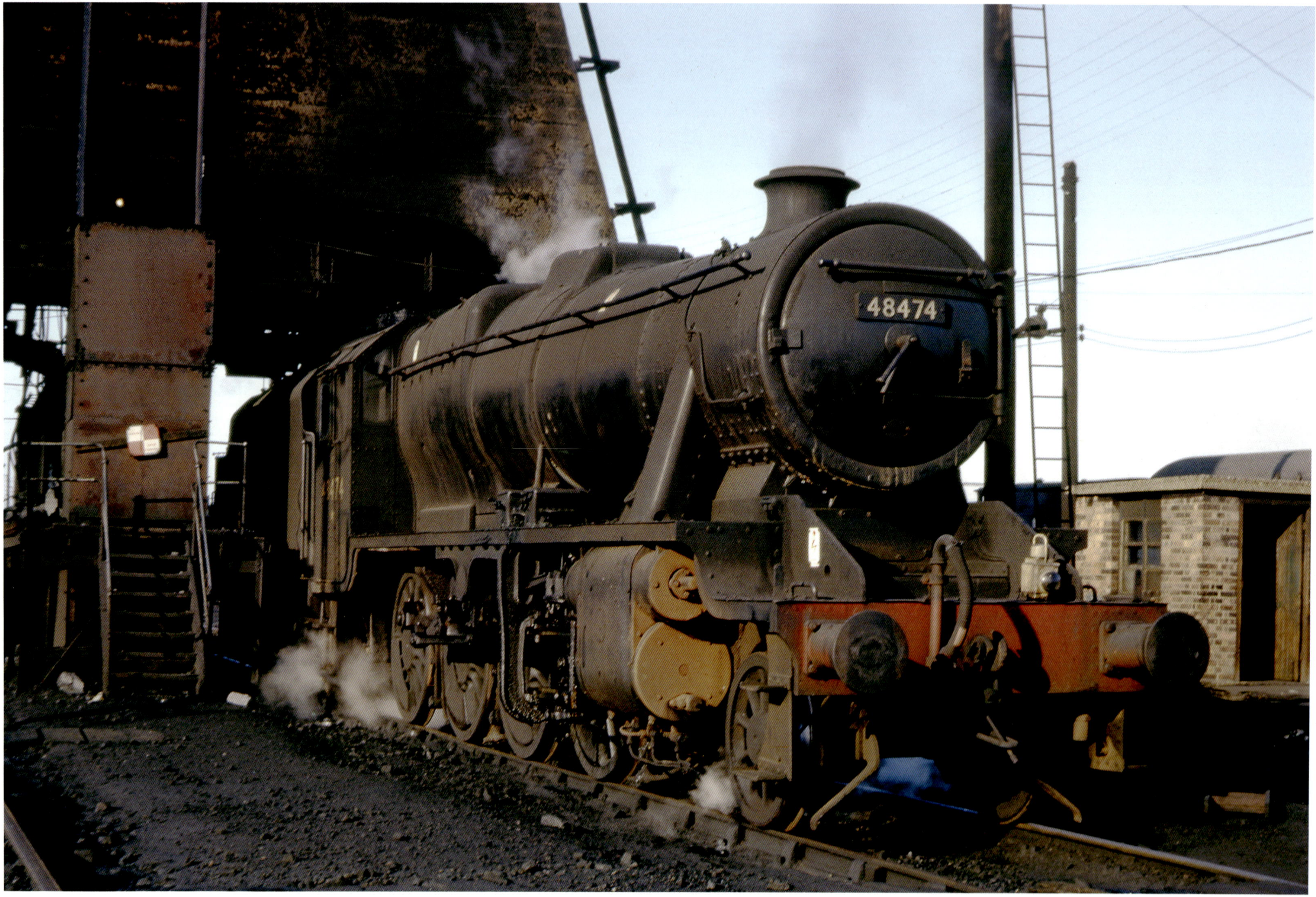
48474

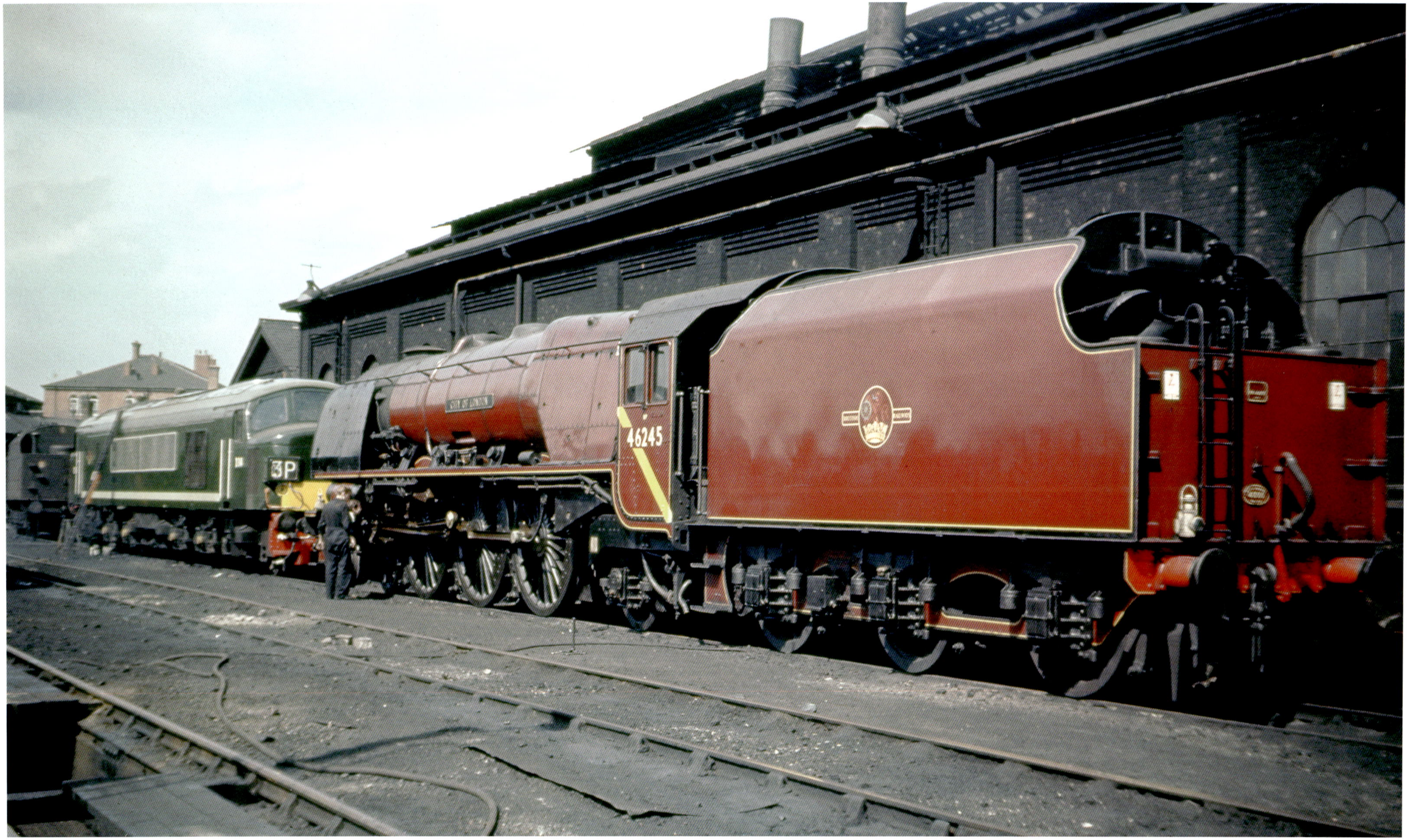

Page left: Still cleanish, well for a Class 8F was 48474 after its last overhaul, under the coaling tower at Willesden on 15 November 1964, also having just taken another charge of coal. This example was one those built at Swindon Works as part of the war effort, although it entered traffic in May 1945, just as VE Day was being celebrated. ***Frank Hornby***

Derby Work's Open Day in 1964 was on 30 August, having just arrived staff look over 46245 City of London, the yellow warning stripes on the cab were added that year to denote that they were banned south of Crewe. It's interesting to note that this banning order seems to have come into operation on 1 September 1964, therefore were these stripes applied at Derby? ***Len Smith***

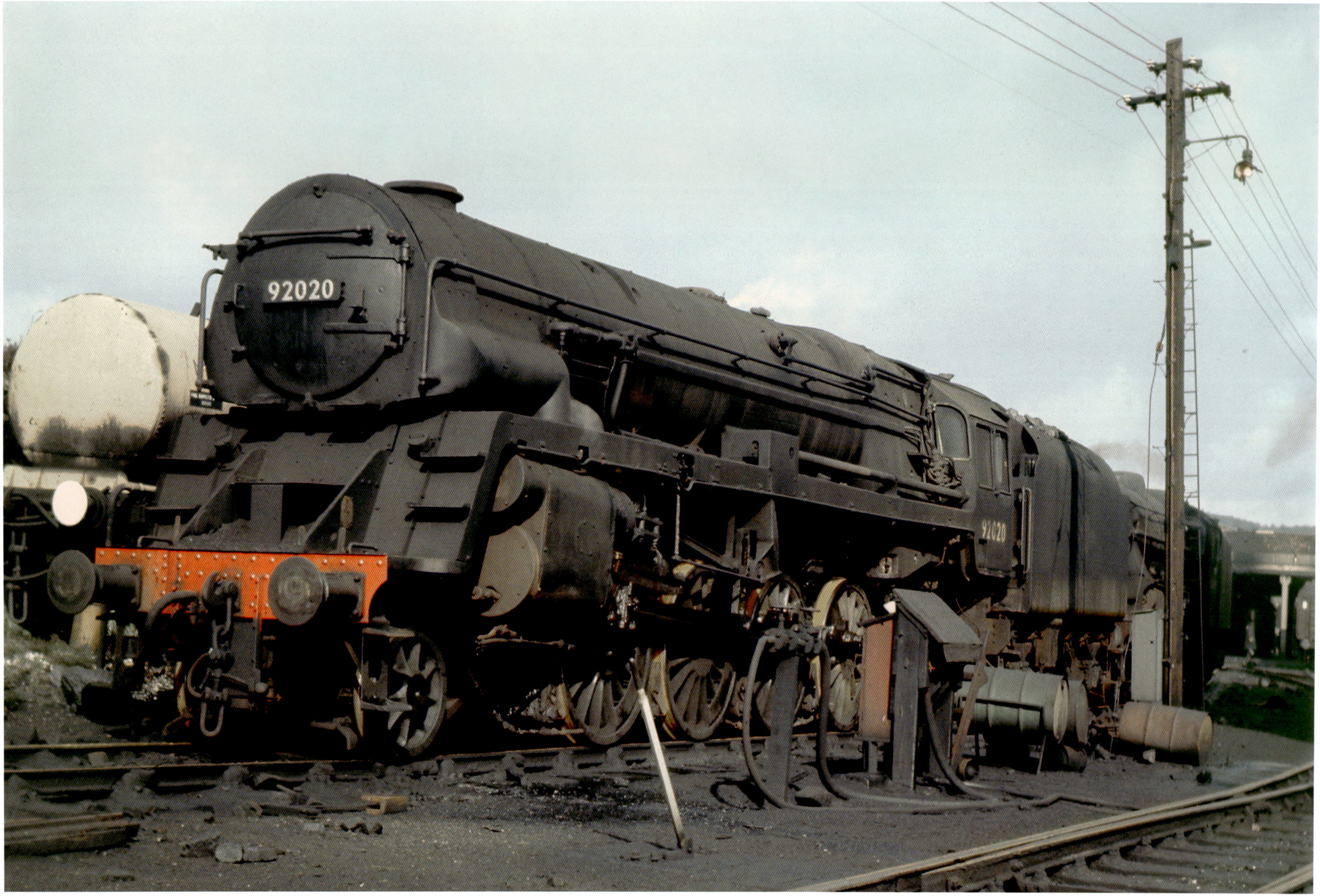

92020
92020

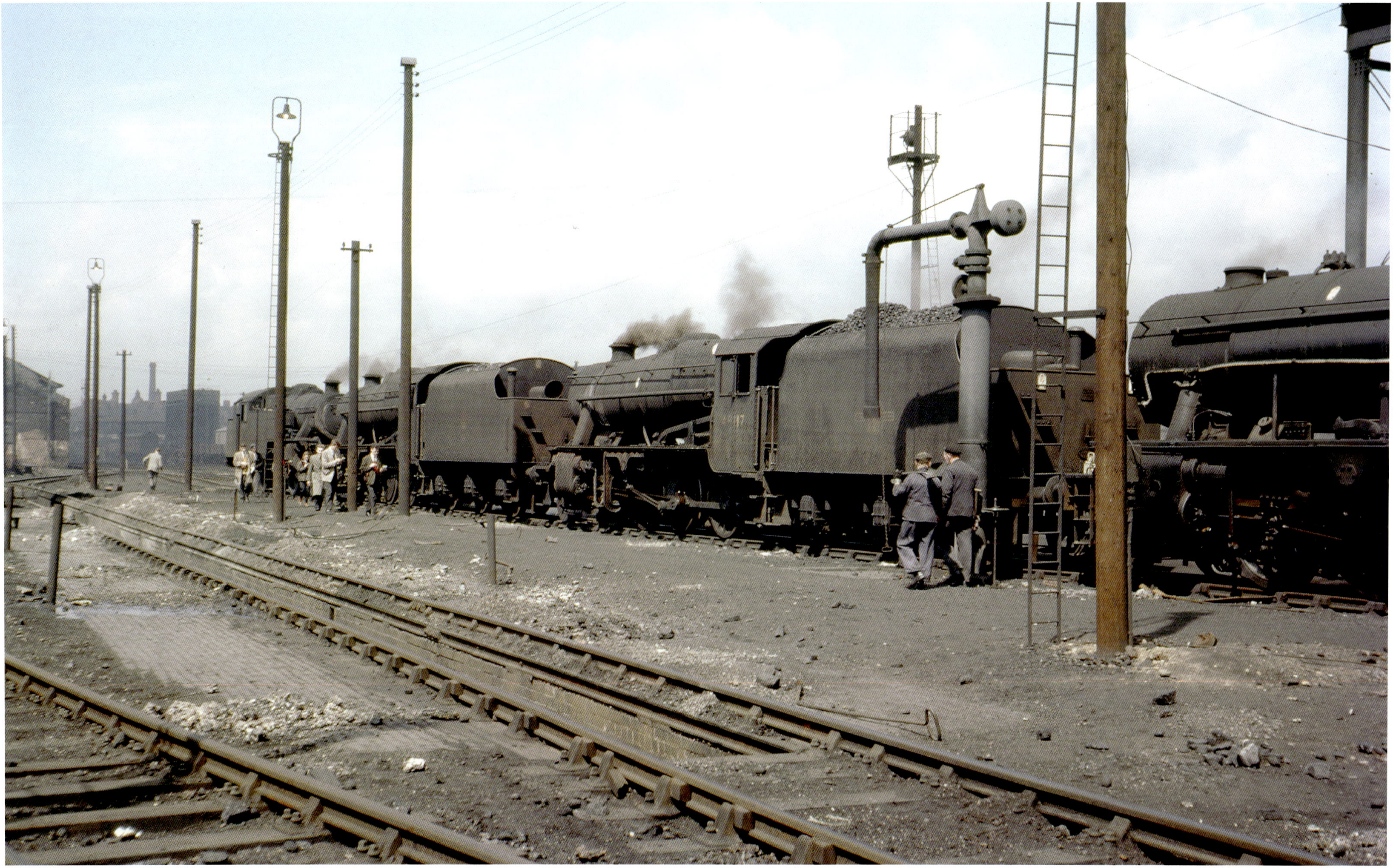

Page left: One of the thrills of every shed visit was a walk along the lines of locomotives in the shed yard to see what was on shed that day, such as ex-Crosti boilered Class 9F, 92020 here at Carnforth on 7 October 1967 which had just been withdrawn. ***Gilroy Kerr***

Two relaxed engine crew head towards their work for the day in May 1963 at 17A Derby, whilst a small group of spotters seek out all the engines in the lines on shed today. ***Win Wall/Strathwood Library Collection***

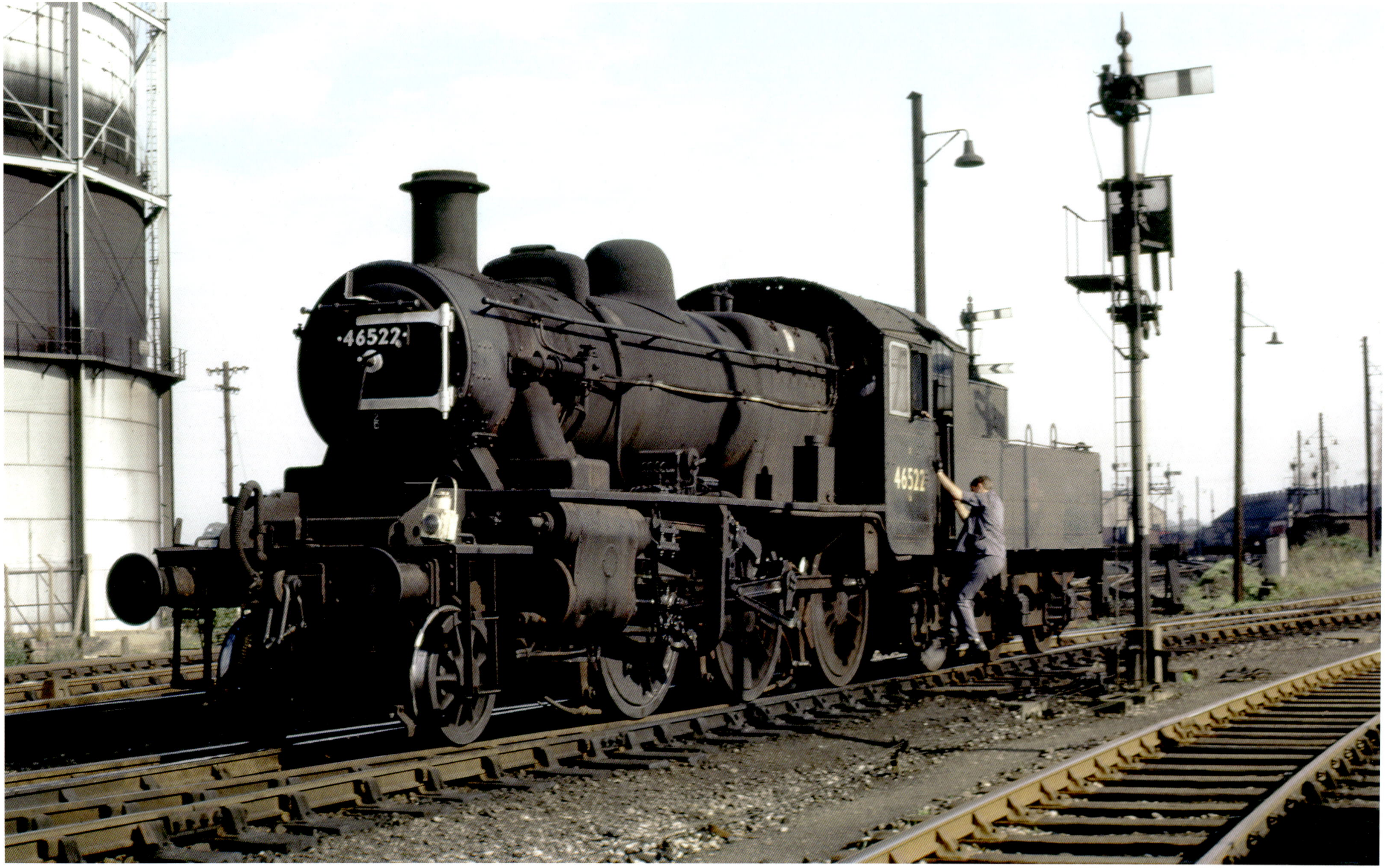

Light engine activity at Banbury on 8 September 1966 with Ivatt Class 2MT, 46522. Now coded as 2D with the London Midland Region since 1963, it was previously a former Western Region shed coded 84C. ***Aldo Delicata***

Opposite: The mock overhead line gantries for staff training purposes frame this view of Fairburn Class 4MT 42081 after a recent works overhaul in 1963, which would see it through no doubt until being withdrawn in May 1967. ***Strathwood Library Collection***

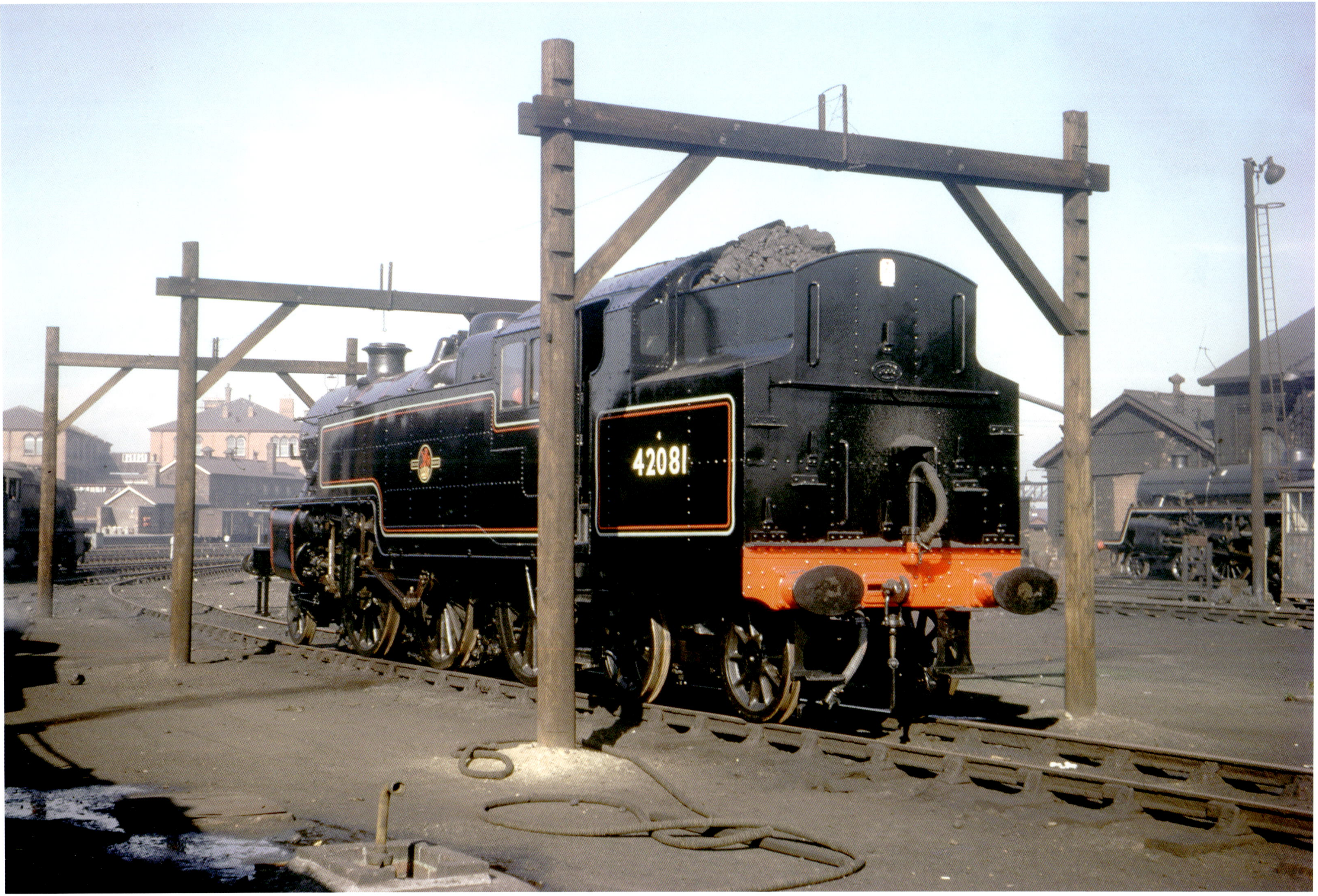
42081

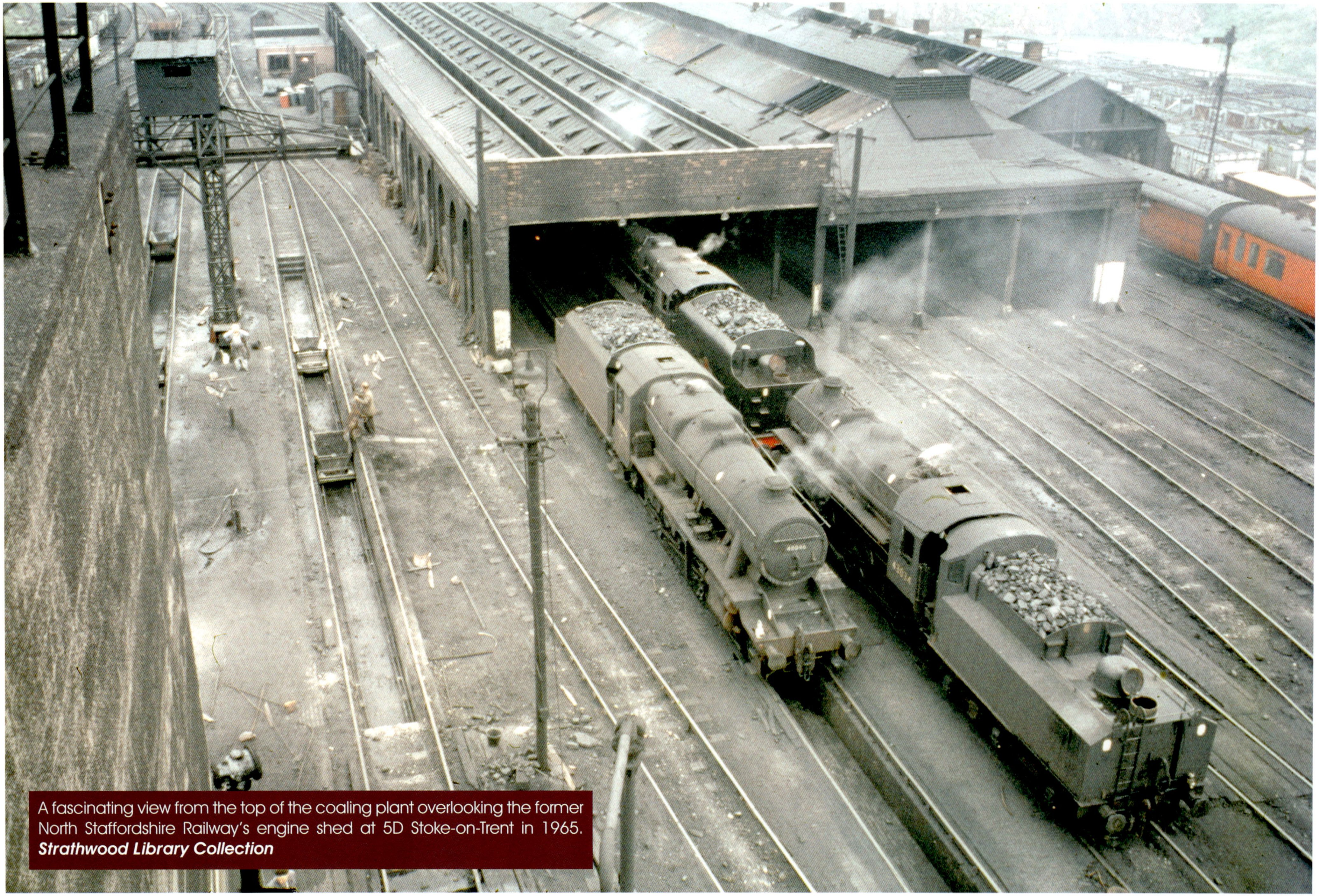

A fascinating view from the top of the coaling plant overlooking the former North Staffordshire Railway's engine shed at 5D Stoke-on-Trent in 1965.
Strathwood Library Collection

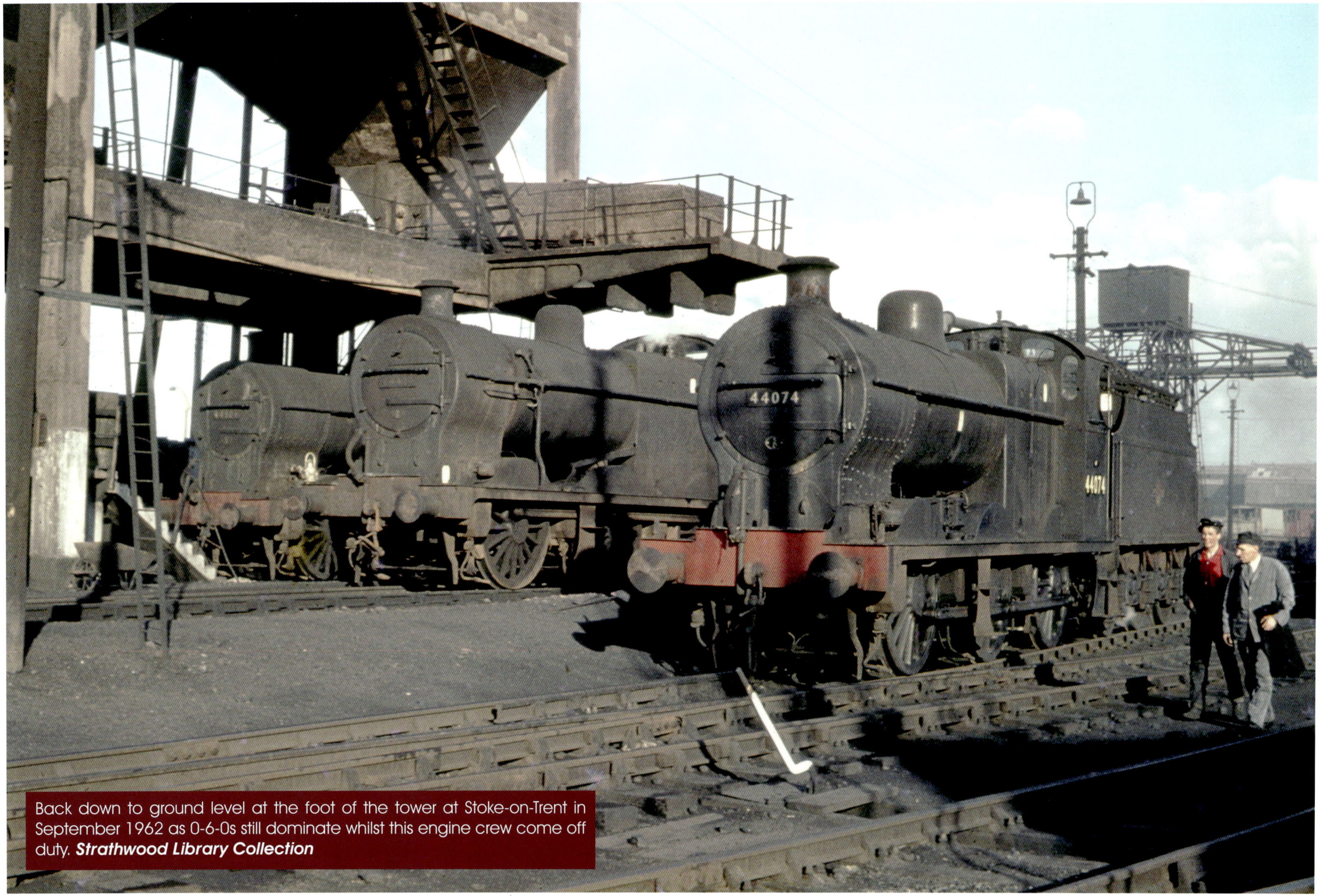

Back down to ground level at the foot of the tower at Stoke-on-Trent in September 1962 as 0-6-0s still dominate whilst this engine crew come off duty. ***Strathwood Library Collection***

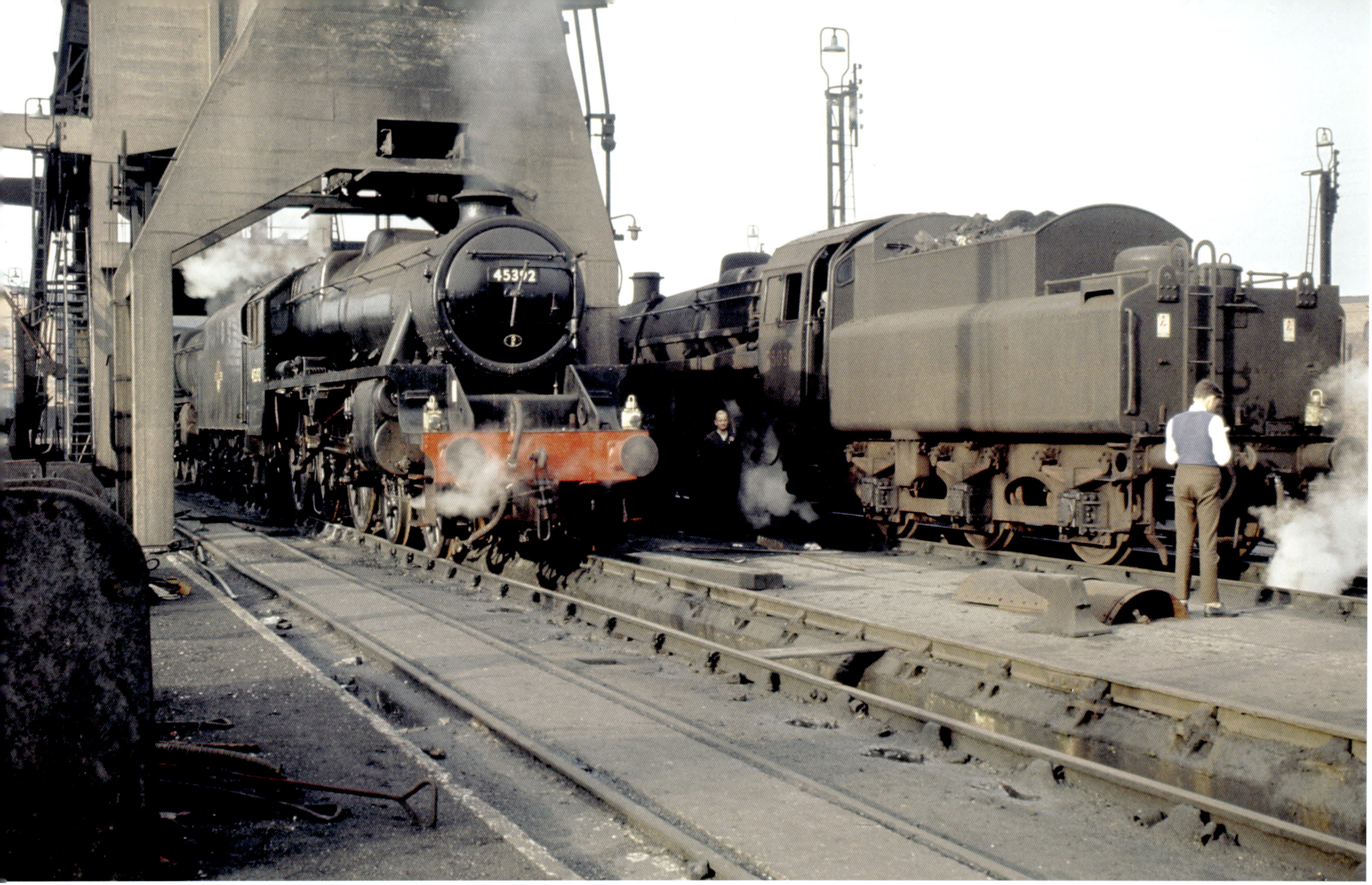

More spotting days, as this party are under the watchful eyes of the yard foreman at Crewe North with Black Five, 45392 under the ash plant tower on 29 October 1964, on what must have been an unusually warm day. ***Strathwood Library Collection***

Opposite: Warm February sunshine also laps the fronts of Black Fives 45382 and 45206 at Newton Heath, as steam enters its last few months throughout the North West in 1968. ***Strathwood Library Collection***

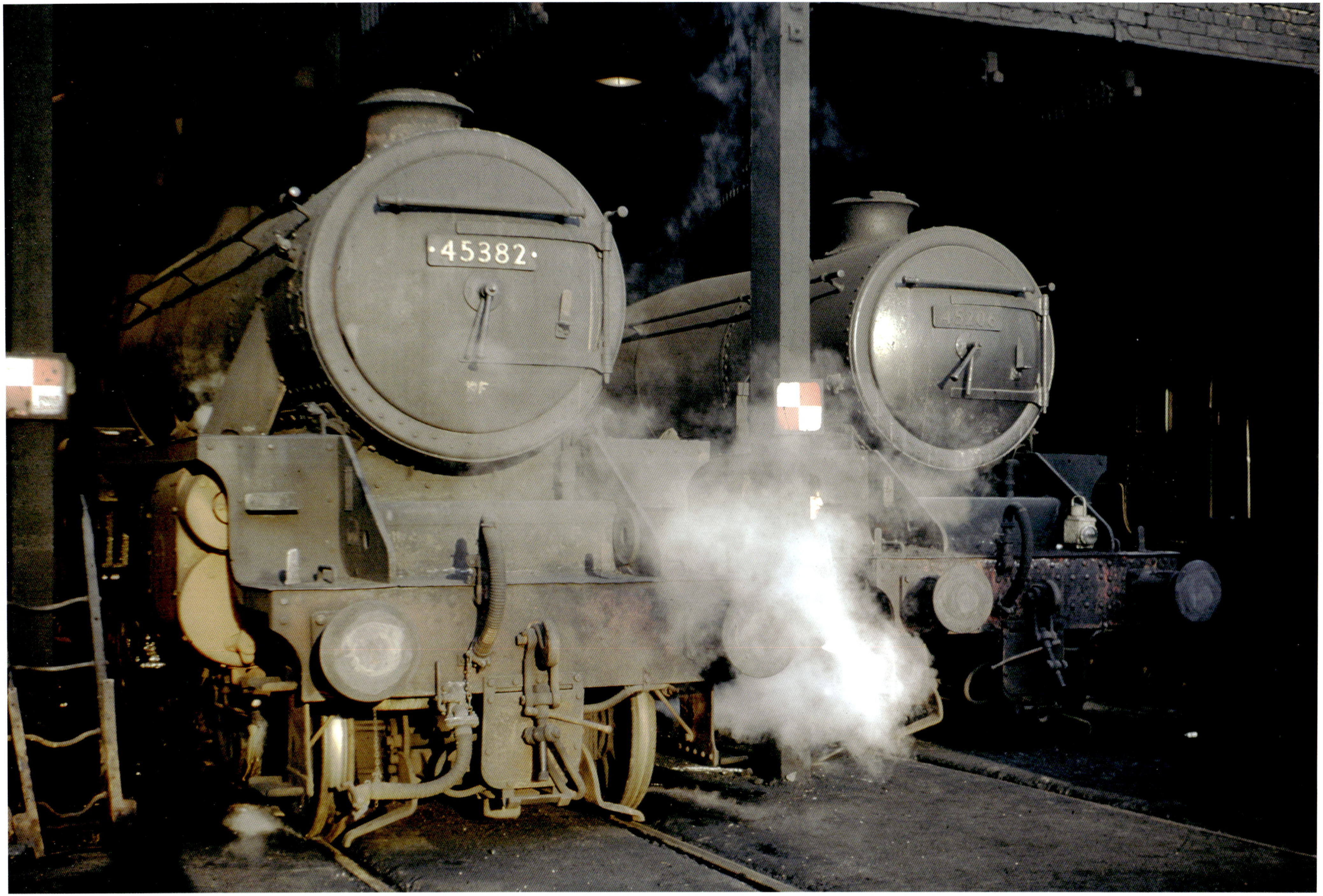
45382

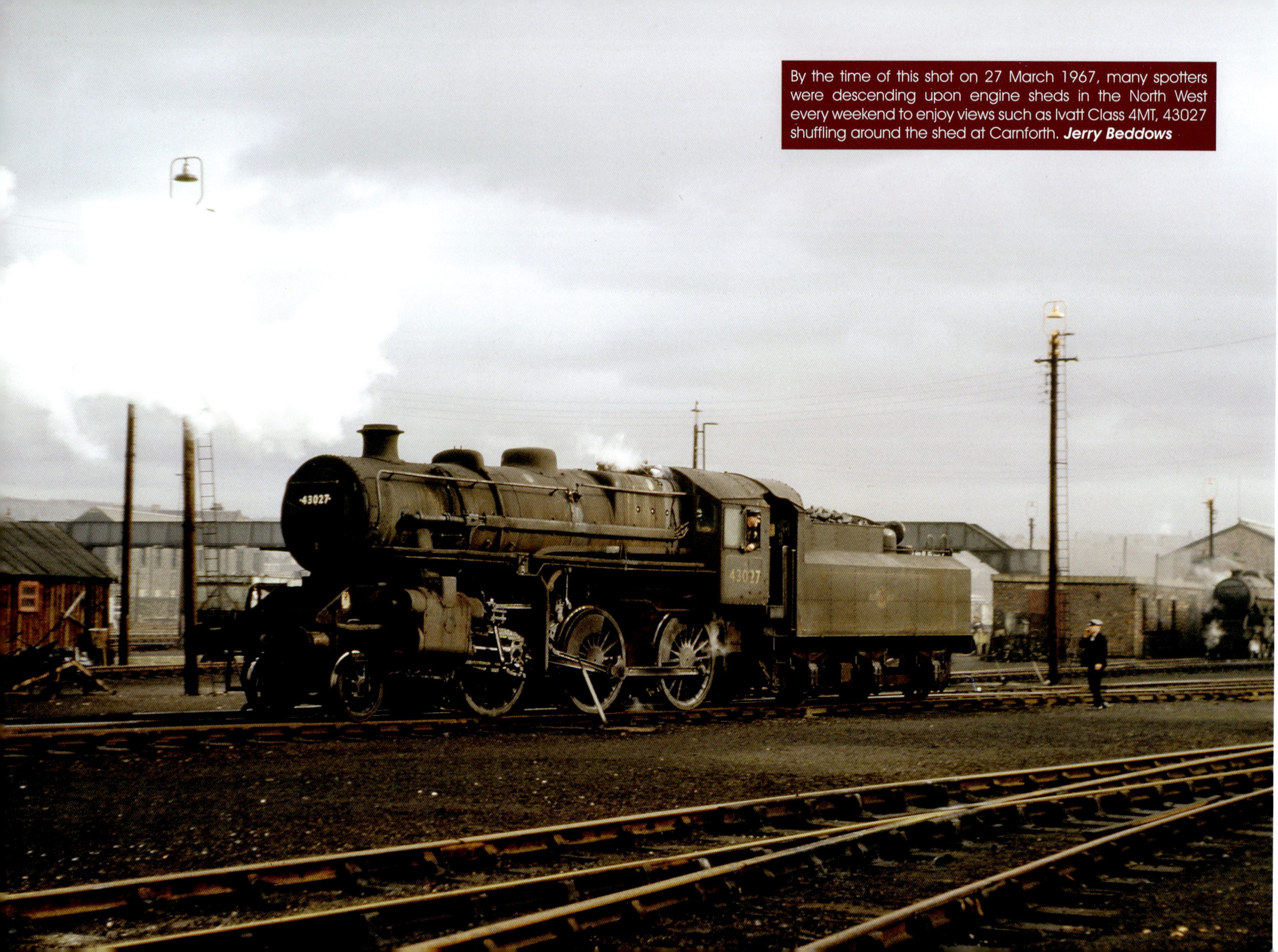

By the time of this shot on 27 March 1967, many spotters were descending upon engine sheds in the North West every weekend to enjoy views such as Ivatt Class 4MT, 43027 shuffling around the shed at Carnforth. ***Jerry Beddows***

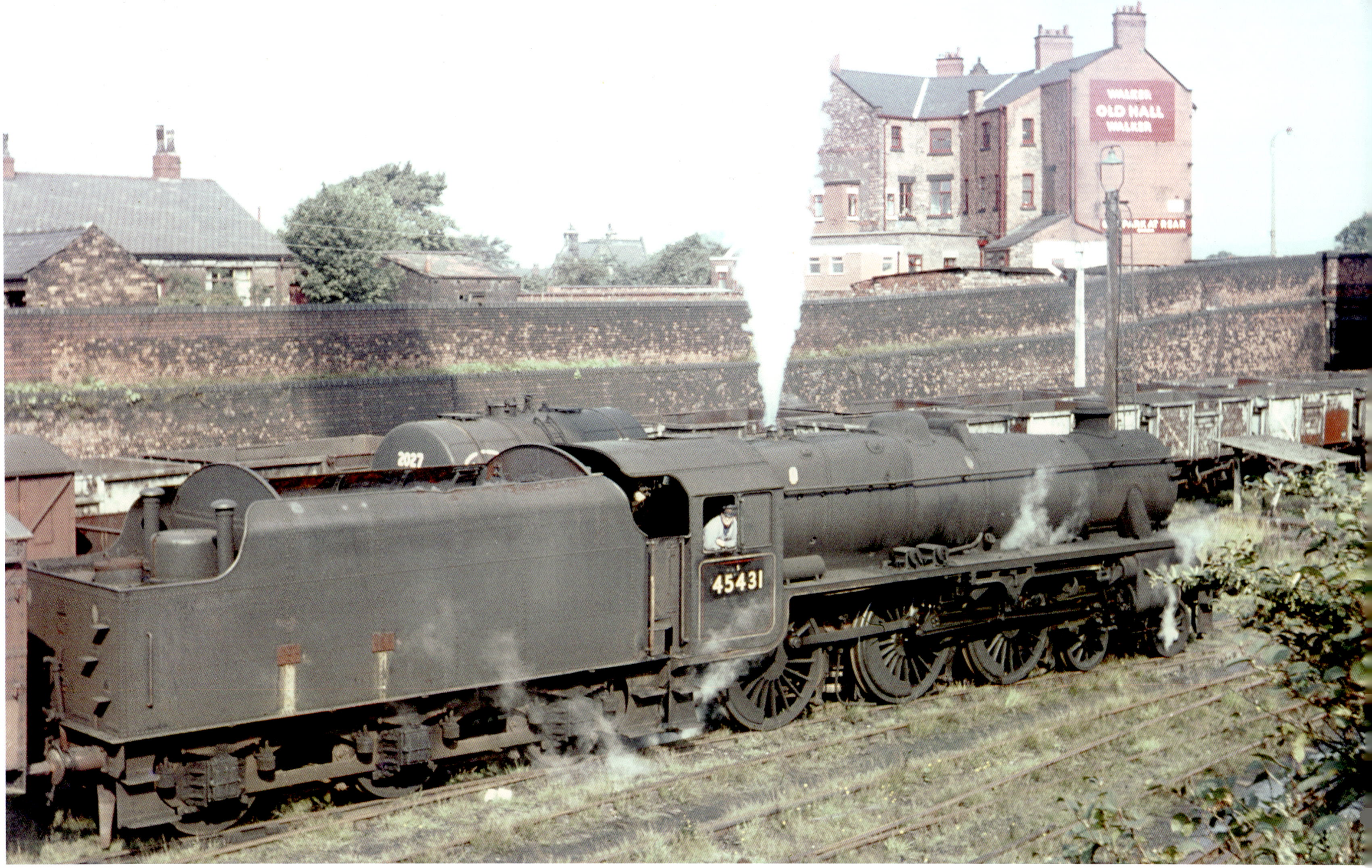

The driver of Black Five 45431 does not look too perturbed about the lack of coal, or the patched up tender of his engine for the day, on 13 September 1967 at Springs Branch. Built by Armstrong Whitworth in November 1937, its working career would end not suprisingly perhaps less than two months after this view. Whilst steam operation finished completely out of 8F Springs Branch on 4 December 1967. ***Late John Green/Strathwood Library Collection***

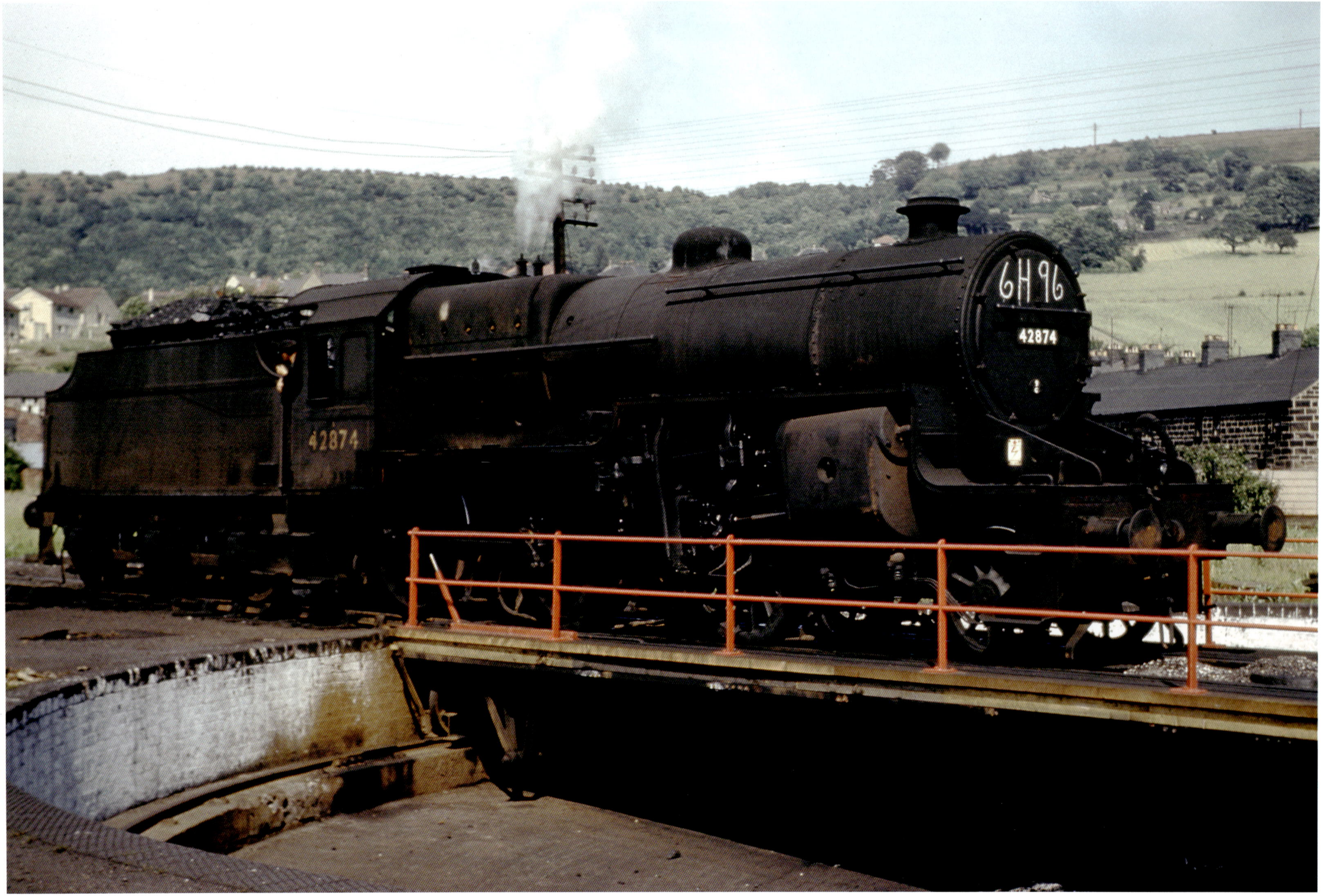
6H96
42874
42874

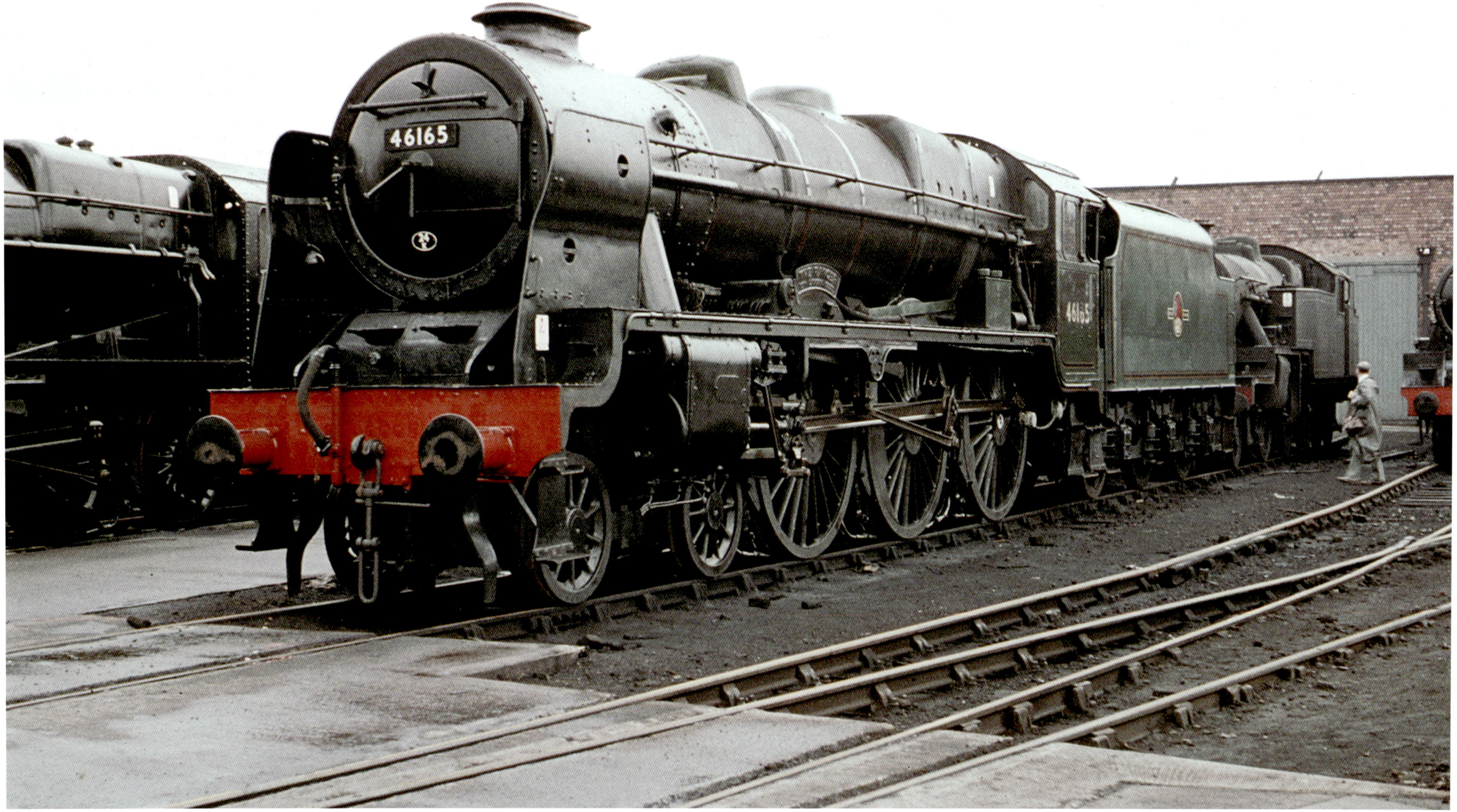

Page left: Rowsley shed is one location not often seen in colour closing to steam on 25 April 1964, although remaining available for further use until 6 March 1967, this early sixties view shows Hughes Crab 42874 rolling off the turntable. ***John Gill***

No repaint just a patch up and clean for Royal Scot, 46165 The Ranger, 12th London Regiment as it awaits a return to service at Crewe Works around 1962. ***Strathwood Library Collection***

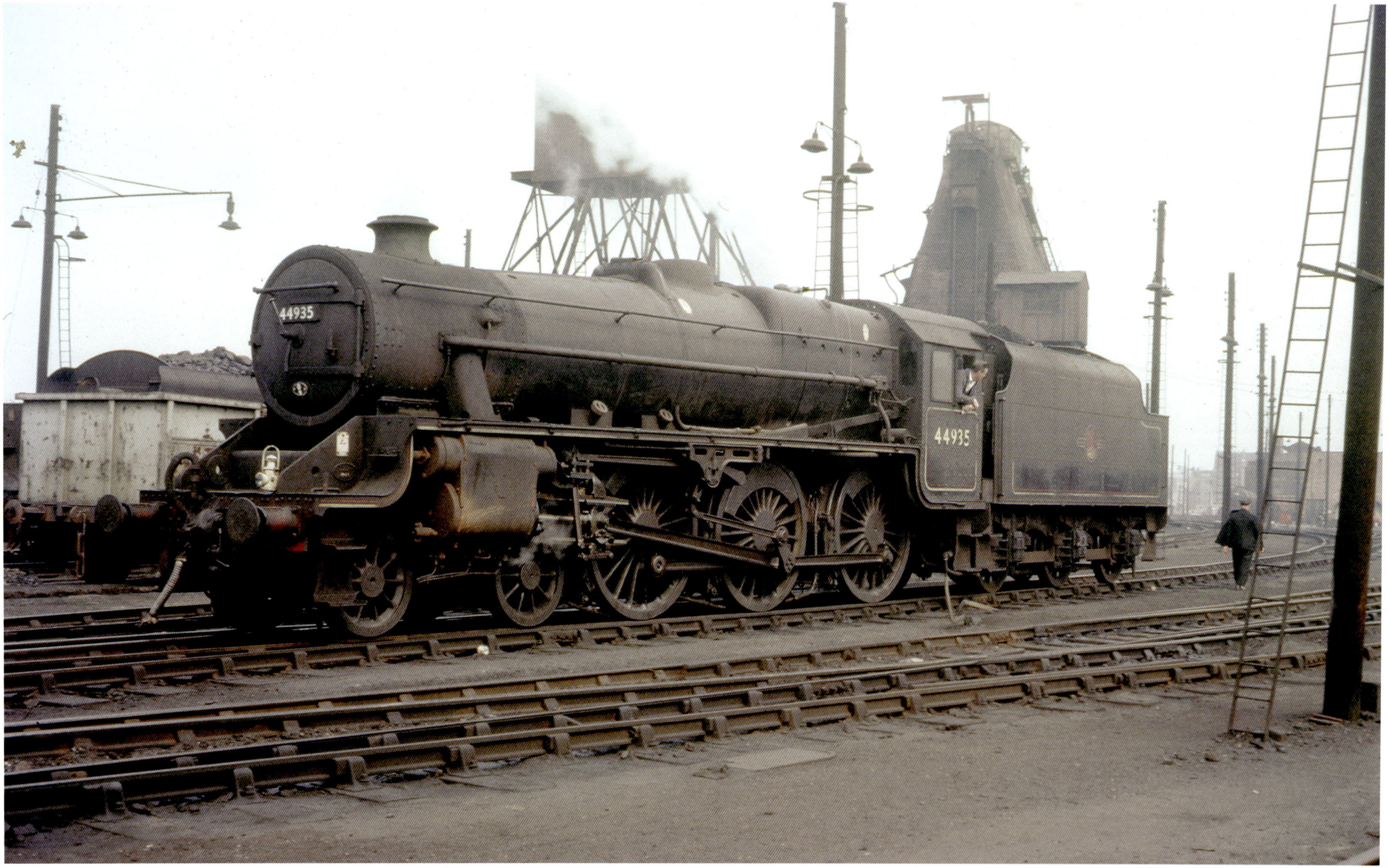

More too and fro at Willesden shed in the last three months of steam activity here on 3 June 1965, as Horwich built Black Five, 44935 takes up a new position in the shed. ***Strathwood Library Collection***

Opposite: Just a few yards away on another visit in March 1964 we can enjoy the resplendent 46240 City of Coventry in its last year of existance. ***Frank Hornby***

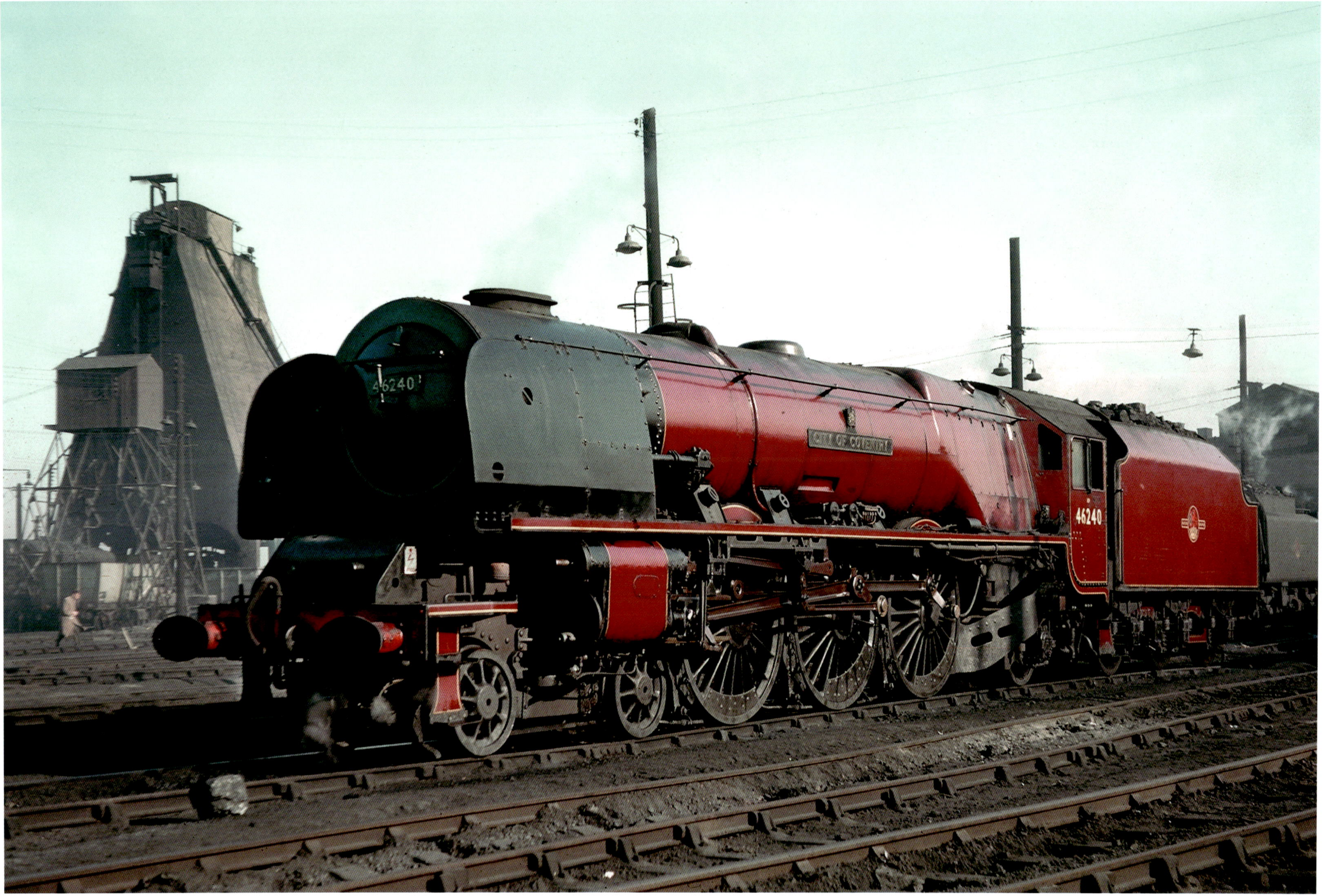
46240
46240

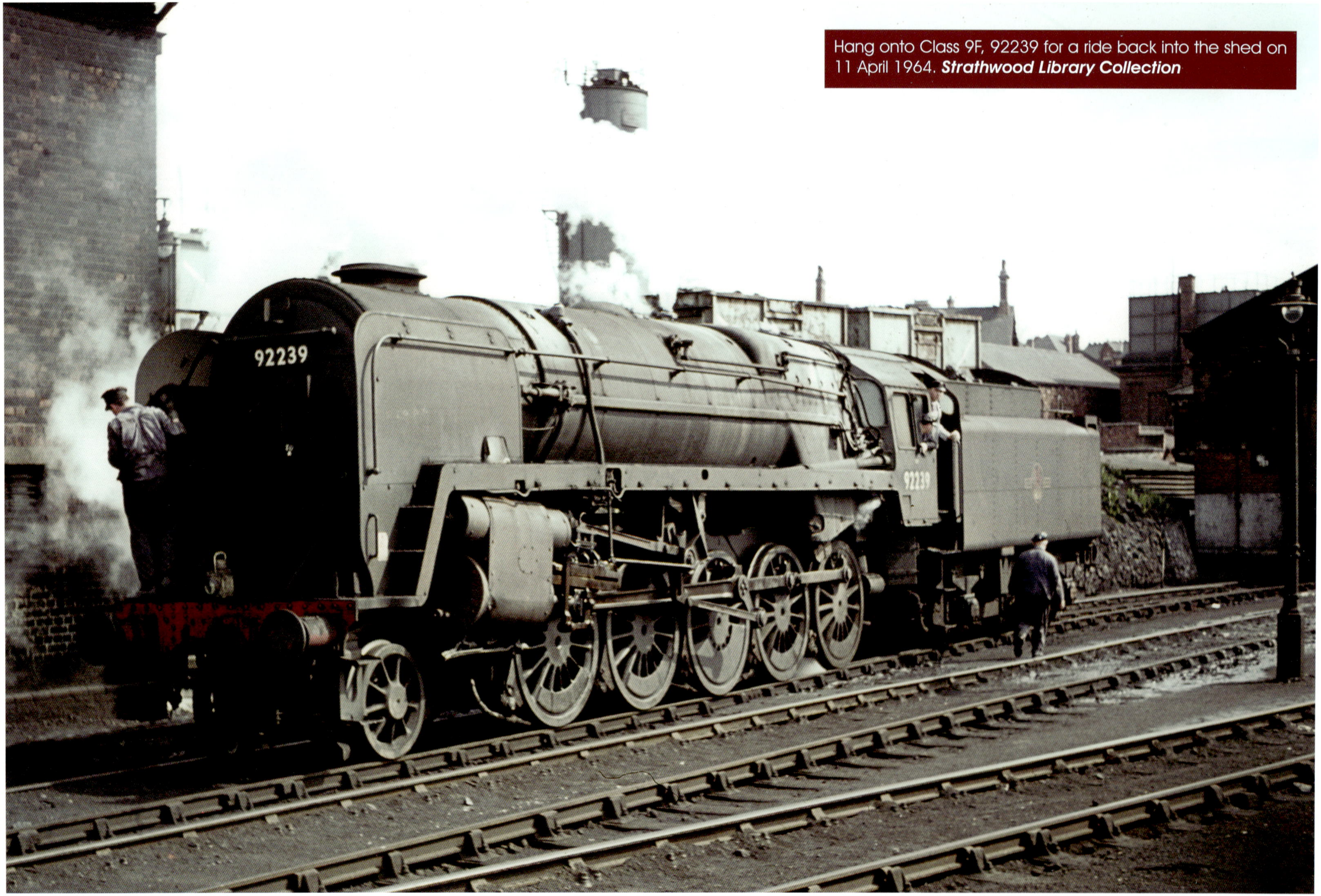

Hang onto Class 9F, 92239 for a ride back into the shed on 11 April 1964. ***Strathwood Library Collection***

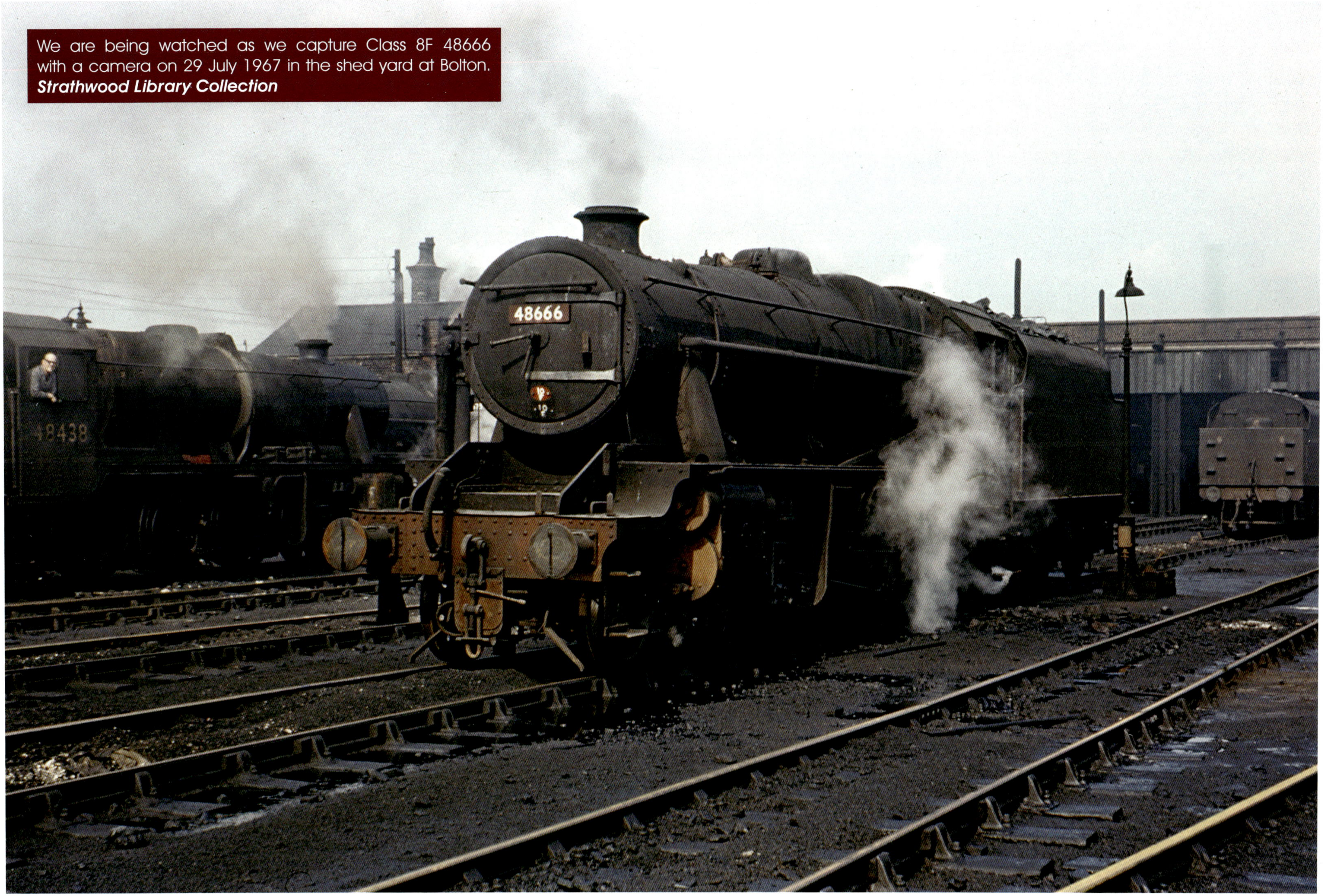

We are being watched as we capture Class 8F 48666 with a camera on 29 July 1967 in the shed yard at Bolton. ***Strathwood Library Collection***

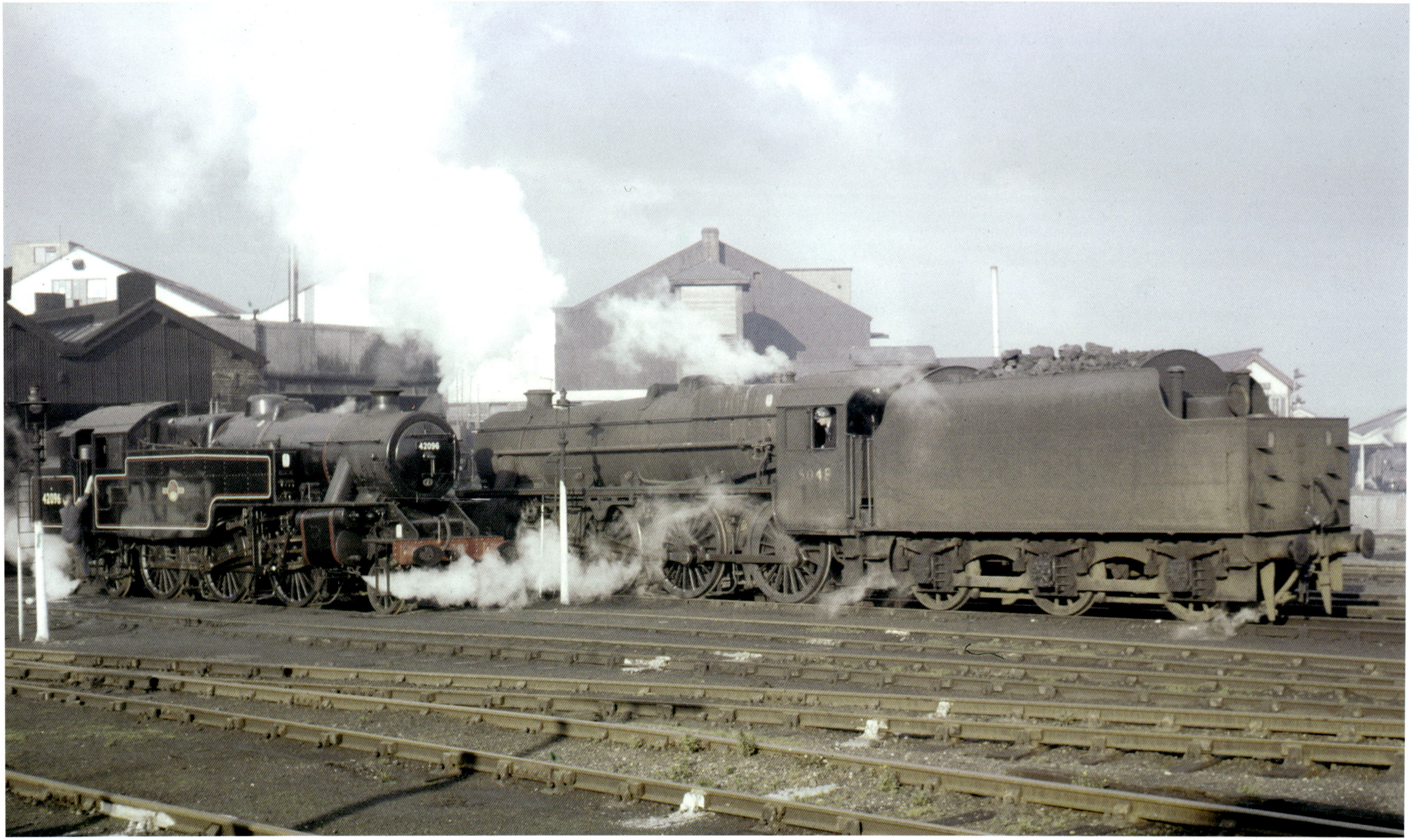

The shed yard at 1C Watford appears very busy at this moment in December 1962, as a recently ex-works Fairburn Class 4MT 42096, and a somewhat filthy Black Five 45048 engage in actvity to help fight off the cold snap that was approaching that winter. ***Win Wall/Strathwood Library Collection***

Opposite: Limescale stains from an internal steam leak are highlighted by the sunshine in this view on 15 July 1964, as Class 9F 92106 is ready for its next run northwards from Willesden. Whilst it was not only the Class 9Fs that were tragically shortlived, but there was just one full year that all 251 of the class were available for traffic, and that was in 1963. ***Strathwood Library Collection***

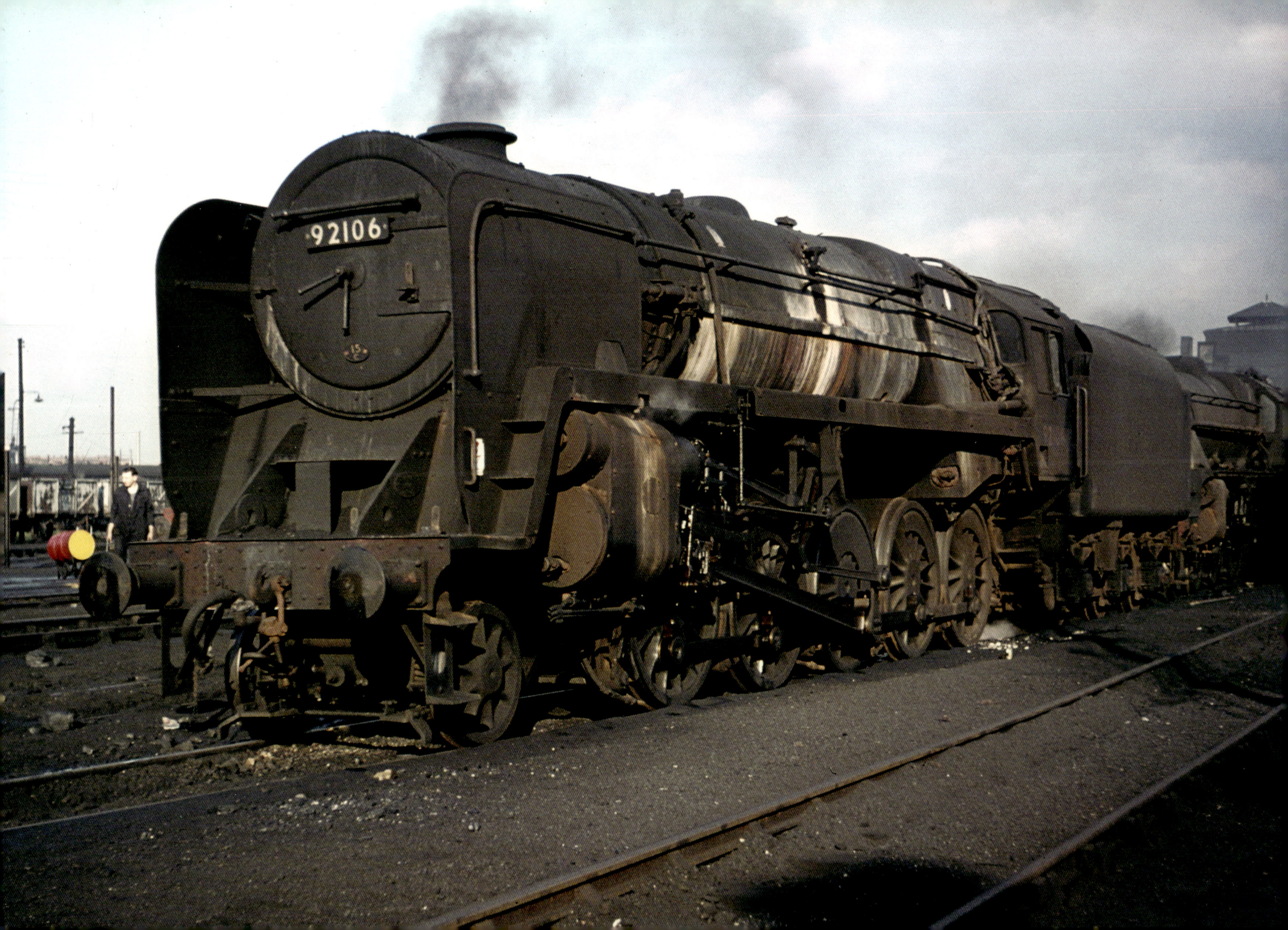
92106

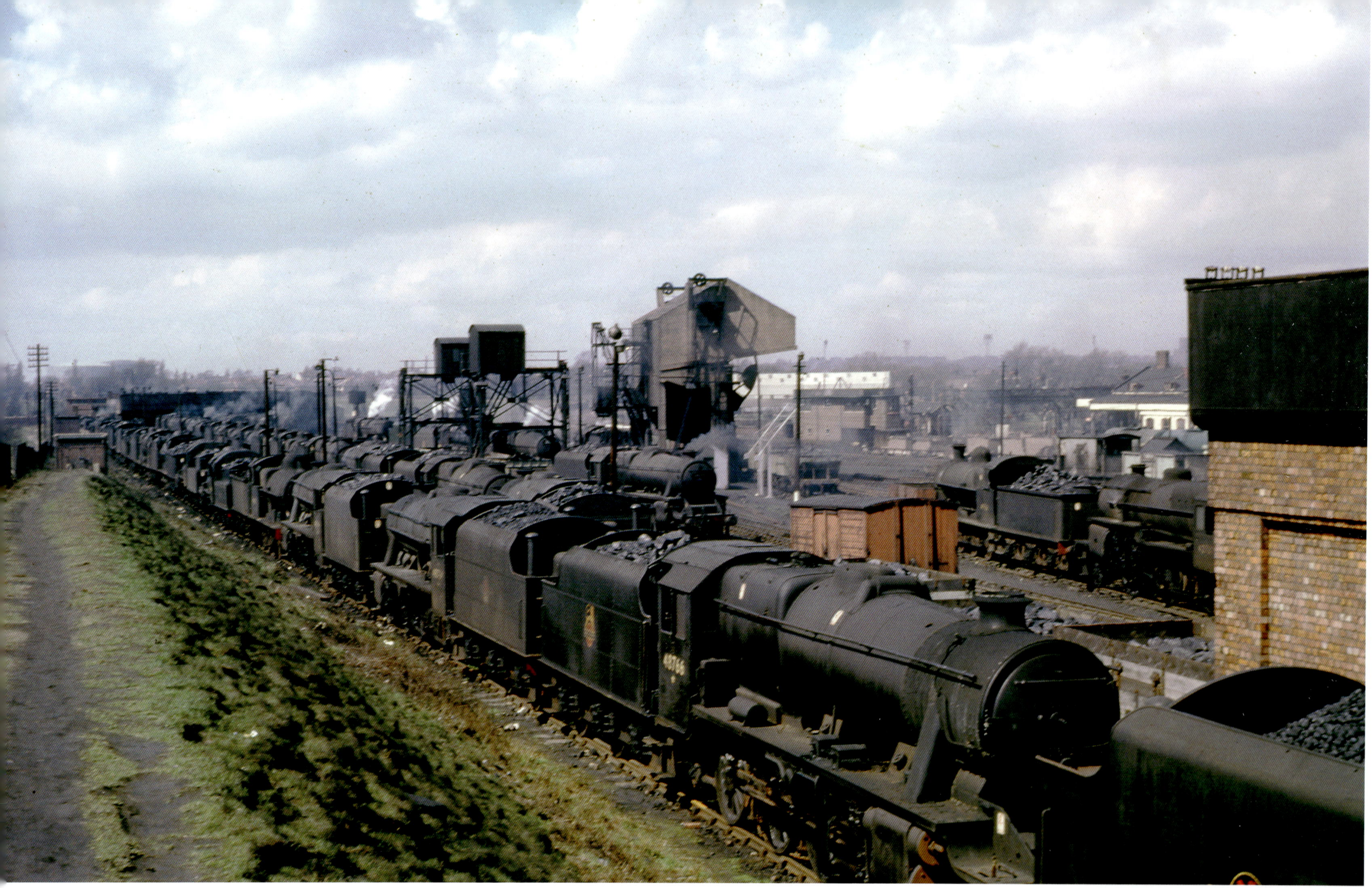

An attractive line up awaits our visit to Bescot on a Sunday in the late 1950s, it will certainly take a while to get around and note this lot down. ***Strathwood Library Collection***

Opposite: Wolverhampton's Oxley shed was now coded 2B towards the end and no longer within the reign of the Western Region on 4 March 1967, just two days from its closure. ***Jerry Beddows***

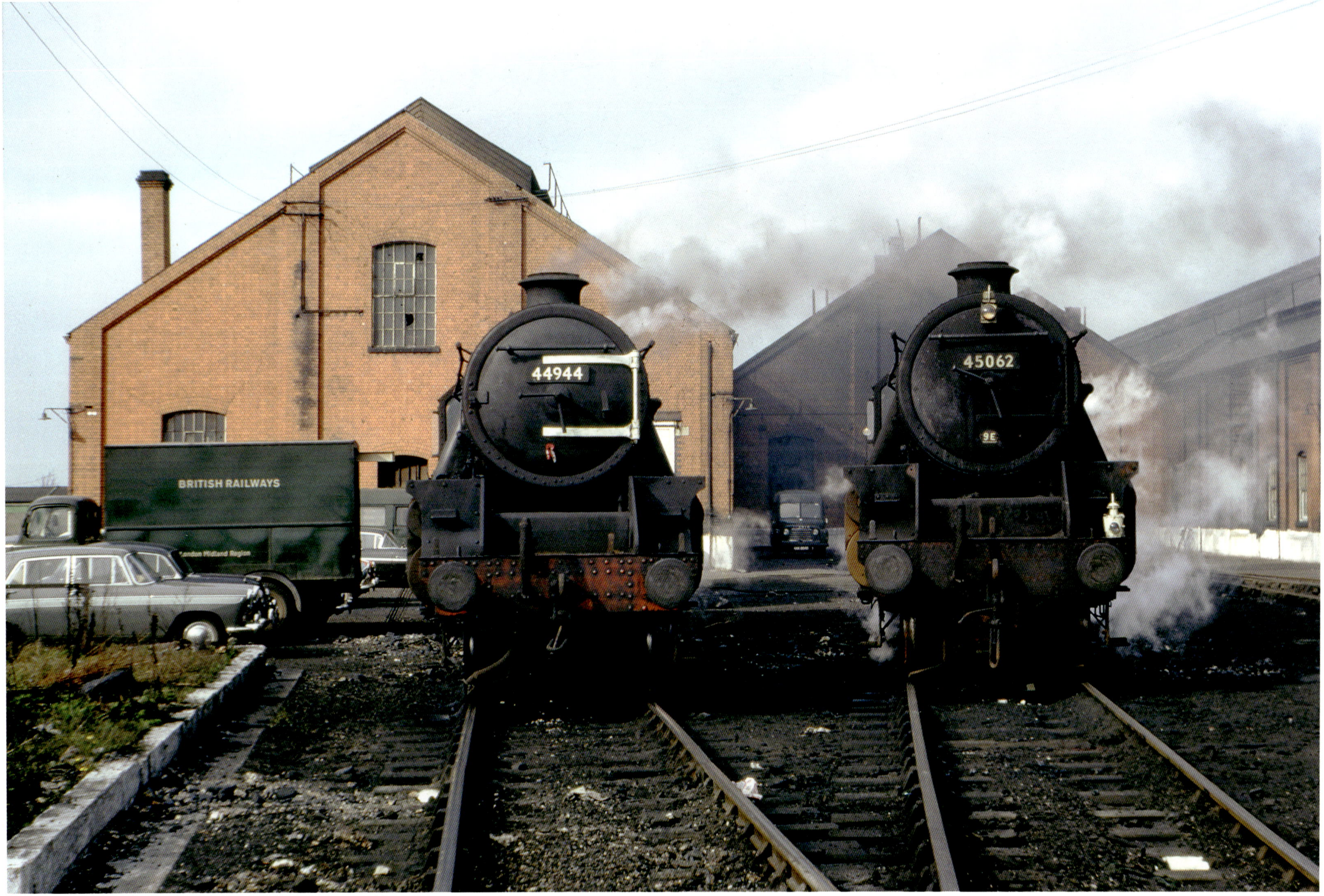
44944
45062
9E
BRITISH RAILWAYS

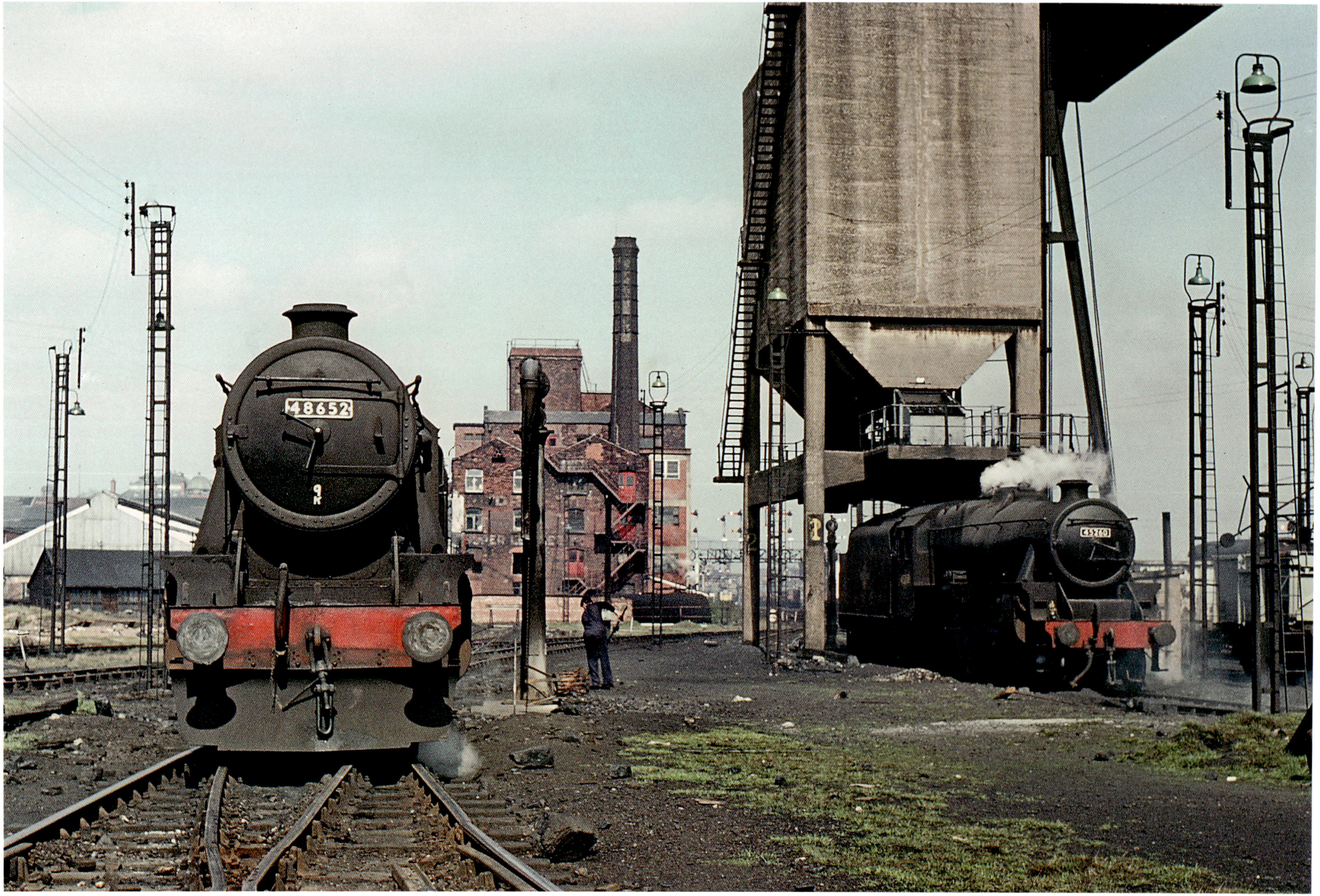
48652

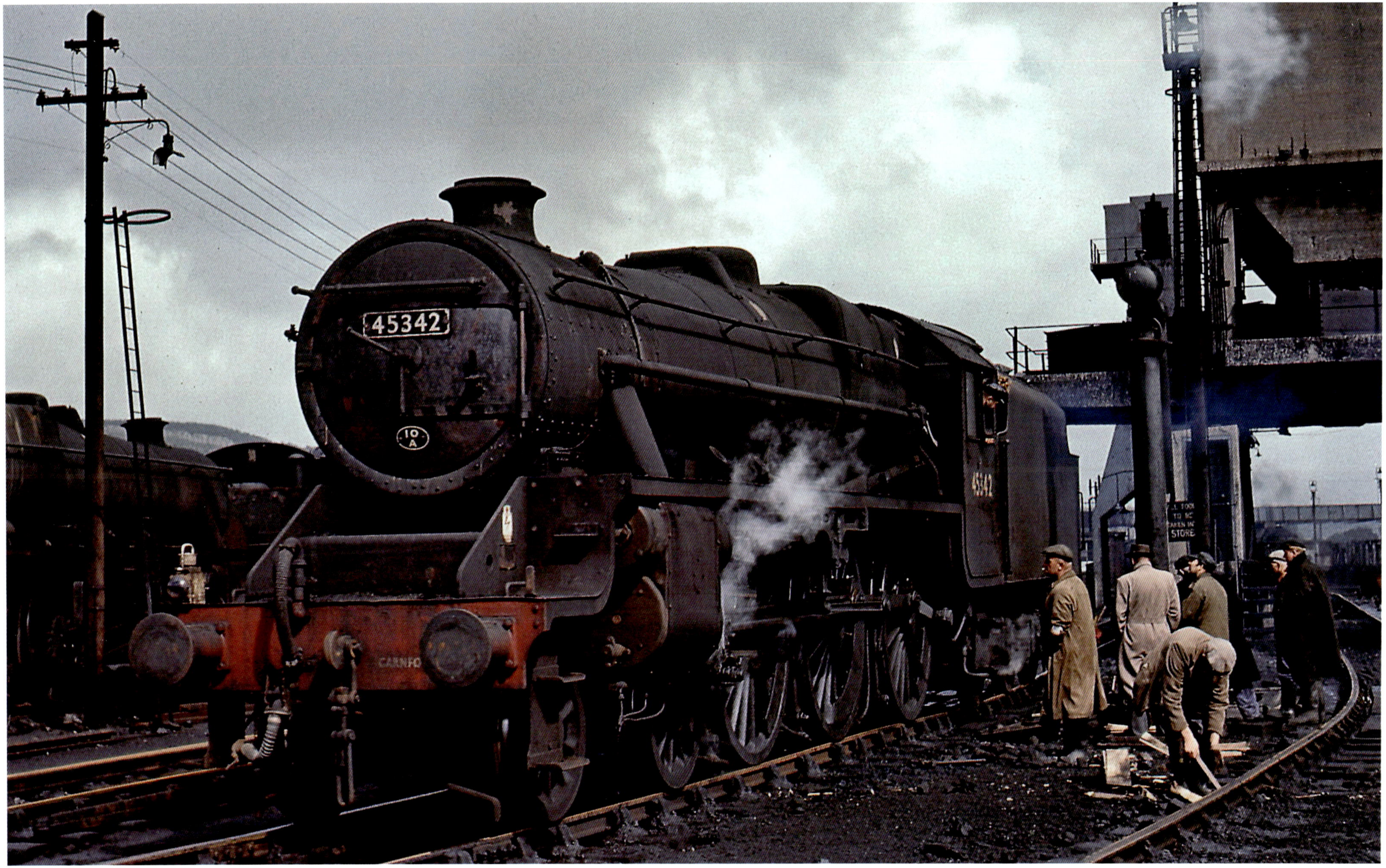

Page left: A bit of tidying up around the water column by the coaling tower at Bolton on 20 April 1968, as Class 8F 48652 and Black Five 45260 look on. ***David Rostance/Rail Photoprints***

More activity around a water column as another Black Five, 45342 prepares to leave Carnforth shed on 3 September 1967. ***Gerald T. Robinson***

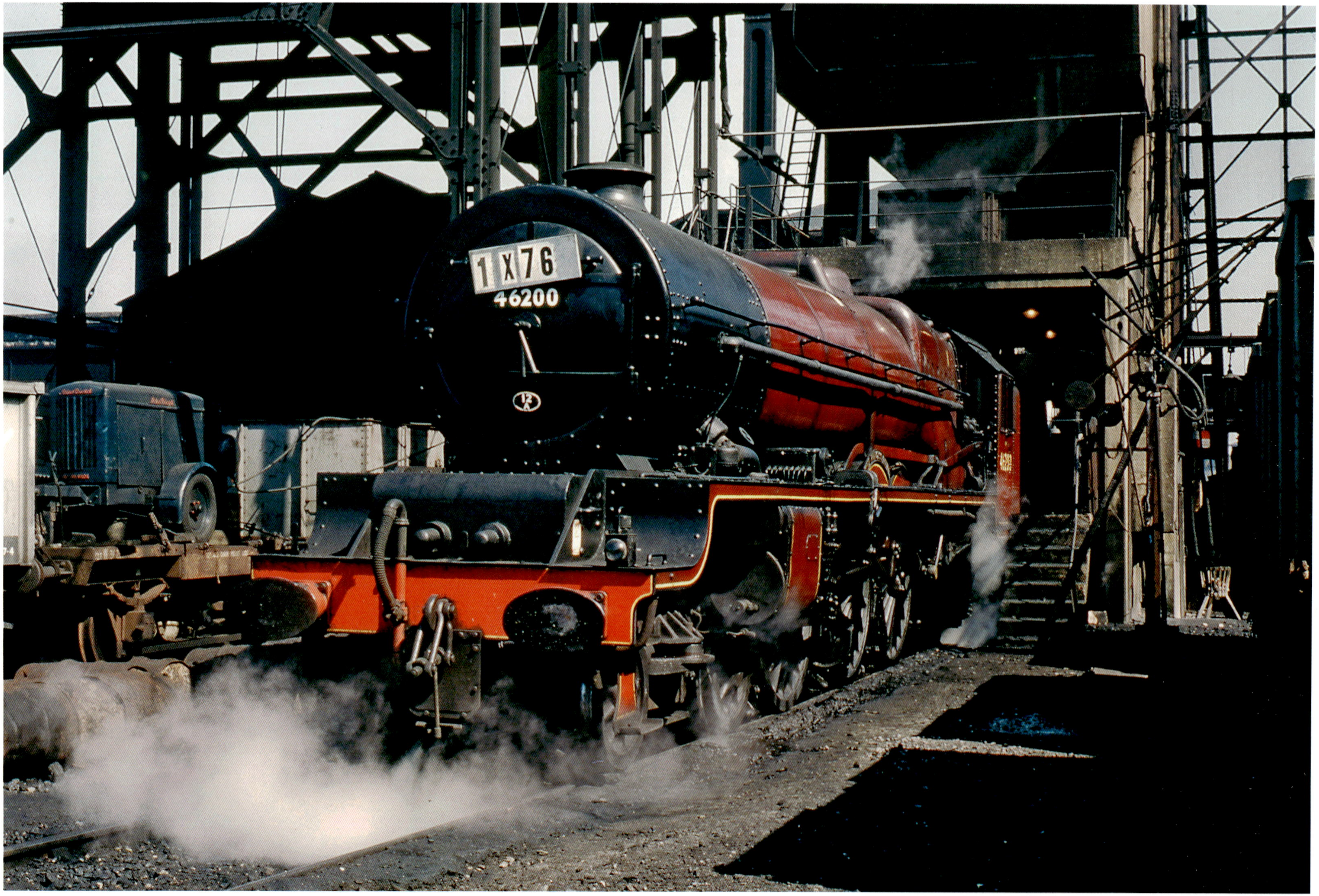
1 X 76
46200

Page left: Many enthusiasts were attracted to photographing steam locomotives by coaling facilities, another such example is here at Camden on 3 June 1962, with 46200 The Princess Royal having arrived after hauling a special from Carlisle earlier that afternoon. ***Dave Cobbe Collection/Rail Photoprints***

One of the coaling gang catches a breather at Heaton Mersey on 7 May 1966, having been given the hard way of fueling up a Class 9F such as the ex-Crosti boilered 92027. None of us would enjoy the prospect of shovelling up to seven tons of coal into that tender if it arrived empty. ***Colour Rail***

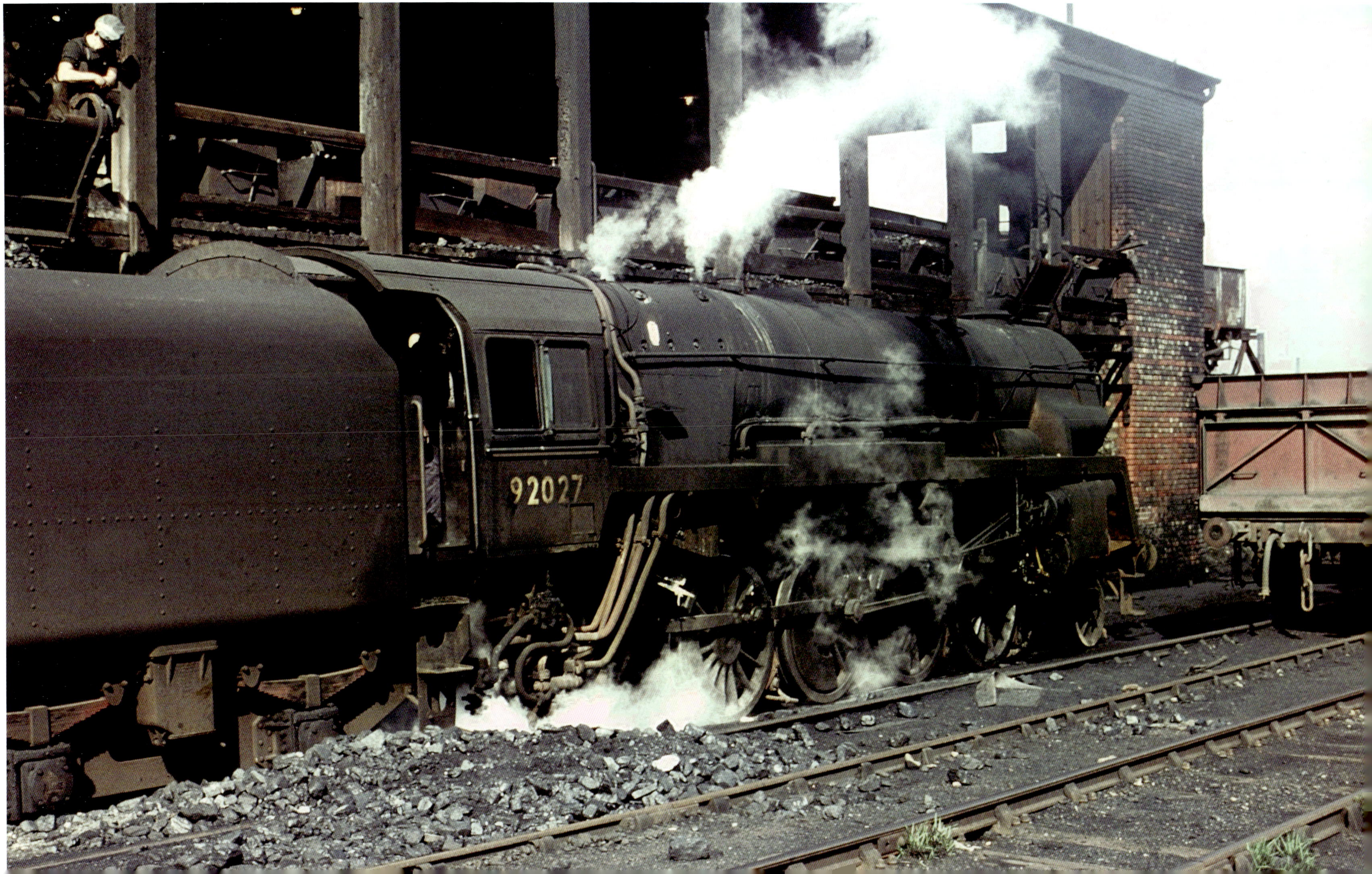

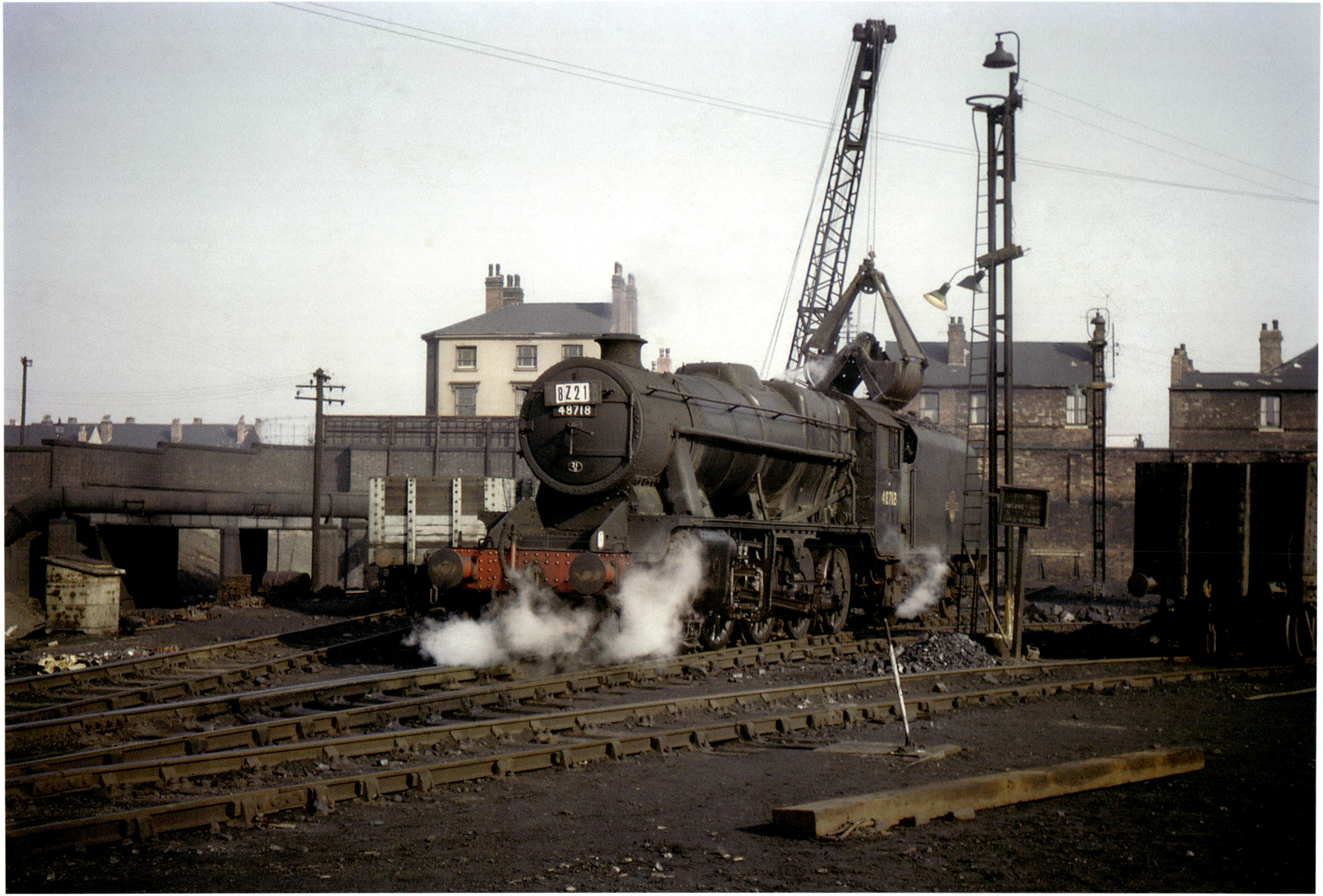
8Z21
48718

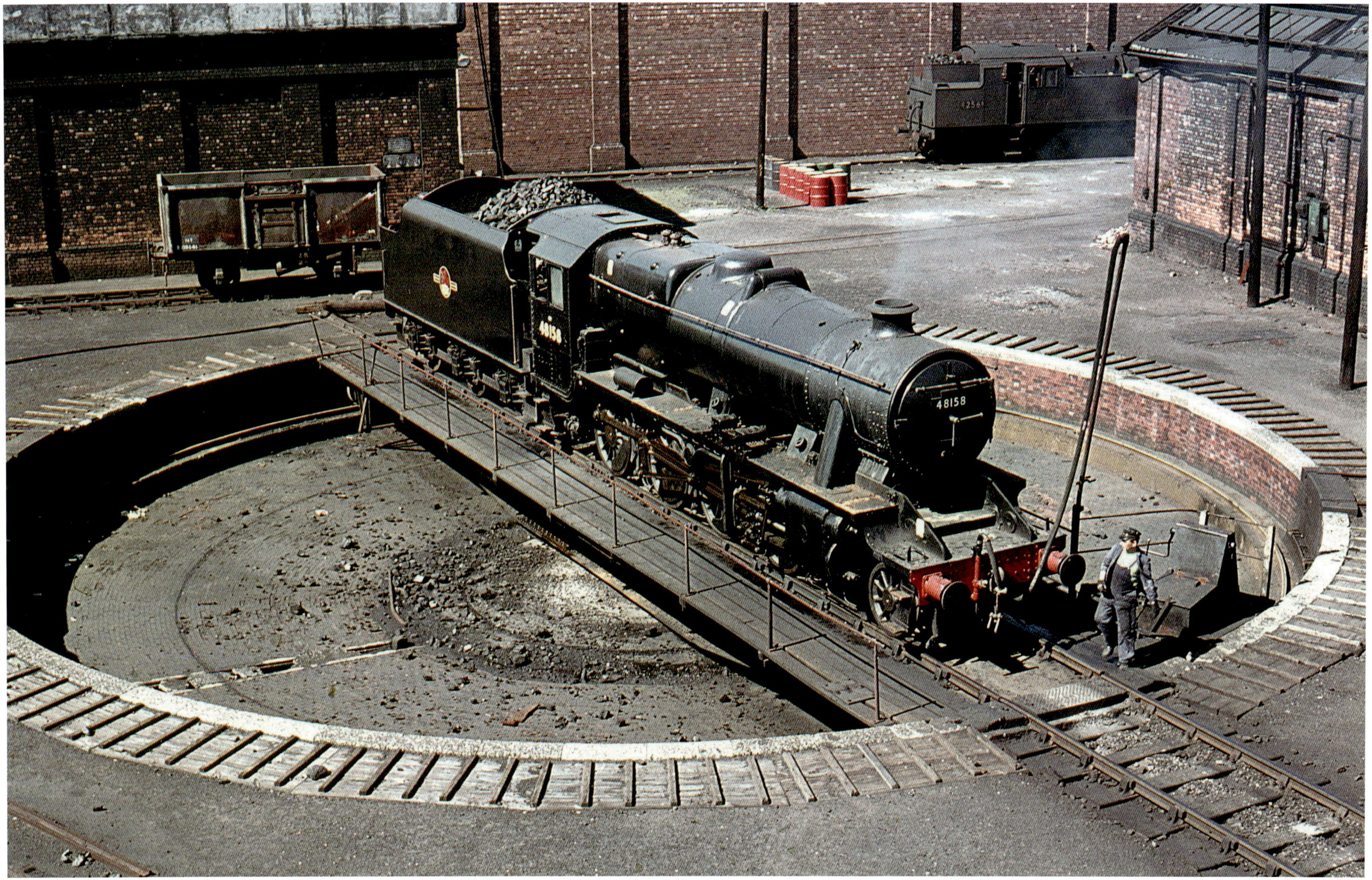

An easier alternative was a coal grab, as here at 21D Aston to fill up Class 8F 48718 on 7 April 1963. ***Rail Online***

Fellow Class 8F, 48158 has already filled up under the same tower we are looking down from at Patricroft also in 1963. ***Late Jim Carter/Rail Photoprints***

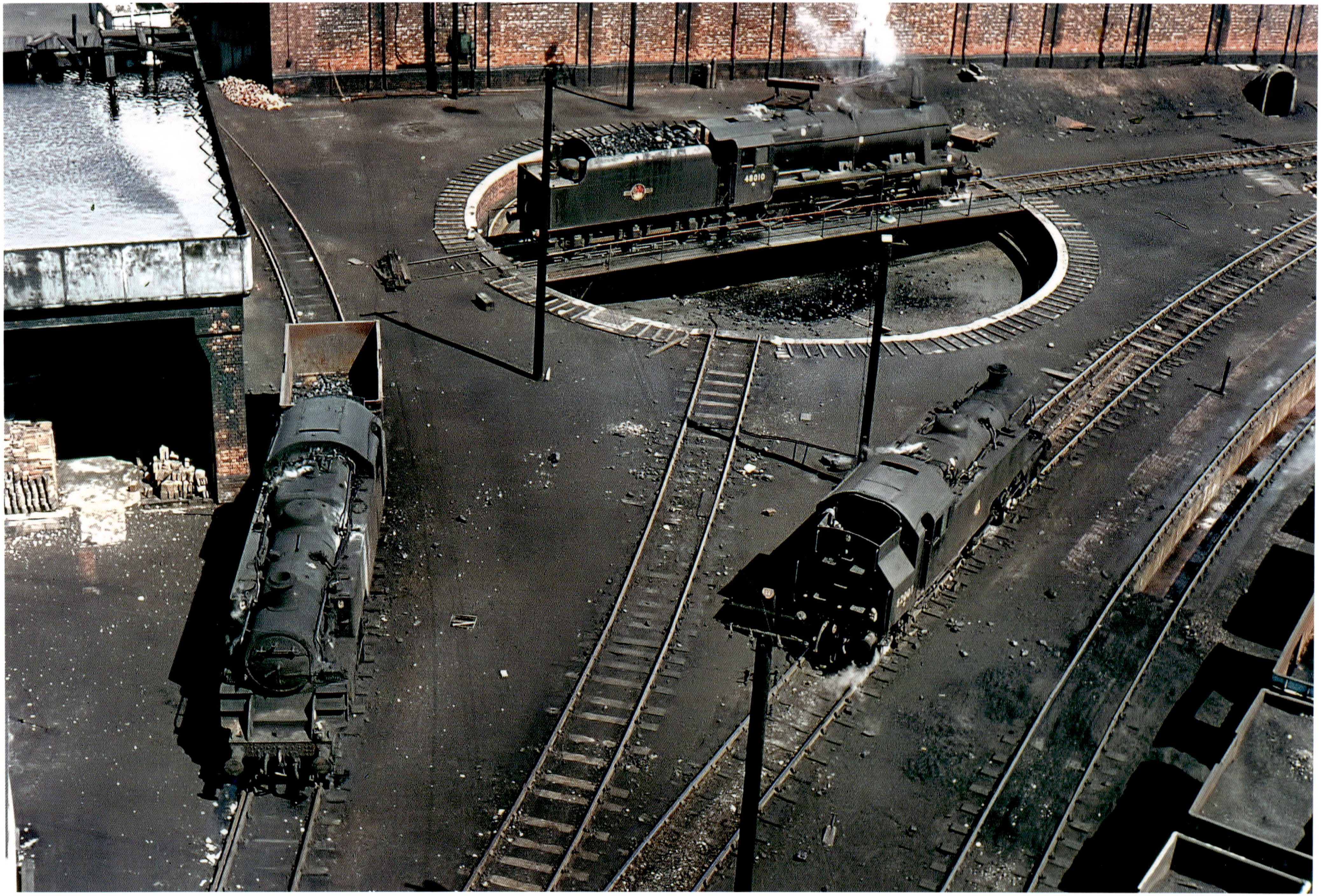
48010

Top Link Work

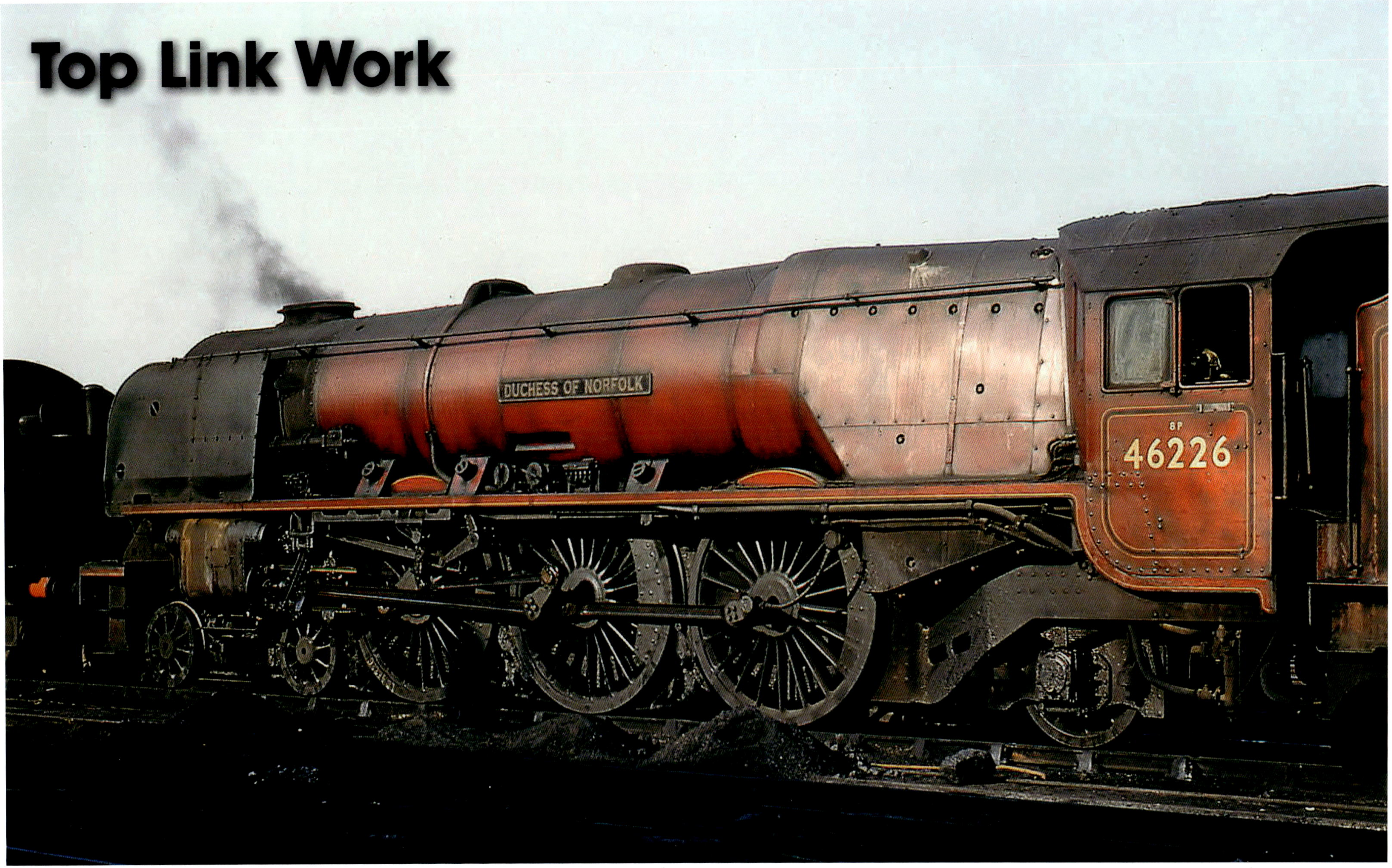

Page left: A further view from a vantage point higher up that same Patricroft coaling plant sees another Class 8F, 48010 flanked by two of the five Standard Class 3MTs allocated to 9H Patricroft in 1965. ***Late Jim Carter/Rail Photoprints***

Evidence of previous clearing out of ash from the smokeboxes of both resident and visiting steam locomotives at Camden, lies alongside the splendid red liveried 46226 Duchess of Norfolk, in September 1959. ***Gerald T. Robinson***

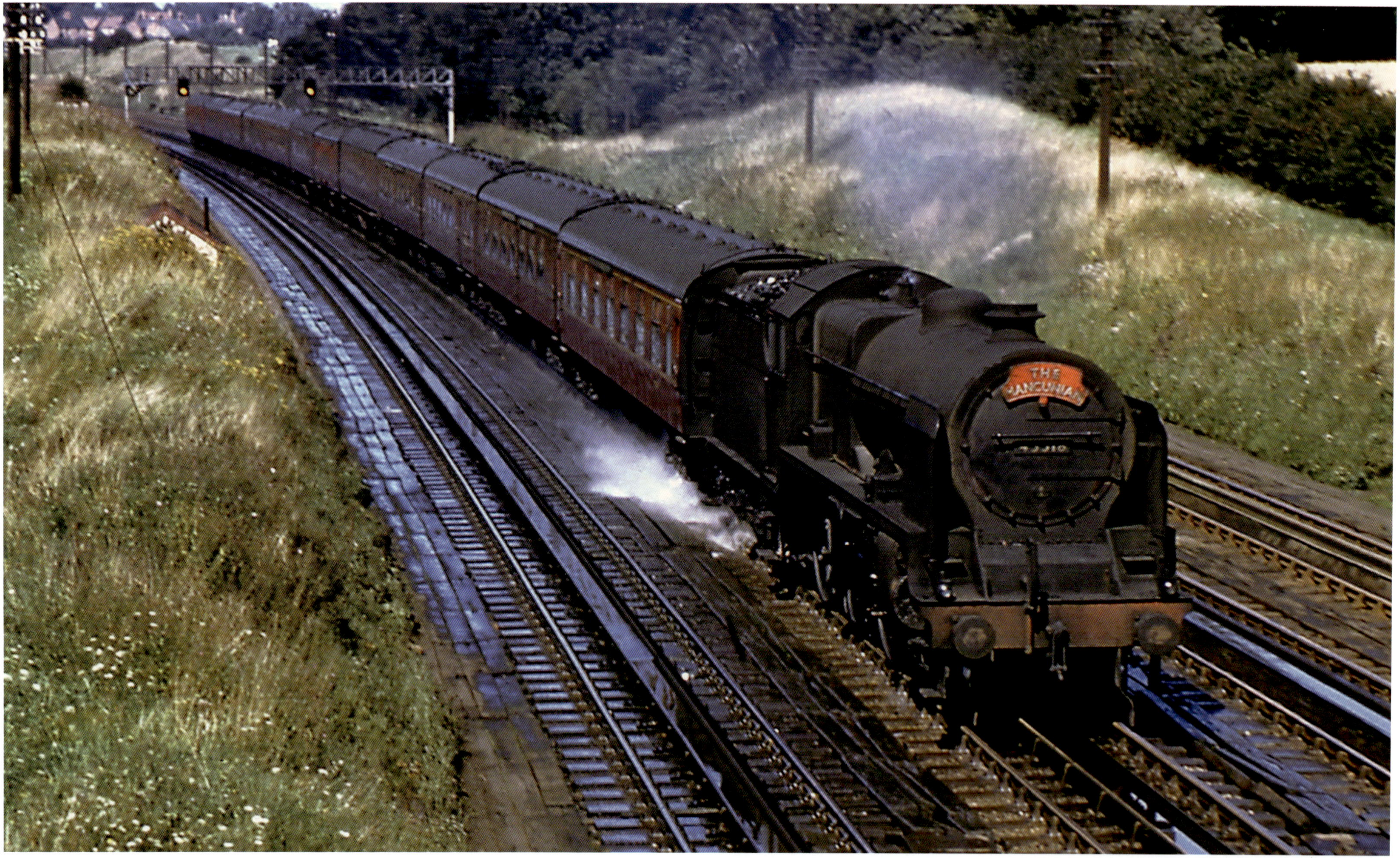

Taking the opportunity of a top up at speed on Castlethorpe's troughs in August 1958, was Patriot 45518 Bradshaw, which seems to be going well with The Mancunian which was the 09:45 departure from Manchester's London Road bound for Euston. ***Trevor Owen/Colour Rail***

Opposite: A frozen moment in time at Preston in July 1961, with Coronation 46227 Duchess of Devonshire halted at signals, this fine locomotive was twenty three years old at this time, and would remain in service for only another seventeen months. ***Colour Rail***

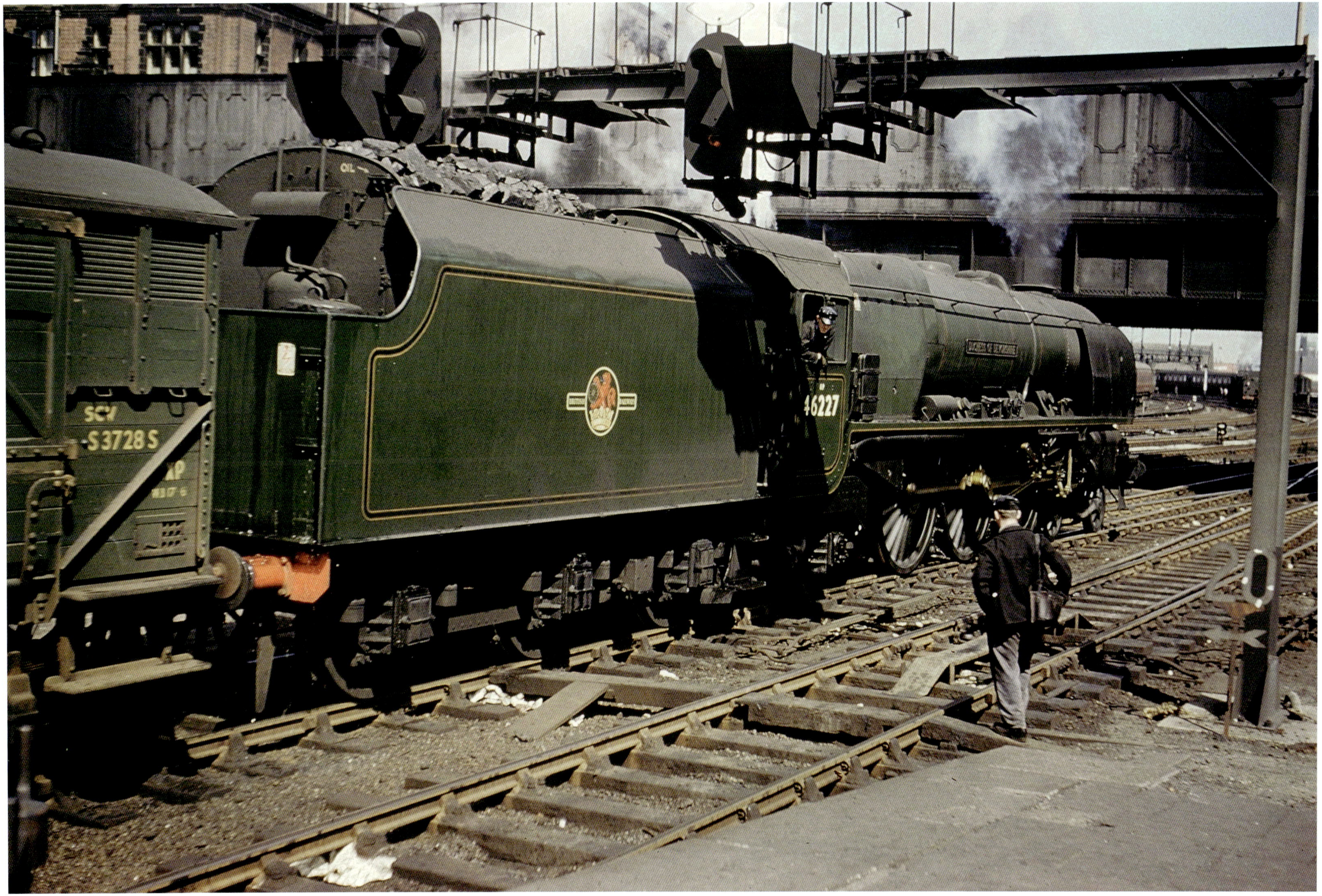
OIL
46227
SCV
S3728 S

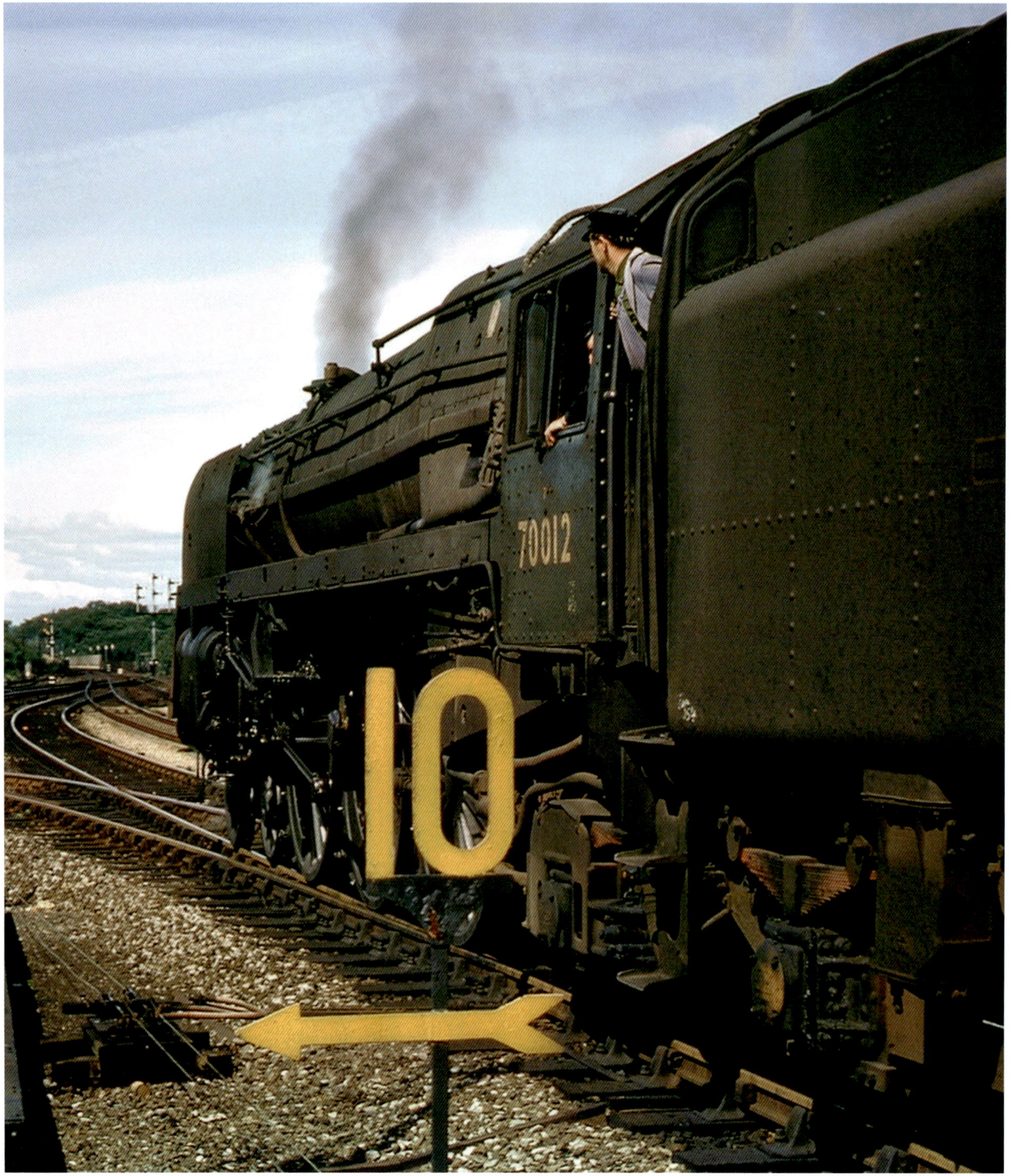

Sadly the John of Gaunt nameplates have been removed by the time of this view at Lancaster on 5 August 1967, with just a little under five months left of it's sixteen year service life left. But on this day the attentive crew have charge of the 10:35 Euston to Barrow express passenger service. ***Bill Wright***

Opposite: Just a few years earlier and we can see how the London Midland Region previously turned out their Britannias, as 70021 Morning Star climbs past Camden Goods Depot on its climb away from London with a Manchester service on 21 July 1962. ***Dave Cobbe/Rail Photoprints***

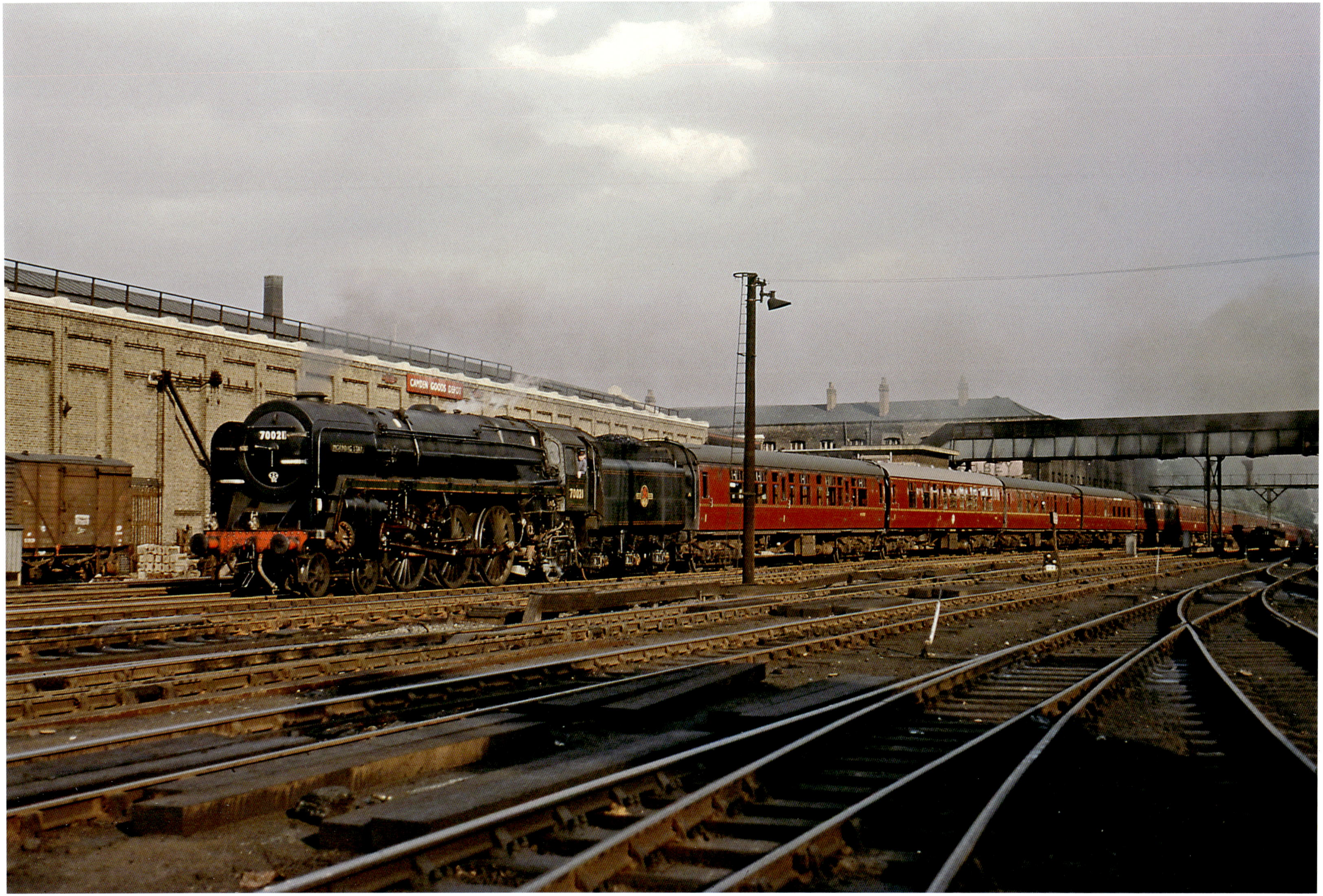
CAMDEN GOODS DEPOT
70021
70021

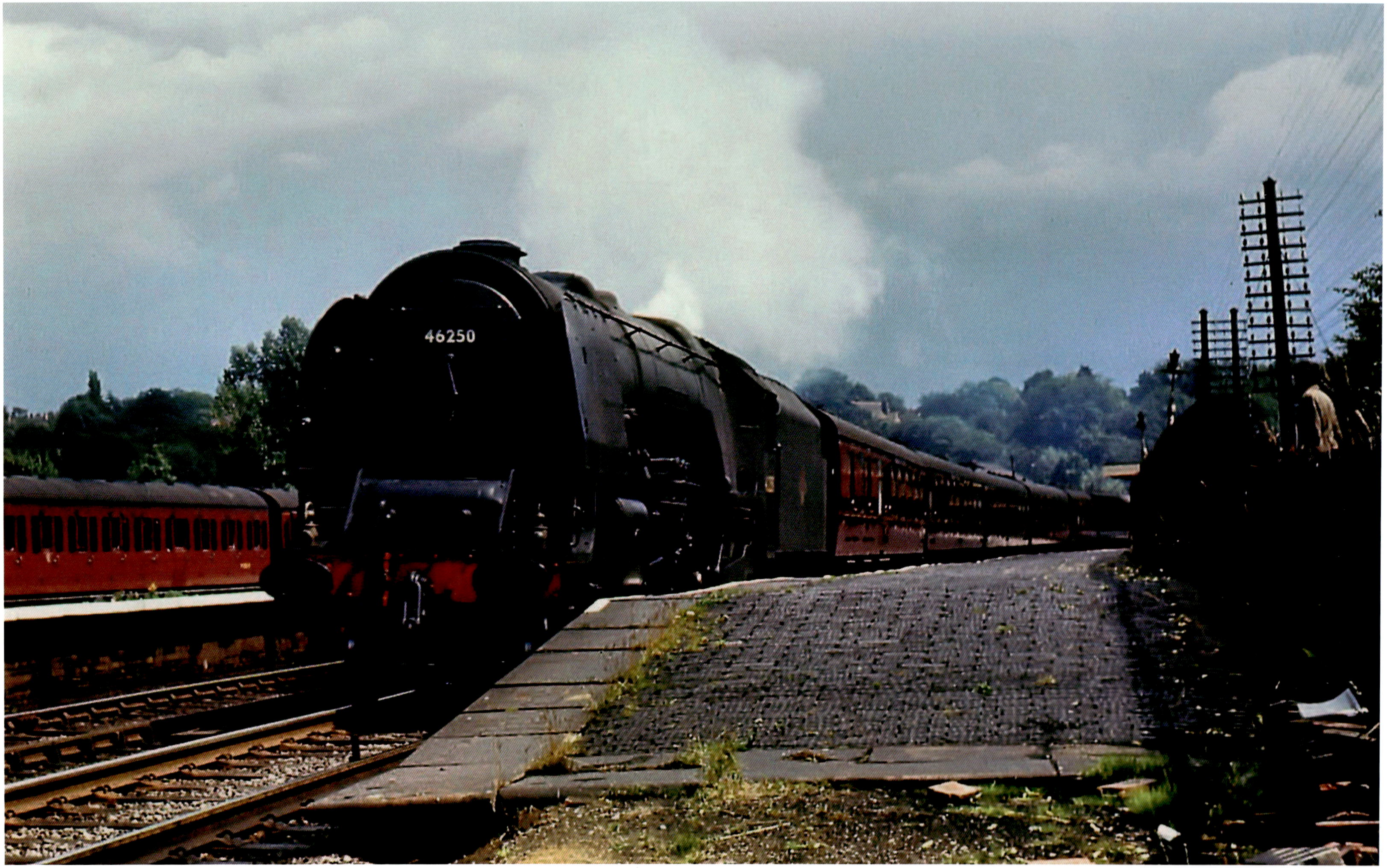

A couple of spectators are on hand to enjoy the passing of Coronation, 46250 City of Lichfield as it hurries through Berkhamsted station with the 13:30 Euston to Perth, on 15 July 1961. ***Gerald T. Robinsion***

Opposite: Another fine Stanier Pacific in green on the turntable at Carlisle Kingmoor, as 46222 Queen Mary is being prepared for her duty on the Royal Scot in 1956. ***Dave Cobbe Collection/Rail Photoprints***

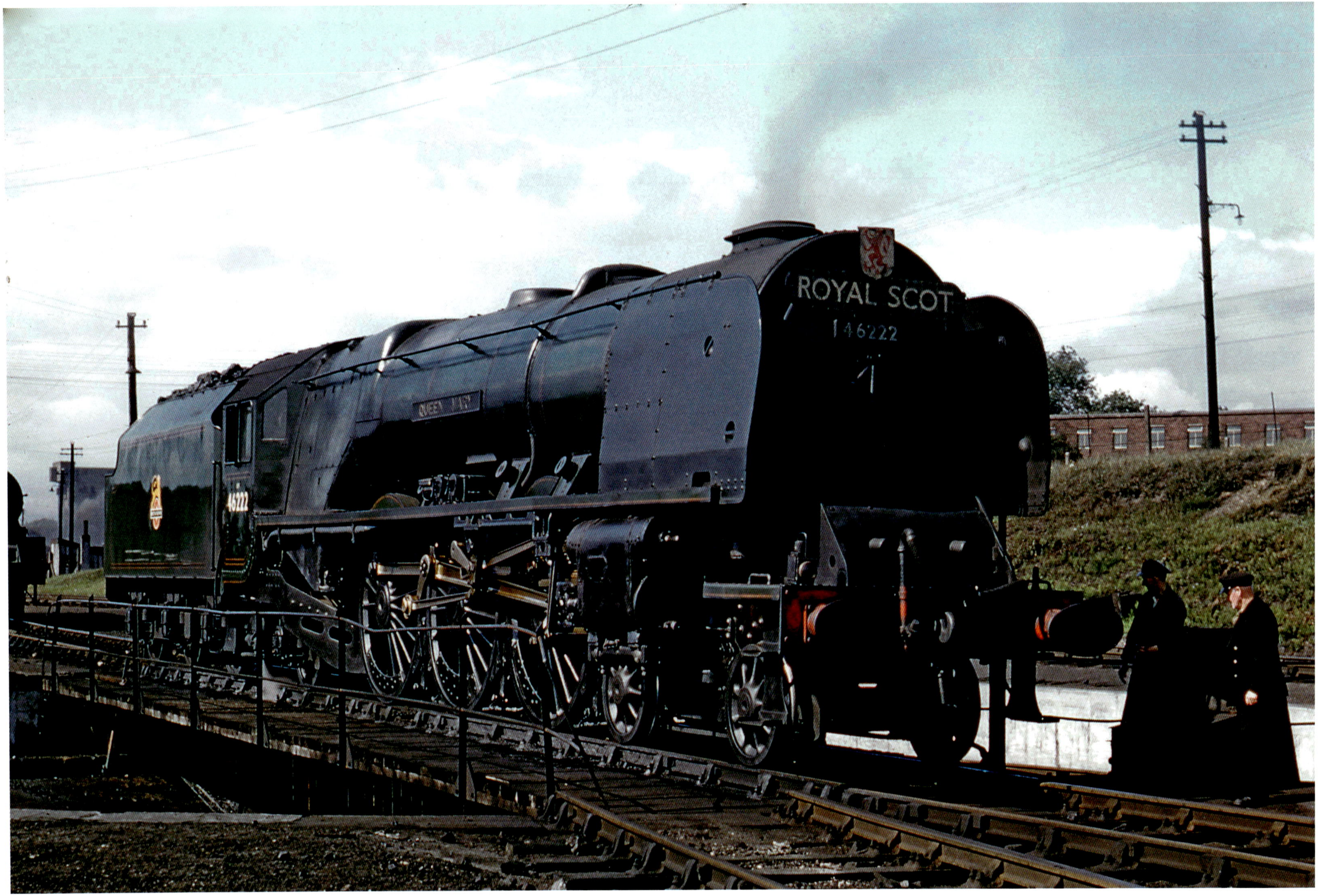
ROYAL SCOT
46222
46222

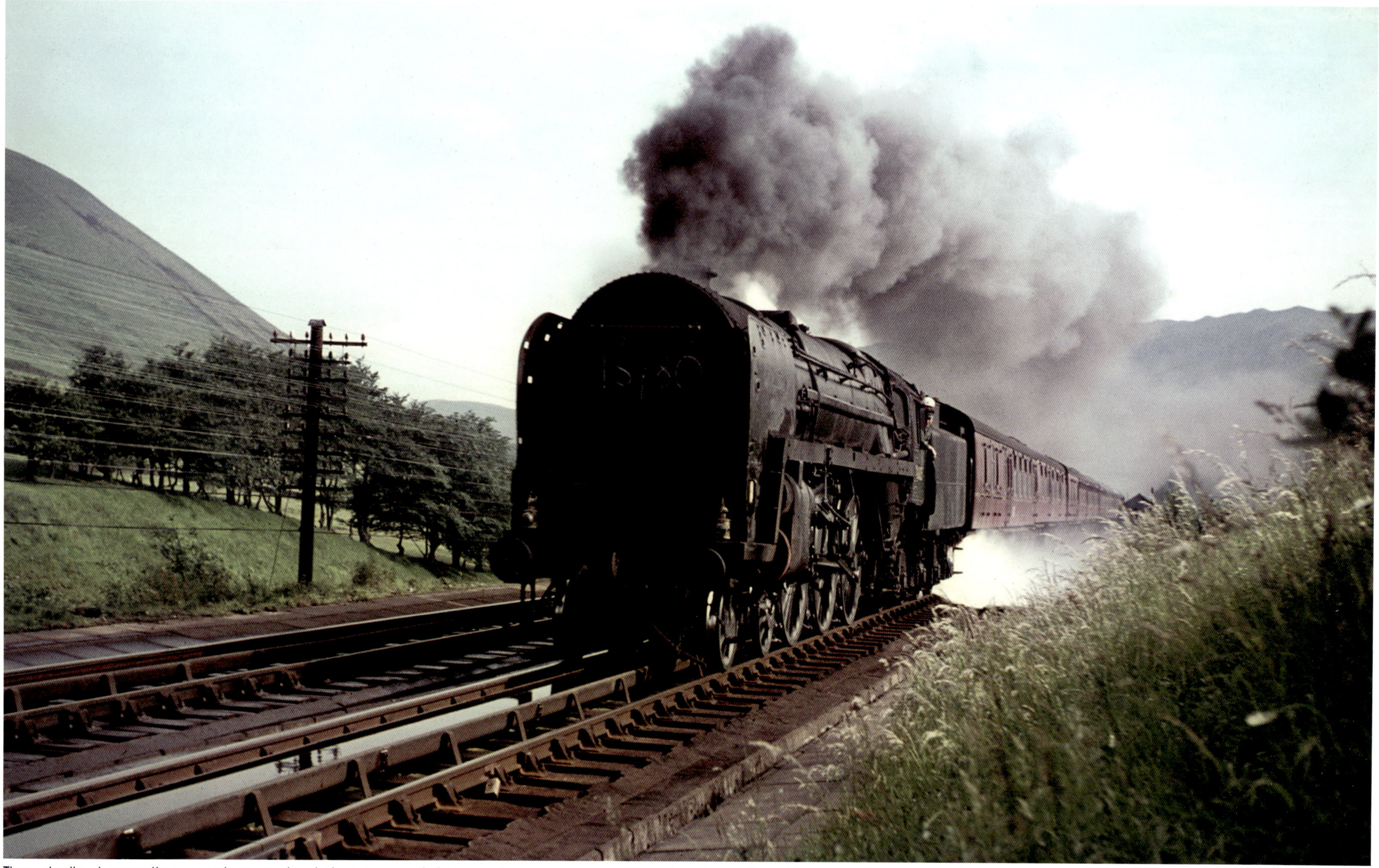

The chalked reporting number and missing nameplates on the once magnificent Britannia 70025 Western Star storming past Dillicar's troughs, do little for the image of British Rail and faith of the travelling public by 1967. ***Strathwood Library Collection***

Opposite: Whereas The Merseyside Express in the competant charge of 46204 Princess Louise, near Hartford with the up working on 12 April 1958, is more the memory we would wish to recall of steam on the WCML. ***Late R. A. Whitfield/Rail Photoprints***

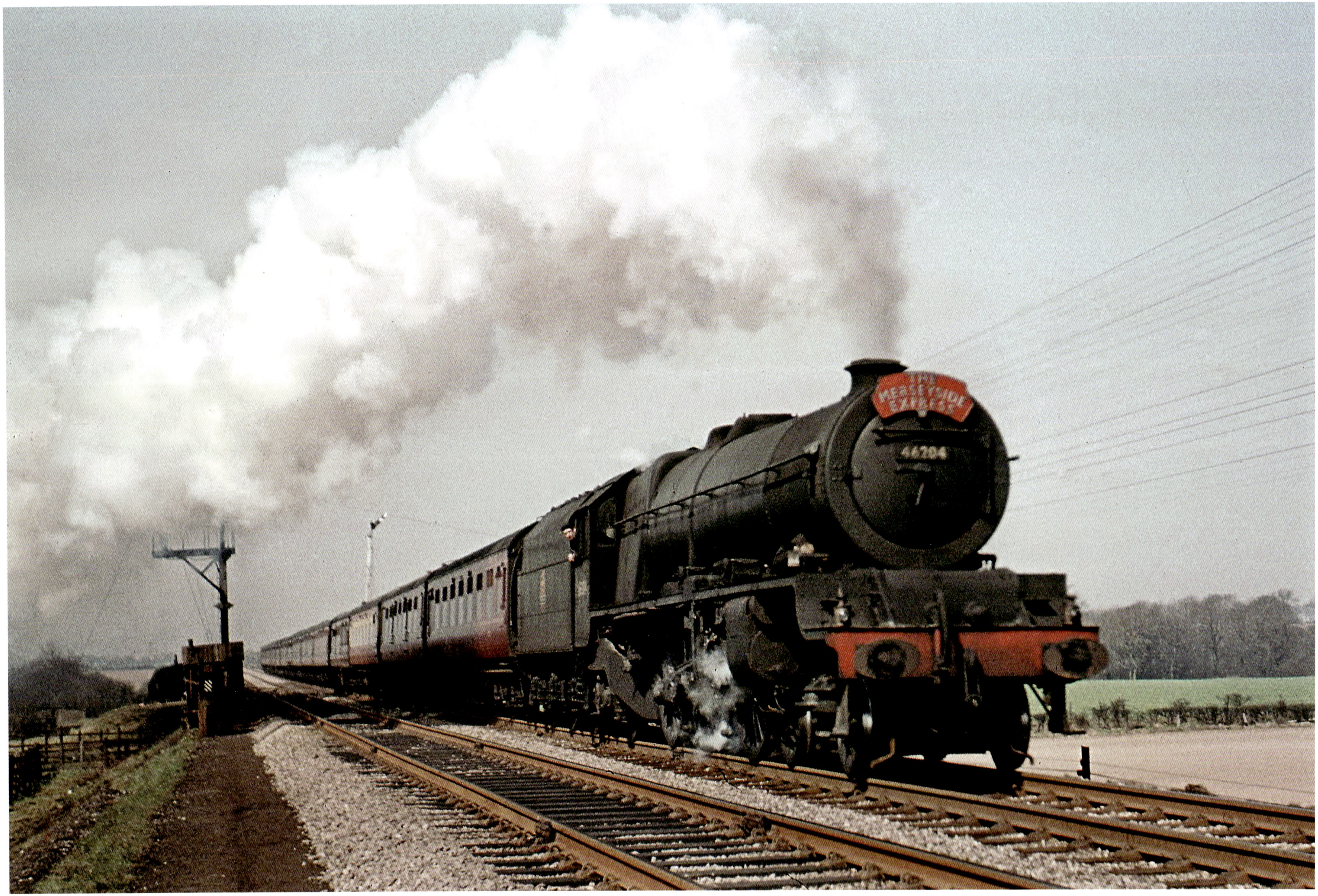
THE MERSEYSIDE EXPRESS
46204

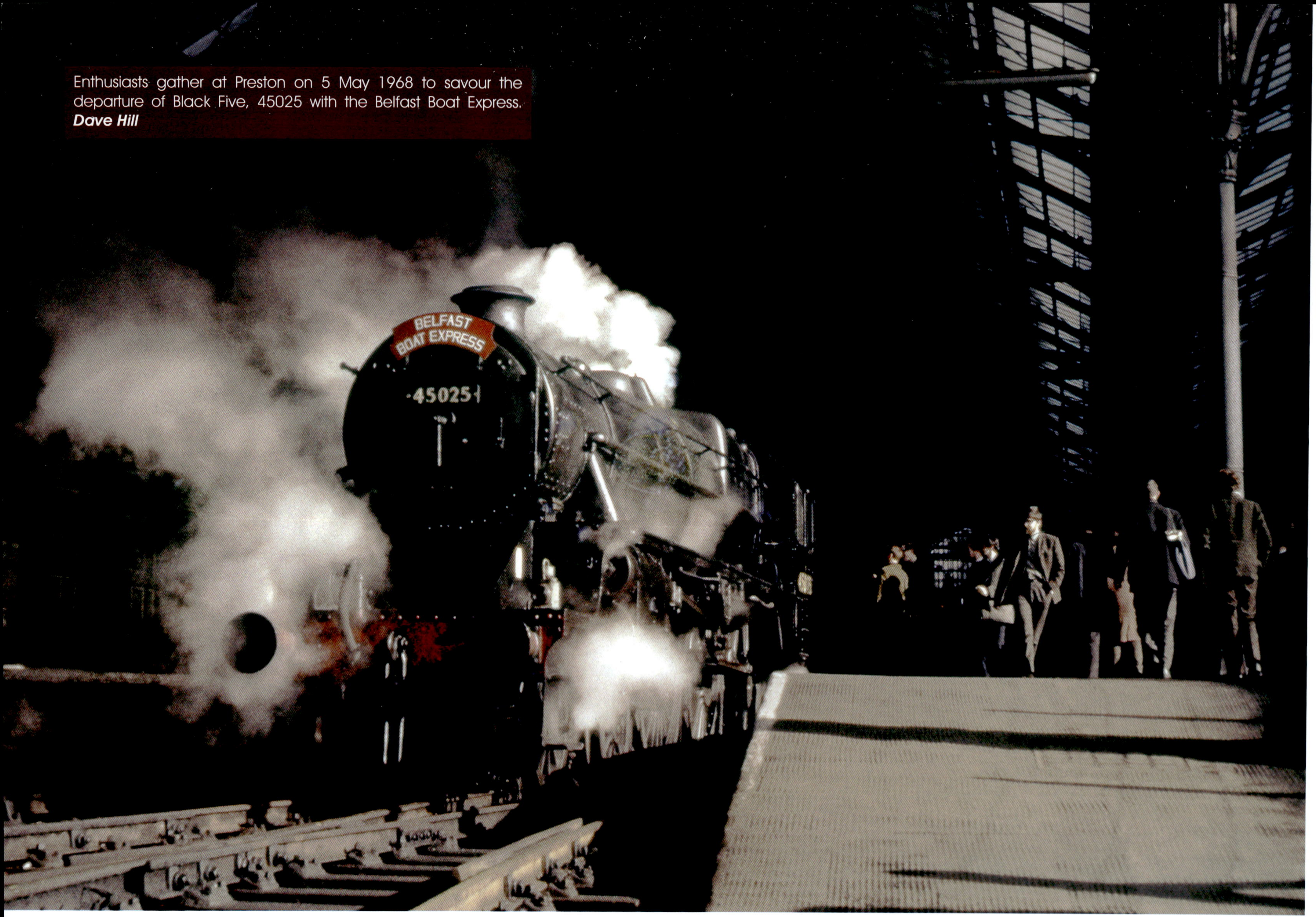

Enthusiasts gather at Preston on 5 May 1968 to savour the departure of Black Five, 45025 with the Belfast Boat Express. ***Dave Hill***

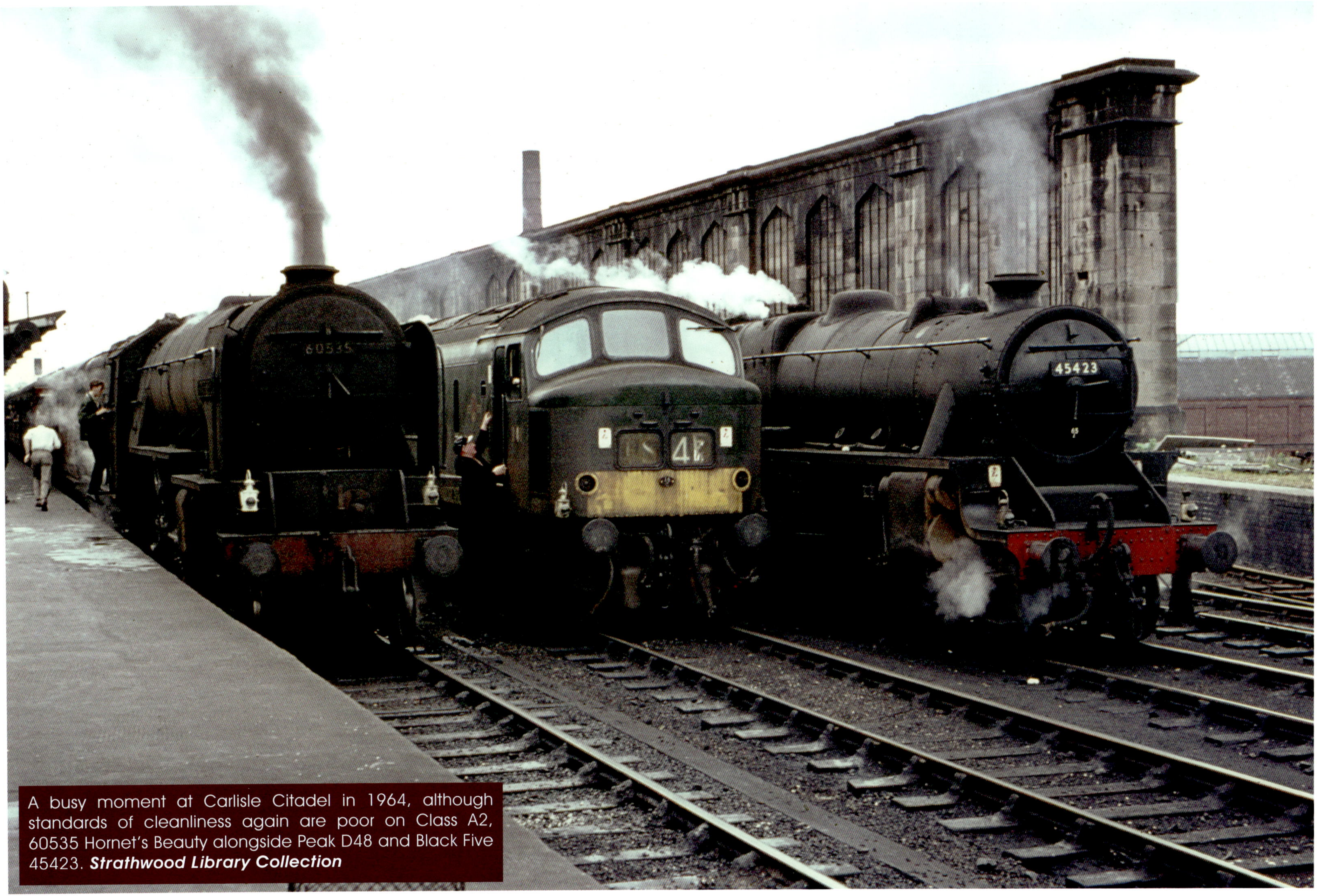

A busy moment at Carlisle Citadel in 1964, although standards of cleanliness again are poor on Class A2, 60535 Hornet's Beauty alongside Peak D48 and Black Five 45423. ***Strathwood Library Collection***

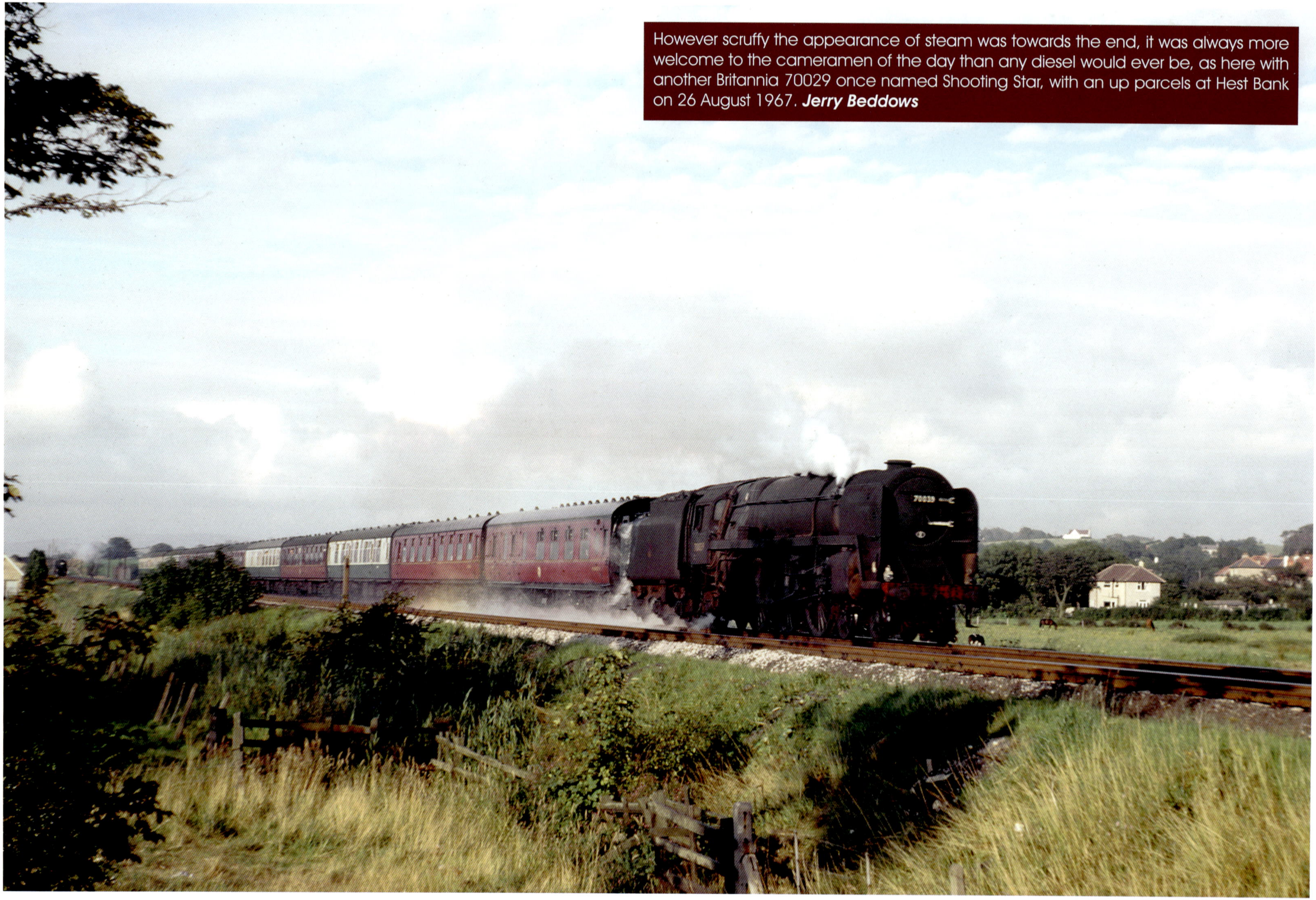

However scruffy the appearance of steam was towards the end, it was always more welcome to the cameramen of the day than any diesel would ever be, as here with another Britannia 70029 once named Shooting Star, with an up parcels at Hest Bank on 26 August 1967. ***Jerry Beddows***

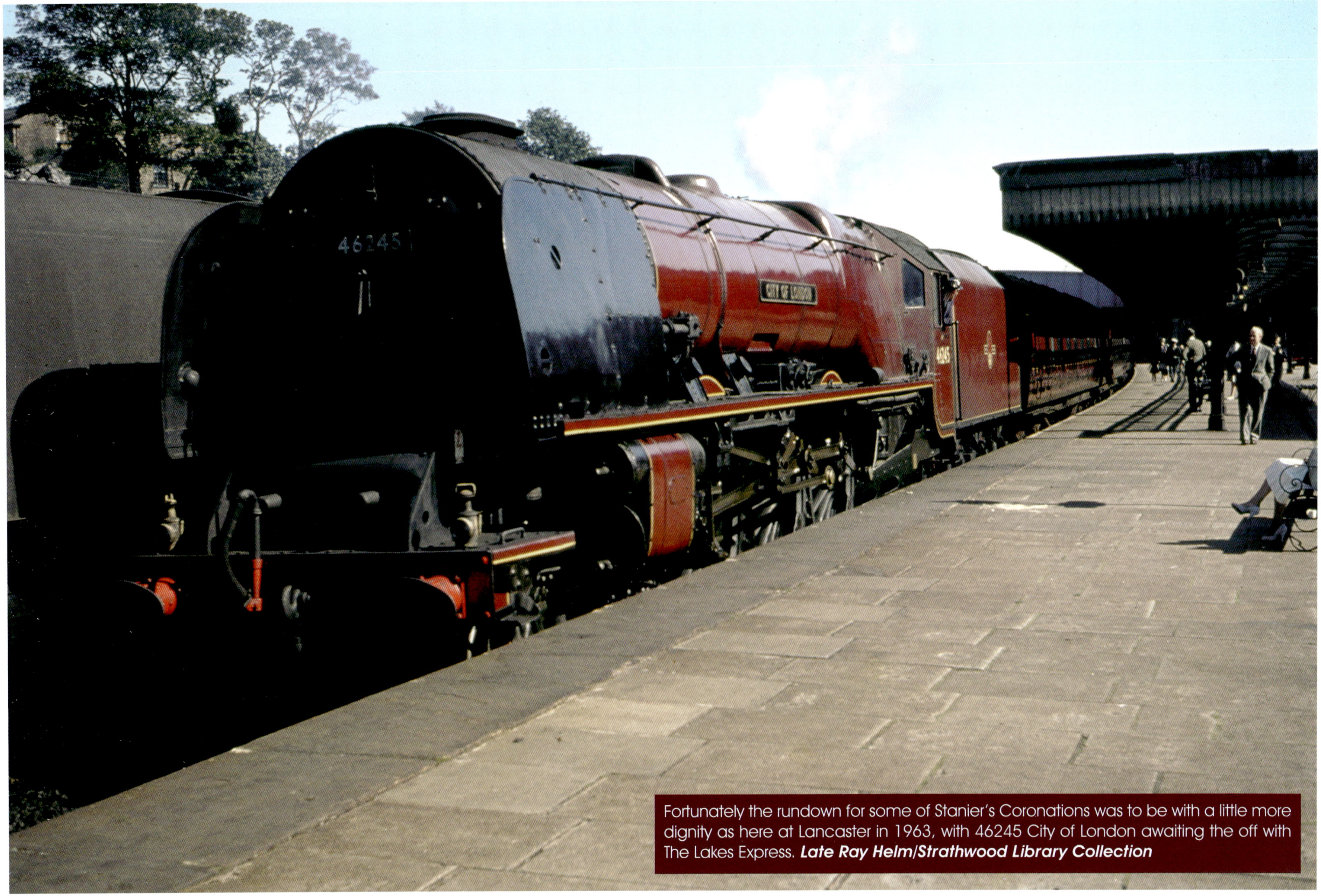

Fortunately the rundown for some of Stanier's Coronations was to be with a little more dignity as here at Lancaster in 1963, with 46245 City of London awaiting the off with The Lakes Express. ***Late Ray Helm/Strathwood Library Collection***

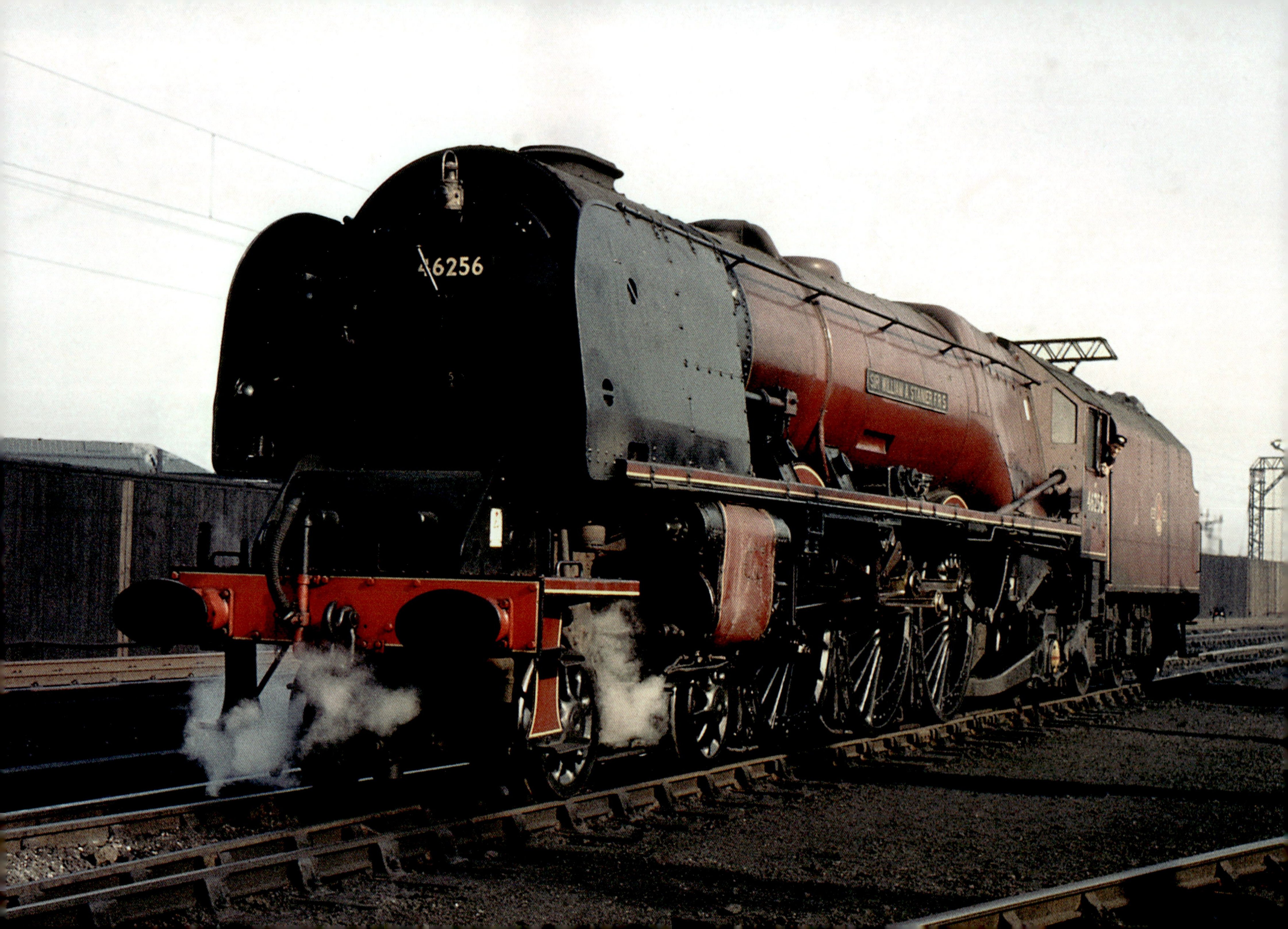
46256

Under the Wires

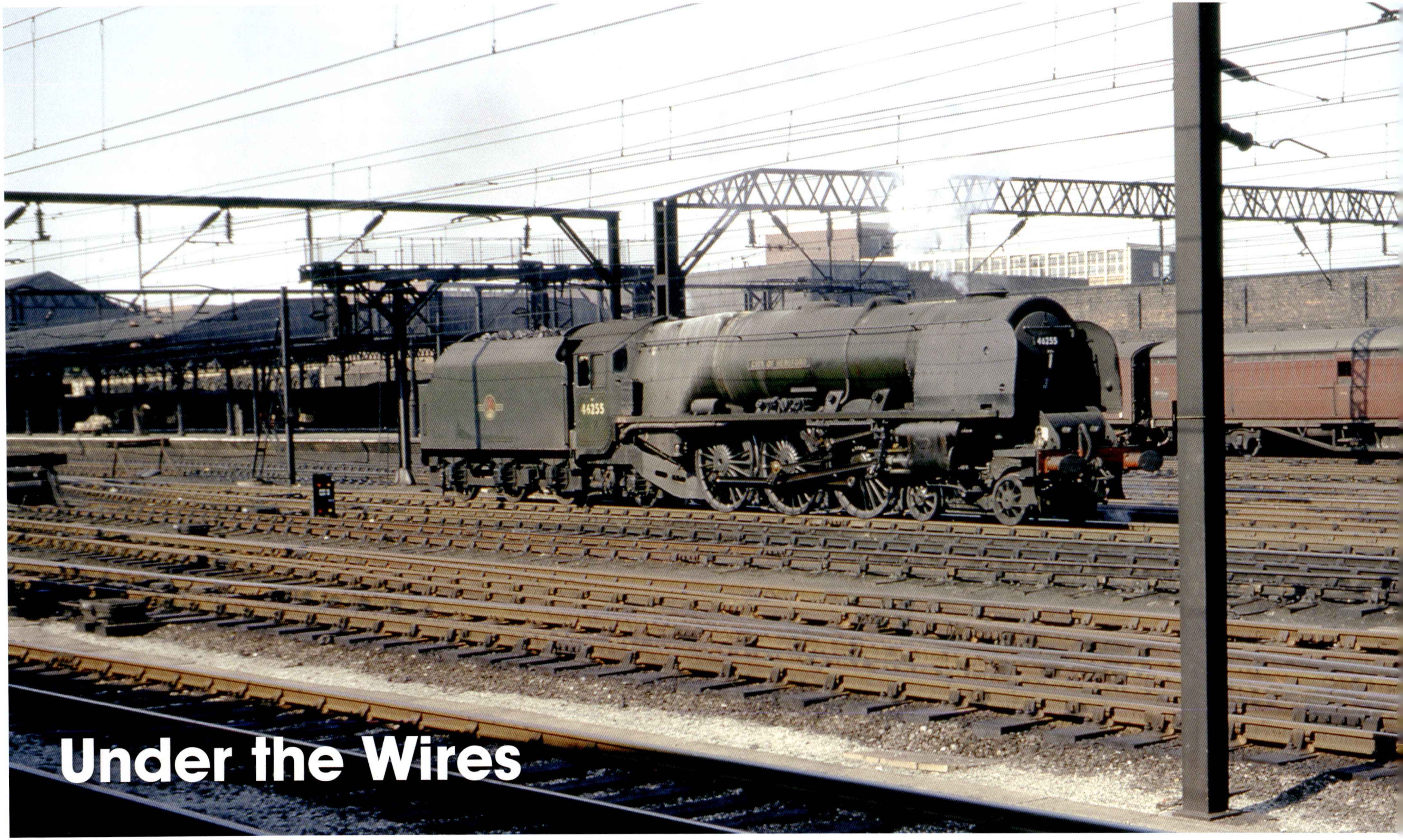

Page left: The wiring that will spell their ultimate demise along with the deliveries of replacement English Electric Type 4s has already begun to encroach upon Crewe North in 1961, but 46256 Sir William Stanier F.R.S. still affords a fine spectacle. ***Rail Online***

Similarly the cats cradle of wiring and masts around Crewe's station throat begin to pose a threat to 46255 City of Hereford on 29 July 1963, already the first few have been withdrawn from service. ***Strathwood Library Collection***

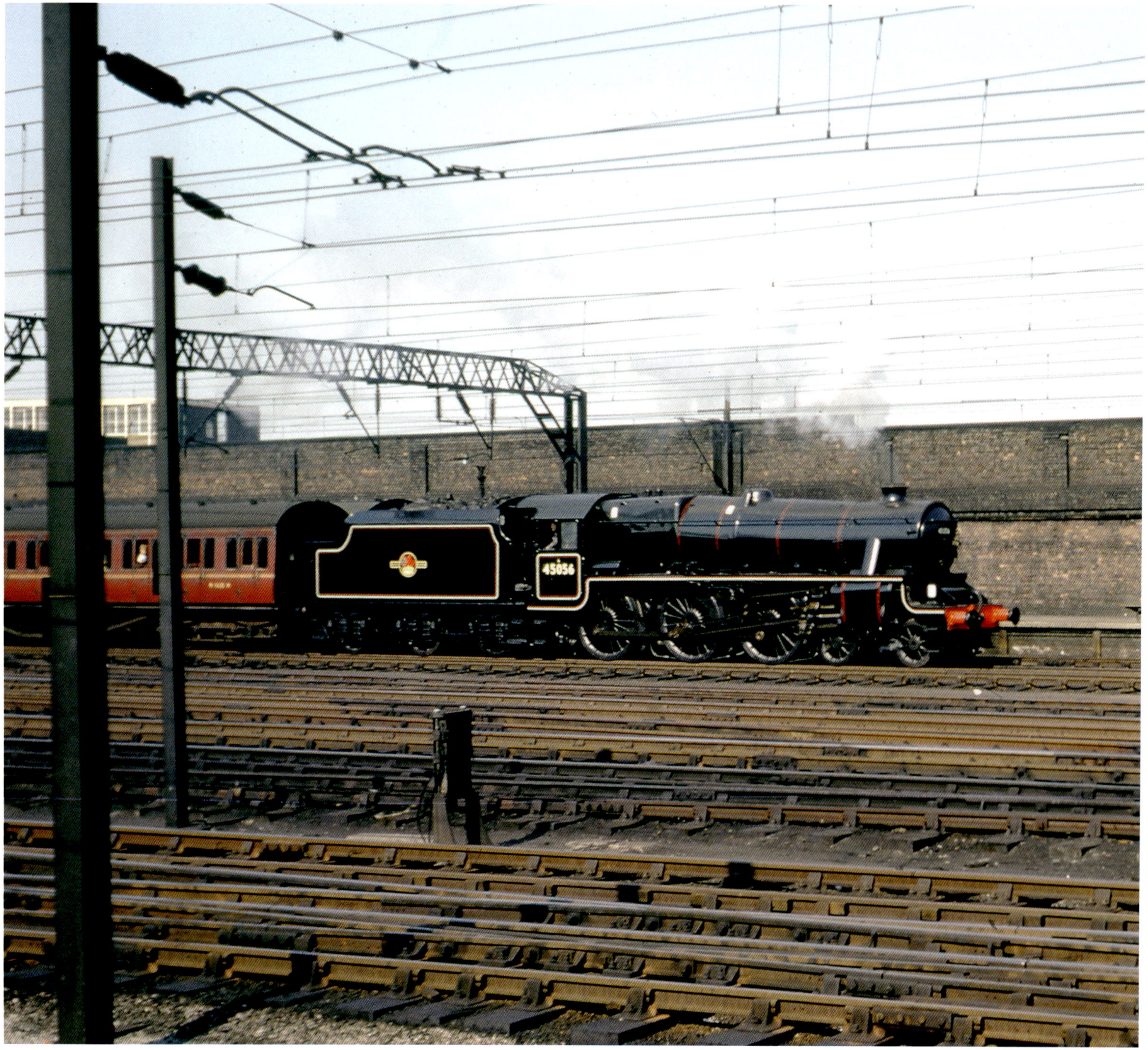

Taken the same day at Crewe was this view of an ex-works 45056, just turned out in first class order, she is put to work on a running in turn which looks like a local stopping service heading southwards to Stafford and Rugby. ***Strathwood Library Collection***

Opposite: In contrast the appearance of Class G2A, 49361 at Rugeley Trent Valley with a special on 22 June 1963 is somehow a sad comparison. In fairness, this normally freight only locomotive kept good time during the day really as the early evening shadows were starting to lengthen, as the Stephenson Locomotive Society tour of Birmingham and South Staffordshire was coming to a conclusion. ***Edward Dorricott***

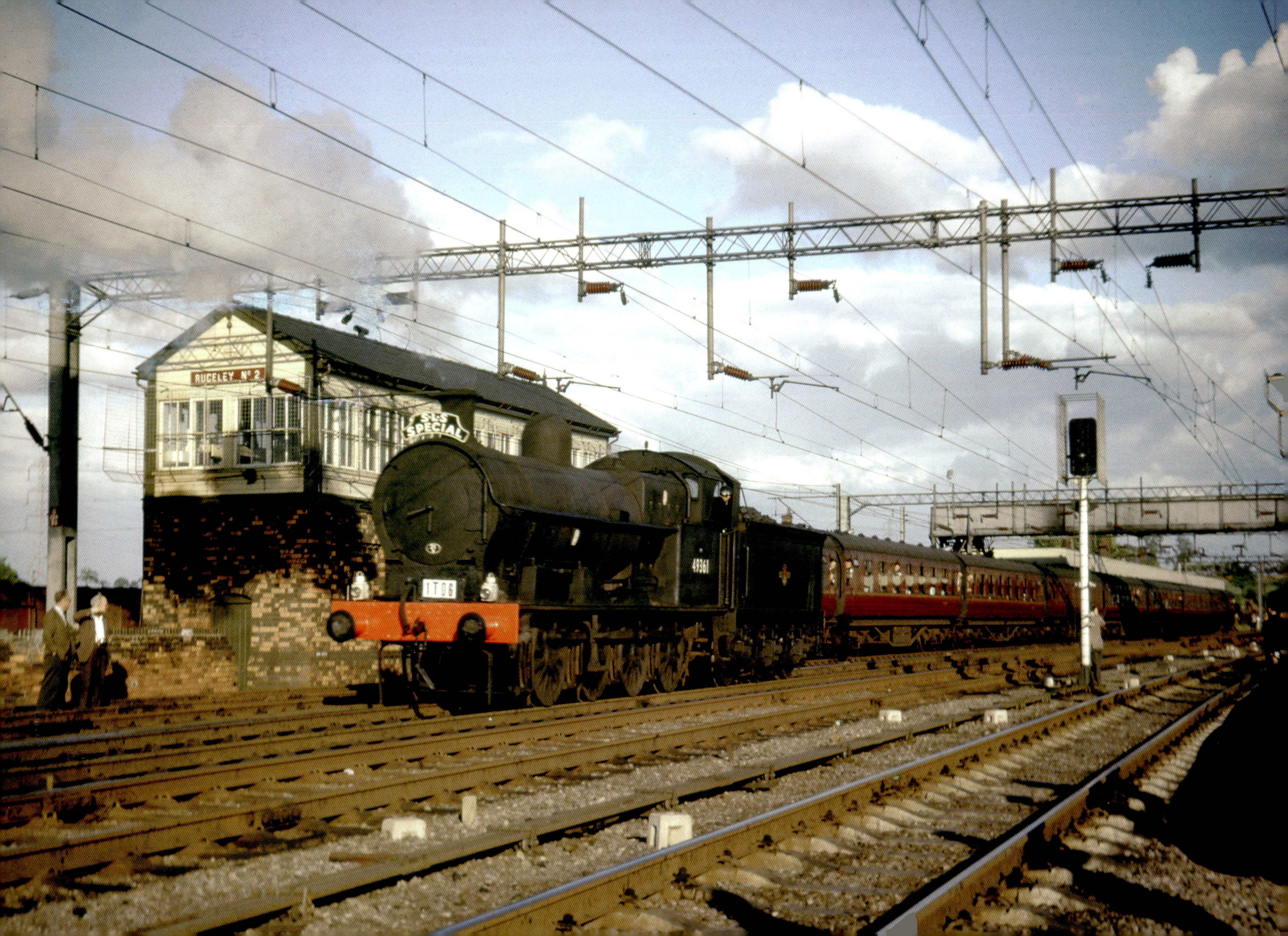

RUGELEY Nº 2
S·L·S SPECIAL
1T06
49361

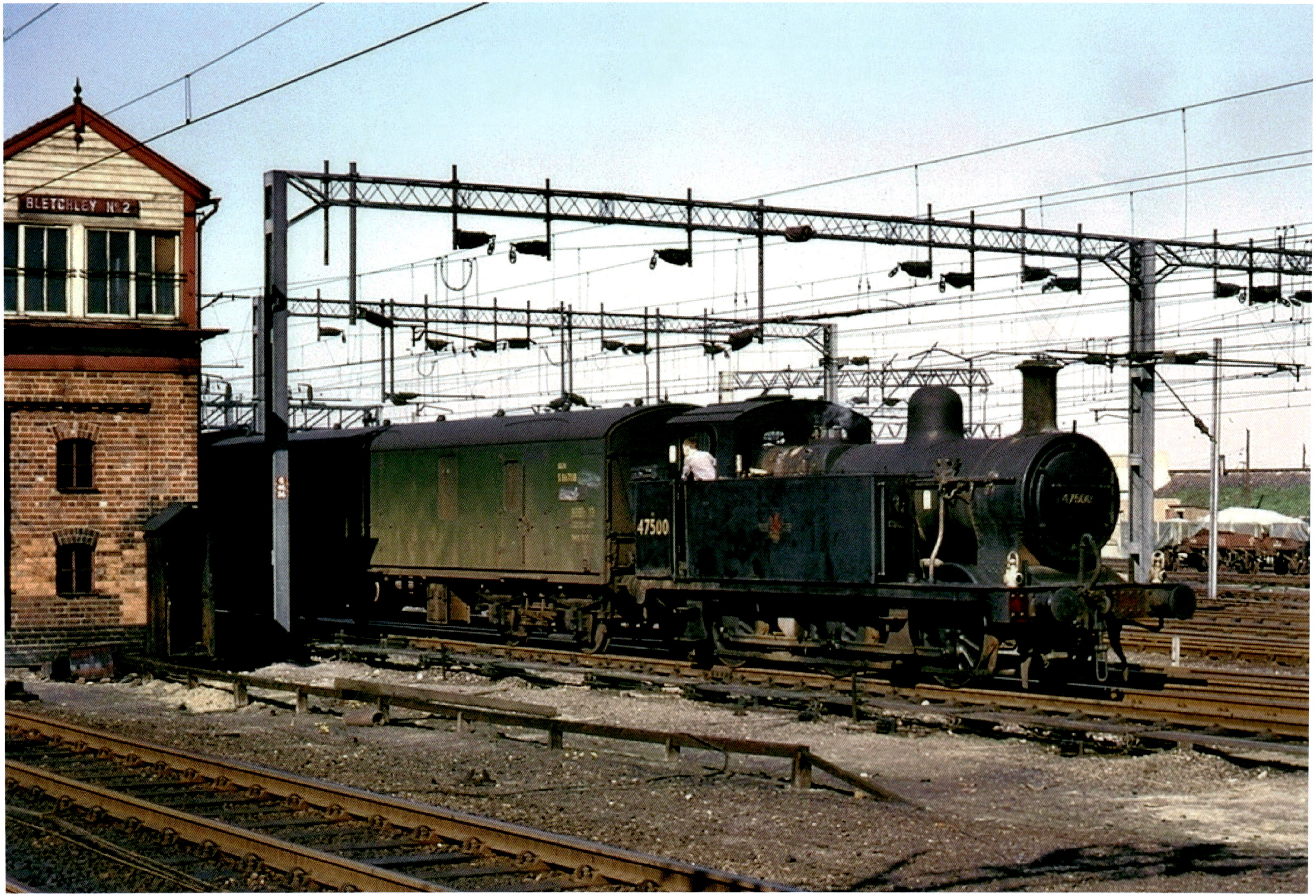
BLETCHLEY No 2
47500
47500

Page left: Some recent attempts to clean Class 3F, 47500 stil acting as the station pilot can be seen at Bletchely on 29 March 1965. Sadly this was a sight soon to end, for this Vulcan Foundry product from April 1928 was to be withdrawn in July just a few months after this view. ***Bill Wright***

Electric services were now commonplace at Stockport on 20 April 1968, whilst steam was declining fast in the North West. This is the pairing of Black Fives 45110 and 44949 which have just taken over from Class AL6, E3180 on today's Manchester Rail Travel Society's joint excursion with the Severn Valley Railway Society which will now head to Stalybridge as seen on page 49. ***Strathwood Library Collection***

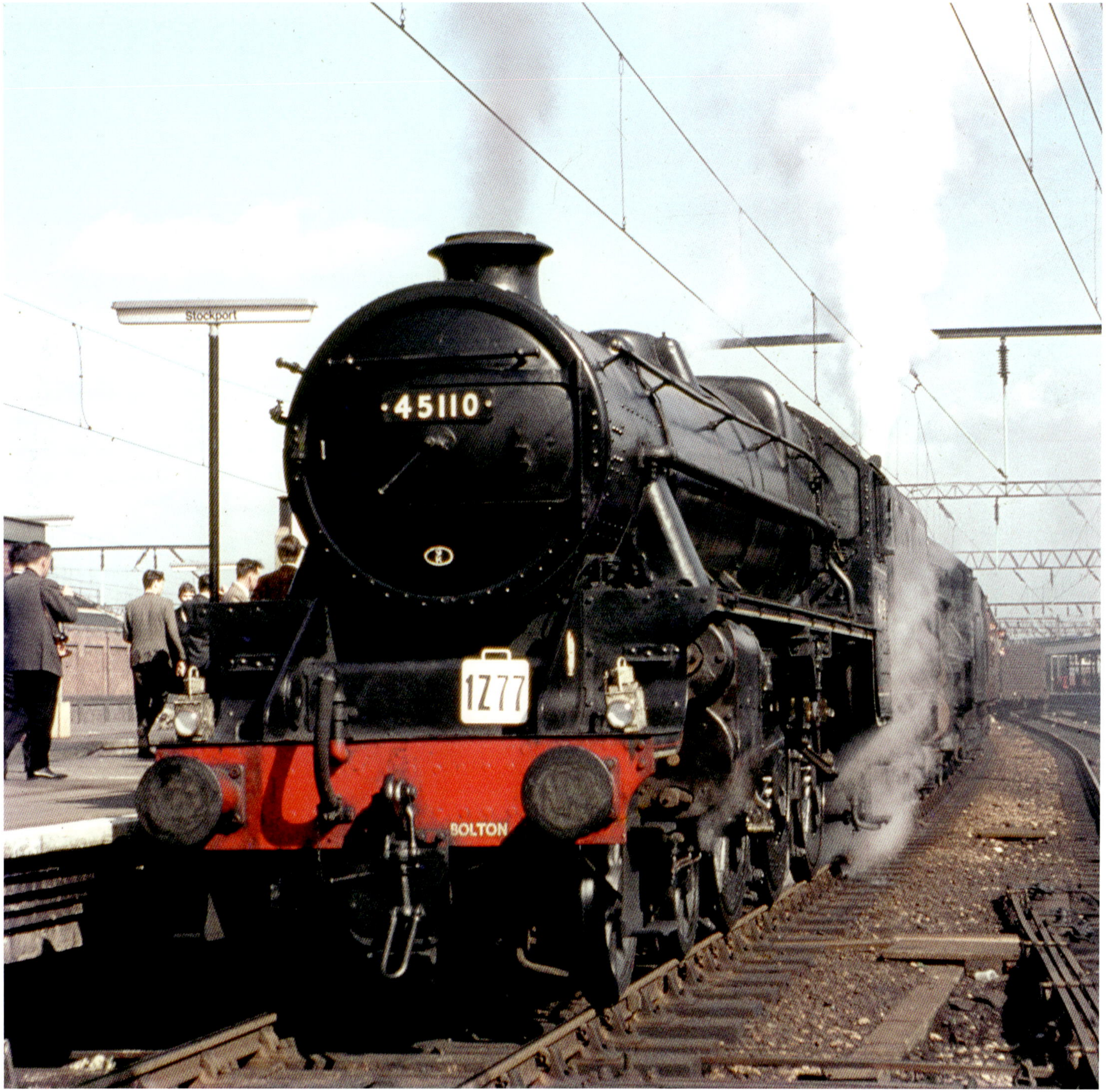

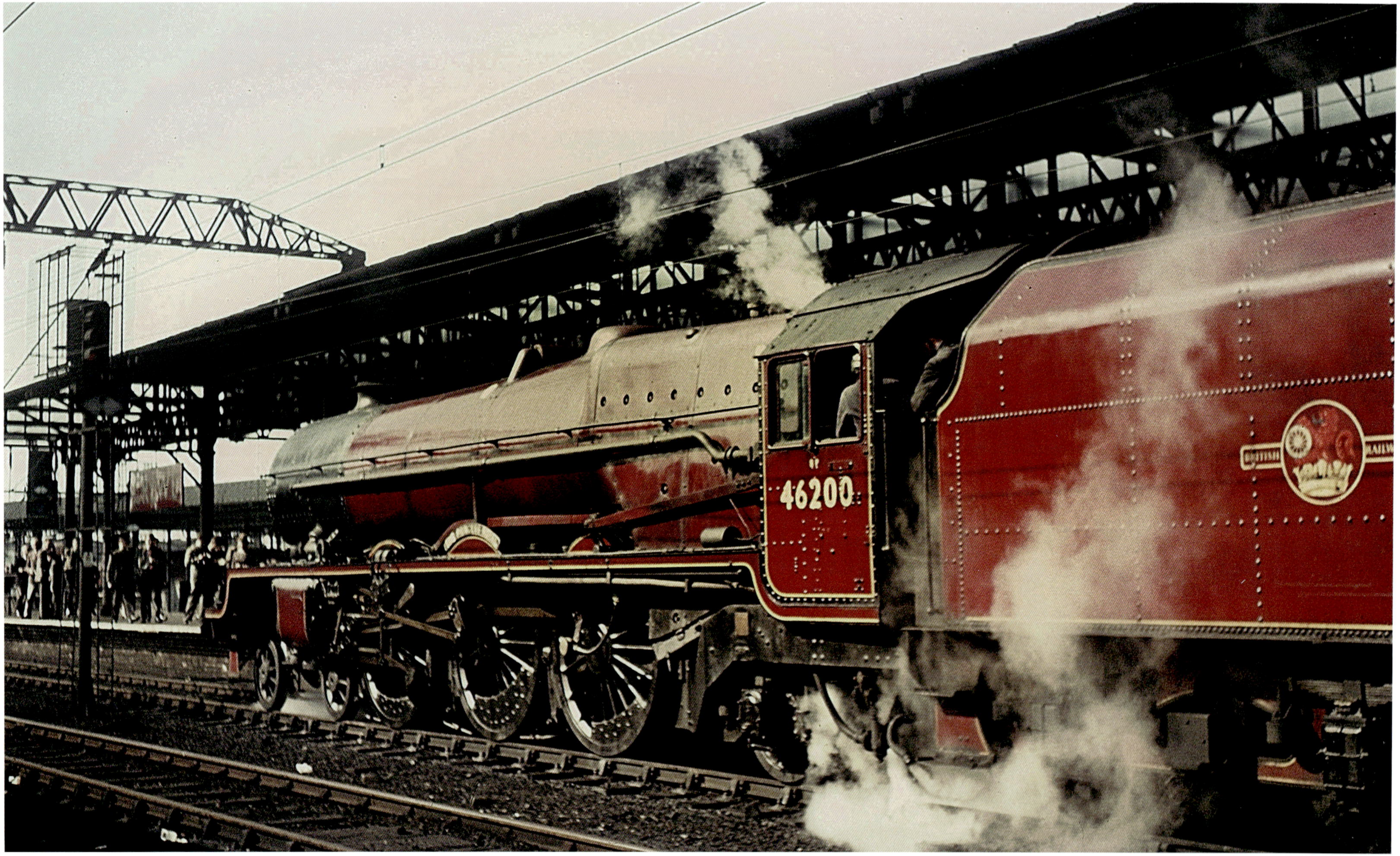

We are into the second day of The Aberdeen Flyer Tour at Crewe on 3 June 1962, and 46200 The Princess Royal still looks great even though we are running a couple of hours down after 46201 Princess Elizabeth had brought the tour south from Aberdeen overnight. ***Colour Rail***

Opposite: Well turned out again at Crewe the year beforehand was ex-works Royal Scot, 46118 Royal Welch Fusilier with an up departure. The Royal Welch Fusiliers were an infantry regiment, founded in 1689 to oppose James II and the imminent war with France. ***Late Alan H. Bryant ARPS/Rail Photoprints***

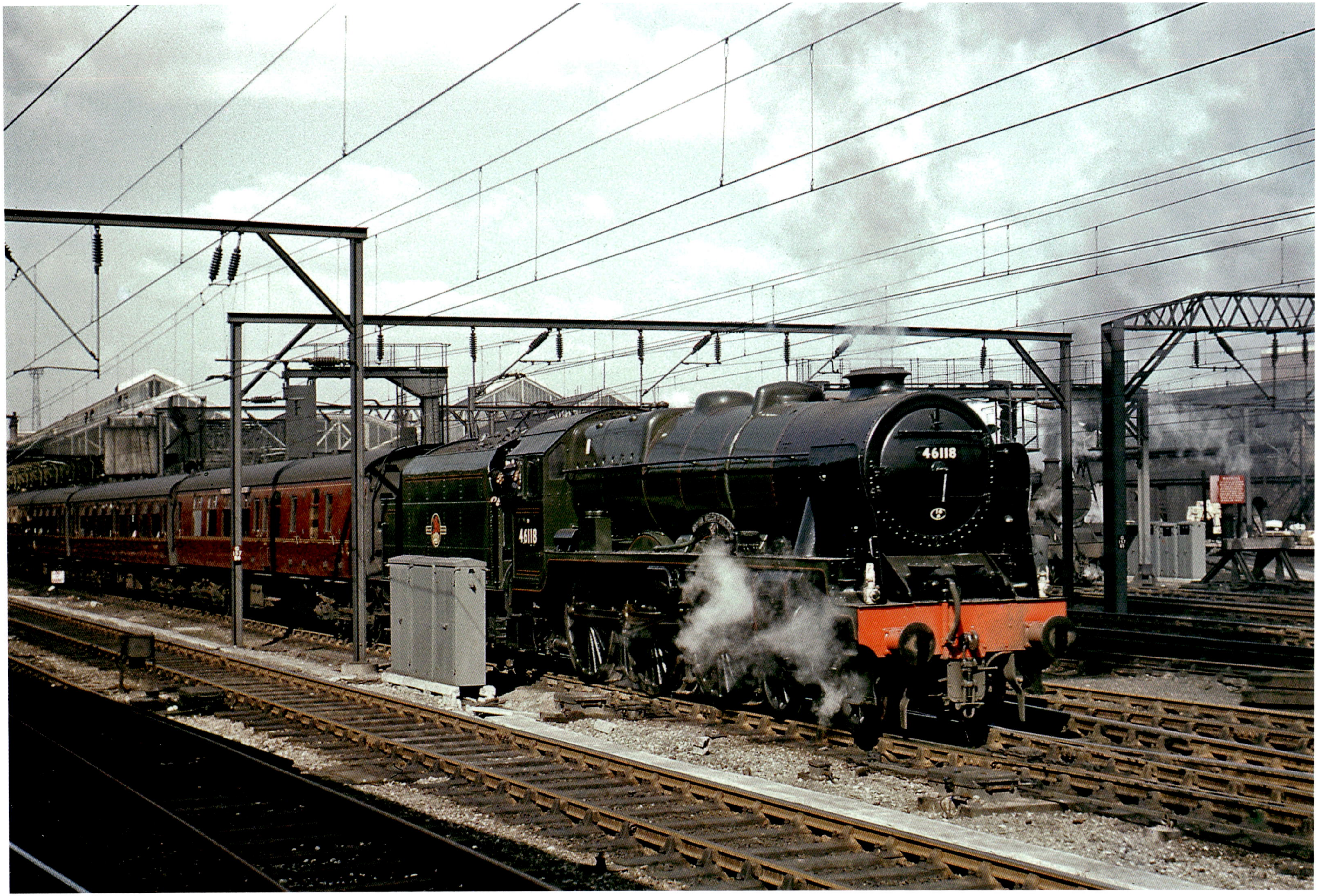
46118
46118

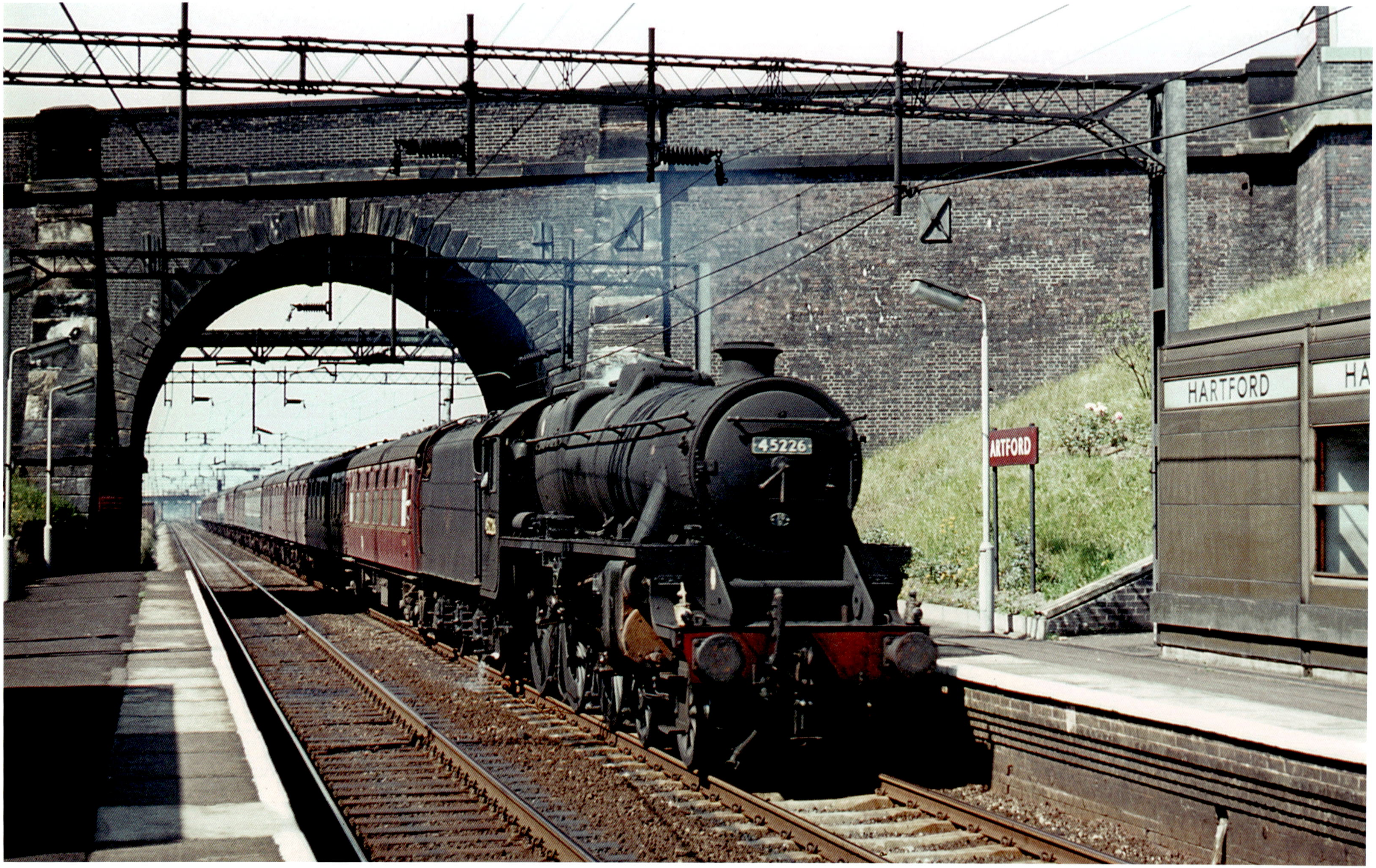

Lostock Hall's Black Five, 45226 heads south through the modernised station at Hartford with an up passenger service on 20 August 1966. ***Late Colin Whitfield/Rail Photoprints***

Opposite: Running light engine from Crewe North to pick up a northbound express in 1961 was 46206 Princess Marie Louise, the following year she would be no more. ***Colour Rail***

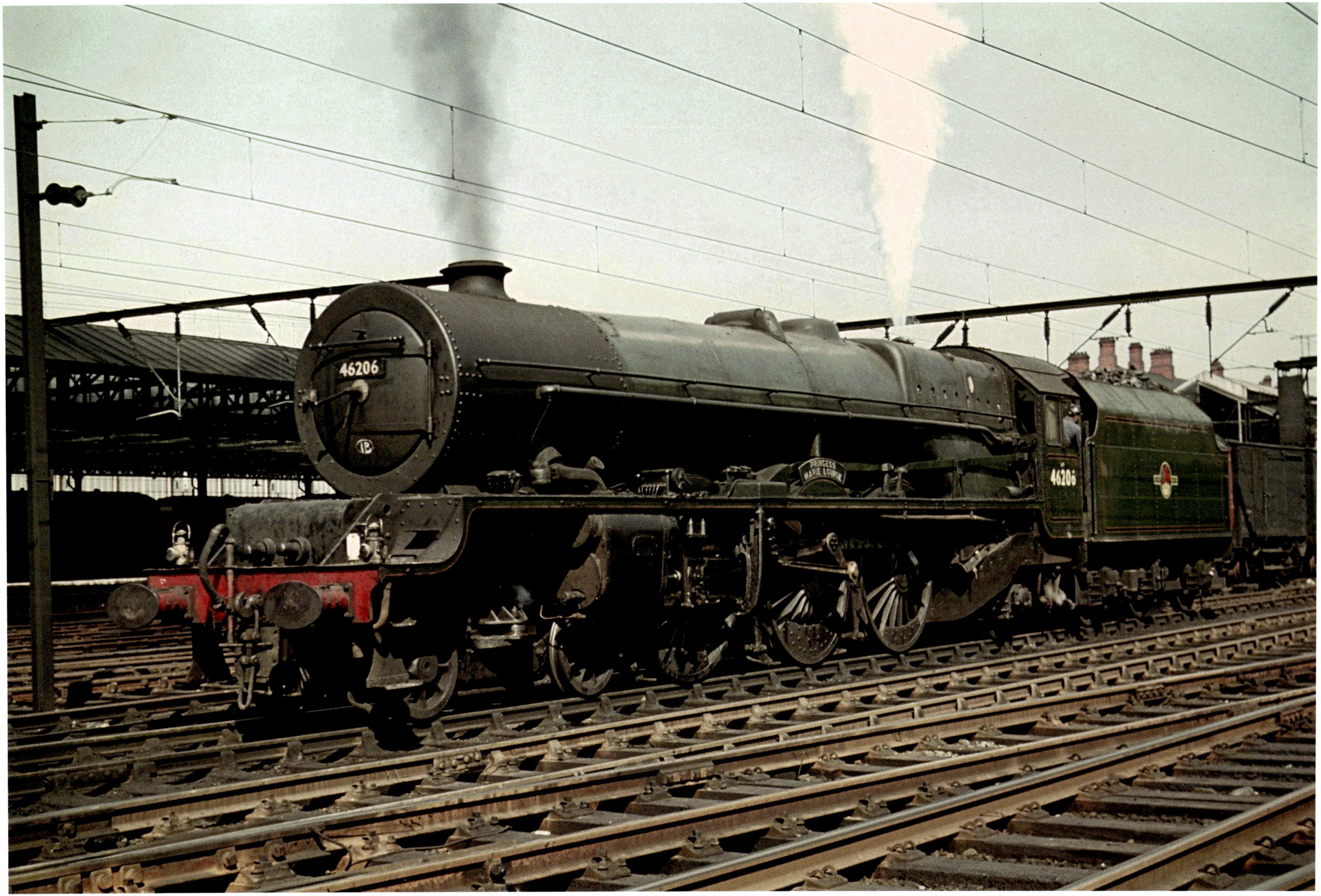
46206
46206

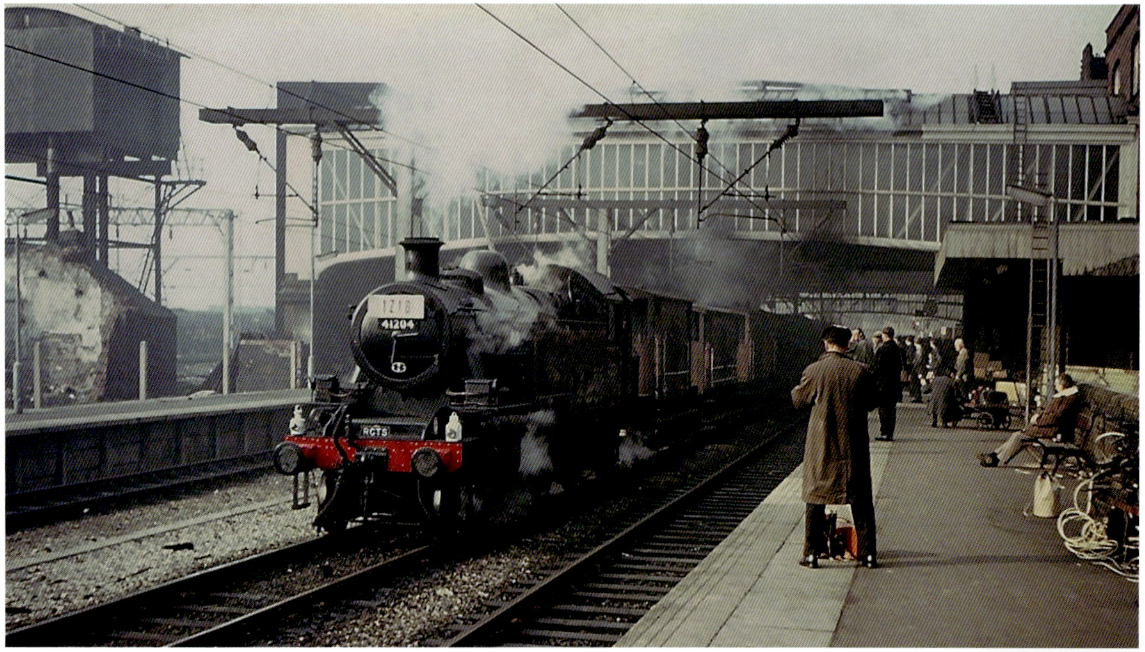

Brake vans and brake van specials are very much a thing of the past now, but they were a good way to run smaller tours back in the steam era. On 29 October 1966, the RCTS ran just such a trip around the Stoke-on-Trent area behind Class 2MT, 41204 seen here heading away from the city. ***George Woods***

Another tour we have already seen on page 47 was the LCGB's Lancastrian caught on camera once again here at Liverpool Lime Street behind Black Five, 45305 awaiting departure at 11.45 on 6 April 1968. ***George Woods***

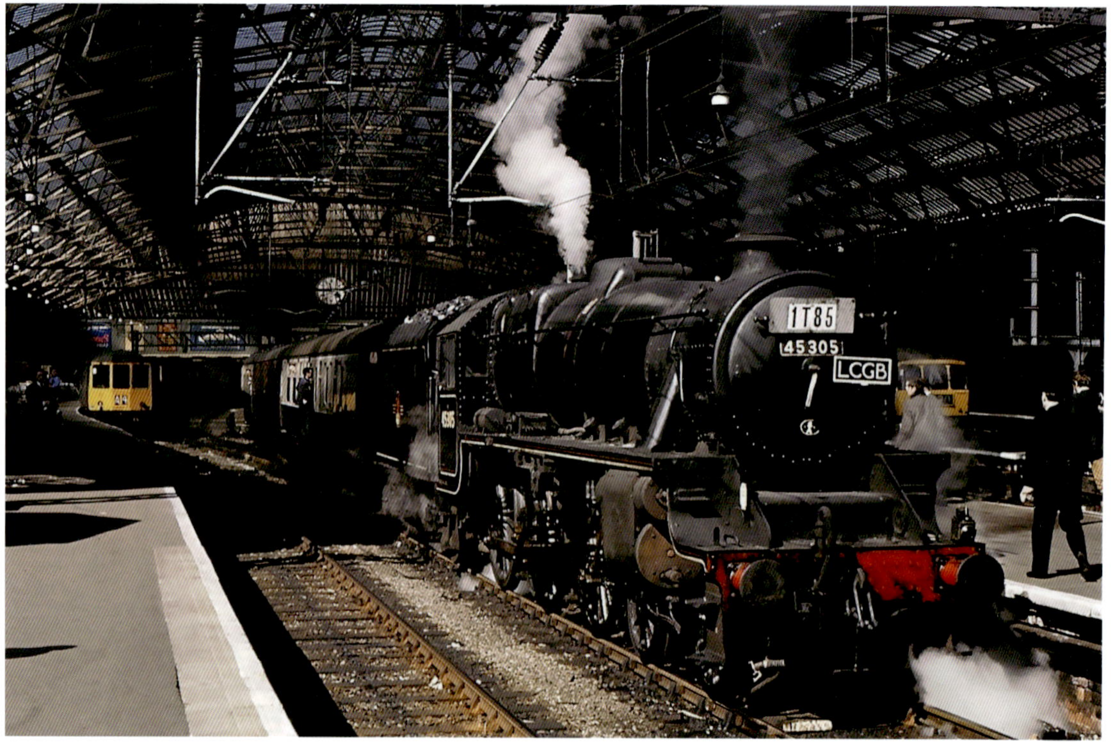

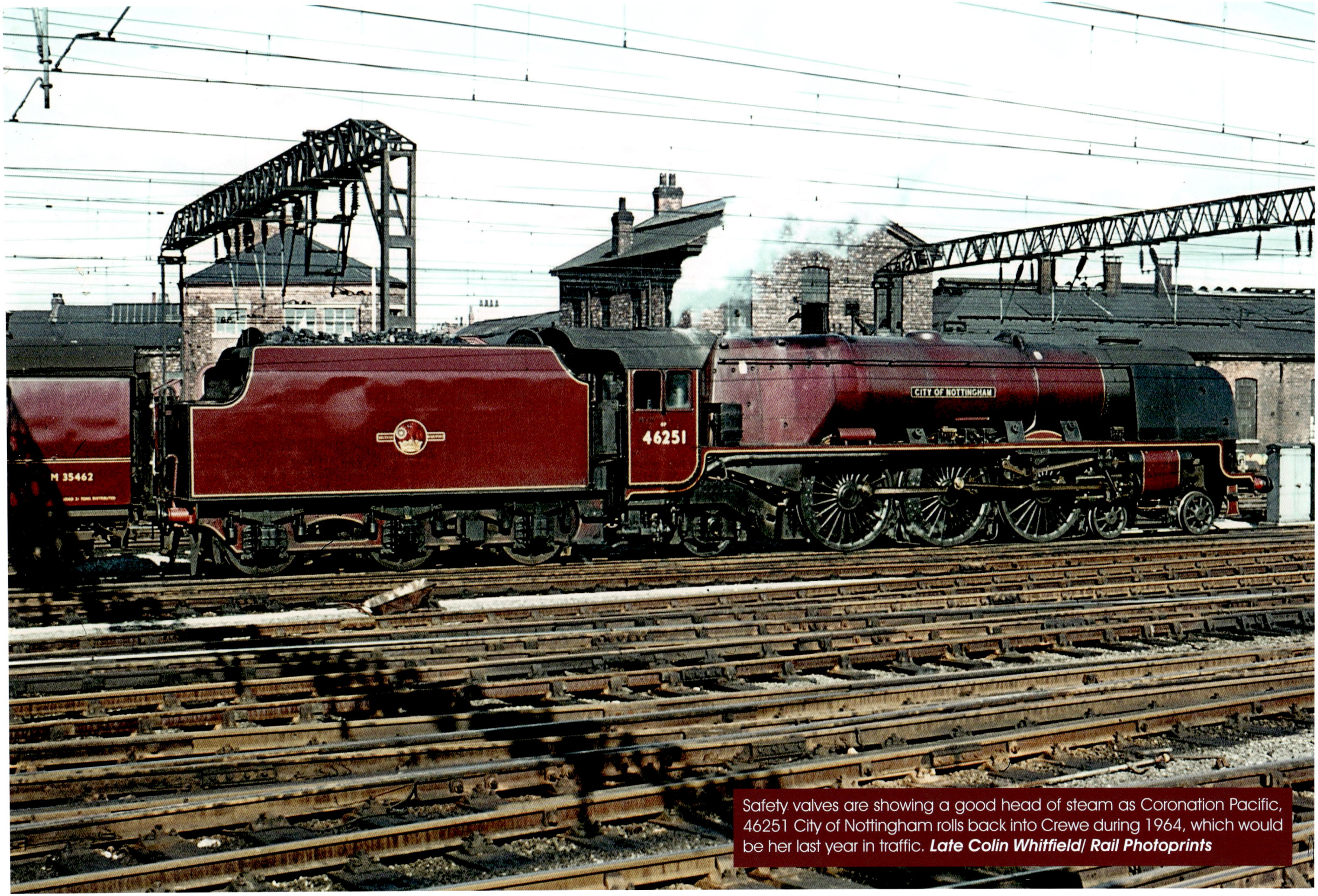

Safety valves are showing a good head of steam as Coronation Pacific, 46251 City of Nottingham rolls back into Crewe during 1964, which would be her last year in traffic. ***Late Colin Whitfield/ Rail Photoprints***

Class 2 Focus

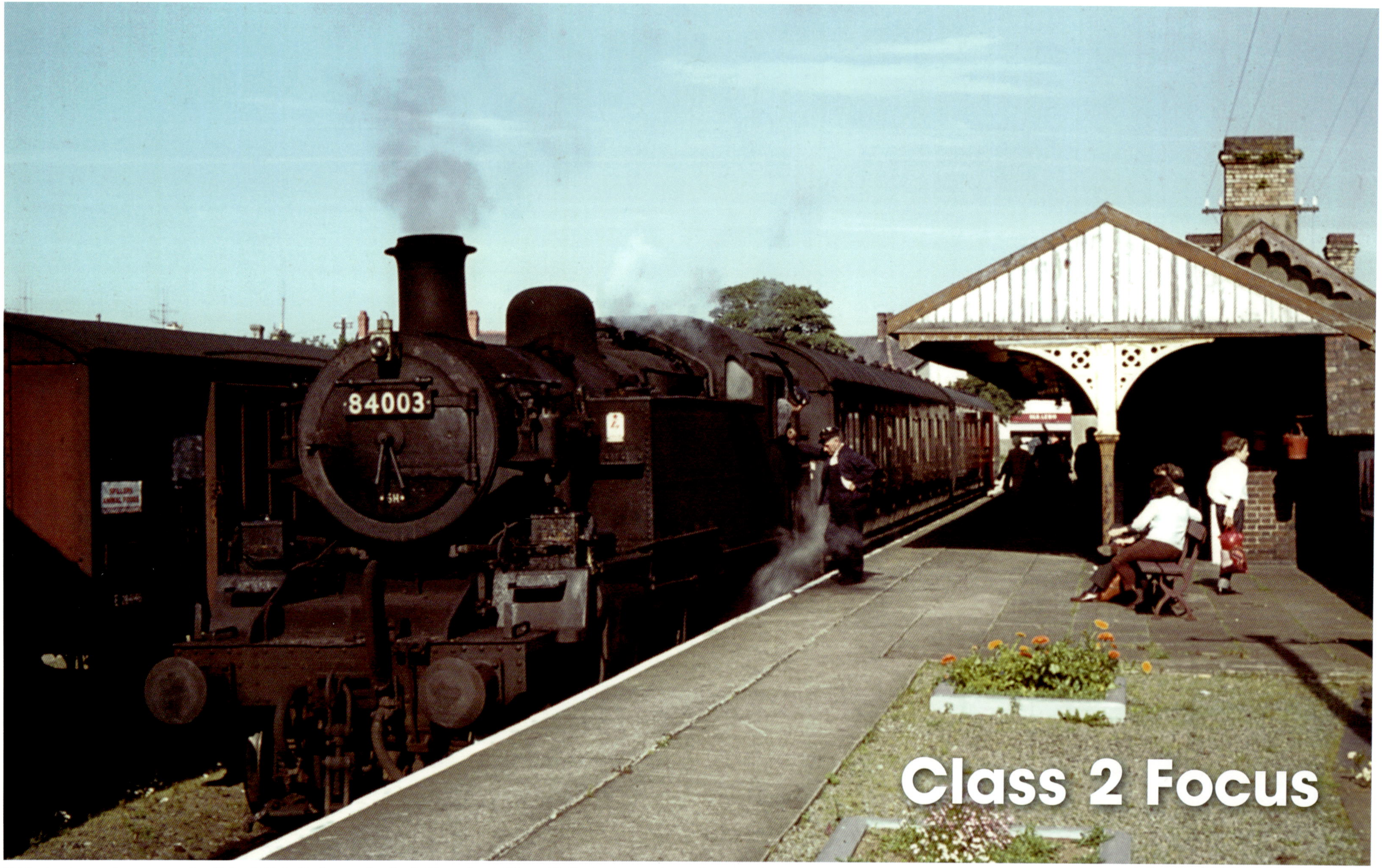

Thirty tank engines were built by British Railways to their Standard Class 2MT design, with 84003 seen at the sleepy terminus at Amlwch on 11 August 1964, being one from the first batch of twenty built at Crewe Works during 1953. ***Douglas Twibble***

Opposite: Thankfully this scene at Crewe South on 27 March 1967, is not as grim as it could have been as this now rusty and withdrawn Swindon built Ivatt Class 2MT, 46512 would be saved for preservation. ***Gerald T. Robinson***

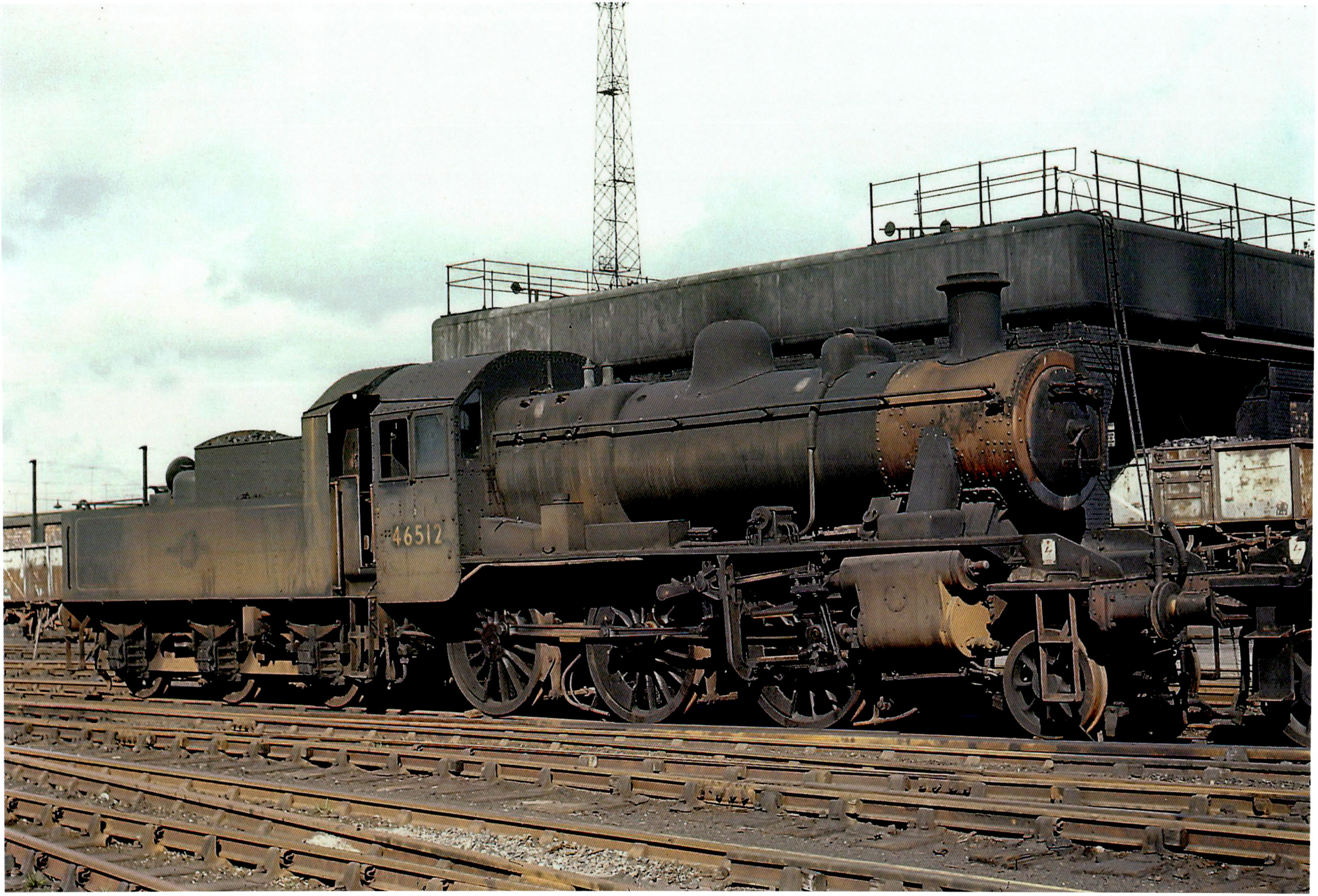
46512

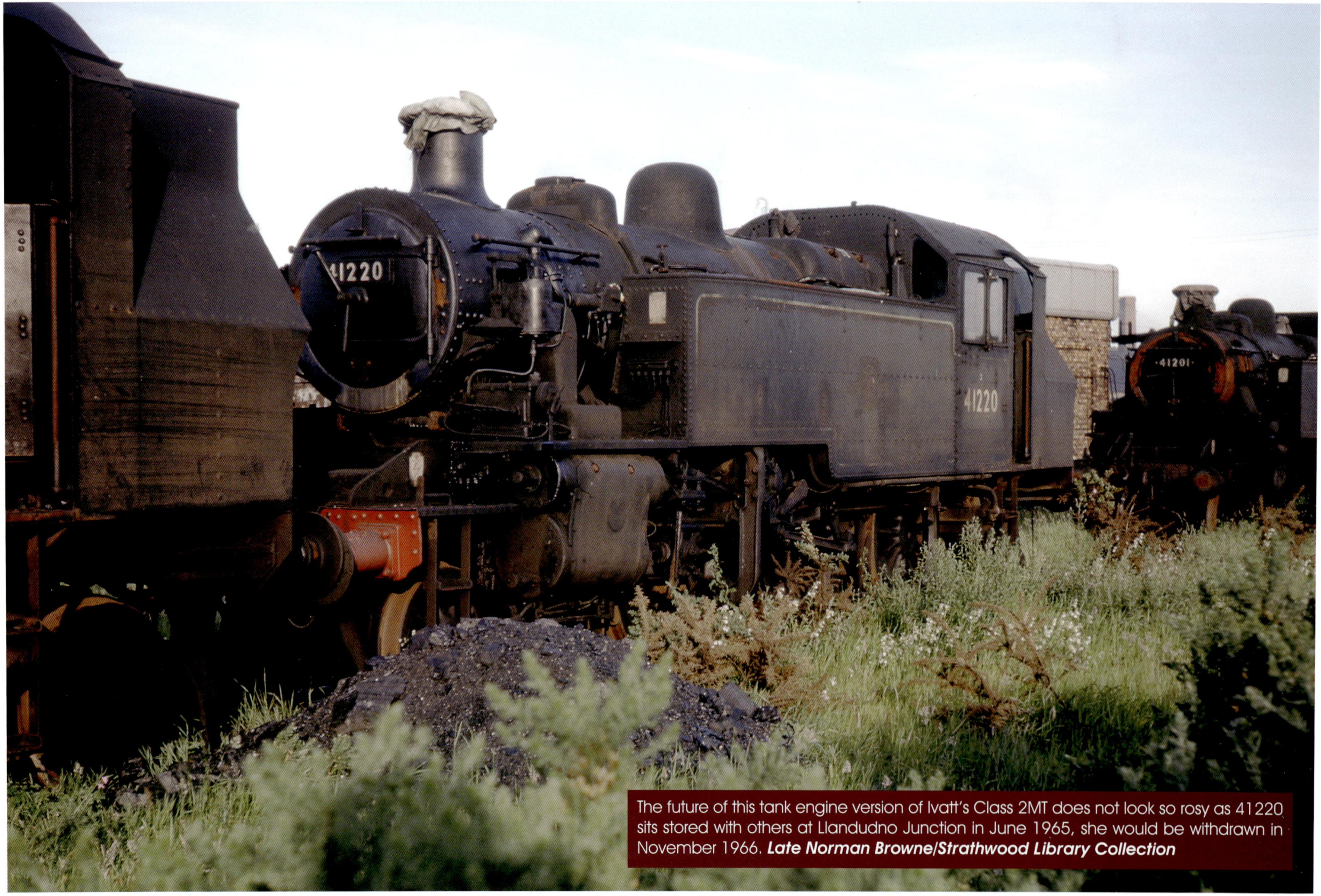

The future of this tank engine version of Ivatt's Class 2MT does not look so rosy as 41220 sits stored with others at Llandudno Junction in June 1965, she would be withdrawn in November 1966. ***Late Norman Browne/Strathwood Library Collection***

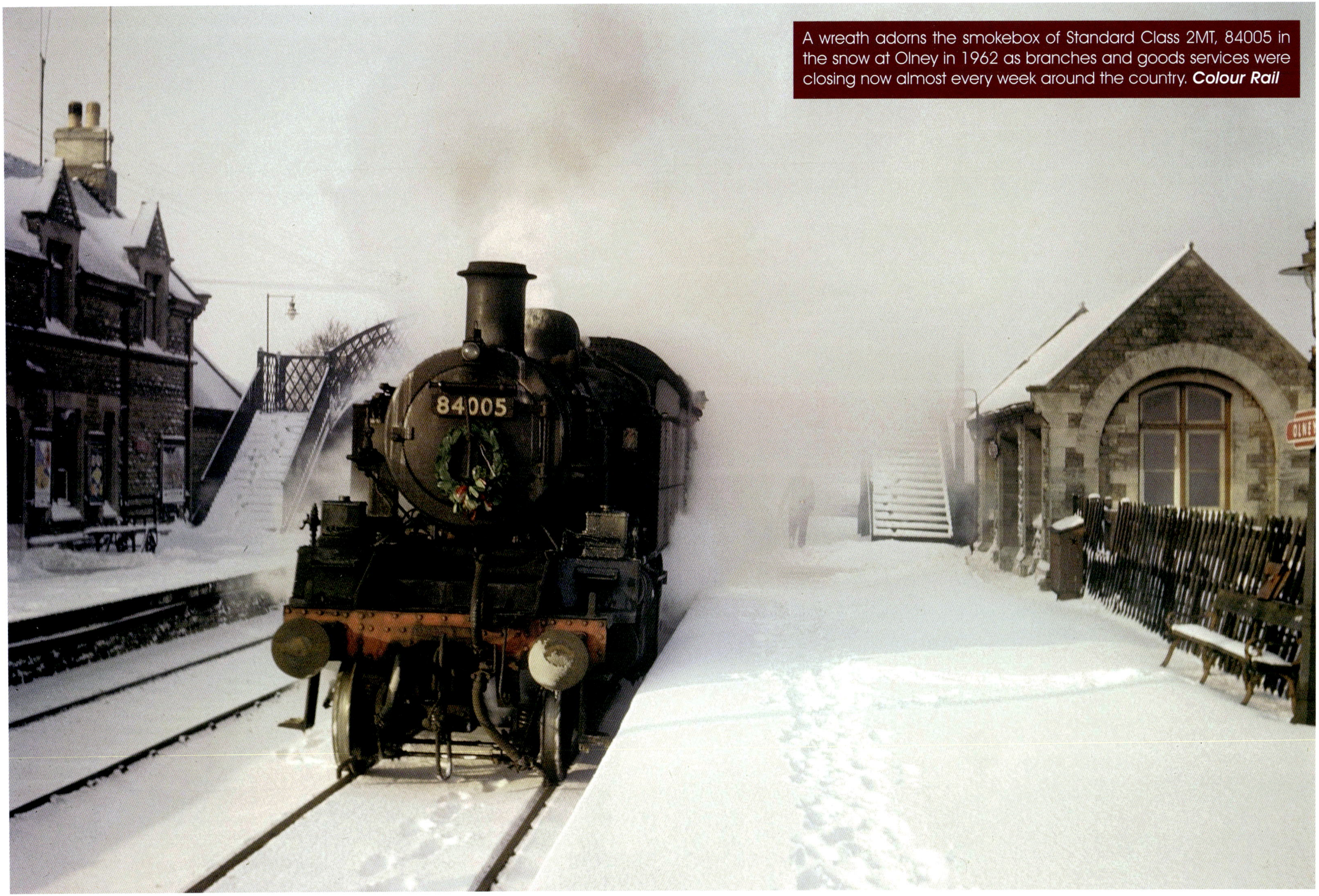

A wreath adorns the smokebox of Standard Class 2MT, 84005 in the snow at Olney in 1962 as branches and goods services were closing now almost every week around the country. ***Colour Rail***

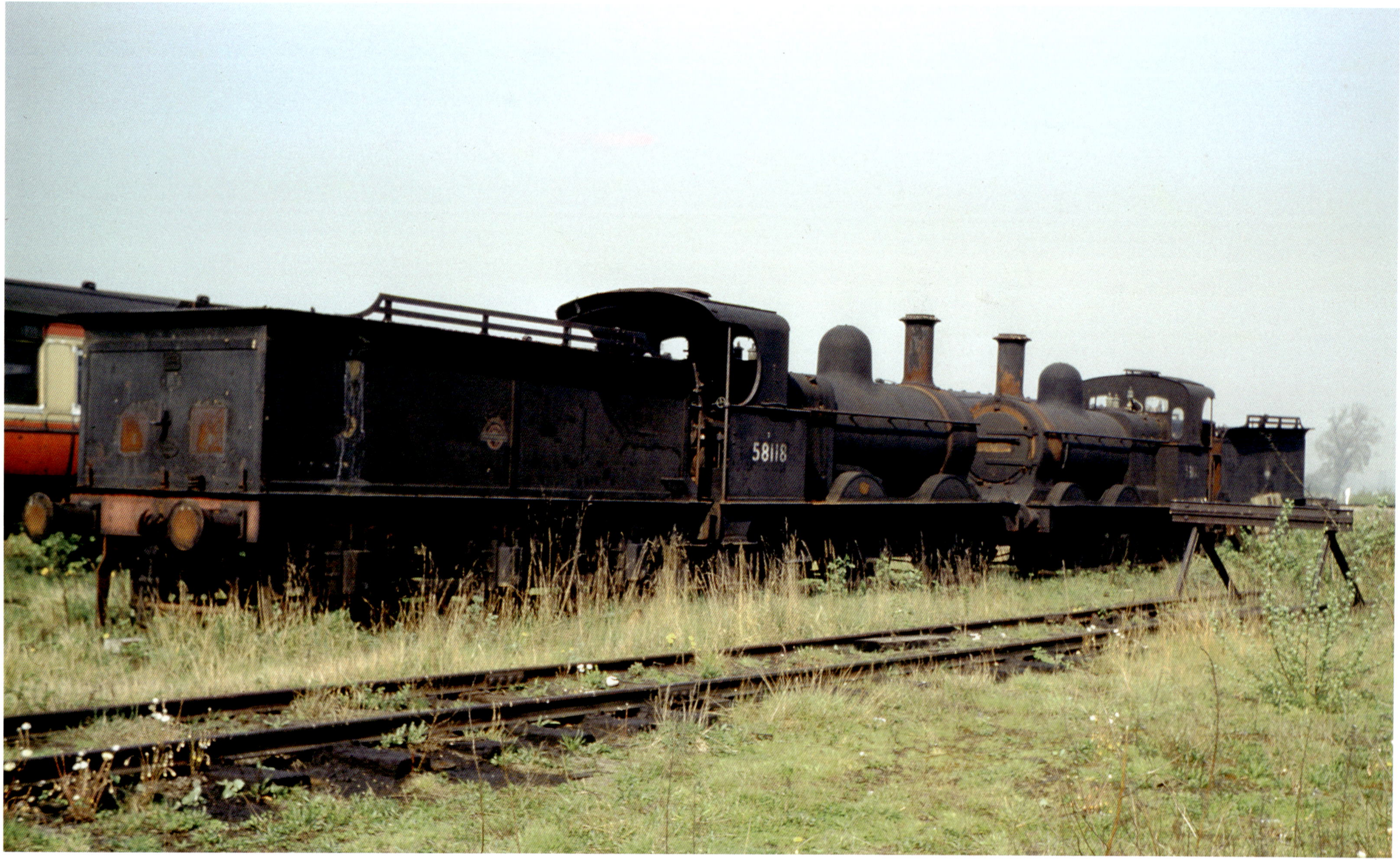

This pairing of former Midland Railway, Class 2Fs, 58118 and 58135 which date from 1875, will have seen much service before their withdrawl and removal to the dump here at Chaddesdon in 1959 for scrapping at nearby Derby Works. ***John Gill***

Opposite: Ninety six of these Johnson designs passed into British Railways service in 1948, with this example 58148 being the last one in traffic when withdrawn in December 1963, and all seemed well at Desford on 22 November just beforehand. ***Tony Butcher***

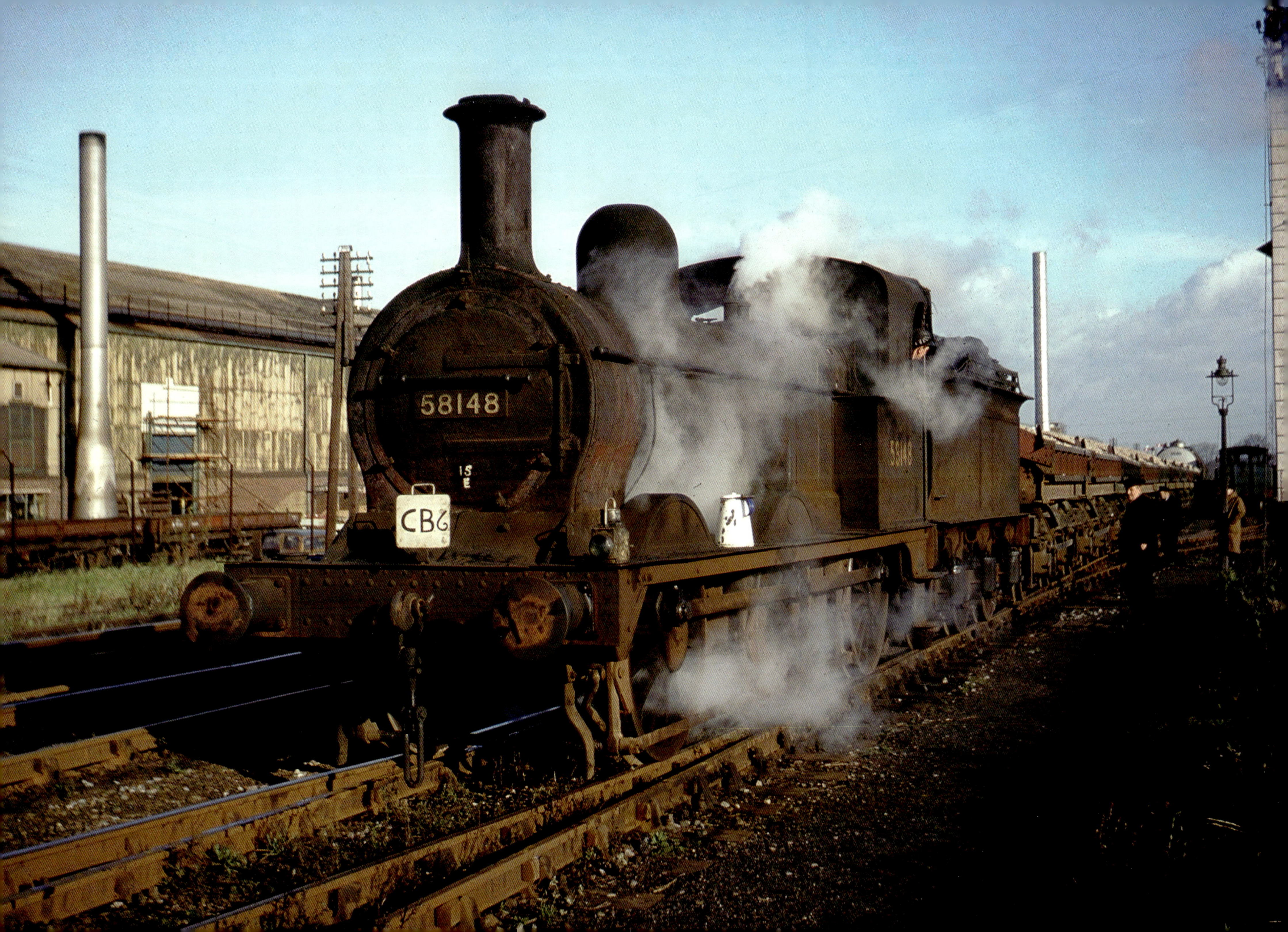
58148
CB6

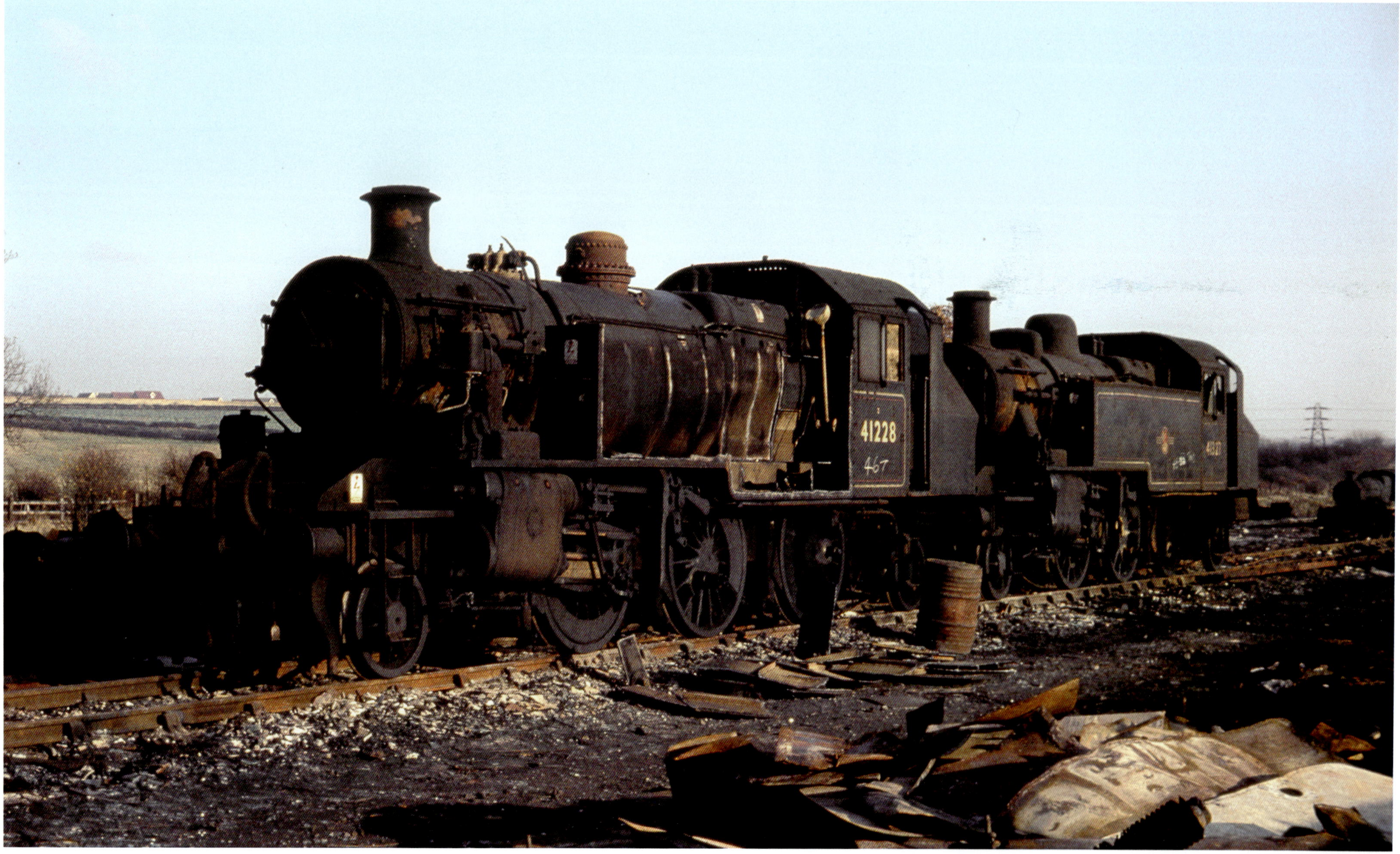

The cutters will resume work again soon on Ivatt Class 2MTs, 41228 and its sister 41327 in 1964 at Cohen's yard at Cransley. The former being from the one hundred and twenty built at Crewe Works and 41327 from the ten built at built at Derby Works. ***Strathwood Library Collection***

Opposite: Shortly before the Chesham shuttles' association with steam was to end we see another motor fitted Ivatt Class 2MT, 41284 at the terminus on 28 August 1961, these had taken over from Robinson Class 2Ps just a couple of years beforehand. ***Douglas Twibble***

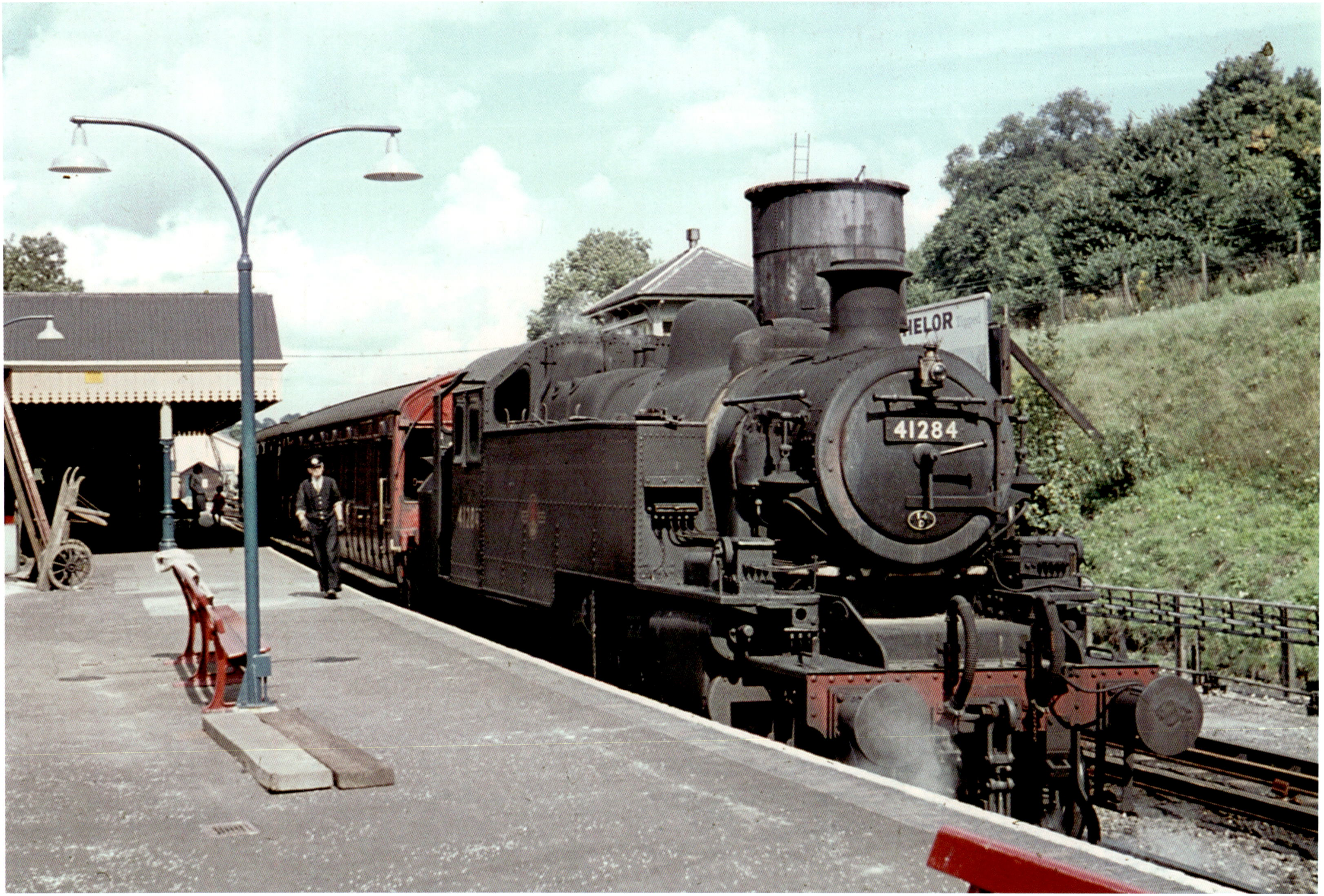
41284

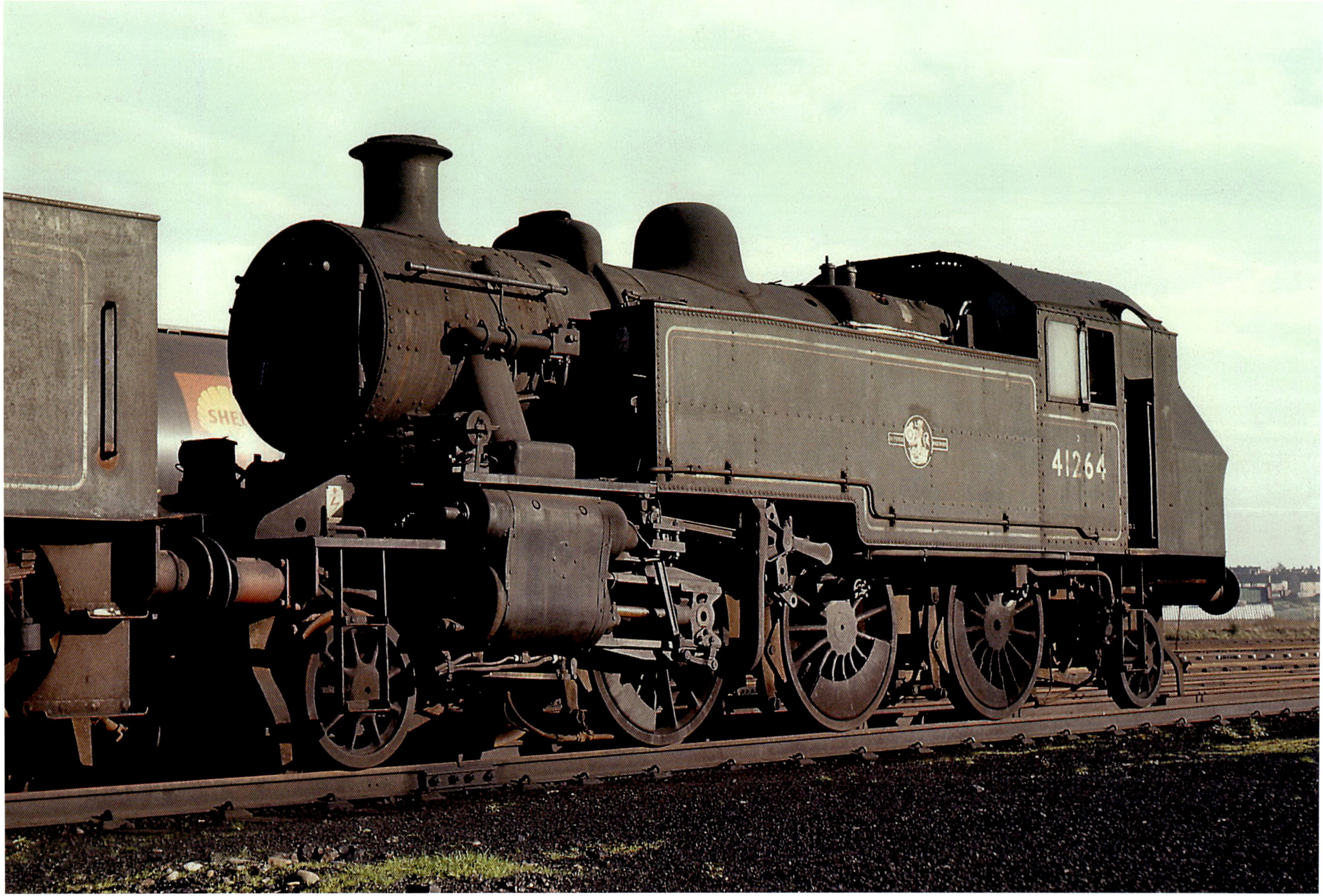
41264

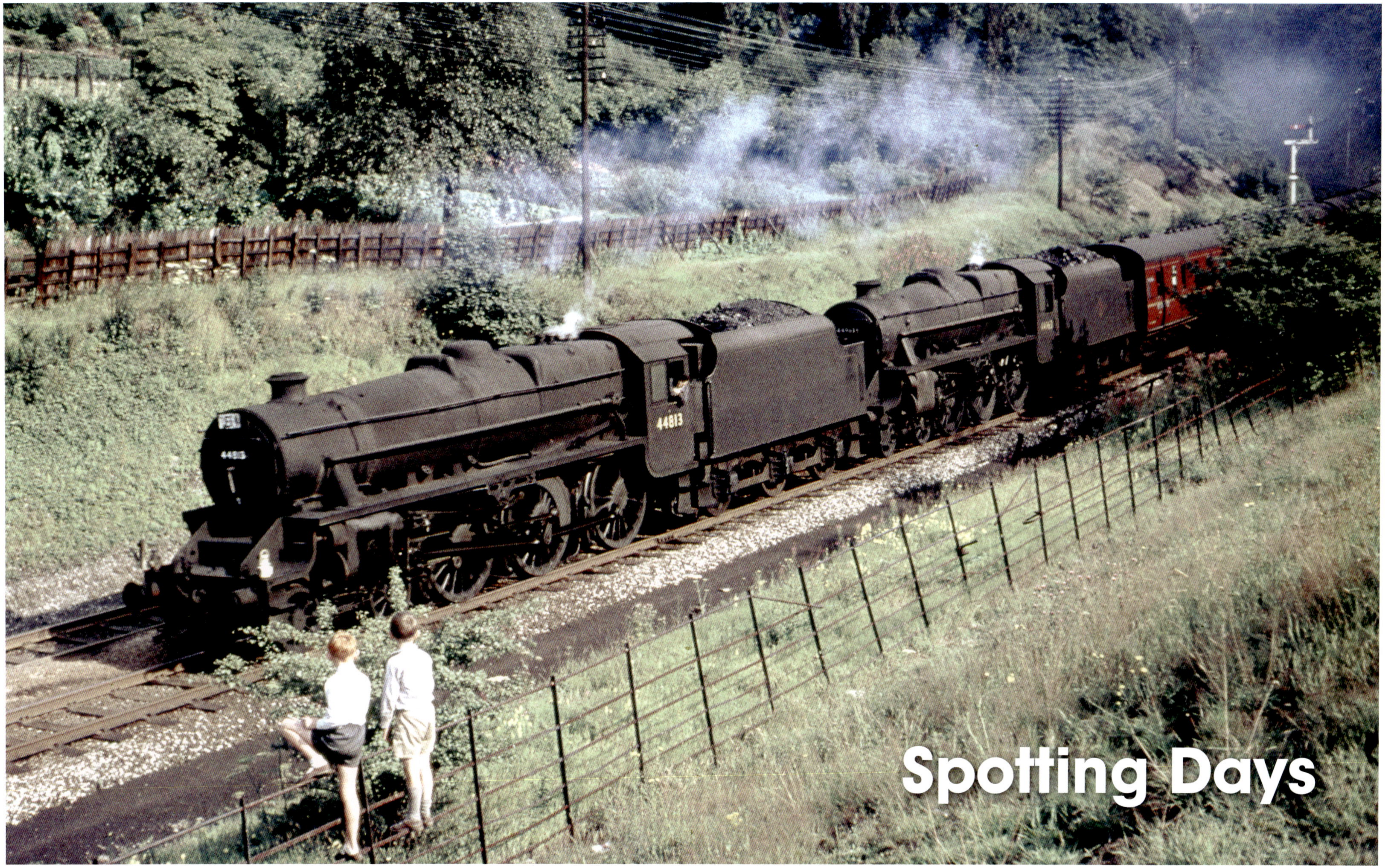

Page left: A good view of the out of service Ivatt Class 2MT 41264, standing unwanted at Carlisle Upperby on 14 October 1967, it had been posted as withdrawn in December 1966. ***Gerald T. Robinson***

This Black Five pairing led by 44813 bring a heavy summer extra around the curve at Dore & Totley heading northwards in 1959. ***Strathwood Library Collection***

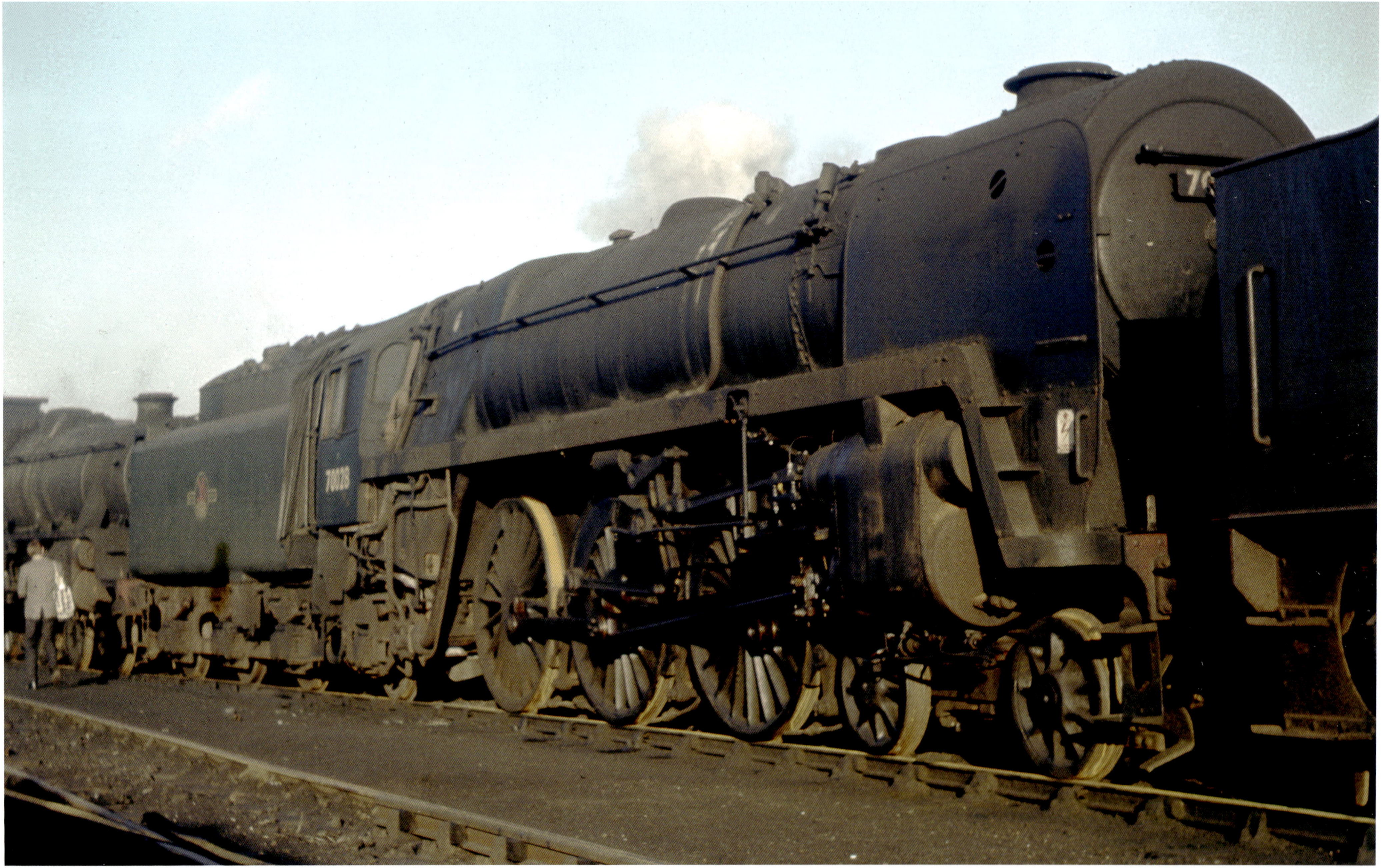

Rust has already formed on the tyres of Britannia, 70028 once named Royal Star over the weekend in September 1965, as this group of spotters make their way around Crewe South. ***Gilroy A. Kerr***

Opposite: Another party of spotters gaze upon the withdrawn Royal Scots, 46160 Queen Victoria's Rifleman and 46132 The King's Regiment, Liverpool at Saltley in 1965. ***Colour Rail***

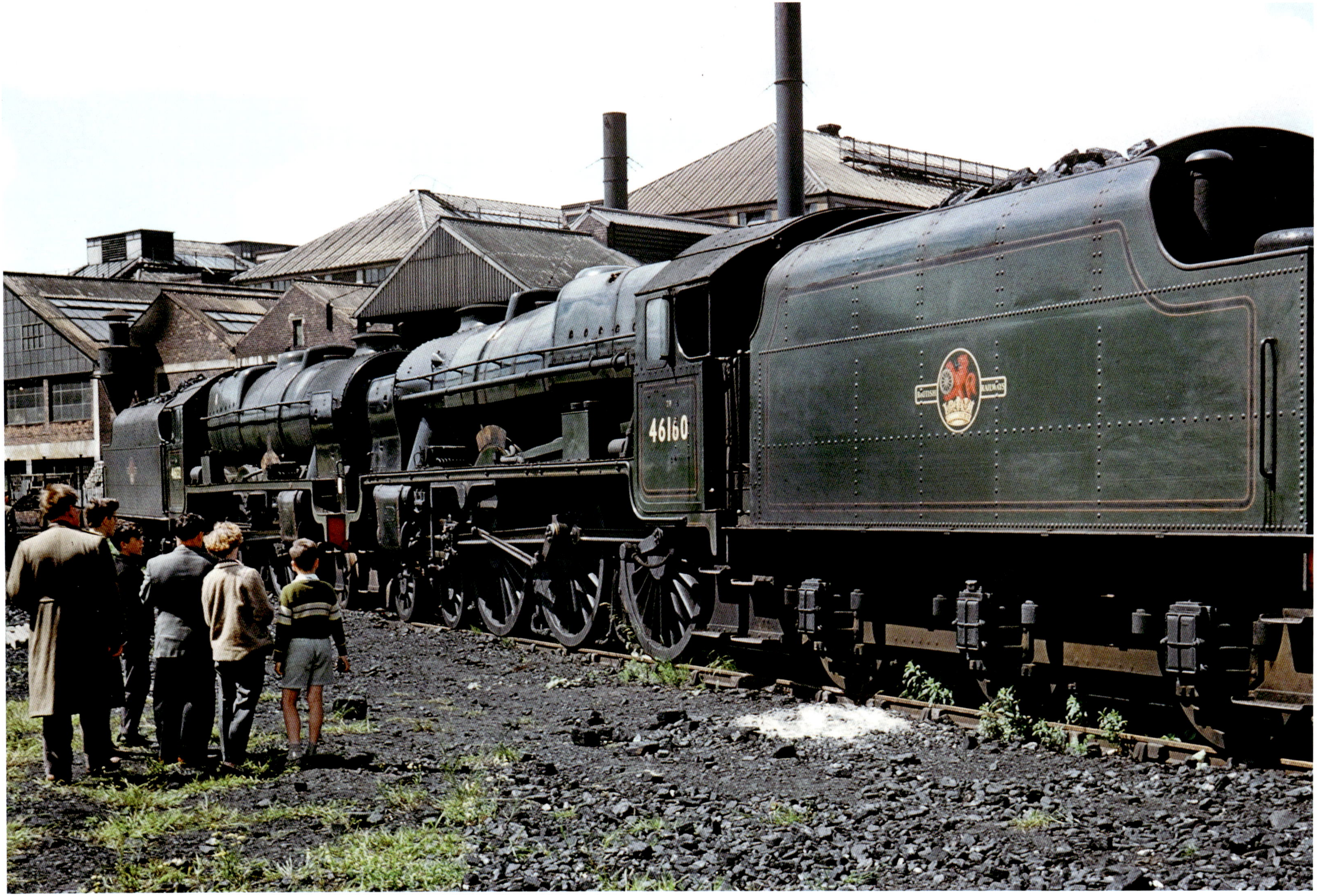
46160

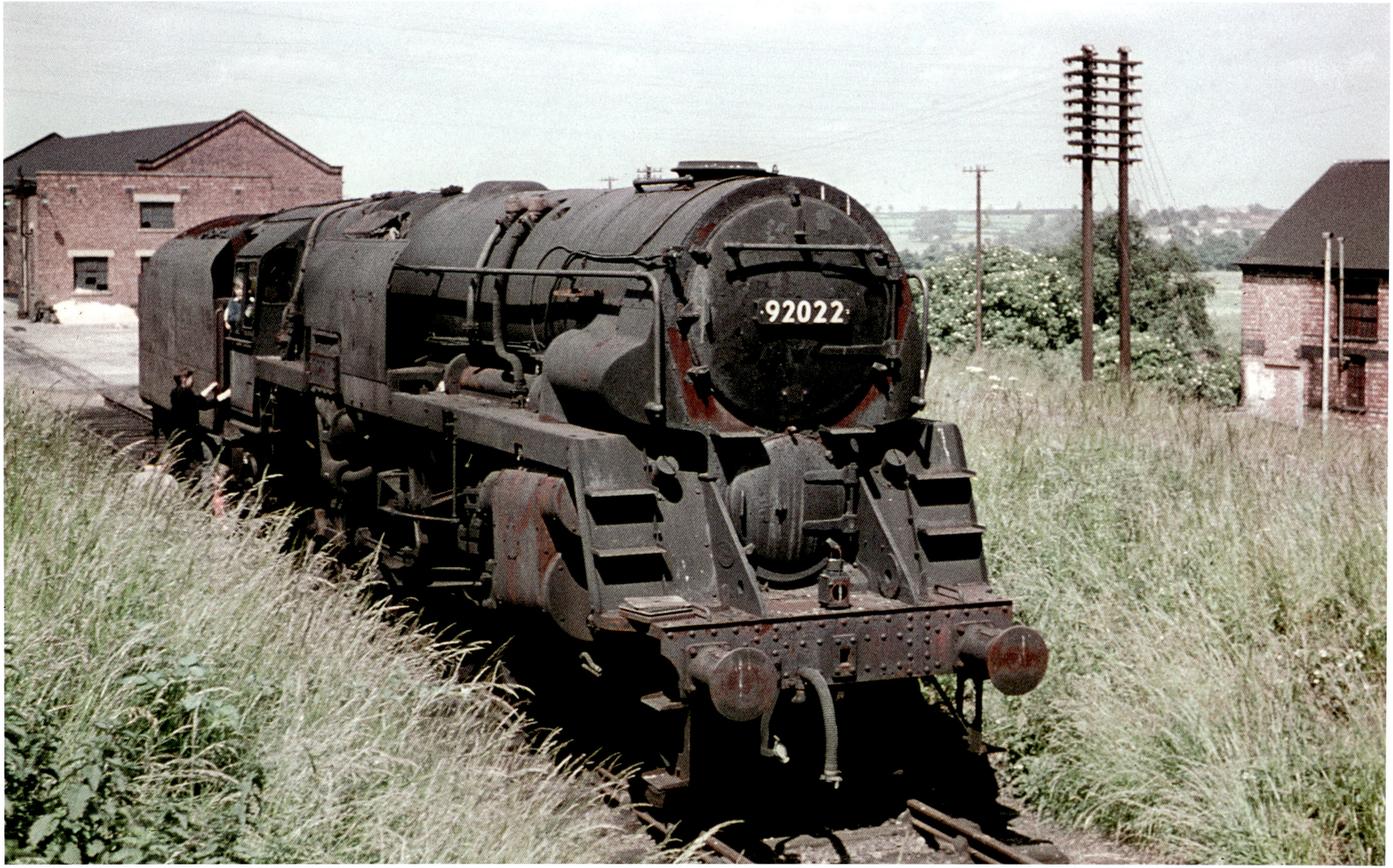

A chance to explore the cab of Crosti boilered Class 9F, 92022 at Wellingborough on 18 June 1961, whilst it awaits the call to Crewe Works for conversion back into a more conventional Class 9F. ***Late Vincent Heckford/Strathwood Libary Collection***

Opposite: Fellow spotters abound in this view at Crewe Works on 8 April 1962, as Royal Scots 46132 The King's Regiment, Liverpool and 46145 The Duke of Wellington's Regt. (West Riding) enjoy what was most likely their last overhauls. ***Frank Hornby***

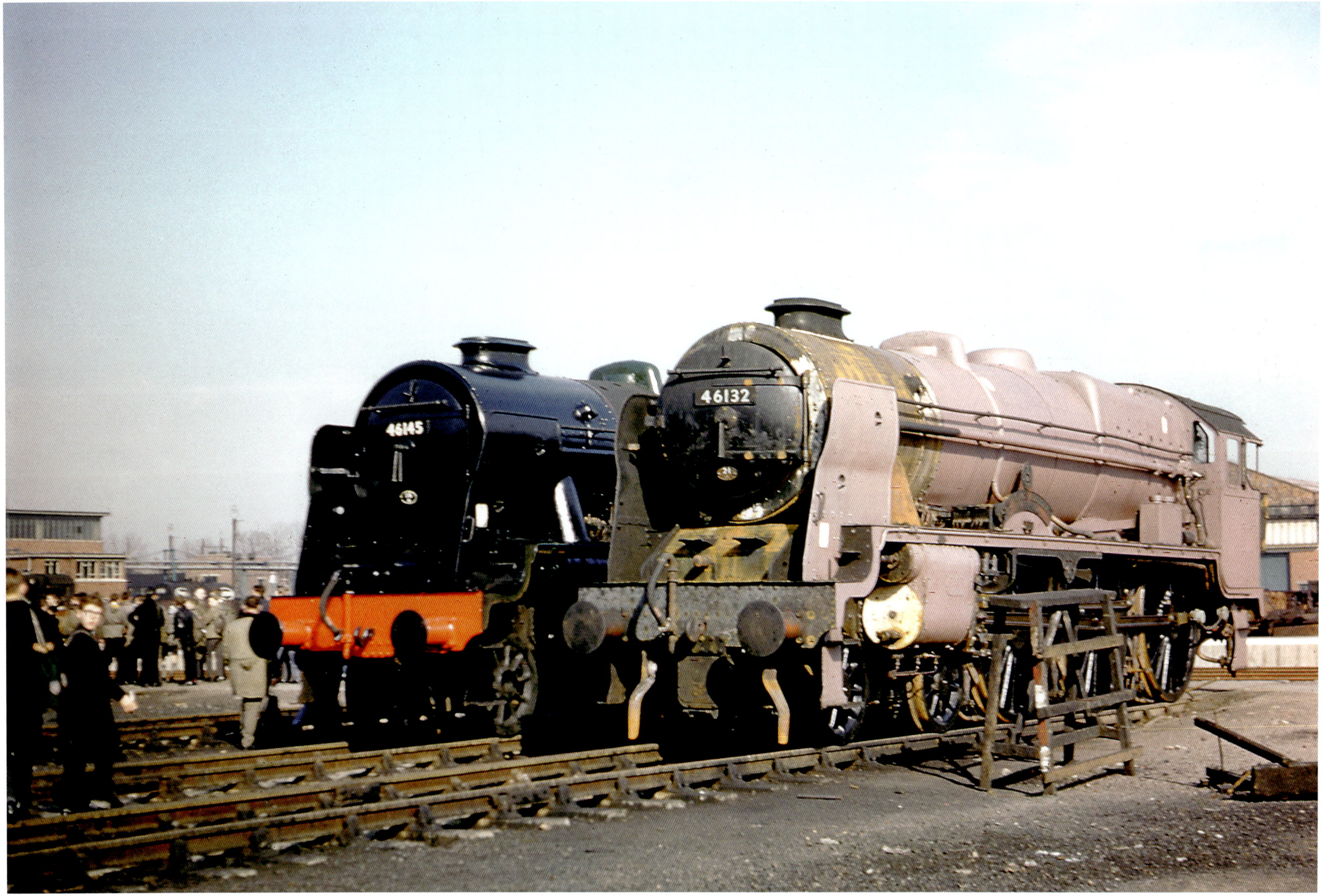
46145
46132

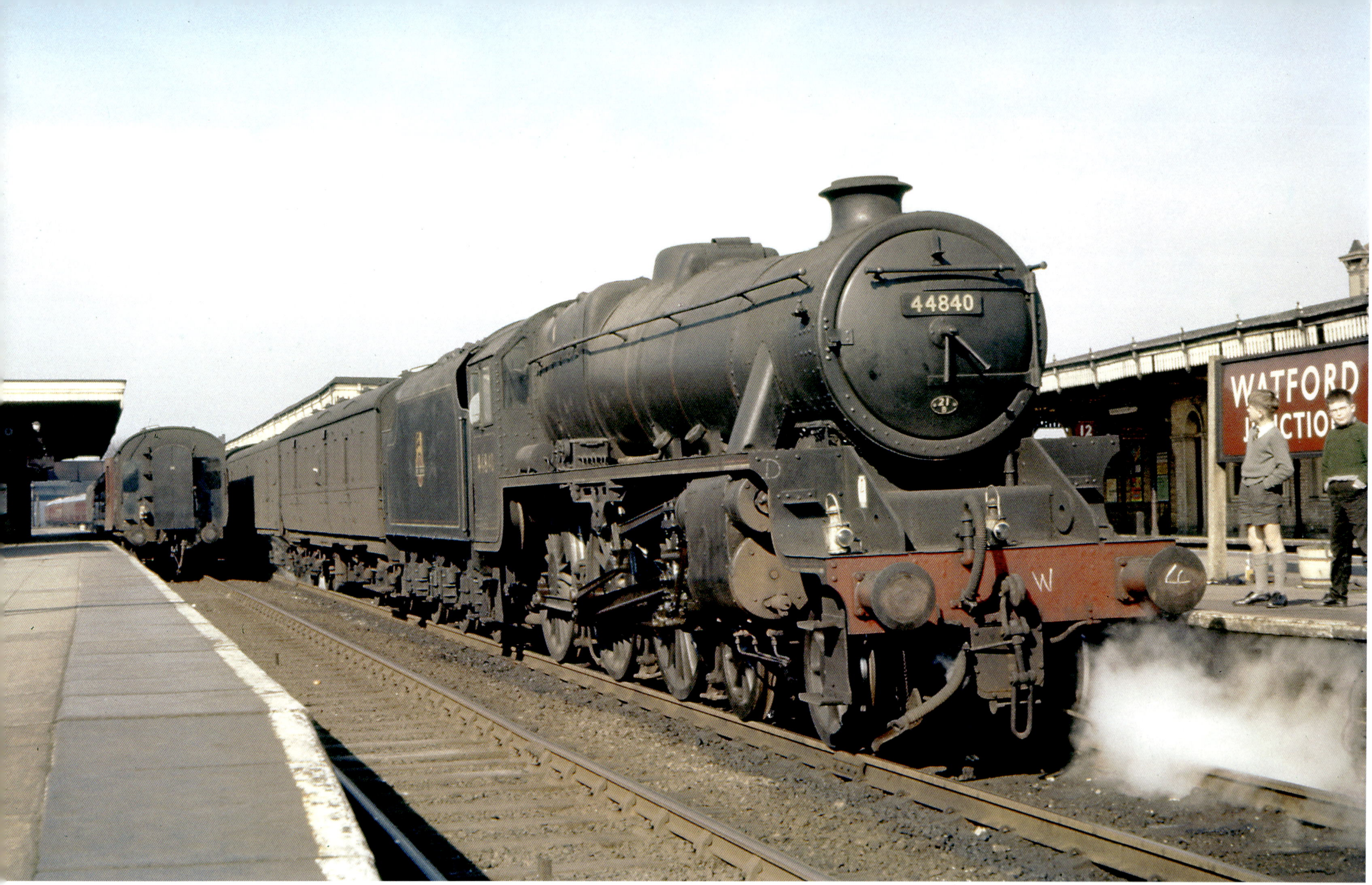

Two lads with hands in pockets are on the platforms at Watford Junction to observe Black Five, 44840 depart with an up parcels on 4 March 1961. ***Frank Hornby***

Opposite: The trackside path at the summit of the Lickey Incline at Blackwell has drawn others in the sunshine of 22 July 1963, as Class 8F 48339 heads southwards down the bank. ***Peter Simmonds***

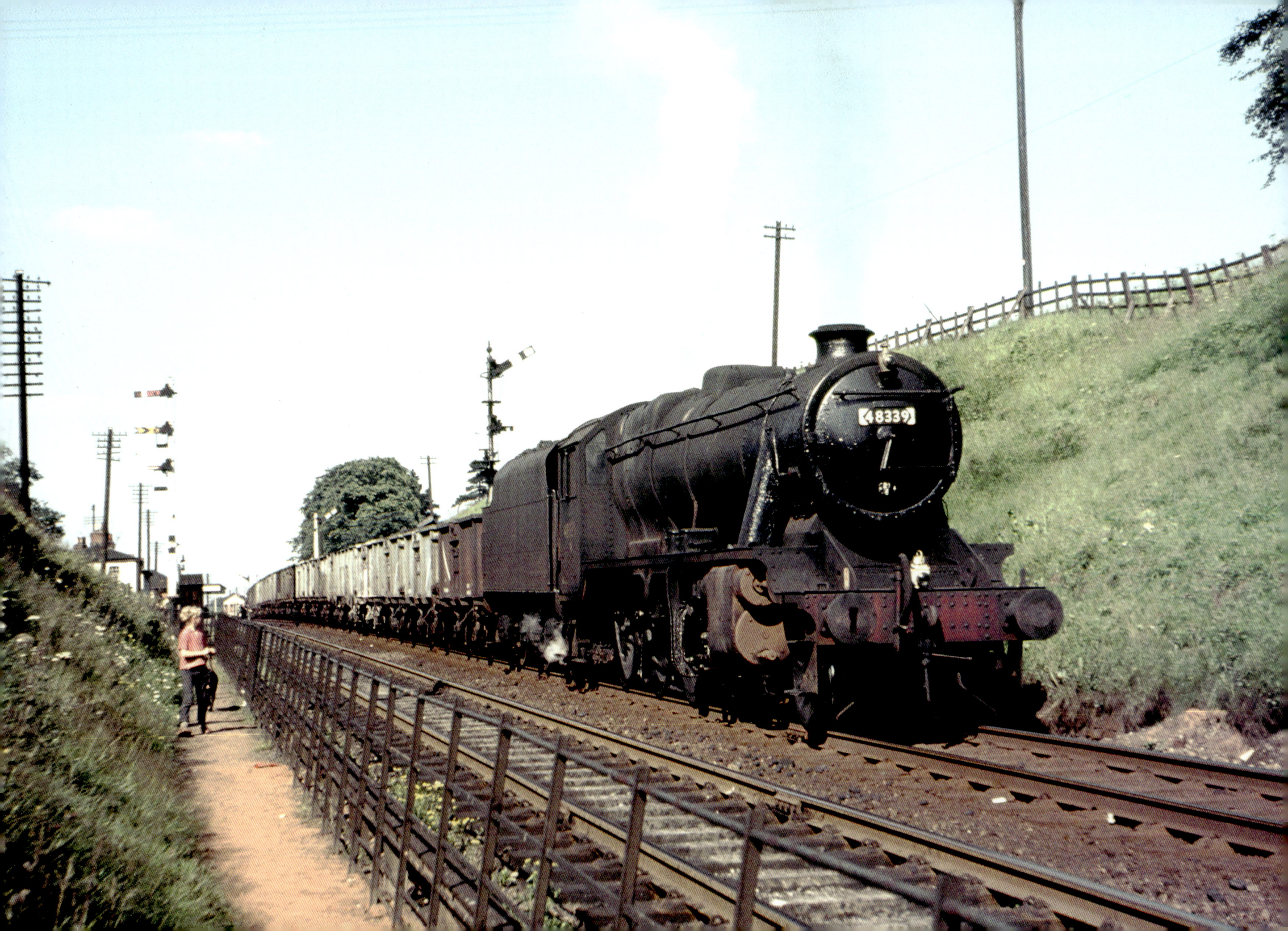
48339

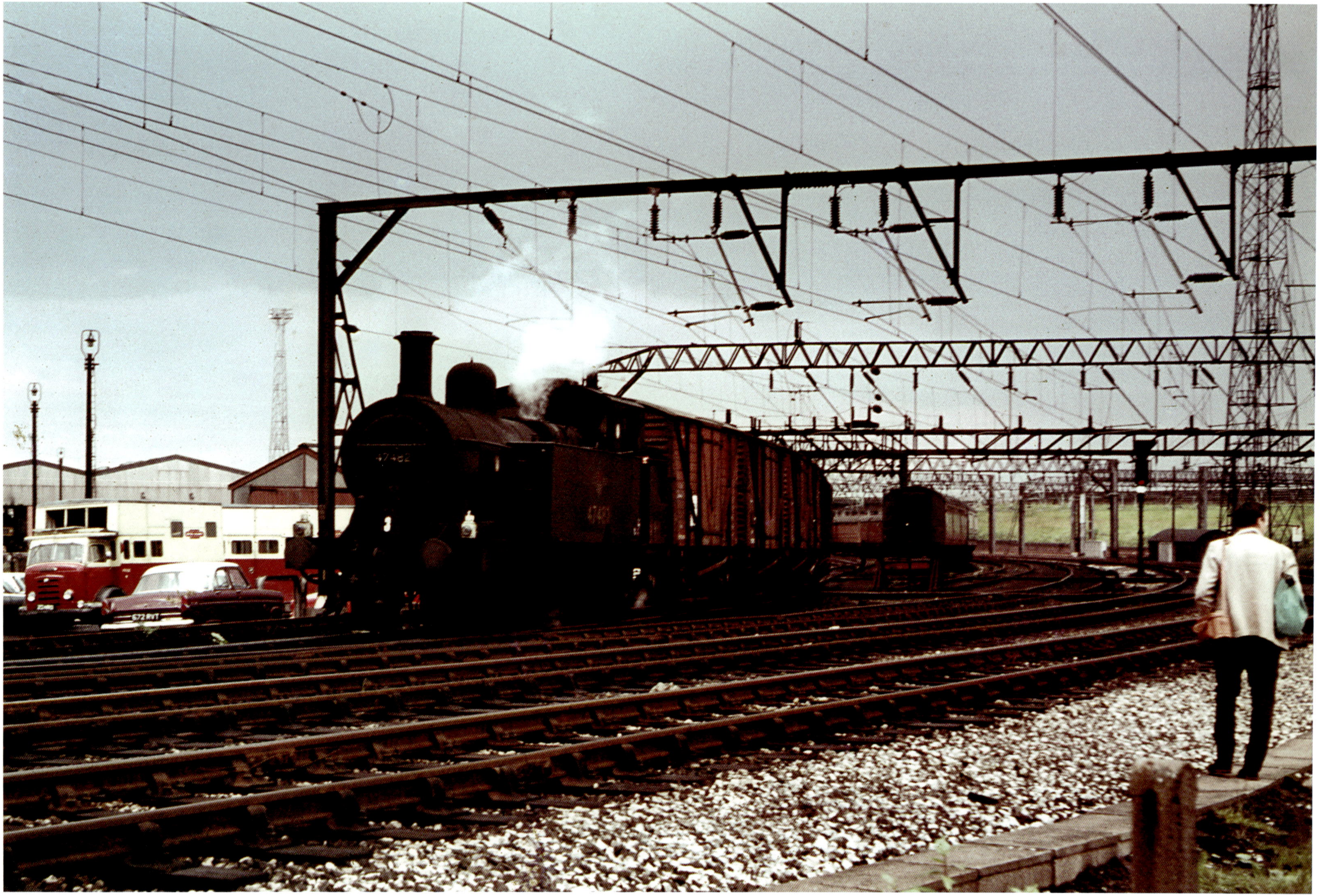
47482
672 RVT

Page left: From a vantage point alongside the Crewe station avoiding lines we are overlooking the new Crewe Diesel Depot and can watch Class 3F, 47482 complete with its distinctive Darlington style larger tankside numbers, engaged in shunting the yard in July 1965. ***Strathwood Library Collection***

The footpath alongside the line just to the north of Derby station could always be replied upon to draw a gathering of spotters, especially in the summer of 1964 as Class 8F, 48084 drifts past Peak, D12 running light engine. ***Strathwood Library Collection***

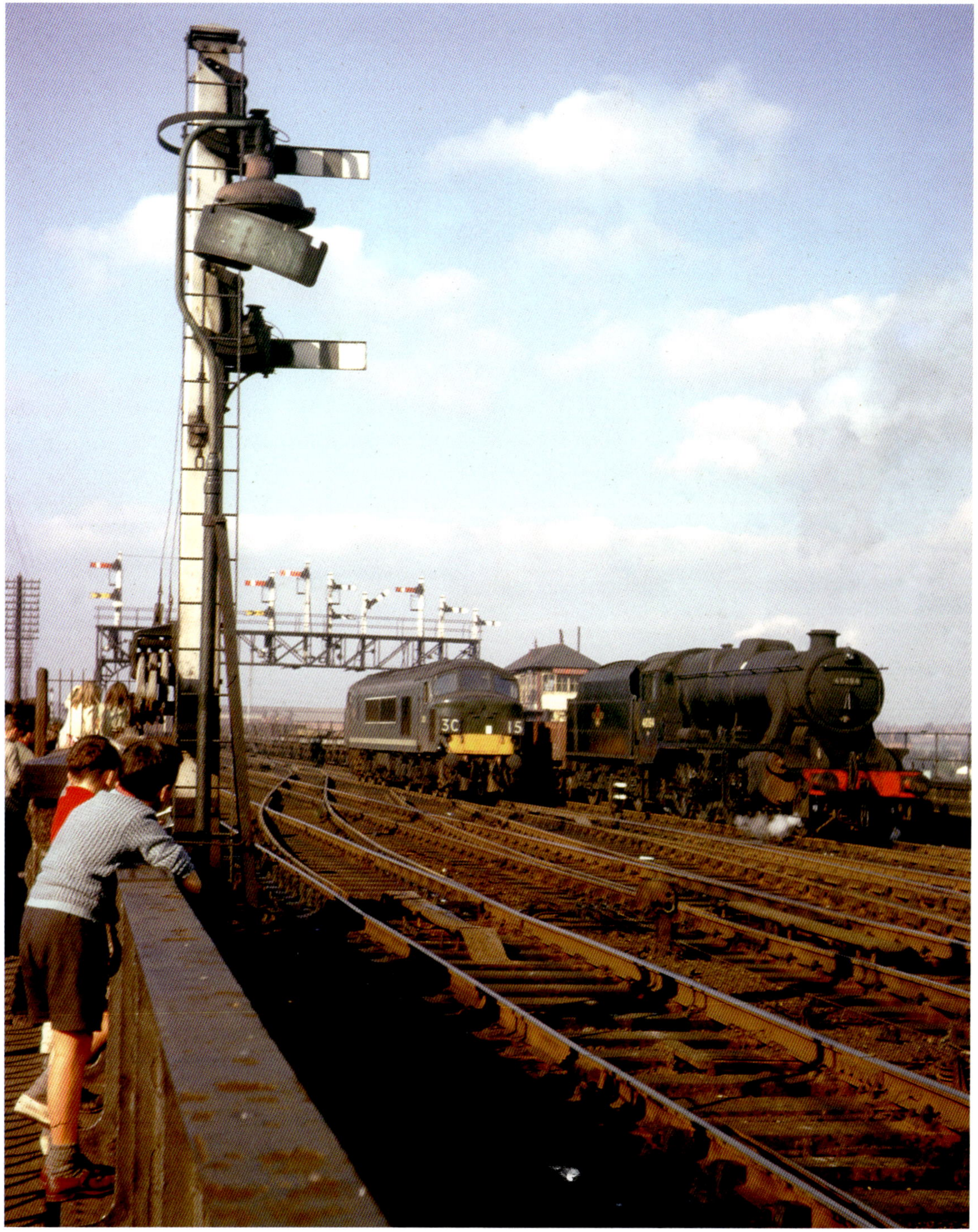

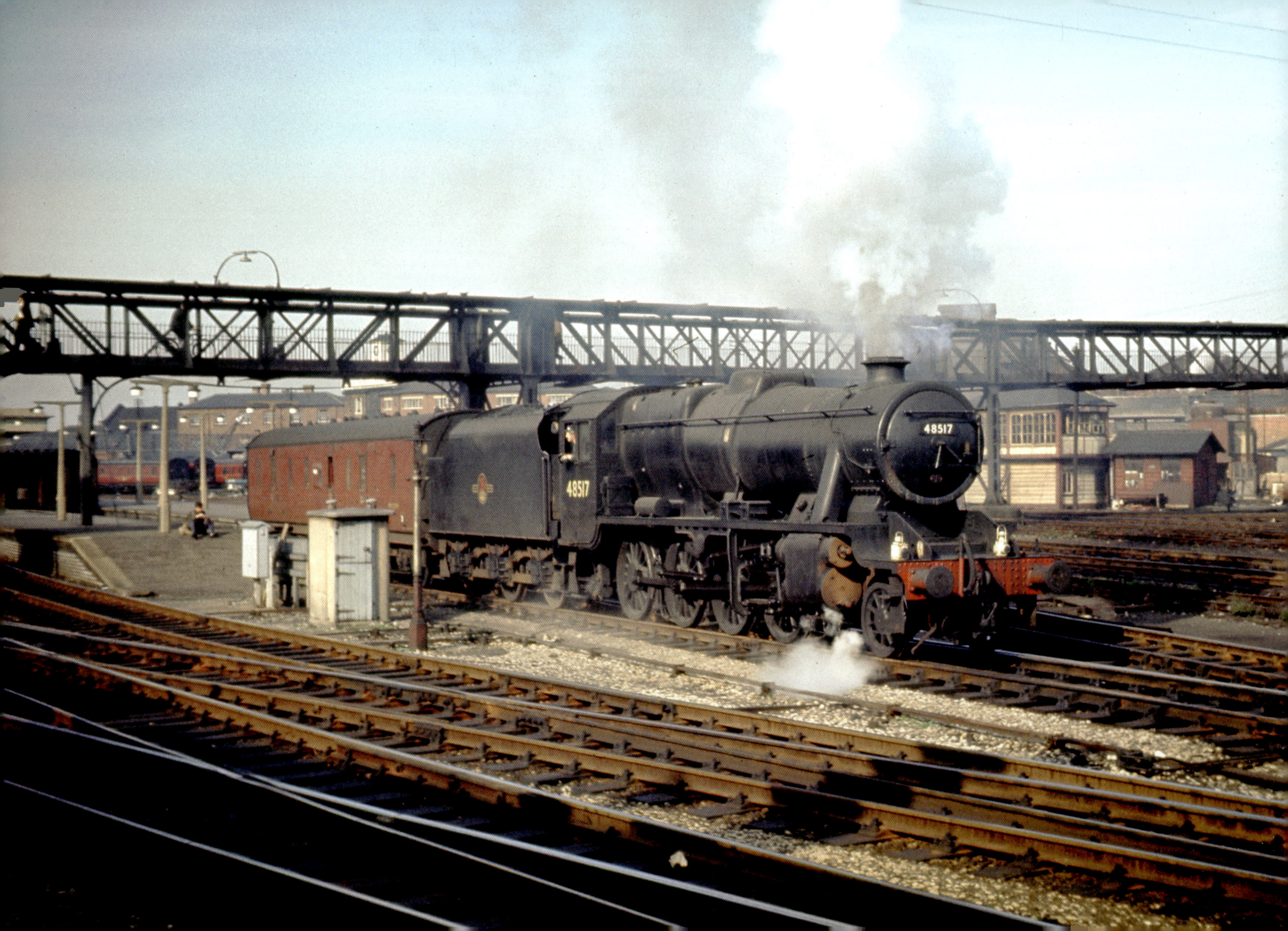
48517
48517

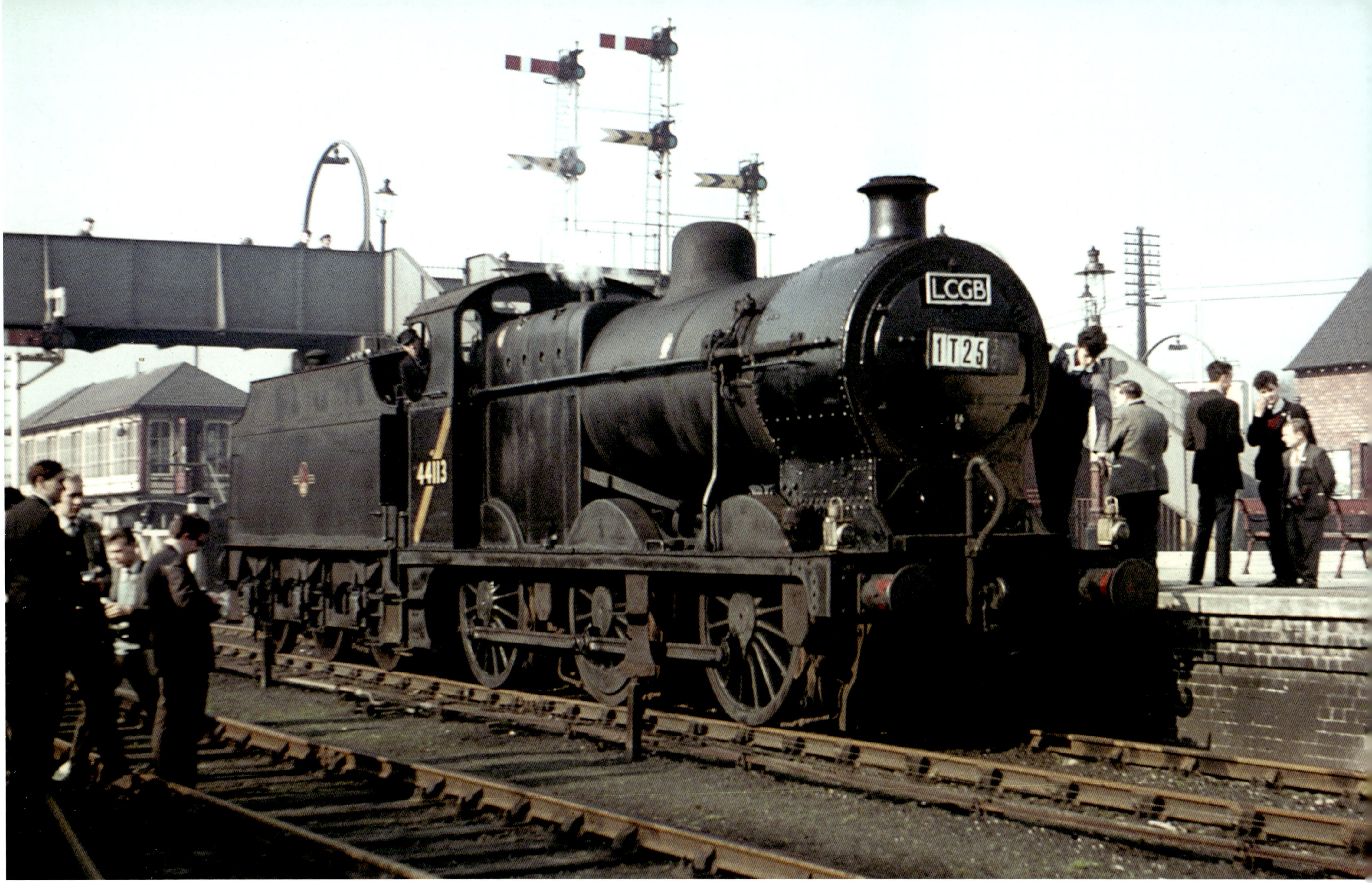

Page left: A lone spotter sits at the platform end at Derby Midland station the same year as another Class 8F, 48517 shuffles about with some parcel vans during a shunting manoeuvre. ***Len Smith***

On 17 October 1965, spotters were free to look out for themselves trackside at Spondon, whilst Class 4F, 44113 runs round on the LCGB's Derbyshire Railtour. ***Strathwood Library Collection***

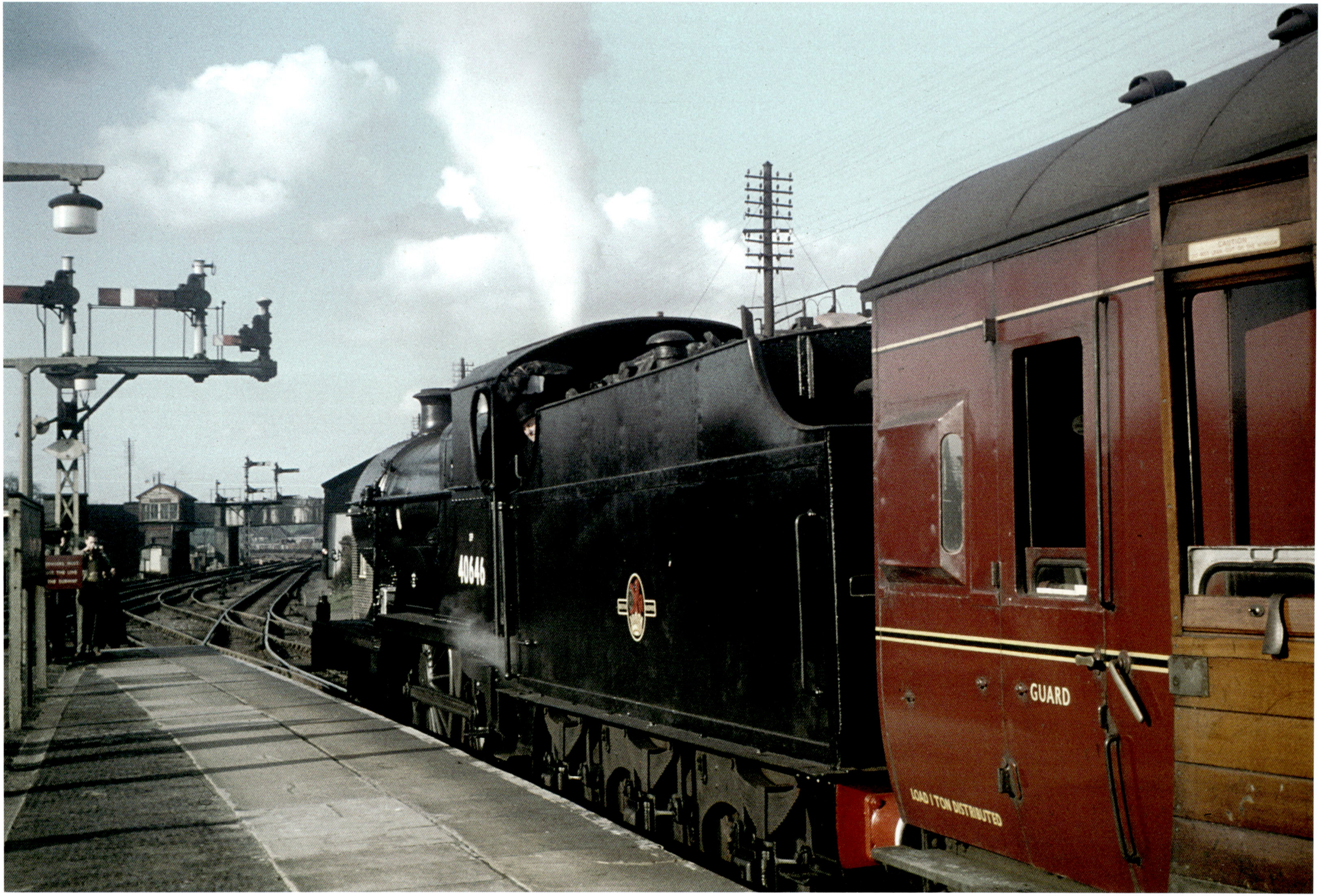
40646
GUARD
LOAD 1 TON DISTRIBUTED

Tender First

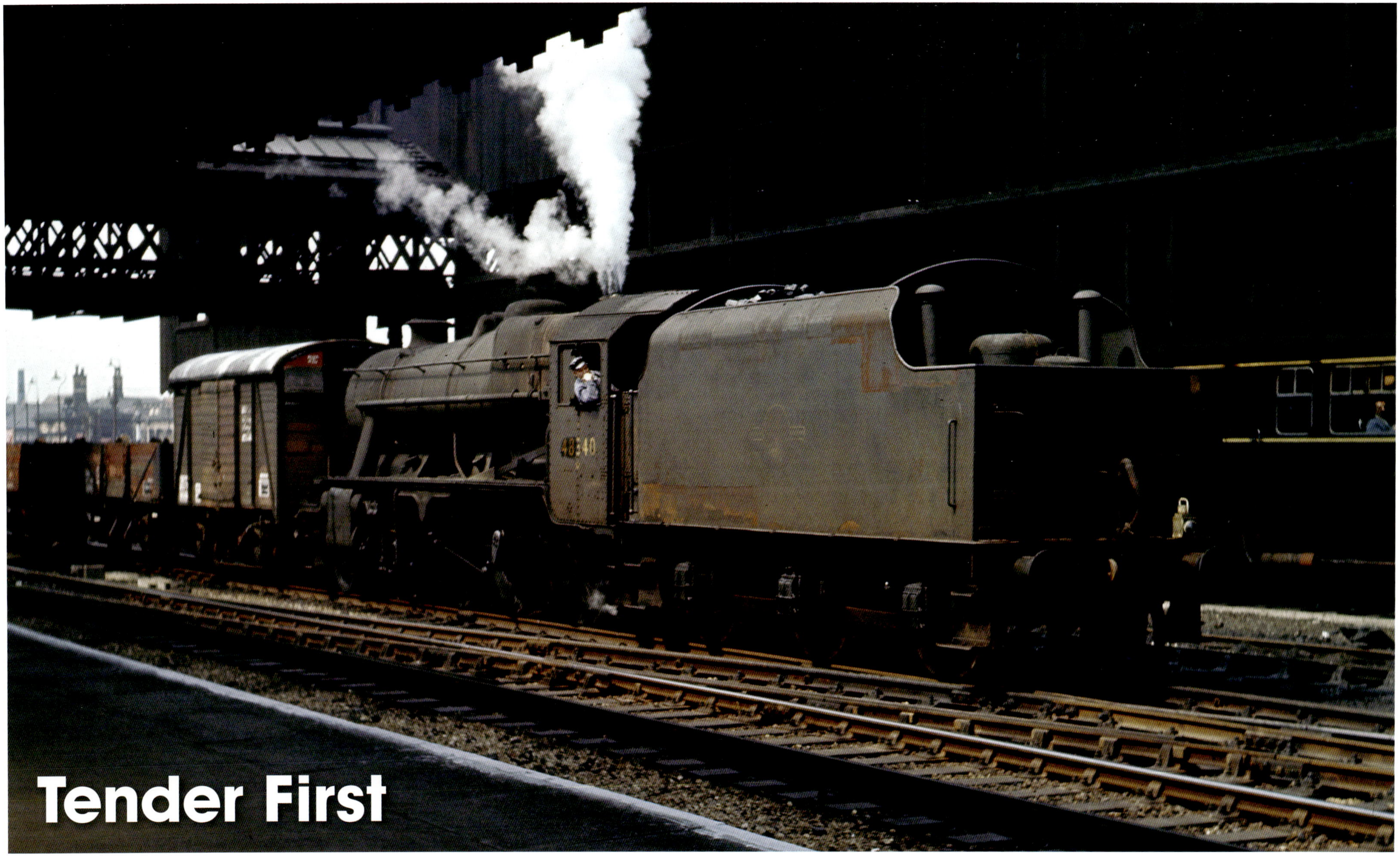

Page left: The chance for a platform end picture cannot be missed at Leighton Buzzard on 14 April 1962, whilst our old friend 40646 waits for departure with the last leg of the Stephenson Locomotive Society's Tour of Seven Branch Lines. ***Strathwood Library Collection***

Rolling tender first down the steep Miles Platting bank into Manchester Victoria on 24 May 1968, the crew of Class 8F, 48340 look very relaxed with their local goods working. ***Gilroy A. Kerr***

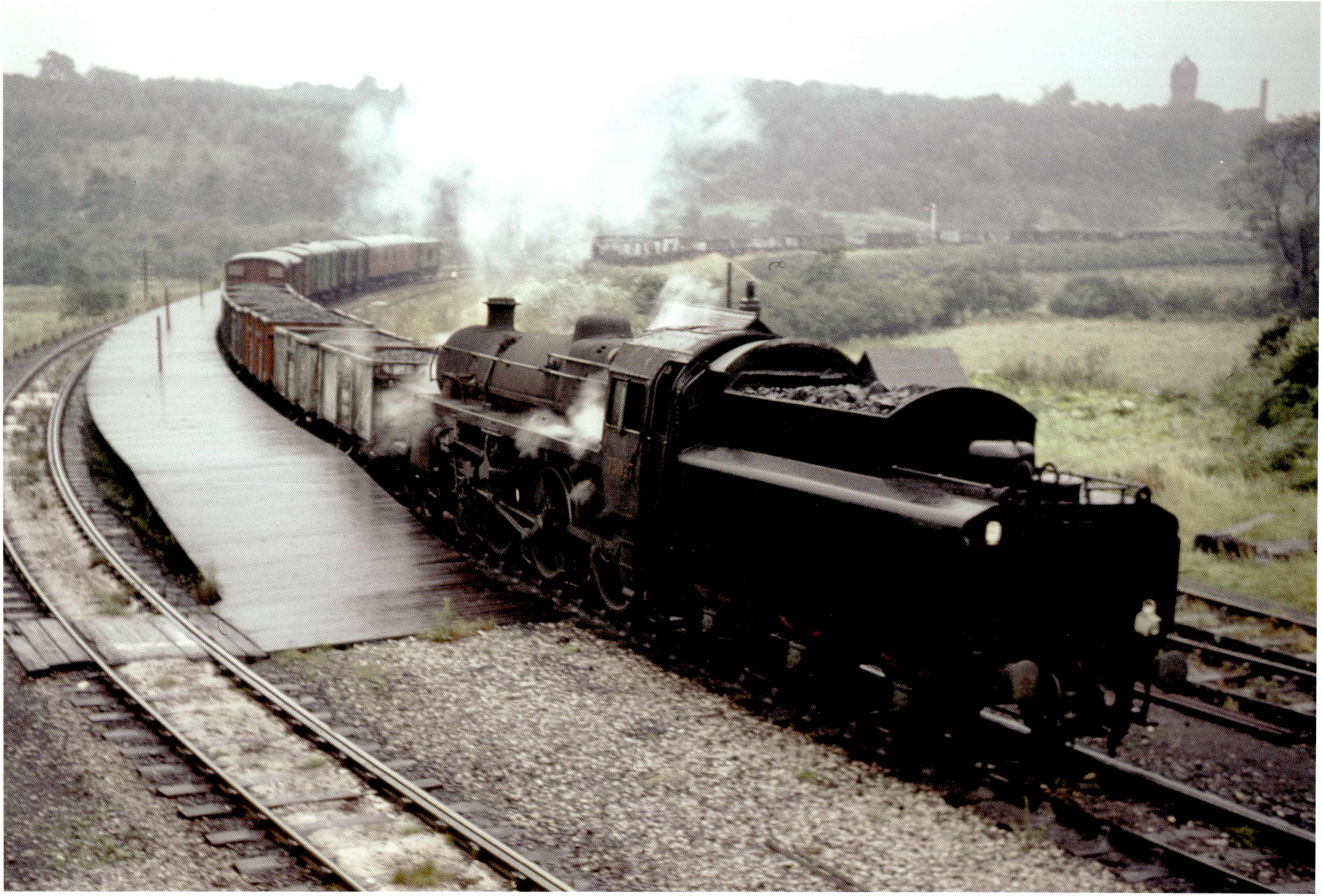

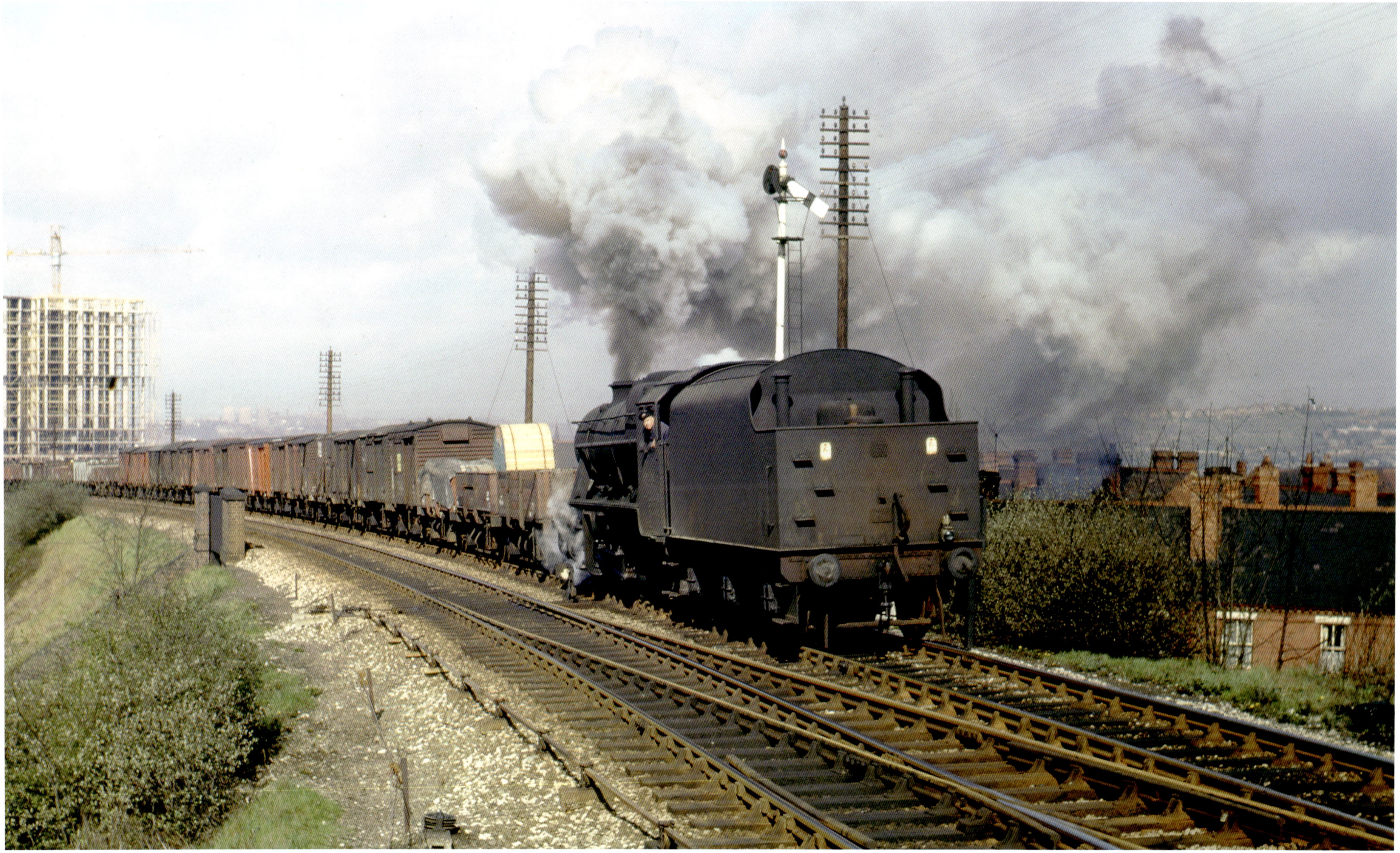

Page left: The cab design of Standard Class 4MT coupled with a BR2 tender could allow the driver and fireman to see where they are going, in theory at least in the rain as here with 75037 at Leek Brook Junction with a goods from nearby Stoke-on-Trent, as seen from the signal box controlling the junction in 1966. ***Winston Cole***

Going well up the grade at Old Hill, near Stourbridge on 23 April 1966 was Class 8F, 48531. Another of these 2-8-0s to have been built away from the London Midland & Scottish Railway as part of the war effort, this time at Doncaster Works in April 1945. ***Jerry Beddows***

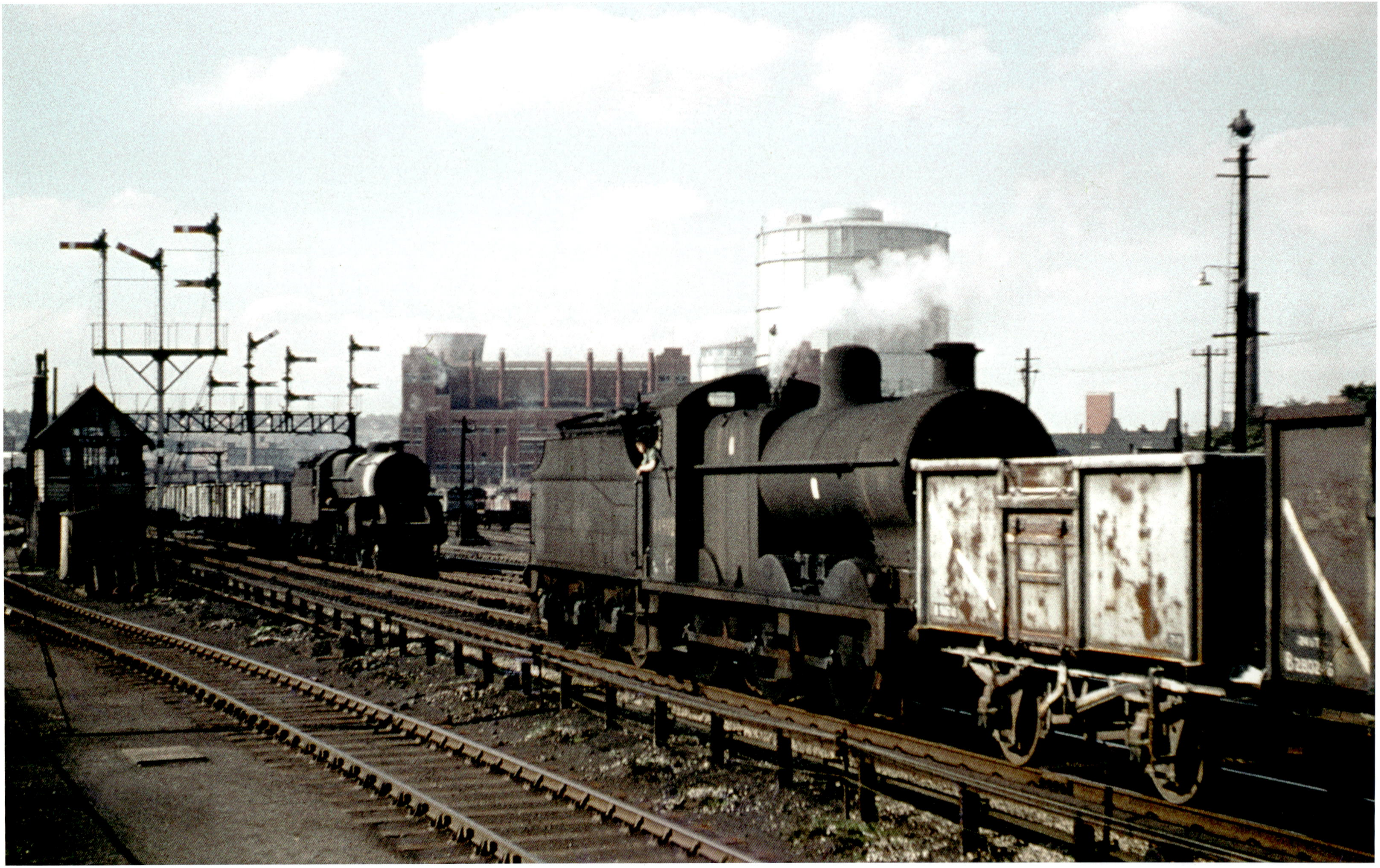

It was still very much an industrialised landscape around Stoke-on-Trent on 9 September 1961, as Class 4F, 44592 is set to pass Hughes Crab, 42891 with their respective goods workings through the city. ***Strathwood Library Collection***

Opposite: A chance for a quiet rest at the platforms for Ivatt Class 2MT, 46440 during the day's pilot duties at Derby Midland station on 5 March 1960. ***Frank Hornby***

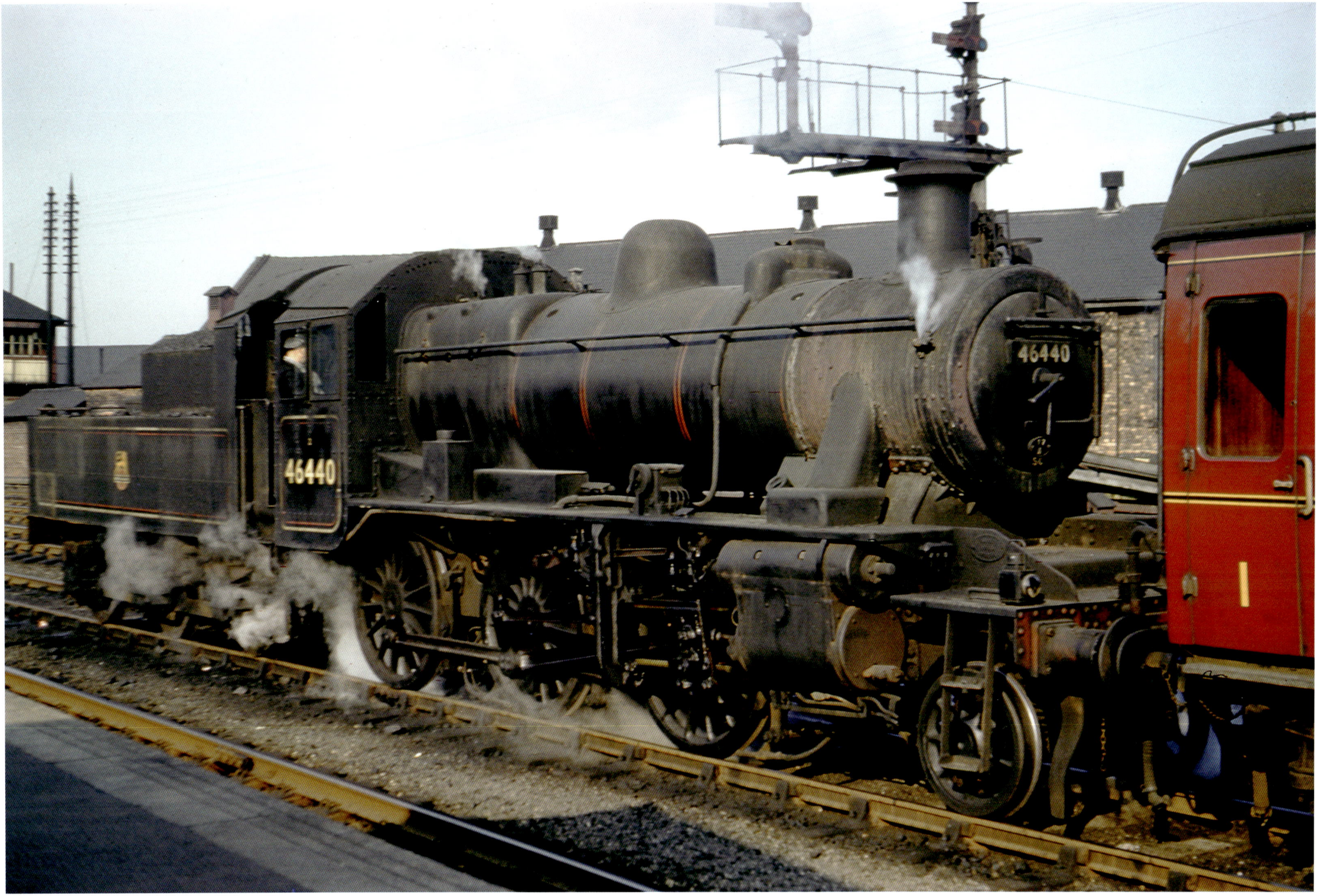
46440
46440

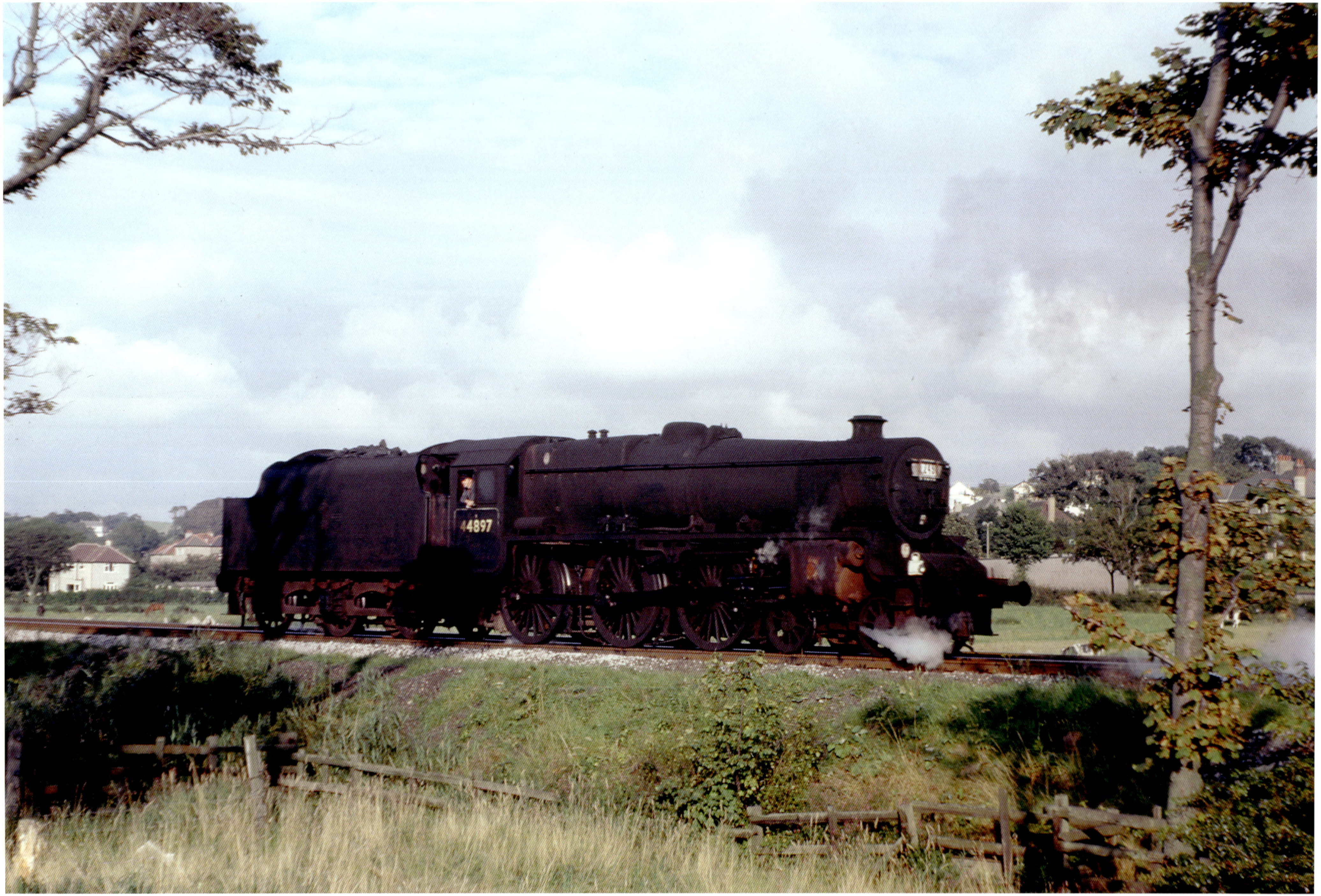
44897

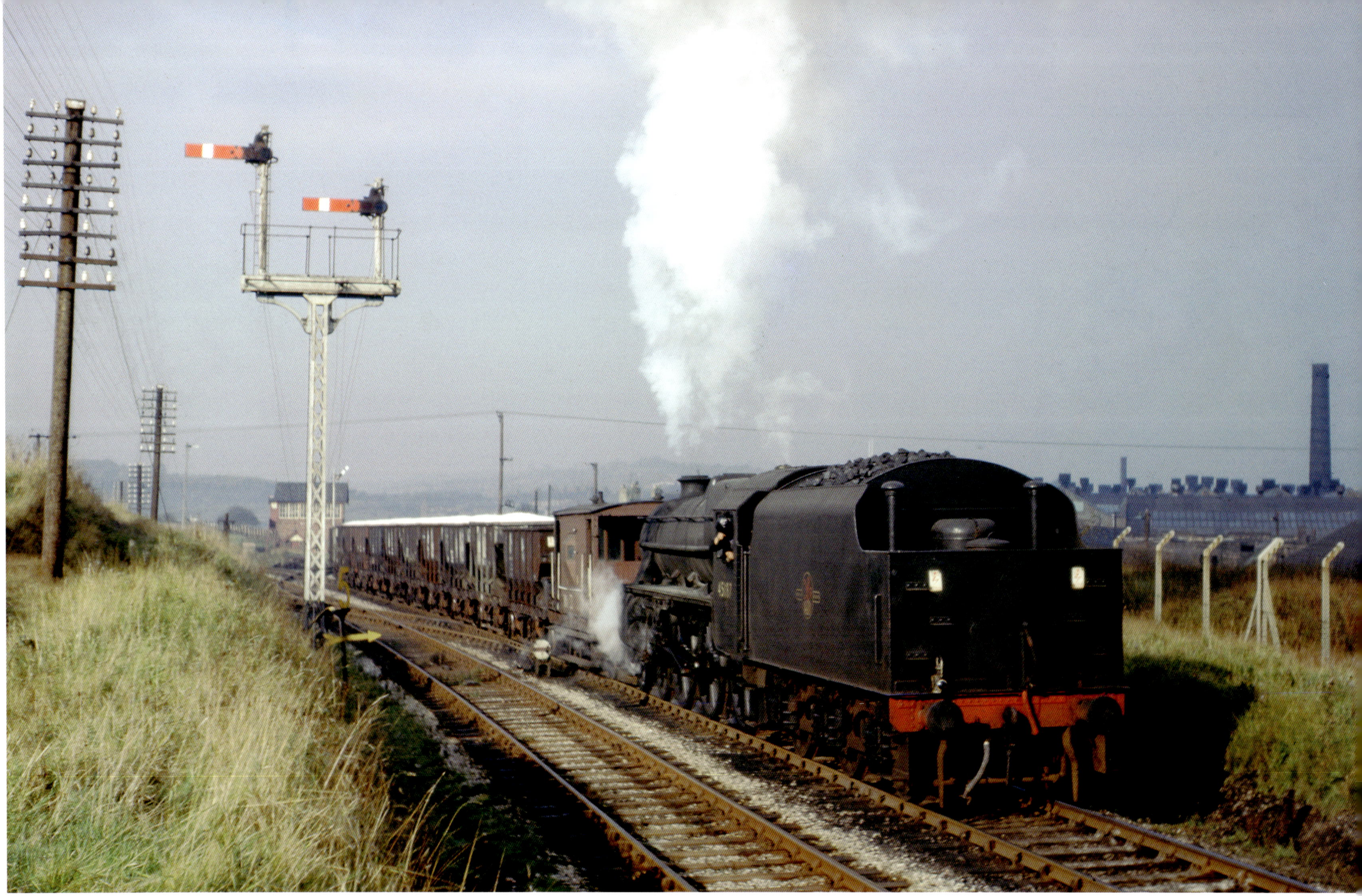

Page left: A tender first light engine movement along the WCML on the down line for the crew of this Black Five, 44897 at Hest Bank on 26 August 1967. ***Jerry Beddows***

Showing a nice clean white exhaust with its load beginning to bite at Milton Junction on 29 October 1966 was another Black Five, this time 45187. ***Jerry Beddows***

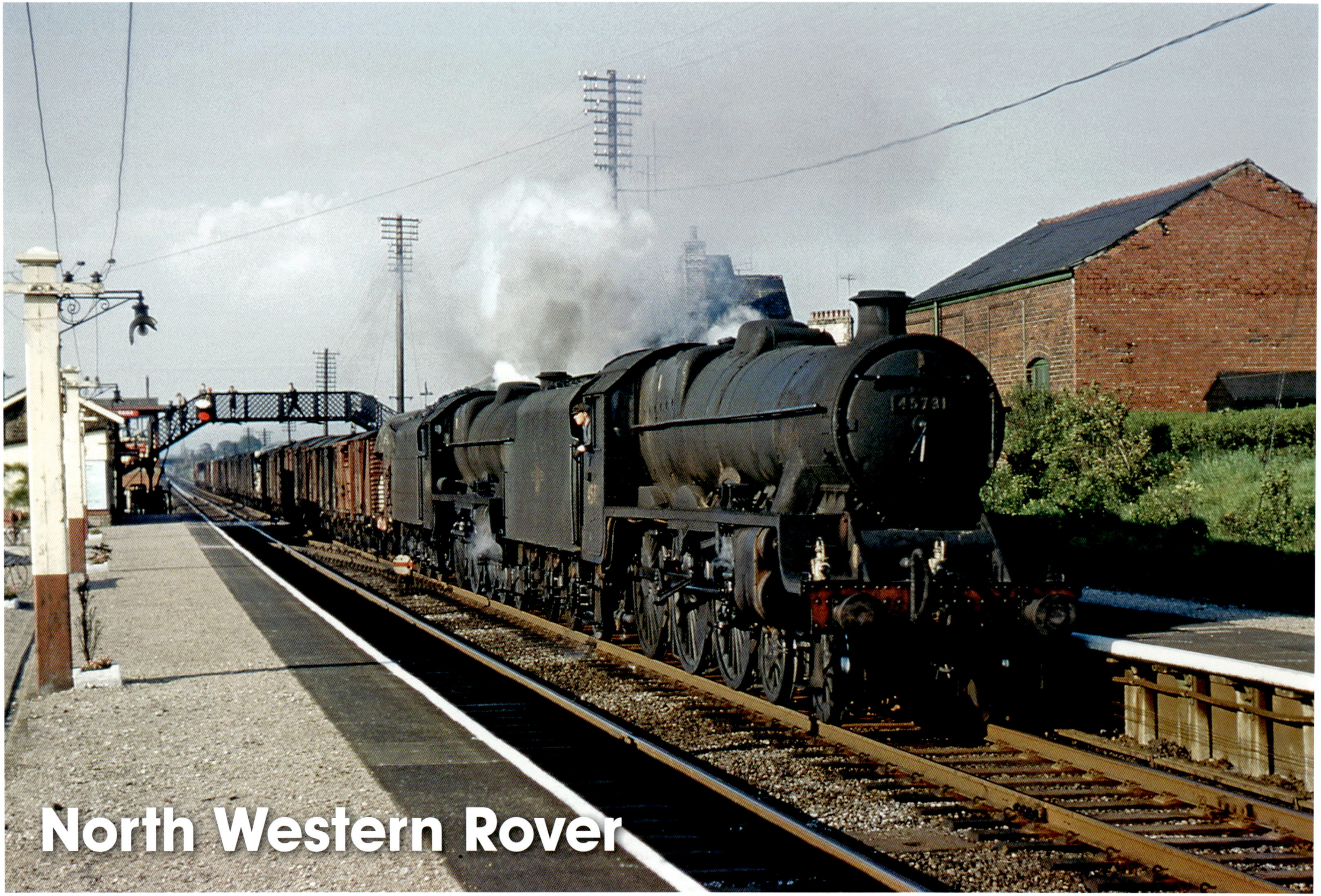

North Western Rover

Page left: Back to Hest Bank once more in June 1962, this time to enjoy doubleheaded Jubilees, led by 45731 Perseverance and an unknown classmate. As they hurry a lengthy freight south through the former LNWR station which closed in 1969. ***Dave Cobbe Collection/Rail Photoprints***

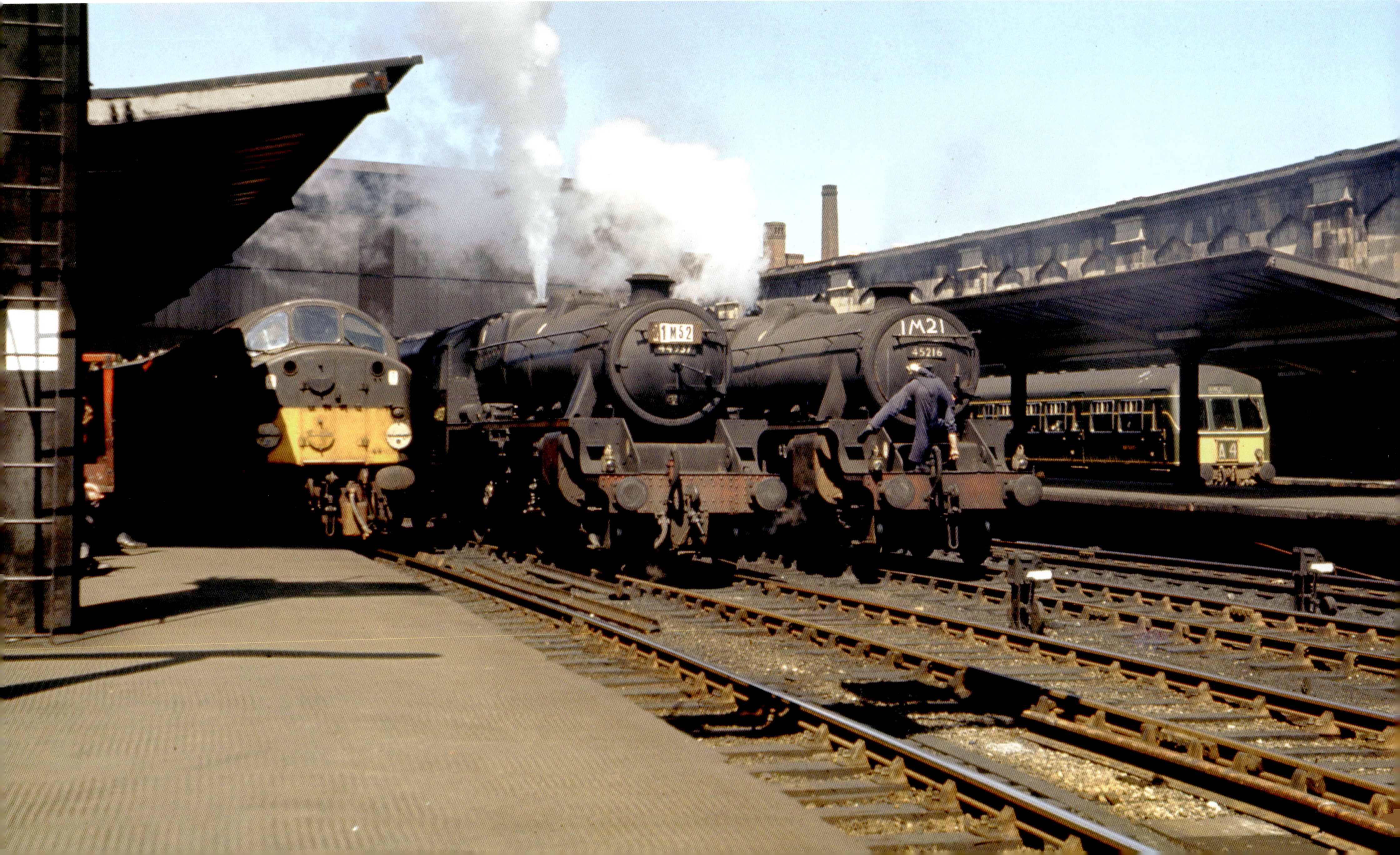

Two Black Fives engaged on extras, blow off loudly to drown out the sounds of the English Electric Type 4 and the Metropolitan Cammell built DMU that sandwich them at Carlisle Citadel in August 1965. ***Strathwood Library Collection***

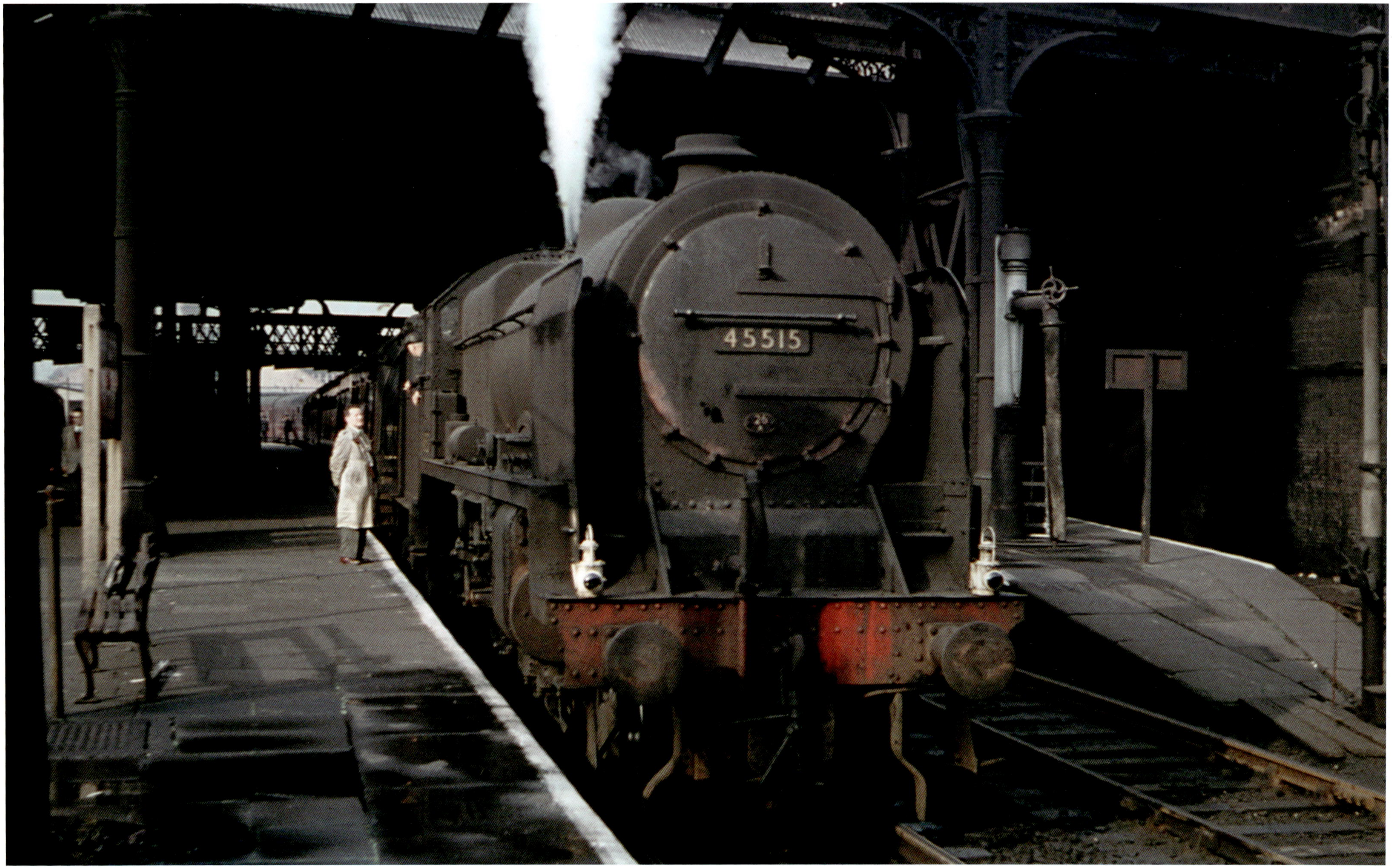

Again plenty of steam is on hand ready for departure away from Manchester Victoria on 23 September 1961, as the driver of Patriot, 45515 Caernarvon awaits the guards green flag and whistle. ***Douglas Twibble***

Opposite: Also casting his eyes back for the right away is the driver of Black Five, 44937 at Warrington Bank Quay on 1 September 1965. This is one of the last few Black Fives to be outshopped by Crewe, in unlined black livery. ***Gilroy A. Kerr***

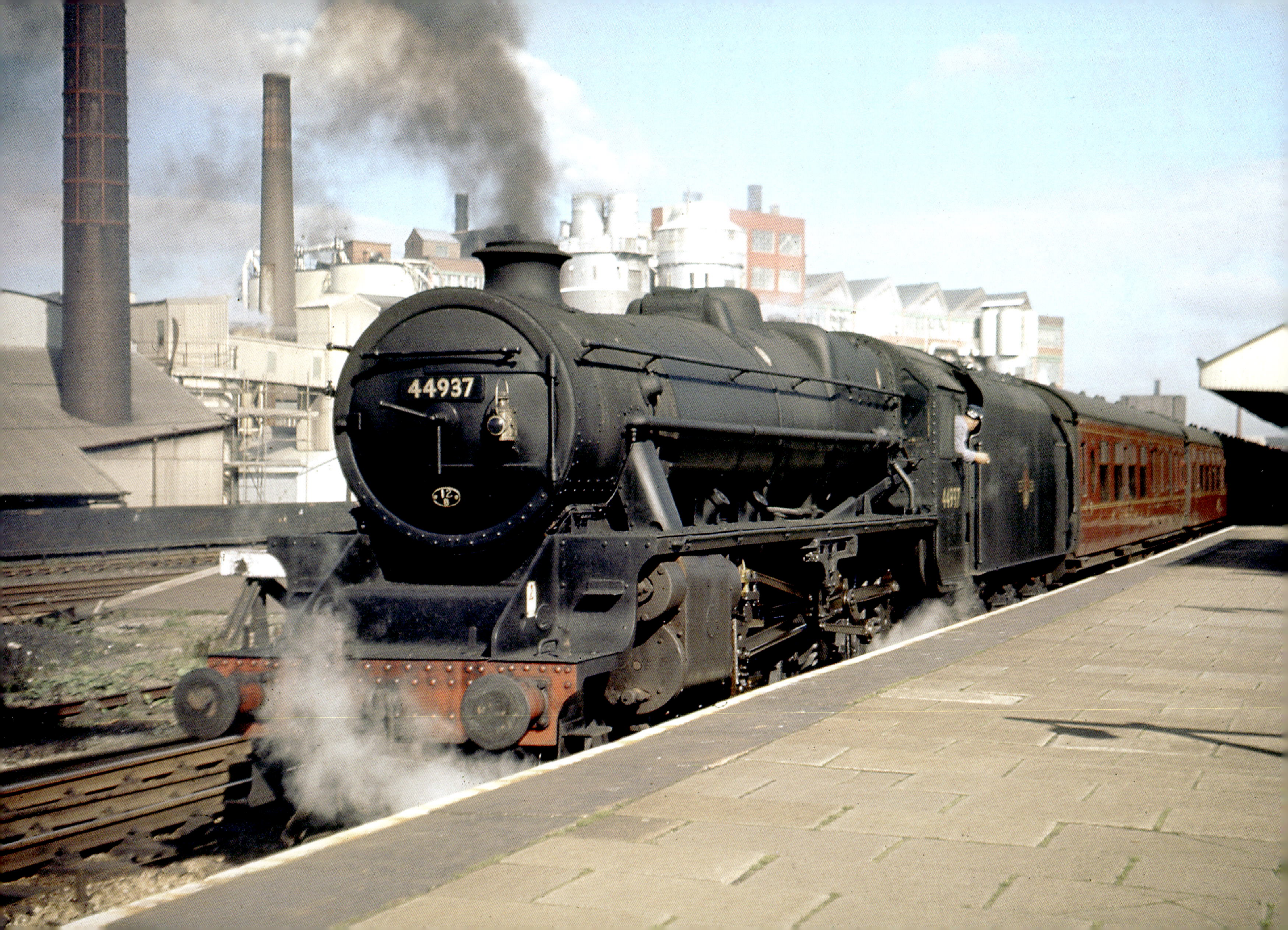
44937

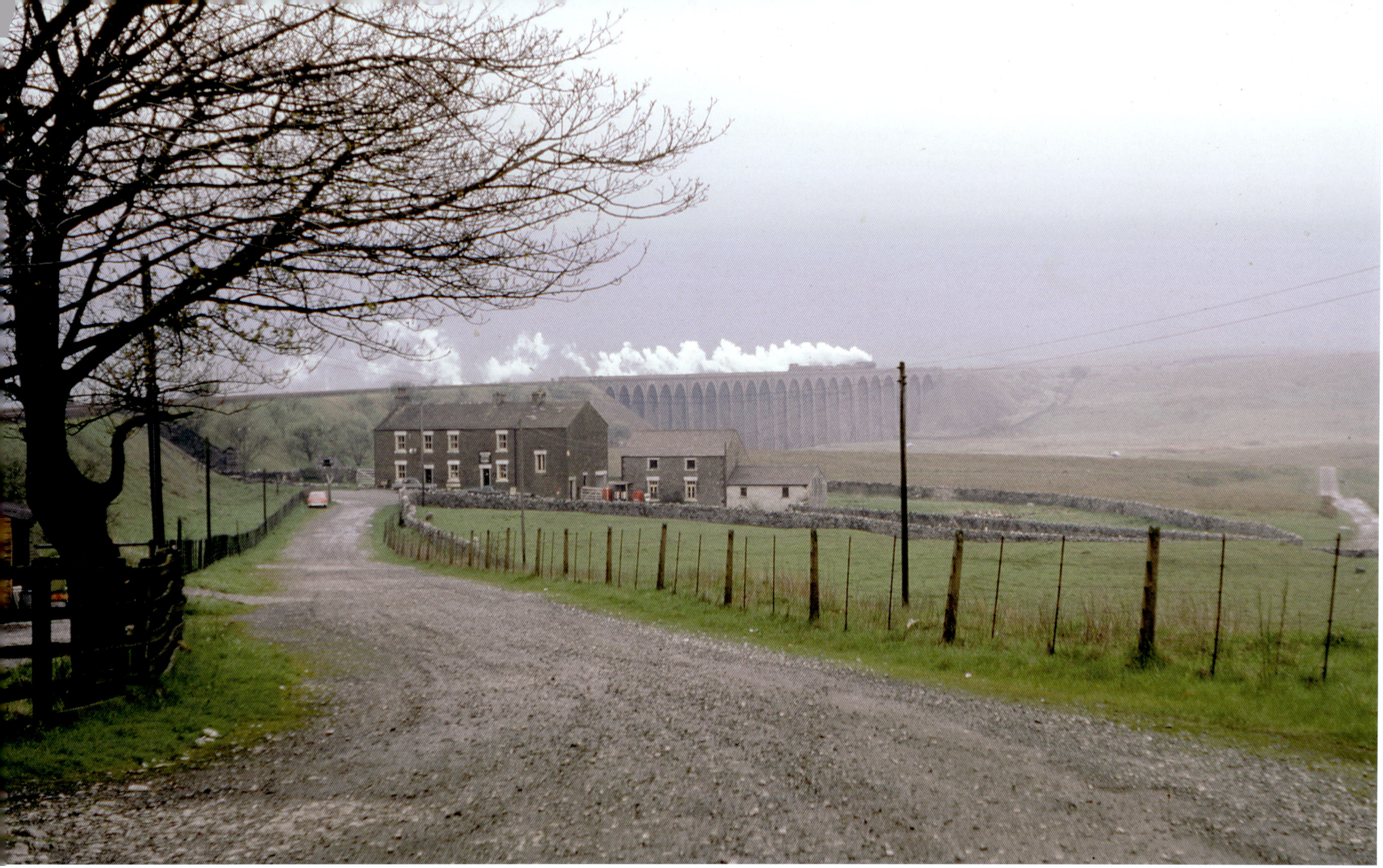

Not so many cameramen opted for the more creative composition, such as this scene looking back at Ribblehead towards the great viaduct on 13 May 1967, as Britannia, 70028, Royal Star ambles off towards the distance into the haze with its easy load on today's pick up goods. ***Strathwood Library Collection***

Opposite: A stoical glare is cast to our photographer from the footplate of one of the few un-named Patriots, 45513 at the north end of Preston station on 1 July 1961. This once fine locomotive would be taken out of traffic at the end of the following summer's timetable and quickly cut up. ***Colour Rail***

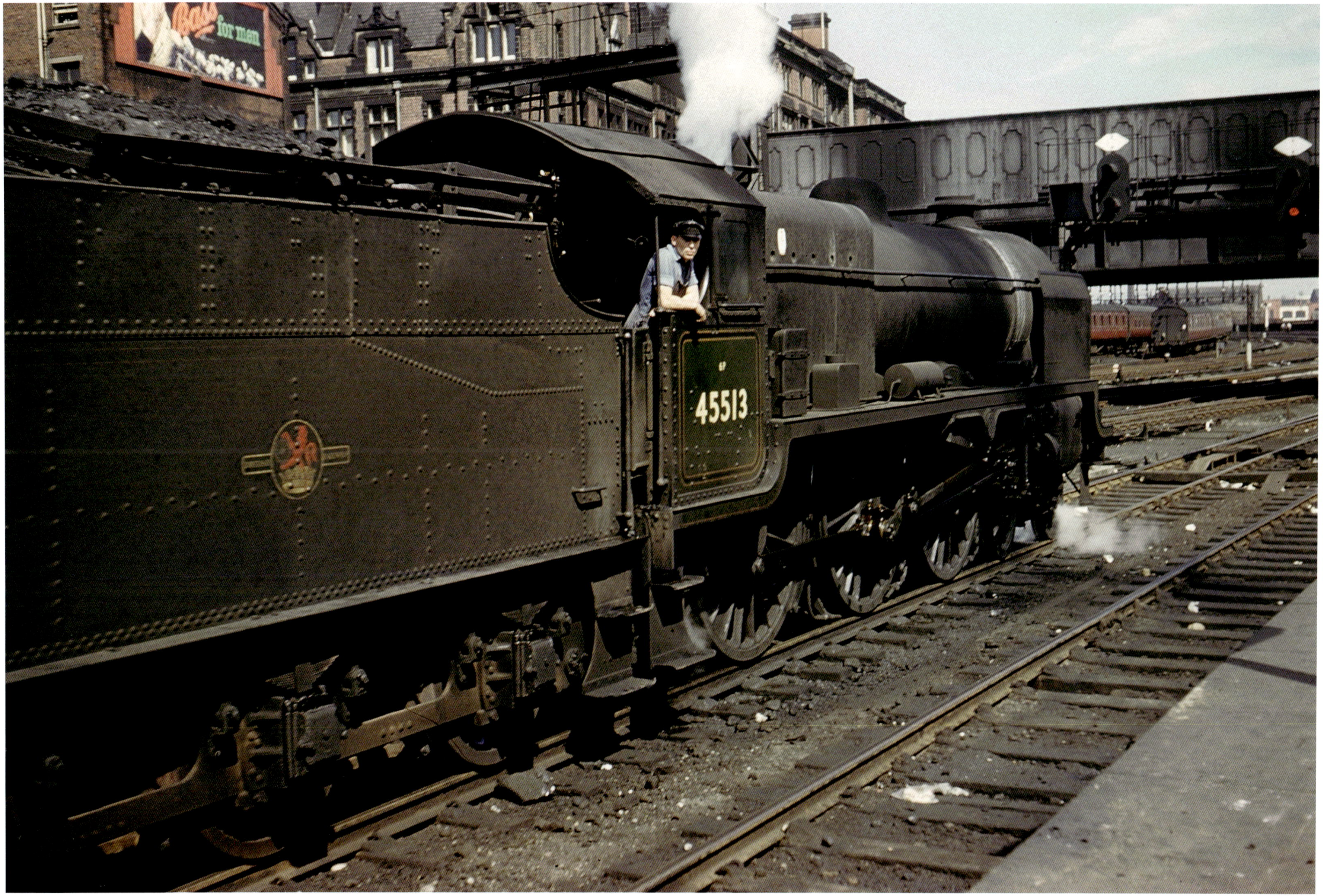
Bass for men
45513

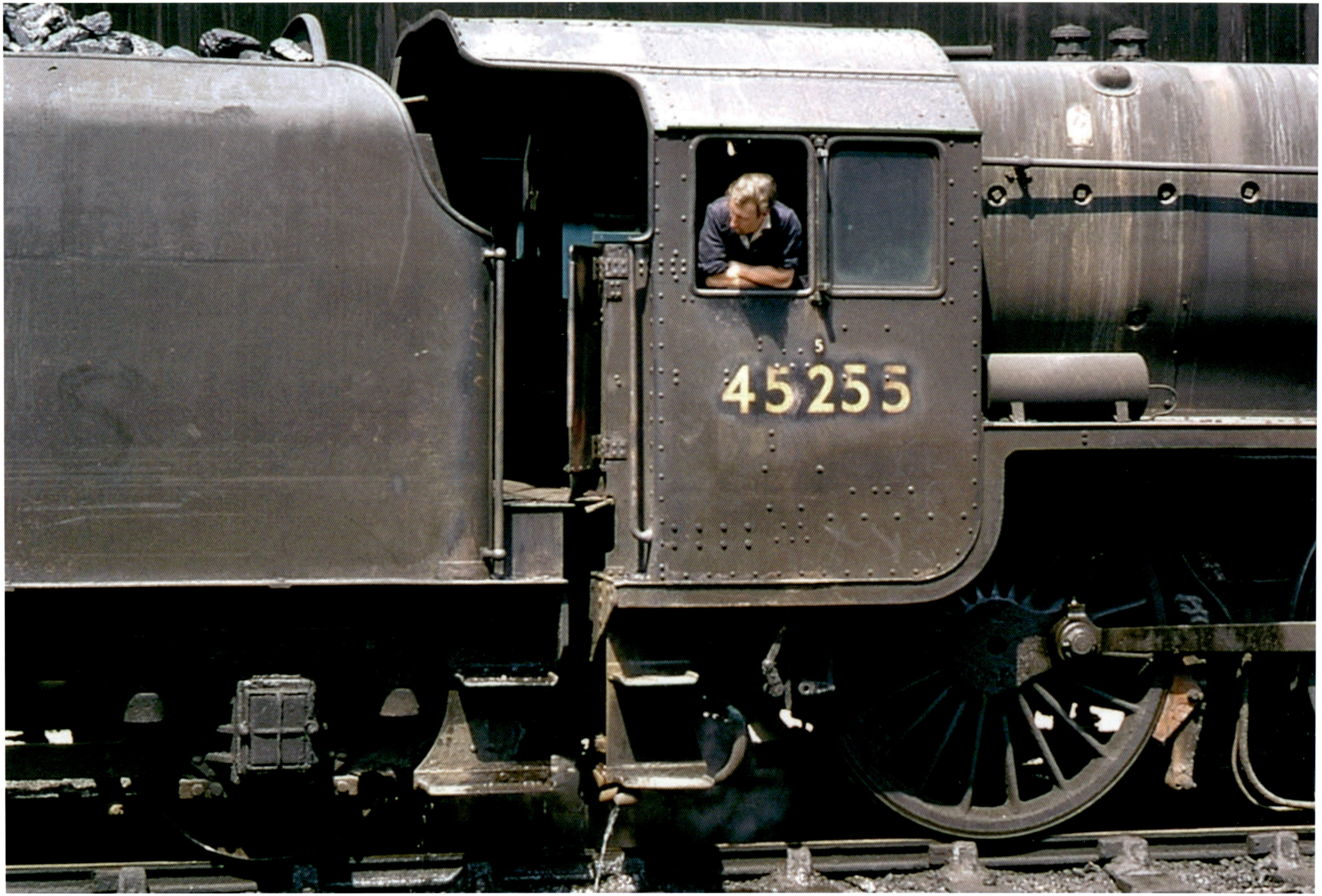
5
45255

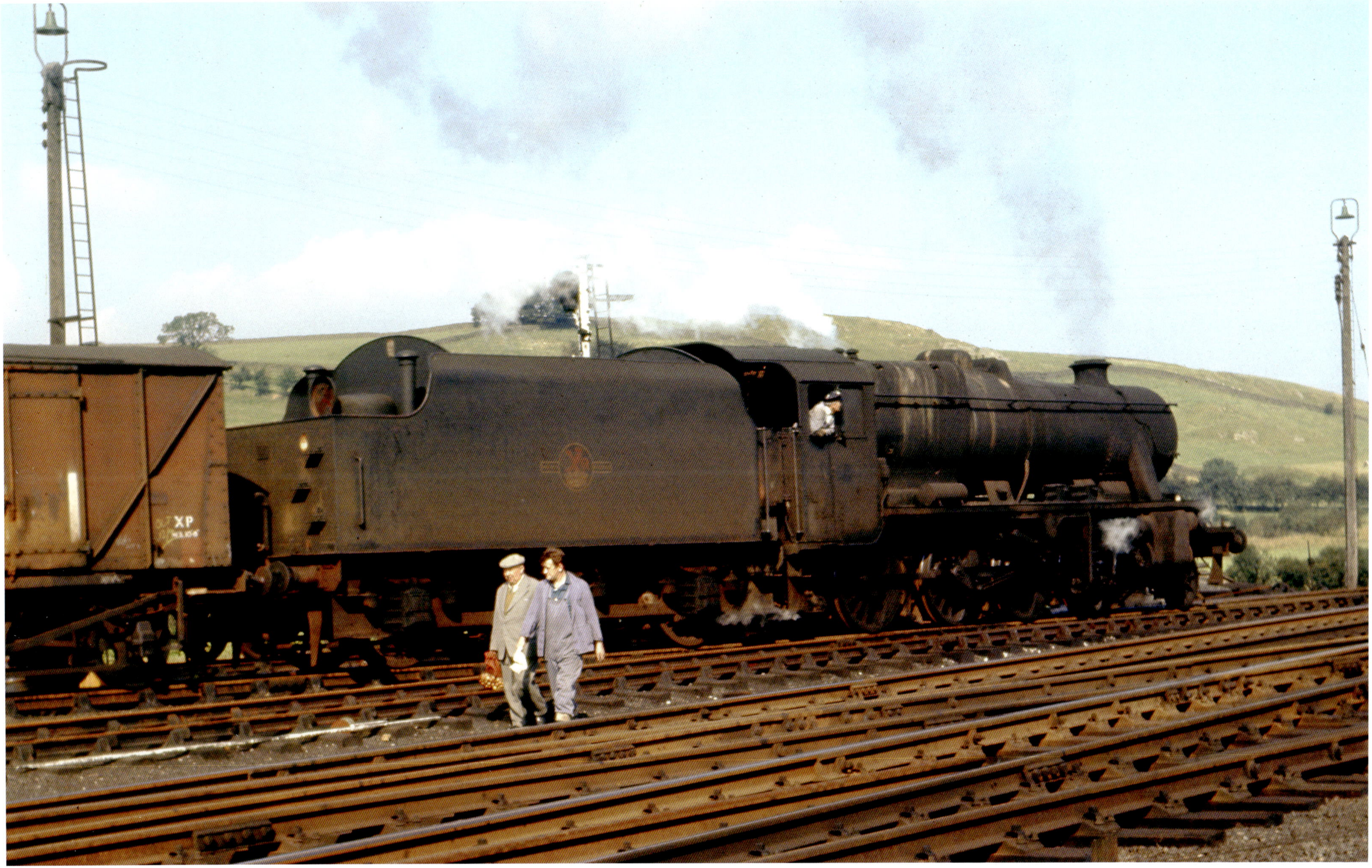

Page left: Taking it easy and enjoying the warm sunshine whilst acting as the bank pilot at Manchester Victoria his eyes gaze towards the injectors on 14 June 1968, this duty will soon pass to Sulzer Type 2s. ***Bill Wright***

We have to hope the departing crew of Class 8F, 48338 have left enough coal in the tender after their changeover at Tebay on 13 September 1967. ***Gilroy A.Kerr***

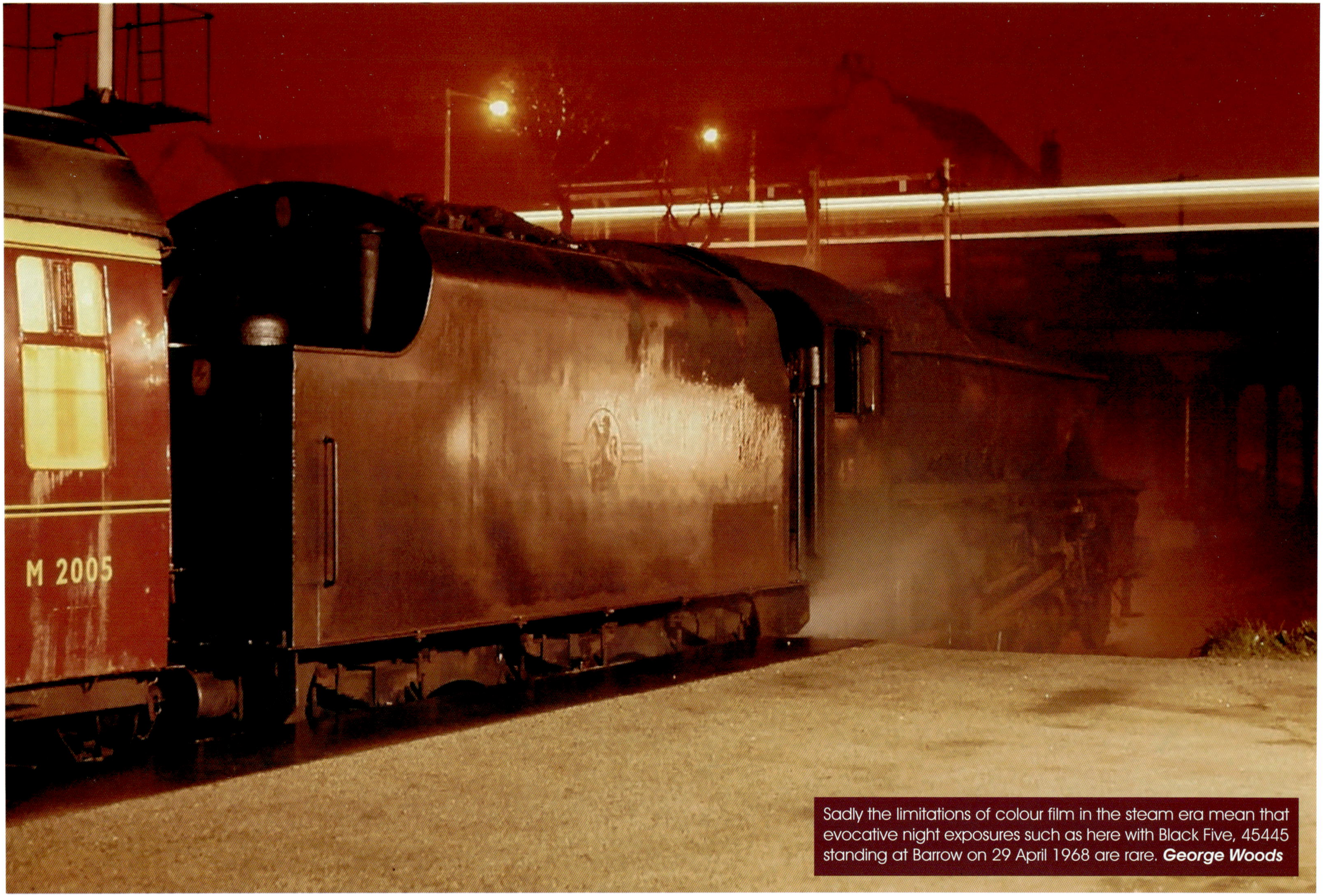

Sadly the limitations of colour film in the steam era mean that evocative night exposures such as here with Black Five, 45445 standing at Barrow on 29 April 1968 are rare. ***George Woods***

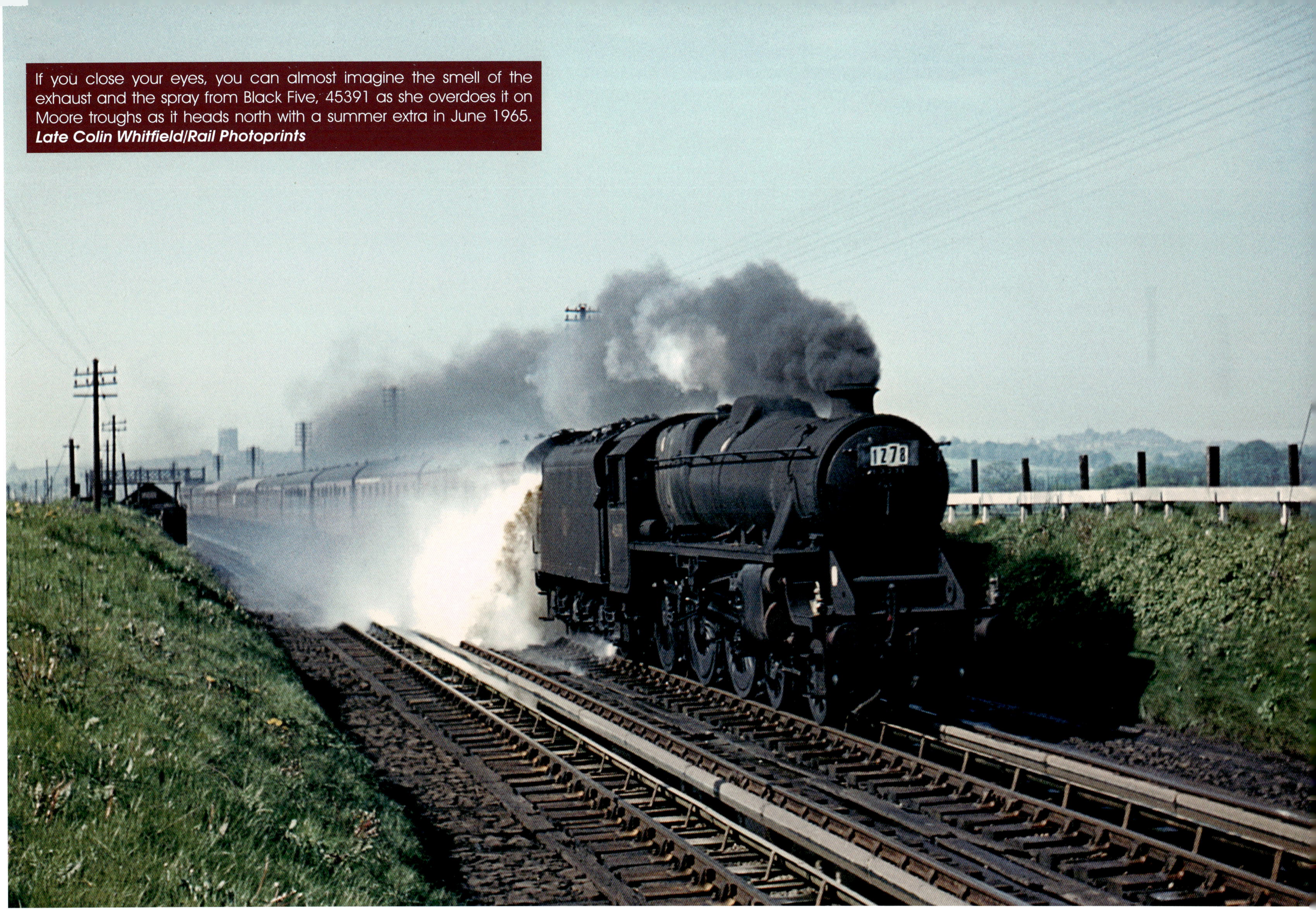

If you close your eyes, you can almost imagine the smell of the exhaust and the spray from Black Five, 45391 as she overdoes it on Moore troughs as it heads north with a summer extra in June 1965. ***Late Colin Whitfield/Rail Photoprints***

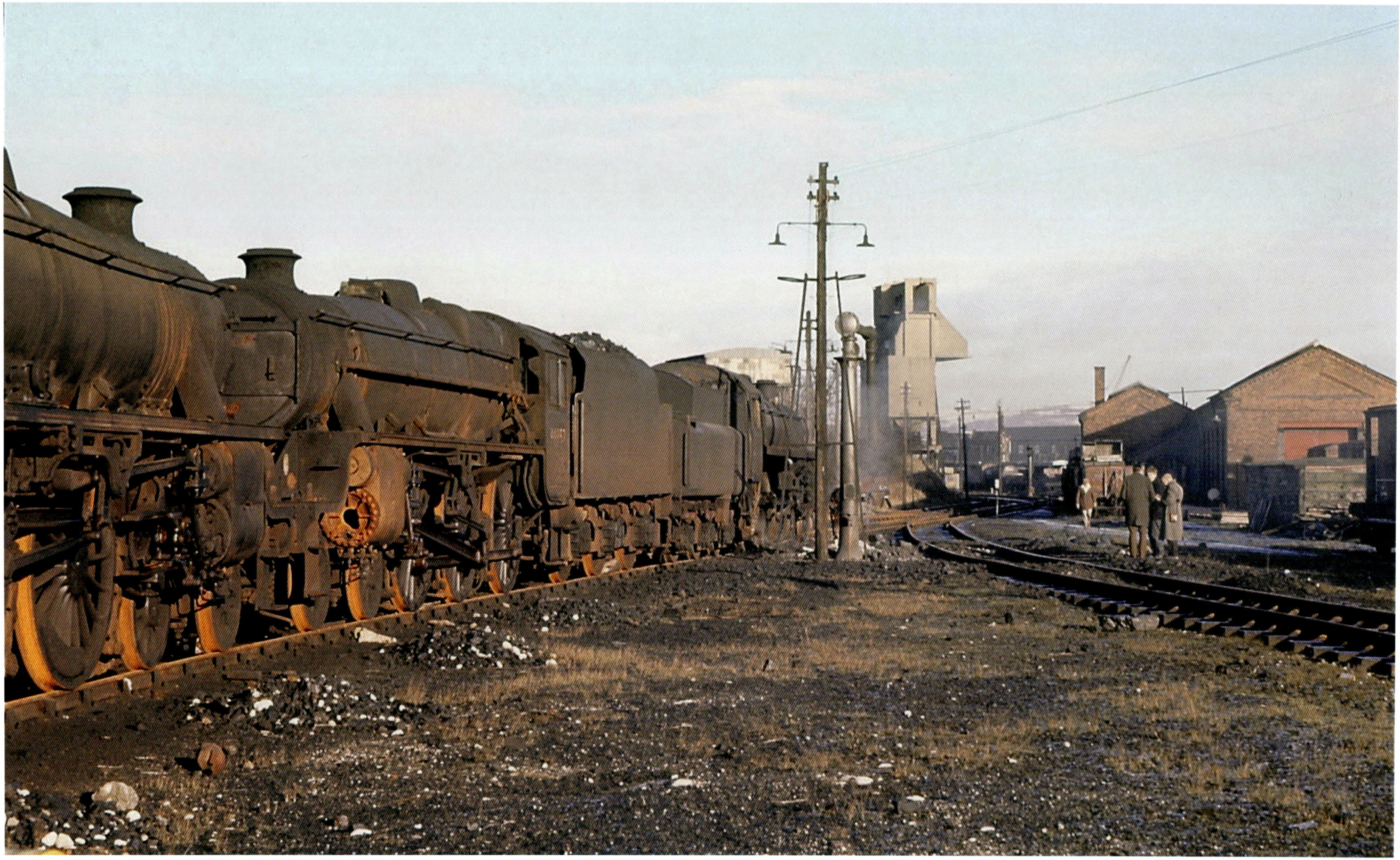

Standing in the cold on the last day of 1967 during a visit to see what Carnforth shed has on offer our party gather to discuss what's next today, as this is set to be the last day for steam on the WCML and nearby Tebay will close completely tomorrow. ***George Woods***

Opposite: A few days later under the overhead wiring at Stockport to witness a little shunting taking place alongside the station with Black Five, 44868 rostered for the job, cameramen will need to grab every opportunity from now on. ***John Gill***

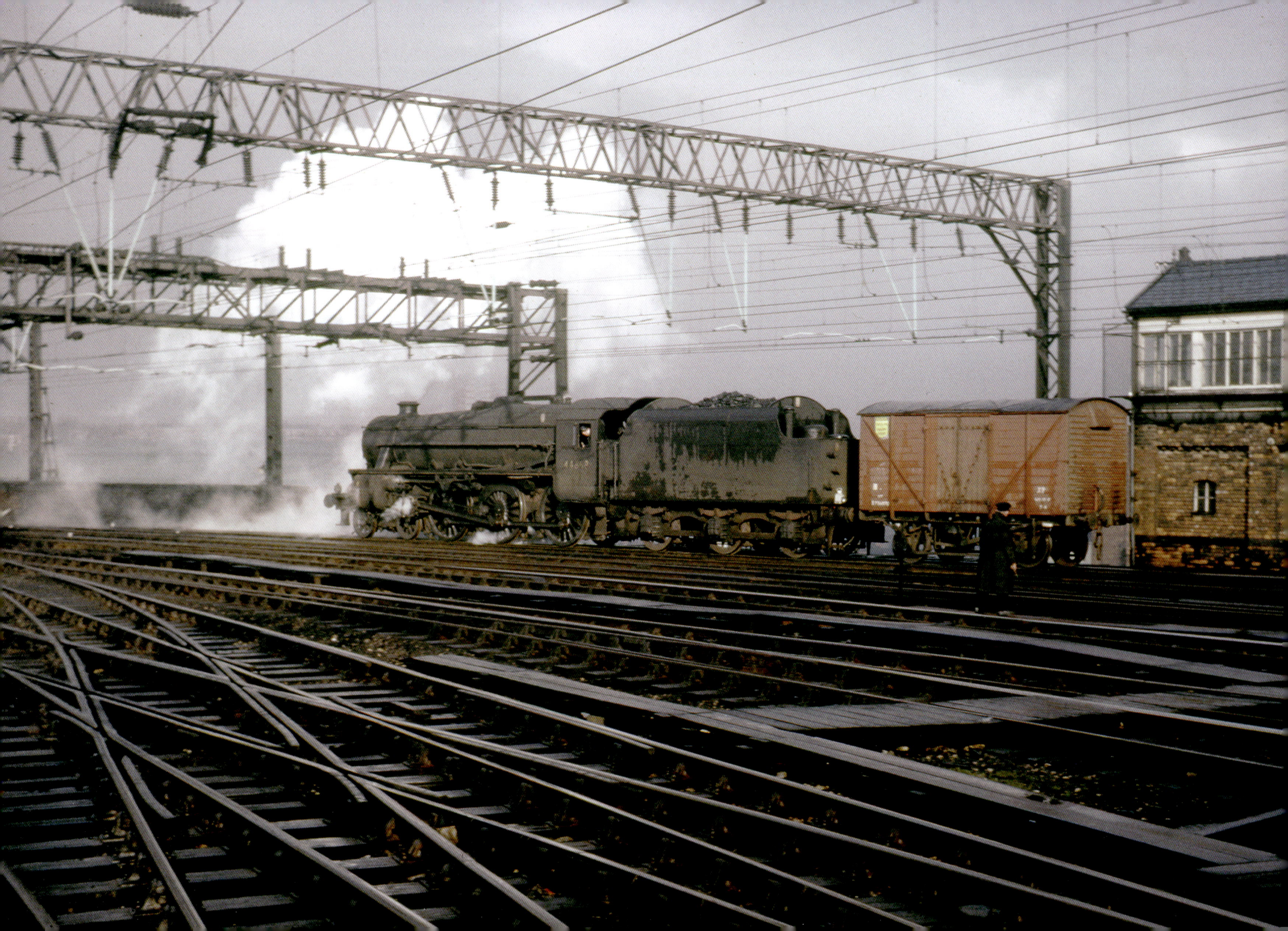

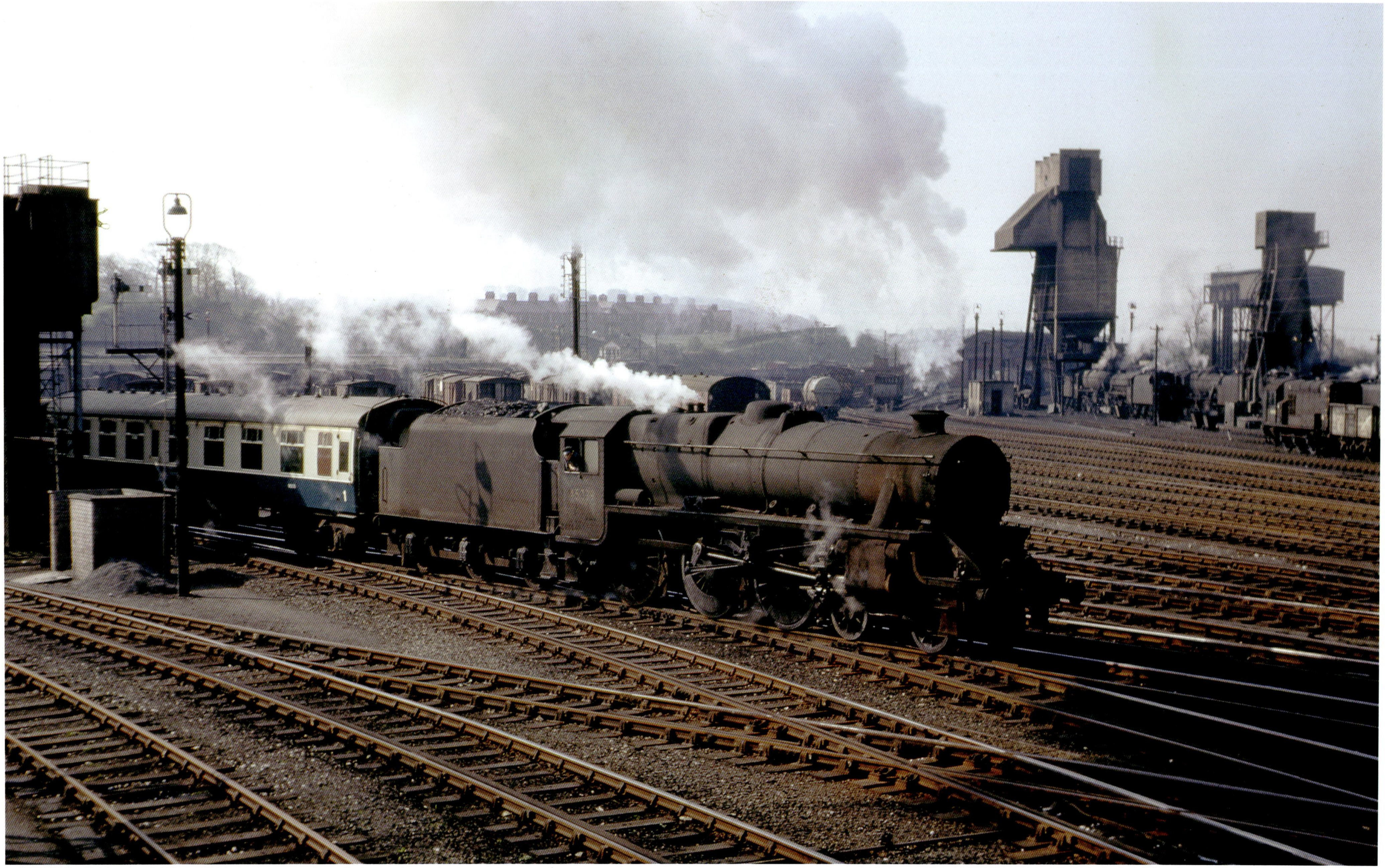

A down passenger service gets away from Carnforth on 29 April 1967, behind Black Five, 45339. Although as spotters our eyes cast towards 10A and what might be on shed today in the background. ***Jerry Beddows***

Opposite: Unusually Ivatt Class 4MT 43131 pilots English Electric Type 4, D313 away from Penrith with a convention special bound for Keswick, on 22 July 1967. ***Chris Davies/Rail Photoprints***

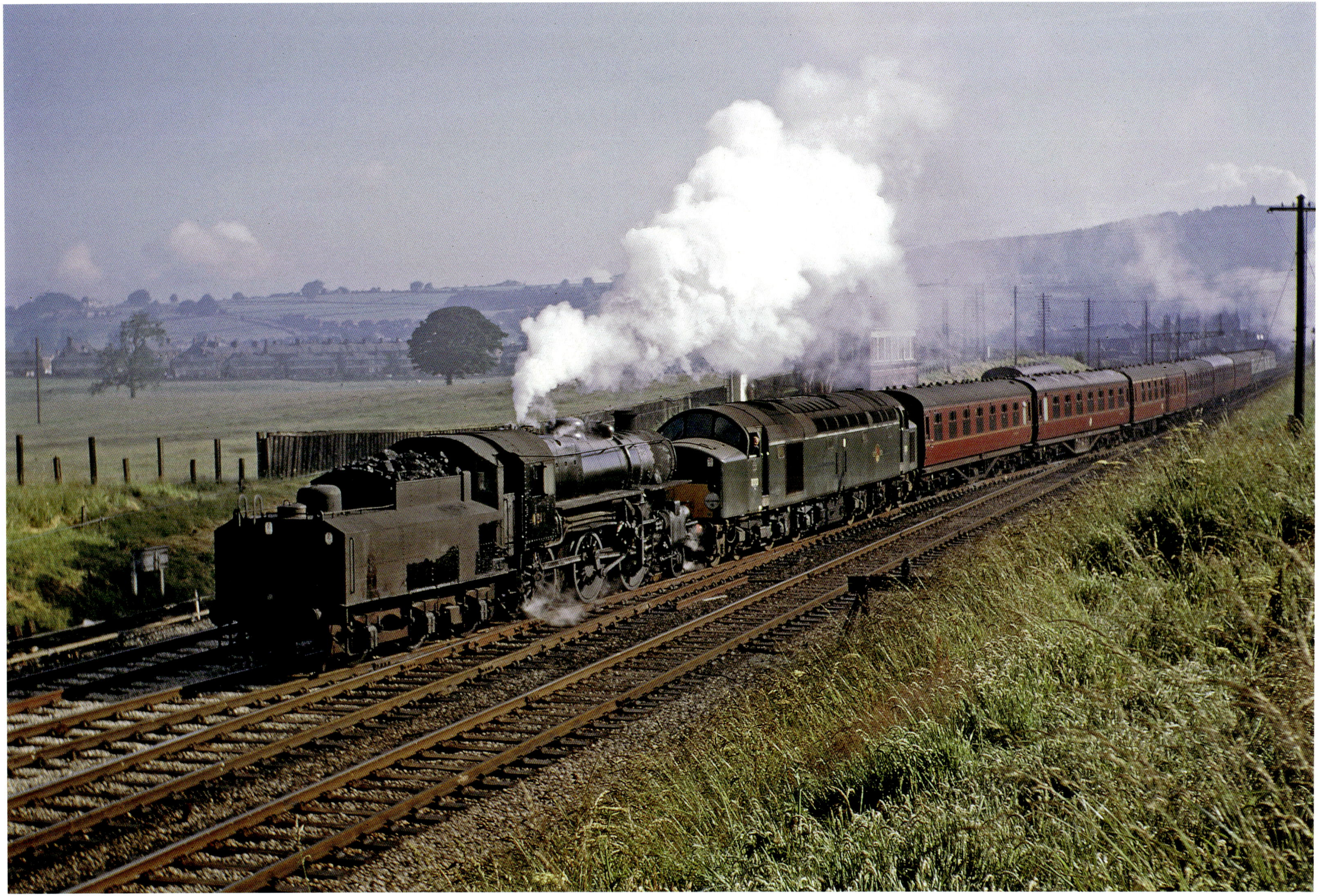

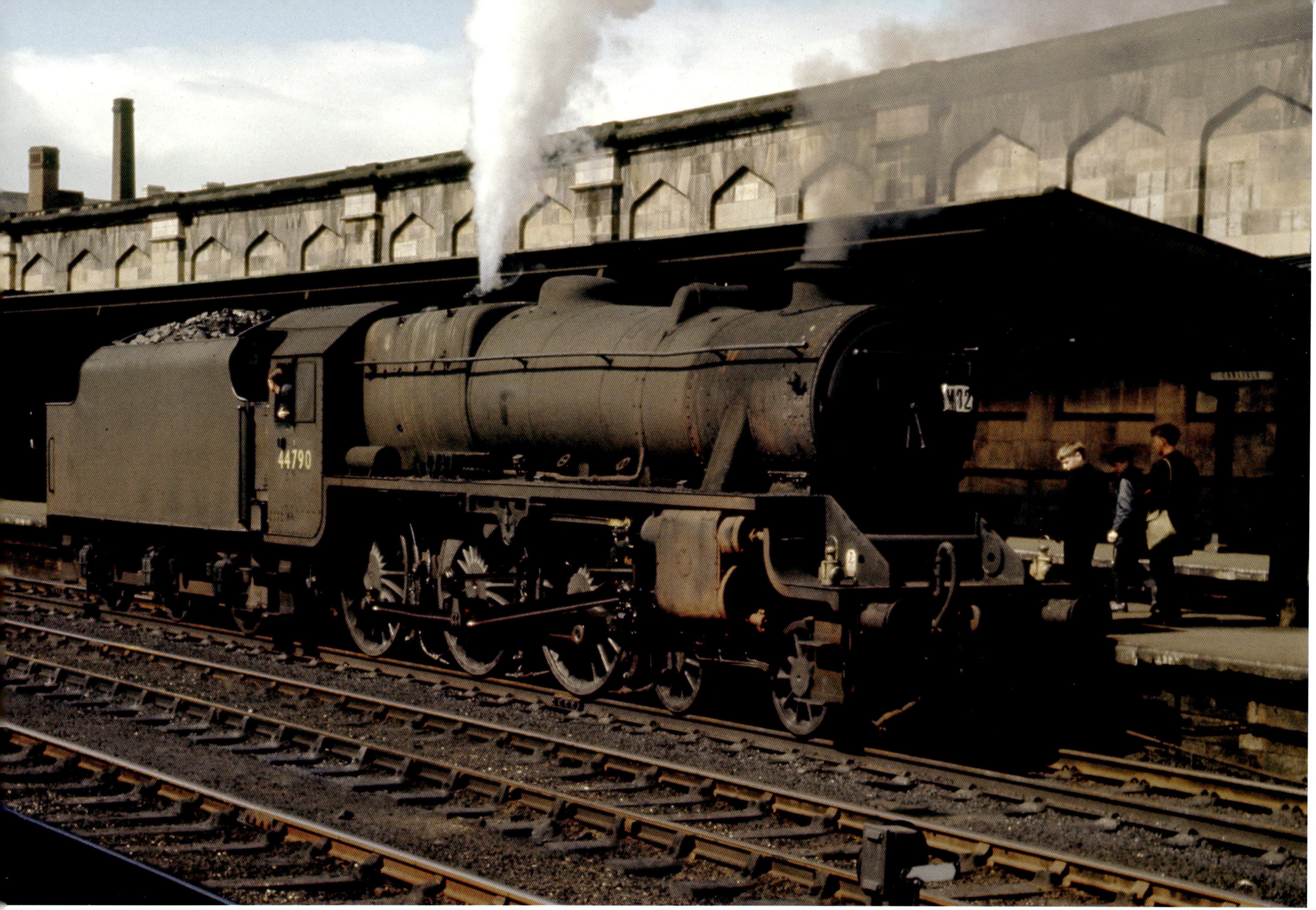
44790

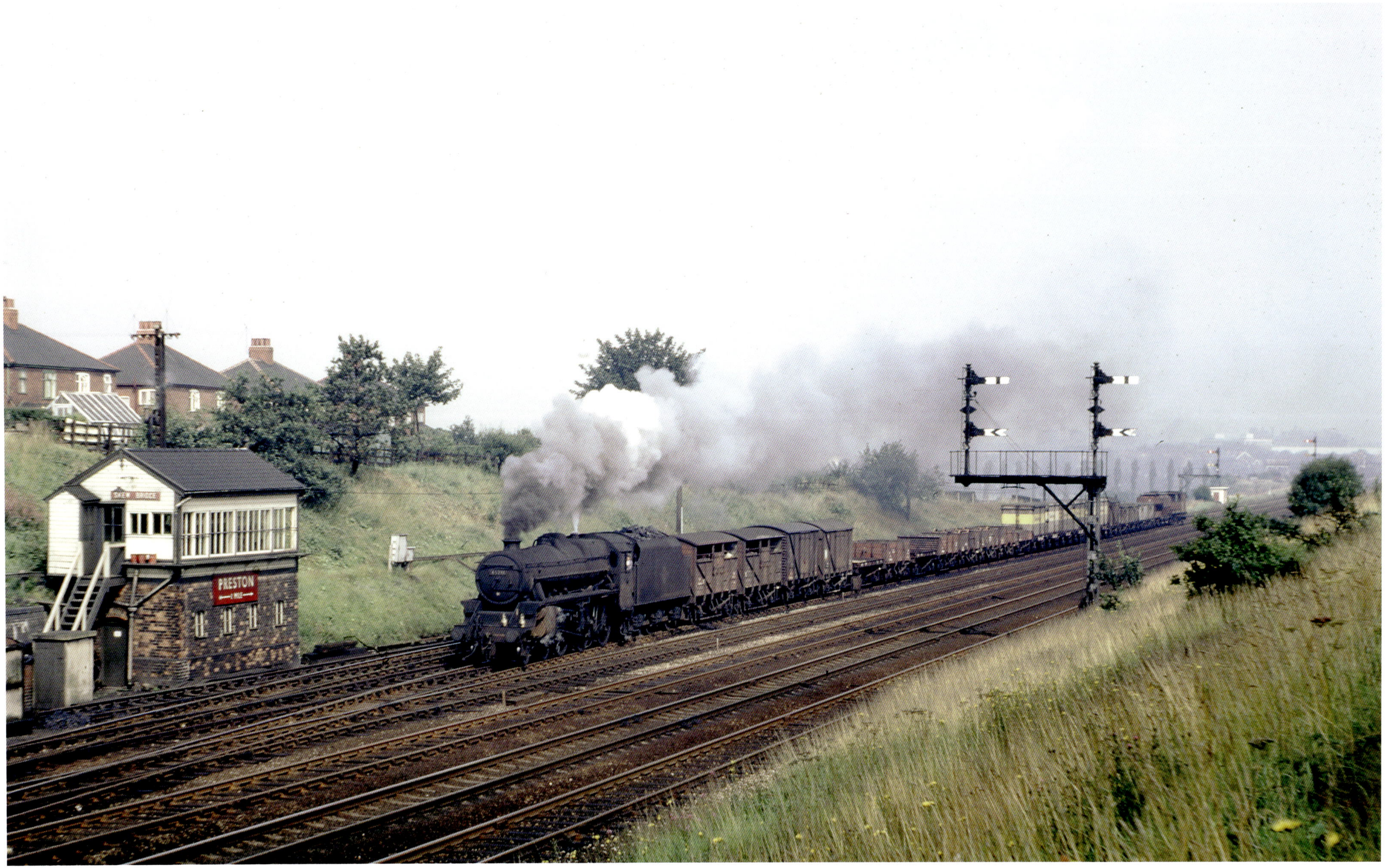

Page left: These lads cast a second glance towards Black Five, 44790 running light past them back along the platforms at Carlisle Citadel on 2 July 1966. ***Gilroy A. Kerr***

A happy vantage point for many enthusiasts in the days of steam was opposite Preston's Skew Bridge Signal Box as another Black Five, 45281 makes its way past with an up freight on 10 August 1967. ***Jerry Beddows***

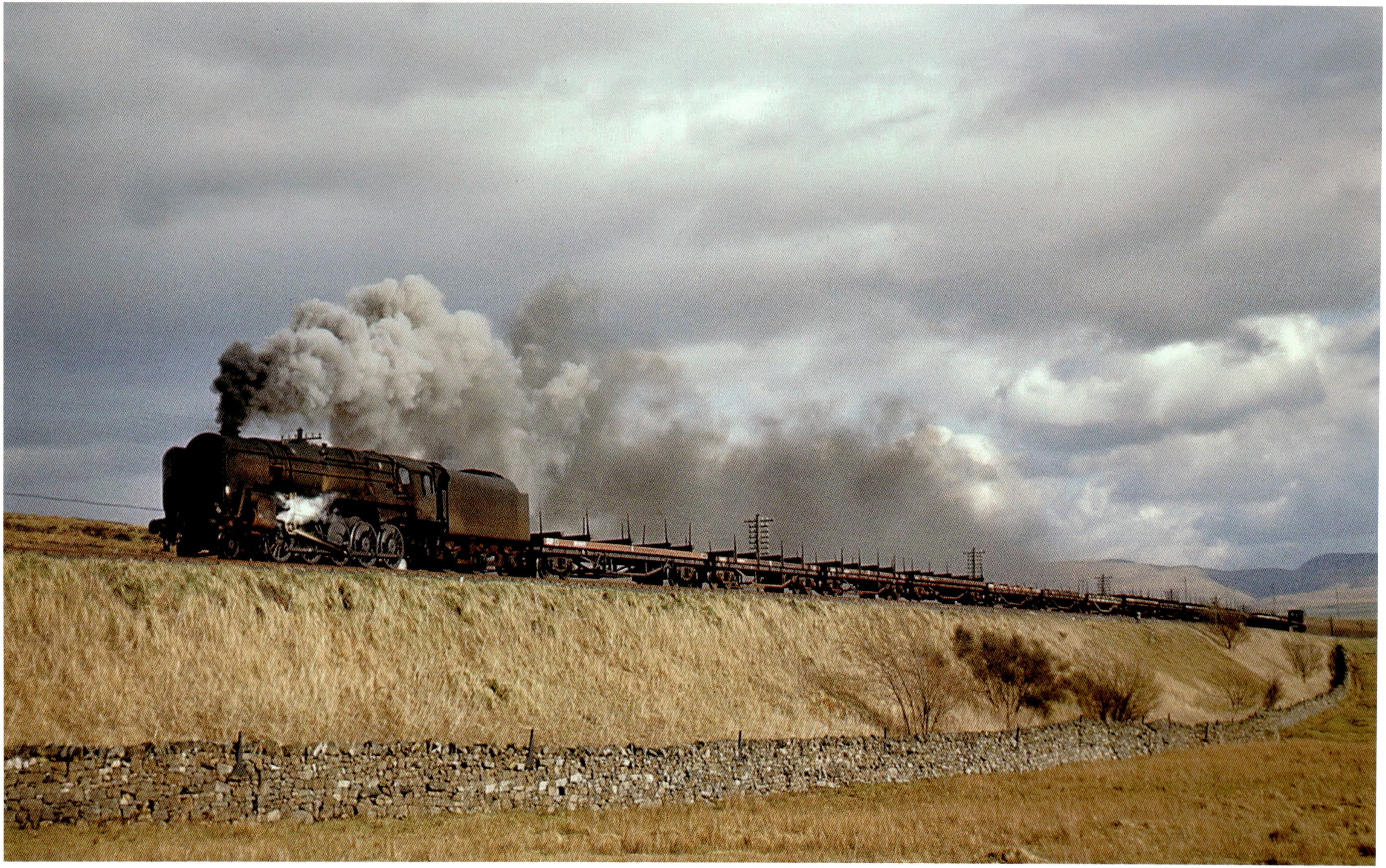

Making a pleasant sight whilst climbing Shap near Scout Green with northbound empty steel flats on 23 March 1967, was Class 9F, 92114 ambling up the bank with power to spare. ***Gerald T. Robinson***

Opposite: Not so many northbound freights could take on the climb up Shap from Tebay without the assistance of a banker such as Class 4MT, 75030 on 6 September 1967. ***Gerald T. Robinson***

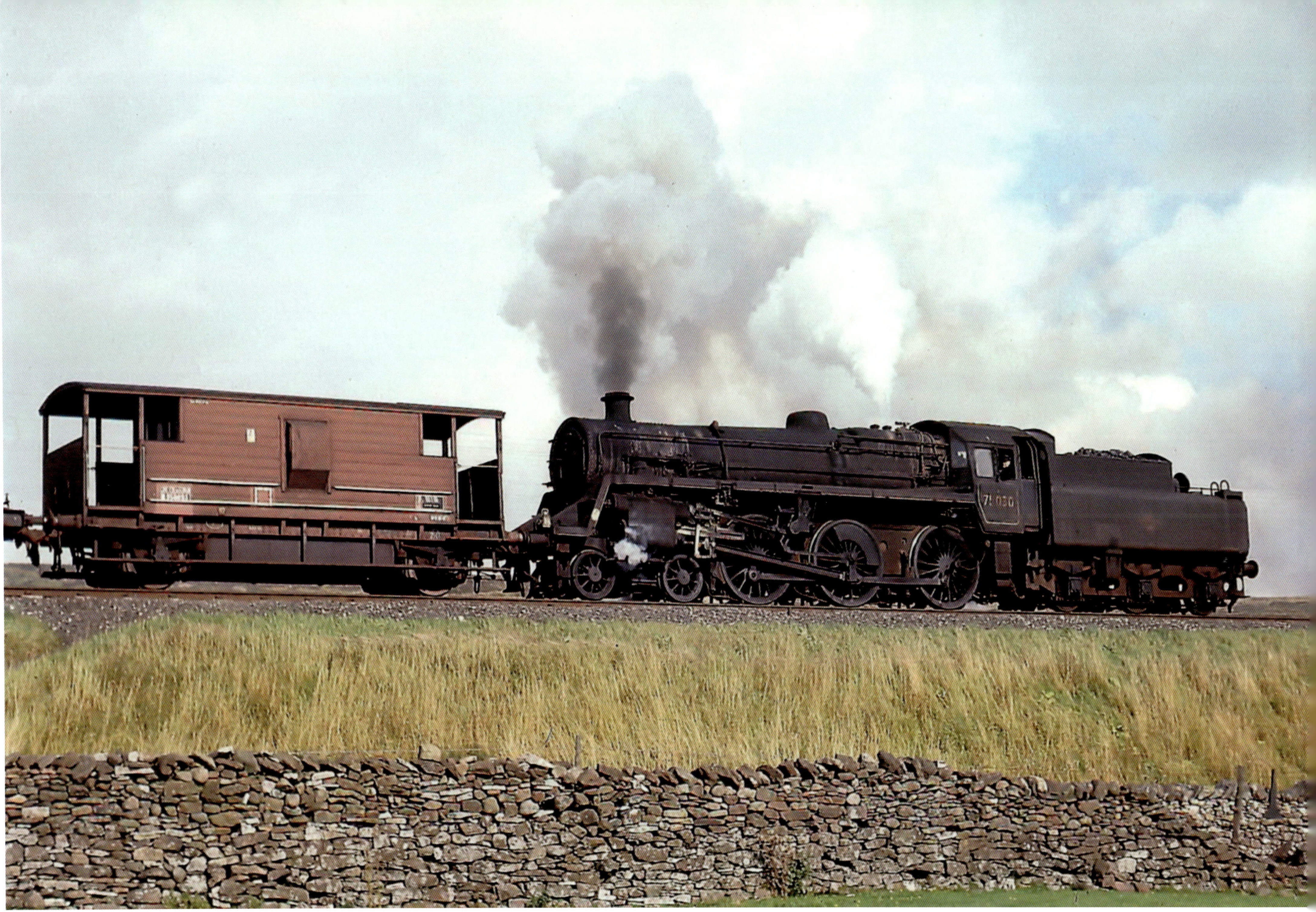

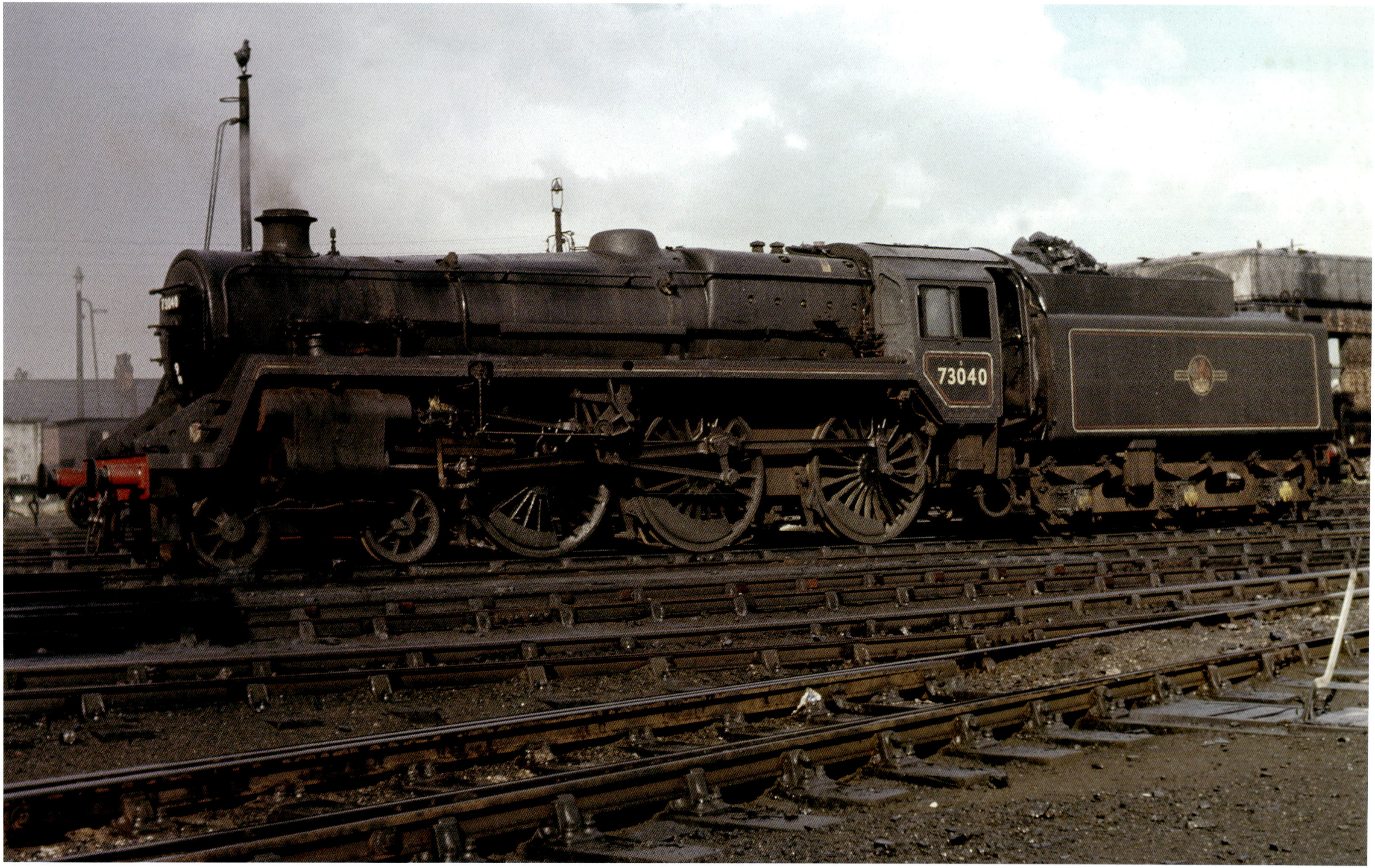

Rolling into the shed yard at 9H, Patricroft on 4 May 1968 was Class 5MT, 73040 facing imminent withdrawal this month and the shed itself would close too on 1 July. ***Gilroy A. Kerr***

Opposite: Its a clear road ahead for Black Five, 44911 with a southbound passenger leaving Carlisle's ever decreasing trackwork behind on 5 August 1967. ***Jerry Beddows***

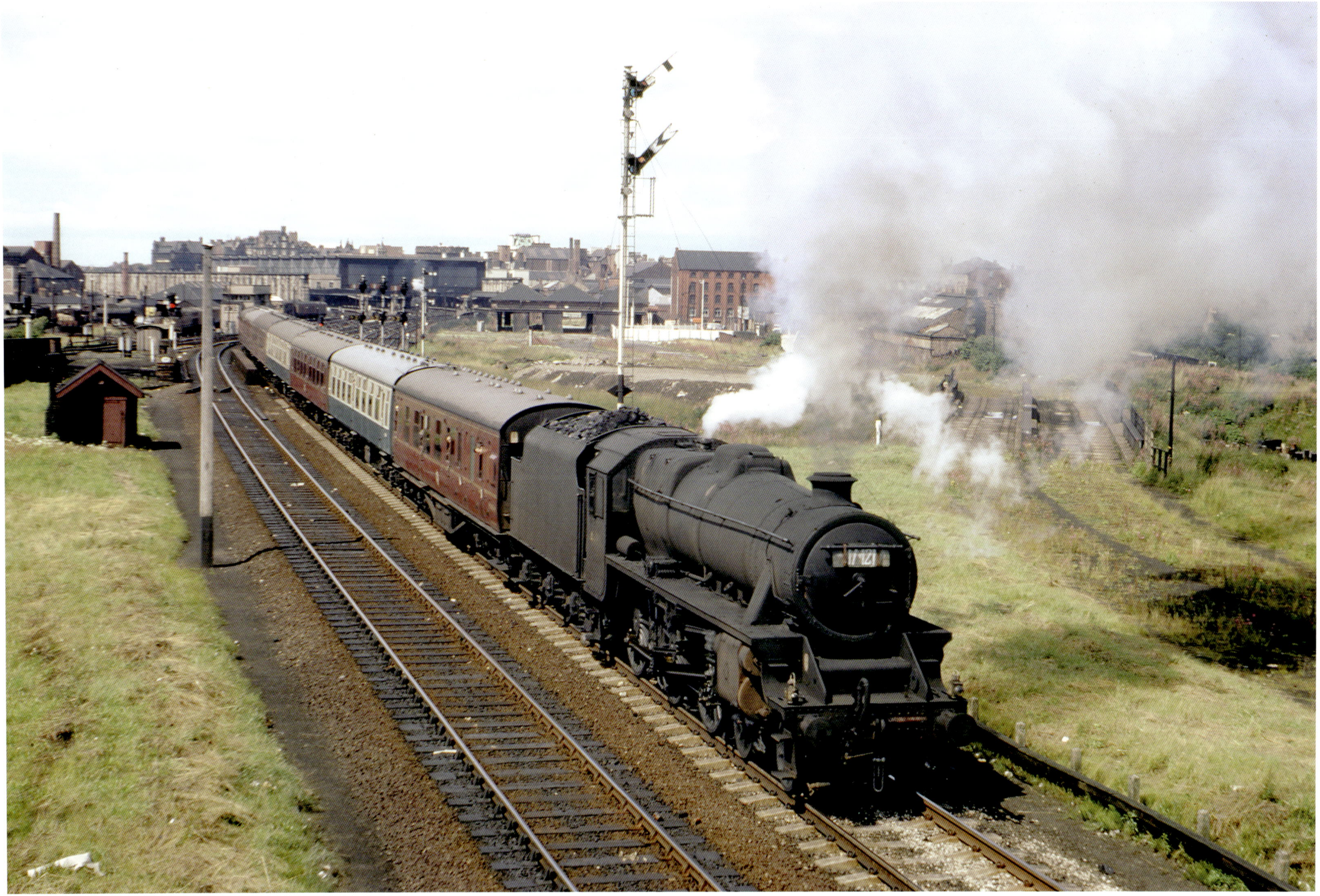

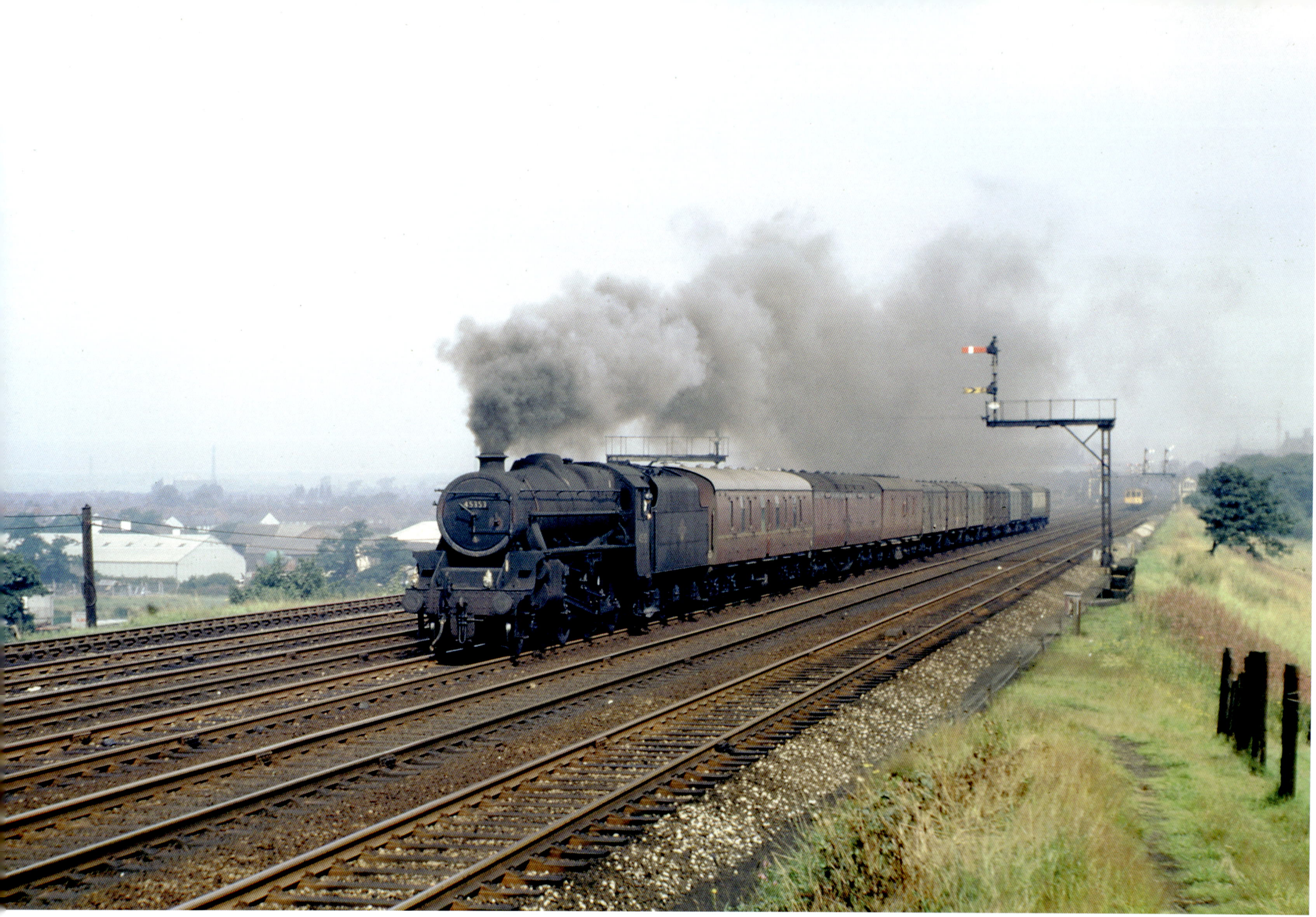

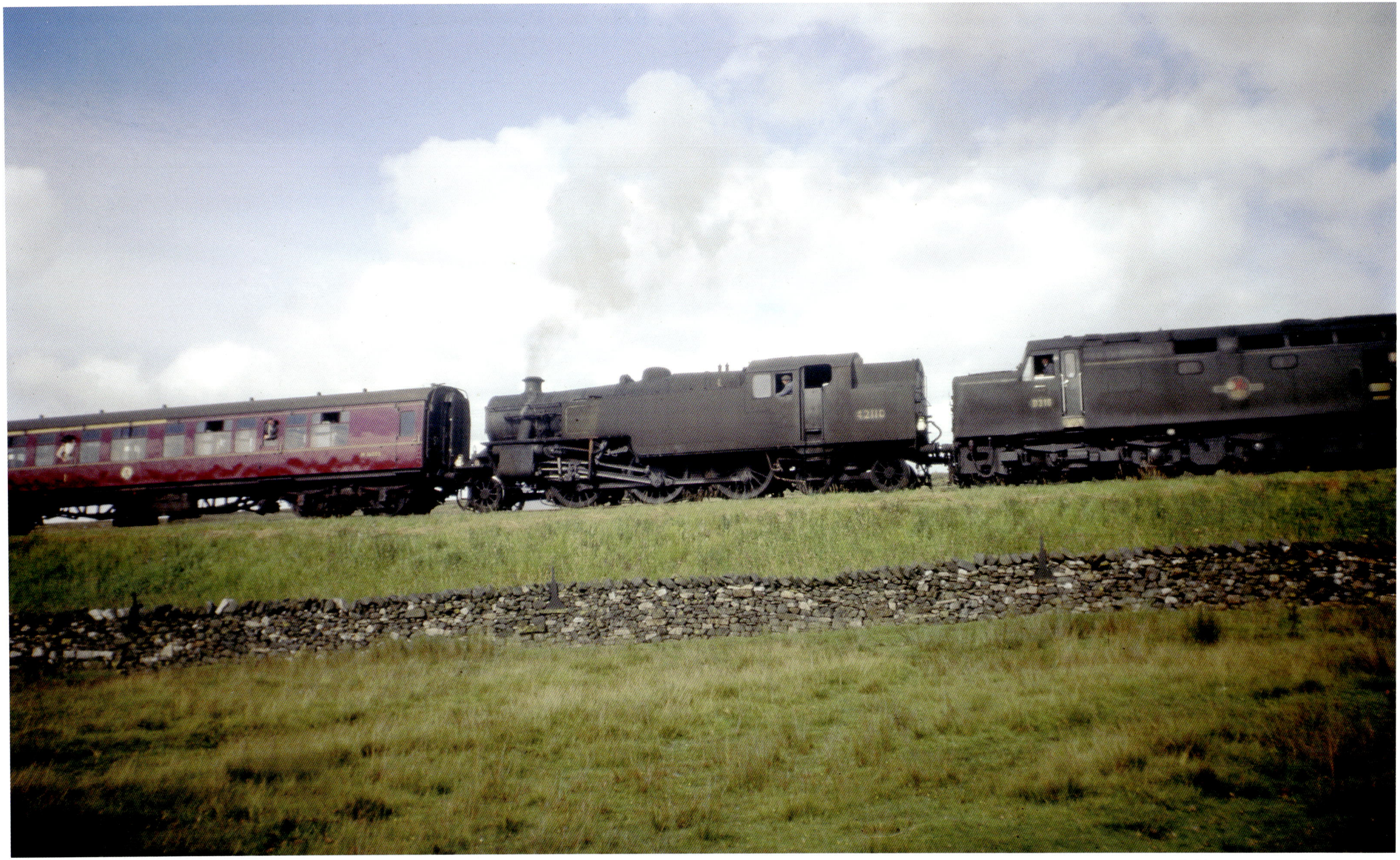

Page left: A return to a vantage point at Skew Bridge once more to enjoy a good view back along the mainlines here as another Black Five, 45353 speeds towards us with an up parcels on 10 June 1967. ***Jerry Beddows***

Permissive block working at Scout Green for the crew of D316 on a Euston to Perth passenger, buffering up to Class 4MT, 42110 one of Tebay's regular bankers after the train engine, D340 had failed on a Birmingham to Edinburgh turn on 25 July 1964. ***Chris Forrest***

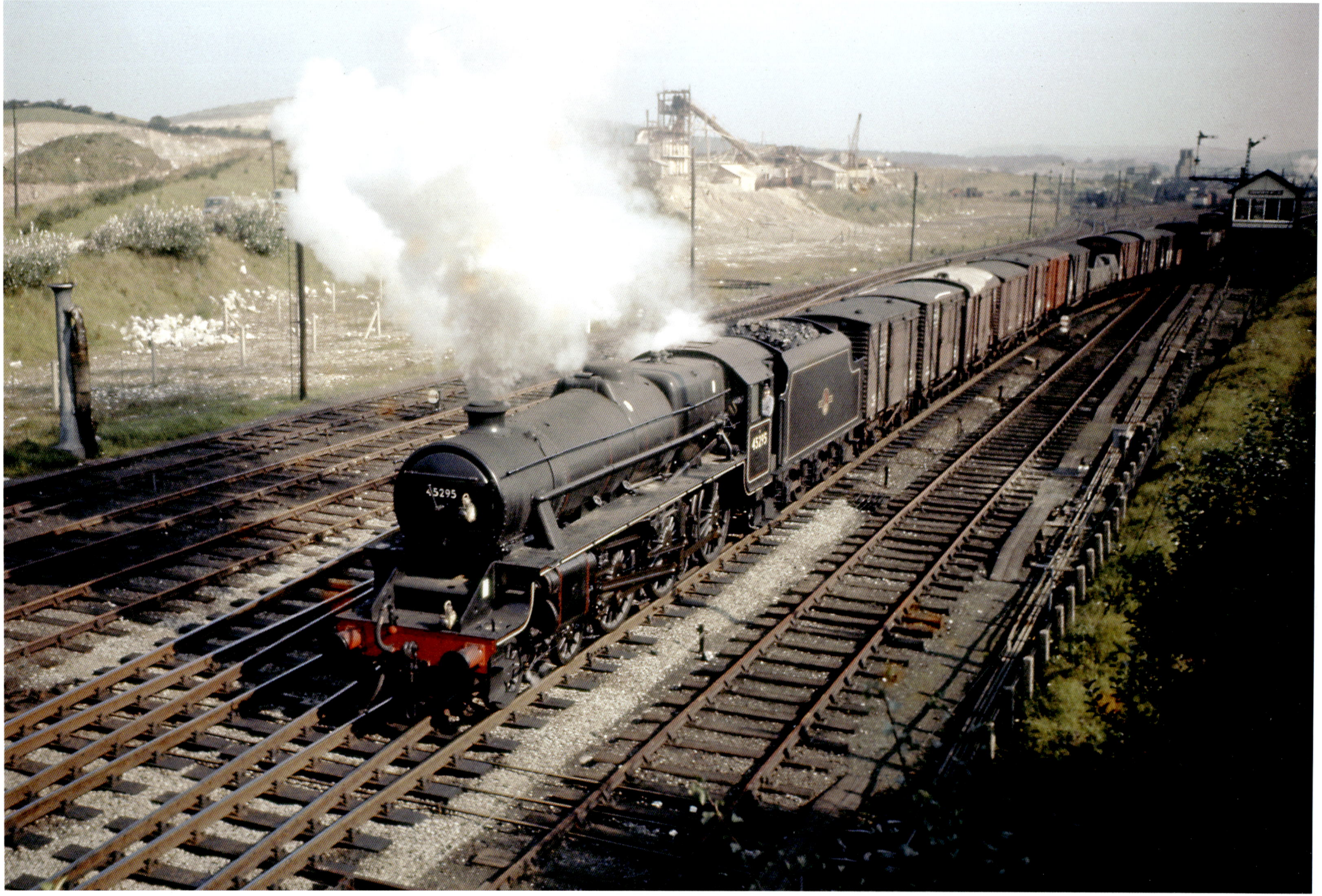
45295
45295

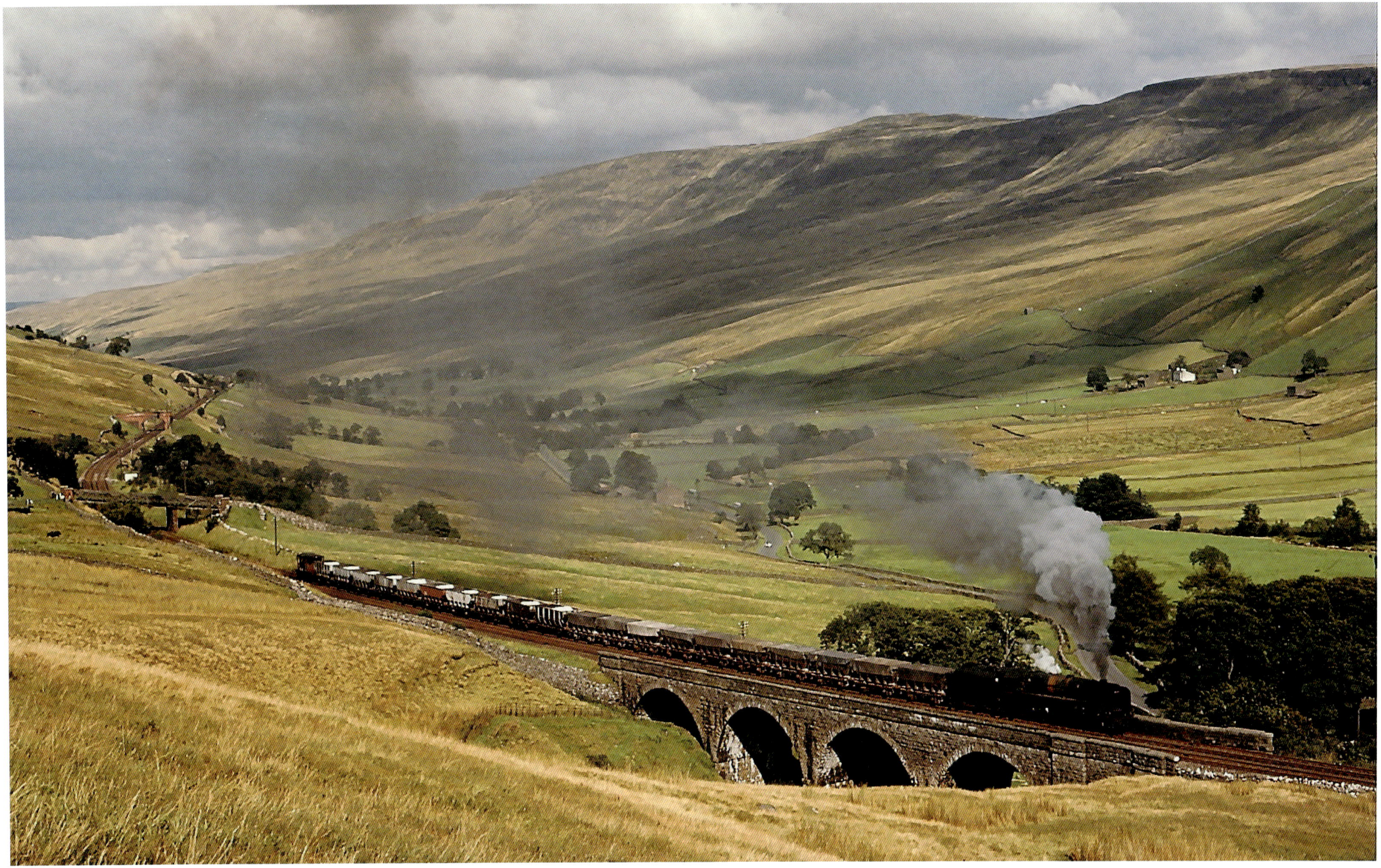

Page left: The signalman has pulled off the home signal for Black Five, 45295 to get away out of the up loop at Carnforth with a heavy southbound goods in 1963. ***Late Ray Helm/Strathwood Library Collection***

As Class 9F, 92058 crosses the short Ais Gill Viaduct on 7 September 1967, the sounds of the distant sheep on the breeze are momentarily interupted in the sunshine. ***George Woods***

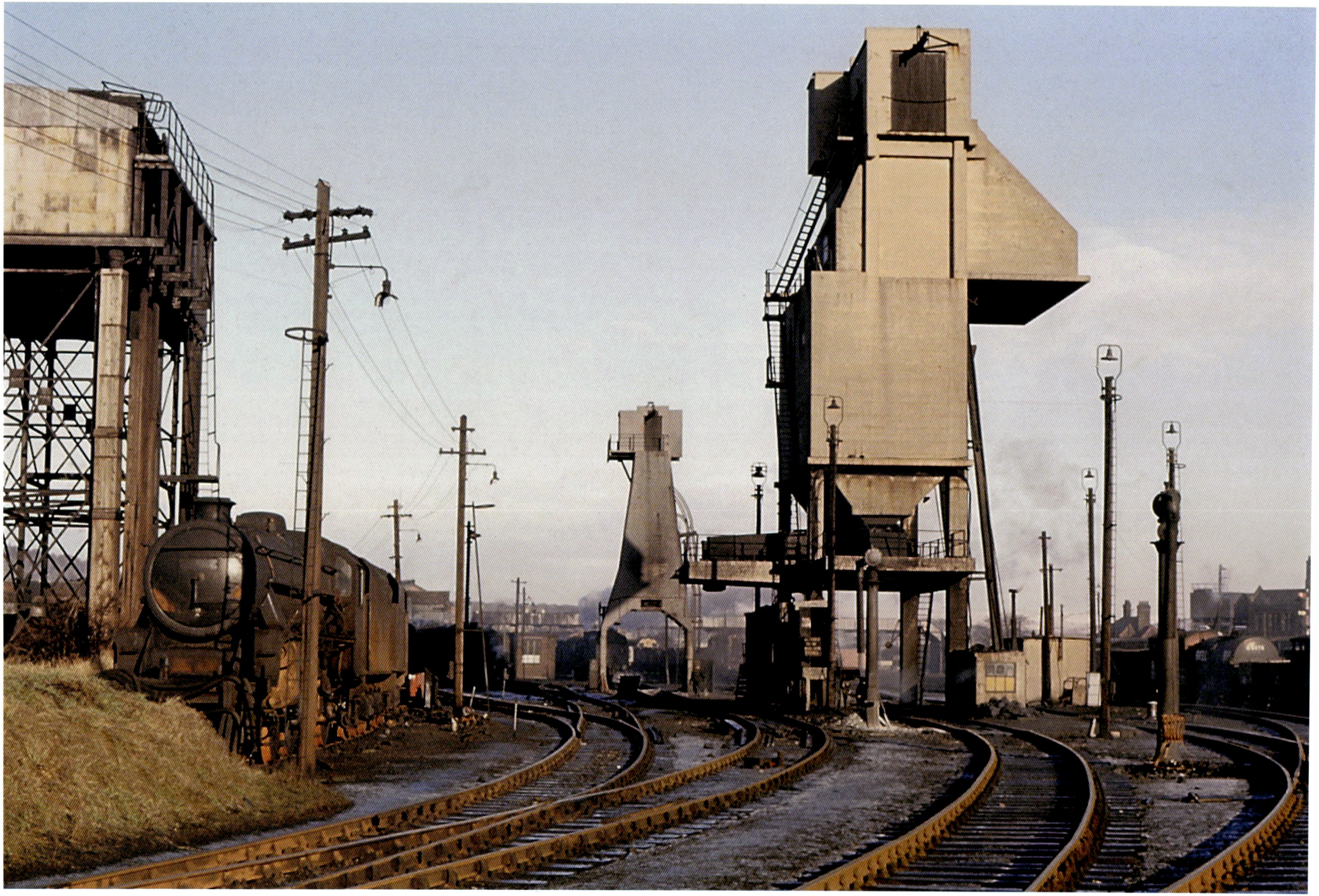

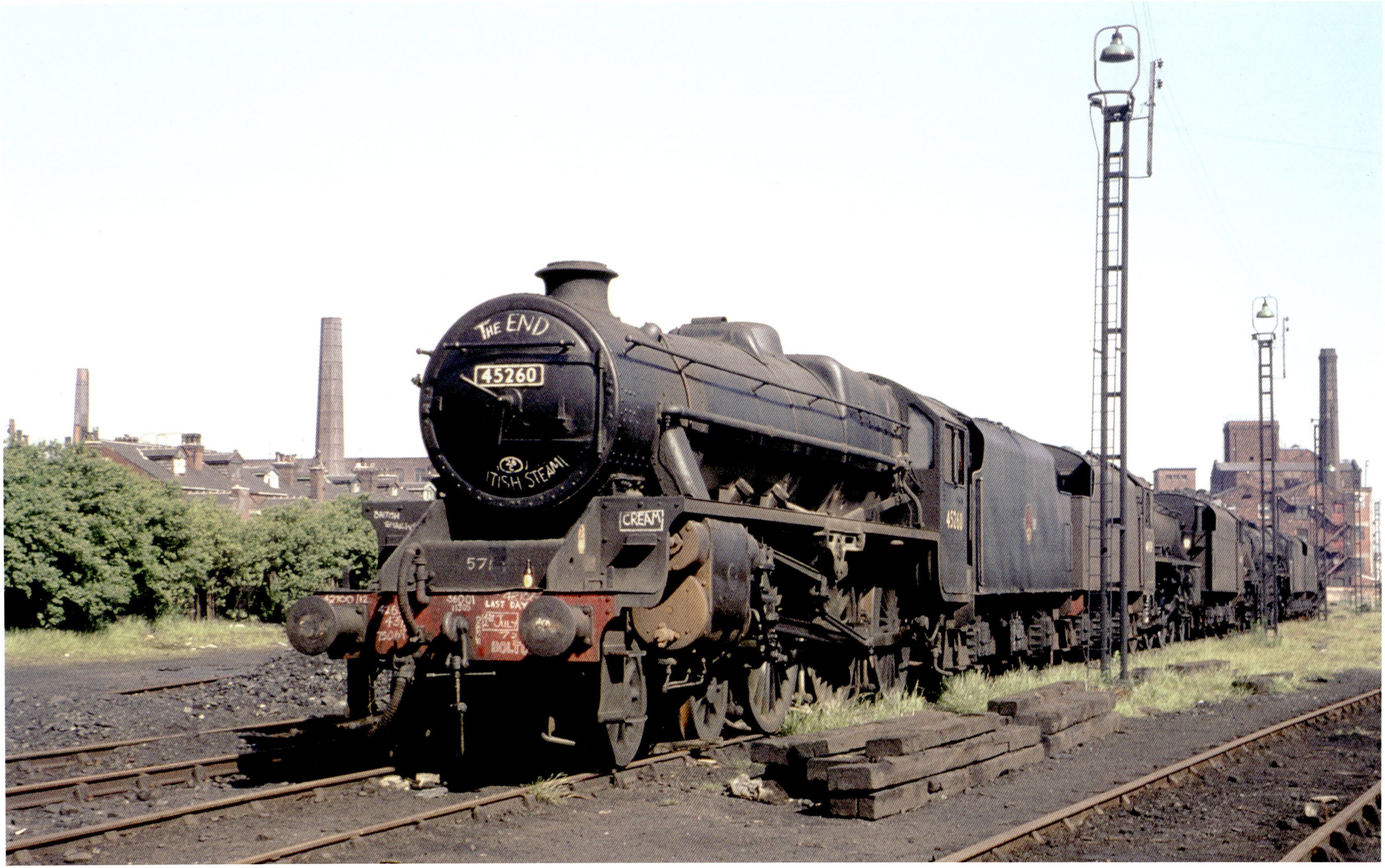

Page left: All is quiet and peaceful around the coaling plant at 10A Carnforth on 31 December 1967, there are more dead engines in the yard than live one's in steam today sadly. ***George Woods***

Another shed to close completely was 9K Bolton on 1 July 1968 , this was the melancholy scene the day beforehand at the end of the yard. ***Strathwood Library Collection***

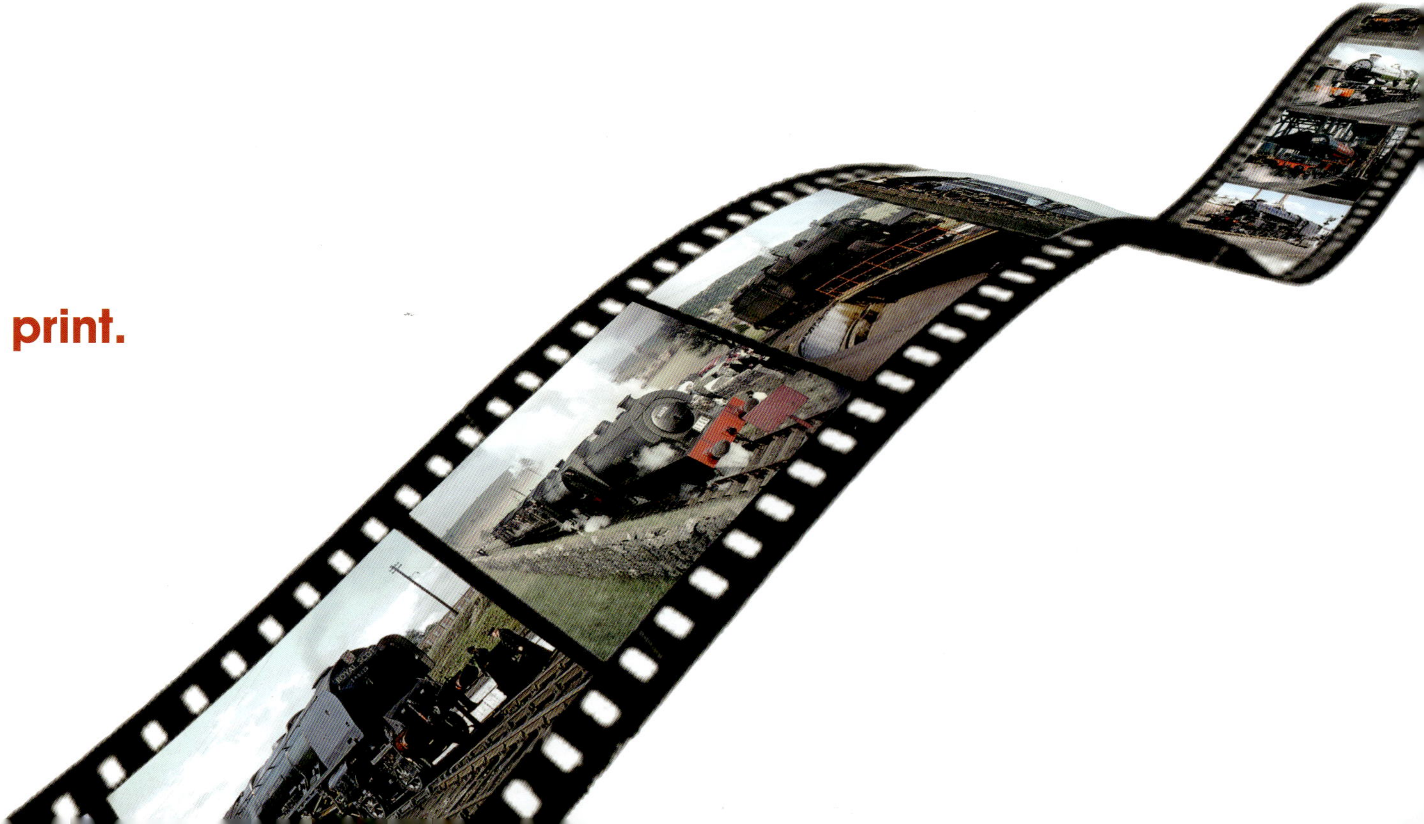